Race in a Godless World

MANCHESTER
1824

Manchester University Press

Race in a Godless World

Atheism, Race, and Civilization, 1850–1914

Nathan G. Alexander

Manchester University Press

The right of Nathan G. Alexander to be identified as the author of this work has been asserted by him in accordance with the Copyright, Designs and Patents Act 1988.

Published by Manchester University Press
Altrincham Street, Manchester M1 7JA
www.manchesteruniversitypress.co.uk

British Library Cataloguing-in-Publication Data
A catalogue record for this book is available from the British Library

ISBN 978 1 5261 4237 5 hardback

First published 2019

The publisher has no responsibility for the persistence or accuracy of URLs for any external or third-party internet websites referred to in this book, and does not guarantee that any content on such websites is, or will remain, accurate or appropriate.

Typeset by Servis Filmsetting Ltd, Stockport, Cheshire
Printed in Great Britain by Bell & Bain Ltd, Glasgow

Contents

v

Figures

Figures

Acknowledgments

I would like to acknowledge that parts of the research for this book were funded by the School of History, University of St Andrews, and the Royal Historical Society.

I am also indebted to the following libraries where I conducted research for the book: the University of St Andrews Library and Special Collections, Bishopsgate Library, Conway Hall Library, the Royal Anthropological Institute Archive, the British Library, the Library of Congress, and the Center for Inquiry Library in Amherst, New York. In particular, I would like to thank the librarians at Conway Hall, who scanned images from the *Freethinker* for me, and Roderick Bradford, who photographed images from the *Truth Seeker* for me.

There are many people who gave feedback on drafts. These include: Gary Berton, Roderick Bradford, John Clark, Felix Driver, Mark Francis, Elliot Hanowski, Minchul Kim, David Livingstone, Chris Moffat, and Mariam Touba. Audiences at conferences and seminars in London, Glasgow, Birmingham, Brighton, Newcastle, and St Andrews listened to early versions of this research and offered feedback. Chris Cameron generously allowed me to see his unpublished manuscript about the history of African American freethinkers in the United States. Ben Hiemstra sparked my interest in this topic a long time ago and has discussed many of these issues with me over the years. Rosario López helped with the writing of the book in more ways than I can count.

Colin Kidd supervised the dissertation on which the book is based, and I am grateful to him for believing in my topic and for offering his guid-

Acknowledgments

ance and support along the way. Richard Whatmore helped bring me to St Andrews and has been a consistent mentor throughout my academic career.

I would also like to thank Alun Richards at Manchester University Press and Jennifer Hammer and Phil Zuckerman at New York University Press for believing in the book and helping me to improve it, as well as the anonymous referees who gave feedback on various drafts. Any errors remain my own.

Finally I would like to thank my family for their continual love and support.

Introduction:
the tangled histories of Christianity,
secularization, and race

The number of atheists and nonreligious people across the globe has never been higher.[1] Secularization – the falling away of Christianity – has occurred over centuries in the West, with far-reaching and sometimes unexpected effects on all aspects of life. These effects extend to race as well, but it remains disputed whether secularization helped open the way for racism or whether it provided new ways to challenge racism. The answer to this question will throw light on a larger one: has secularization been on the whole beneficial or harmful to western societies?

The argument that secularization contributed to the development of racism, sketched in more detail below, goes something like this: Christianity held that all humans were created in the image of God and descended from Adam and Eve, meaning that all humans were literally related. Moreover, the Bible proclaimed that God "hath made of one blood all nations of men" (Acts 17:26, King James Version), which struck at the idea that humans could be divided into distinct biological groups. As the influence of the Christian story began to decline in the eighteenth and nineteenth centuries, however, humans were no longer seen as part of one big family, created by God, but rather as nothing more than another species of animal. From here, the argument goes, it was easy to begin speculating that perhaps different human groups had evolved or emerged separately. If this were the case, it might be possible to arrange these races into a hierarchy or even to consider some as less than fully human. Indeed, many white Europeans and Americans did precisely this in the eighteenth and nineteenth centuries, inevitably placing themselves at the top of the racial hierarchy and justifying racist violence against non-whites. The thrust of this argument is that secularization lamentably allowed for racism to take hold in our modern society.

But there is another story to be told, one in which secularization offered new tools to oppose racism. The argument for this position is as follows: despite Christianity's seemingly anti-racist message, in reality the religion played a crucial role in the emergence of racism through its long history of anti-Semitism and its disregard for non-Christian religions. Africans, for example, were often judged to be irredeemable heathens, and in time as fundamentally separate from Christian whites. These religious divisions, in other words, helped to create and eventually cement racial divisions. Furthermore, Christianity gave divine sanction to slavery and justified the conquest of other groups on the grounds of bringing them civilization and the gospel. Jettisoning the authority of Christianity not only removed this unwarranted sense of divinely granted superiority, the argument continues, it freed people to see humans as they were: not as God's creations, but as highly evolved apes, all descending from a common ancestor. In this view, racism made no sense because races were all part of the same story of evolutionary descent in which superficial physical differences developed over time but had no deeper theological meaning. In contrast to the previous argument, then, secularization could be seen as a boon to the fight against racism since it stripped away irrational Christian ideas about humanity and replaced them with ones based in science and reason.

These two conflicting perspectives about the relationship between secularization and racism – each with a degree of truth – both focus primarily on the influence of Christian ideas about race. They point to the need for an examination of the racial views of atheists, a topic that no historians have yet addressed in any detail.[2] This book tackles precisely that question.

The focus of the book is the second half of the nineteenth century and the early twentieth century in Britain and the United States. There are two reasons for looking at this period. For one, this was the time when racist attitudes in Britain and the United States attained prominence.[3] Racial science, with its emphasis on racial classifications based on physical and mental features – such as measurements of the skull – came to the fore in this period, in tandem with the emergence of the new disciplines of anthropology and ethnology, and more generally the triumph of science as the leading authority on the natural world. New racist doctrines defined whites as the superior race and western society as representing the pinnacle of civilization. These ideas emerged as western countries were beginning to industrialize and gain untold wealth, in part through imperial domination. Pseudo-scientific hierarchies of race and civilizational judgments helped to justify colonial conquests of supposedly inferior non-white people and the enslavement and subsequent oppression of black people, and this domination only served to reinforce the notion that white racial superiority must be true.

This period also saw a burgeoning popular movement of atheists and other nonbelievers on both sides of the Atlantic which challenged the authority of Christianity and the Bible, and instead championed a rational and scientific view of the world. For several centuries there had been those, called freethinkers, who rejected the ideas of Christianity, and even some atheists who rejected the idea of a God altogether.[4] Yet these individuals mostly moved in upper-class circles and did not seek to organize themselves or win converts among the masses. Nineteenth-century freethinkers, on the other hand, banded together in various organizations and sought to convey their irreligious message to all segments of society, particularly the lower classes. These new organizations inserted themselves into the public sphere by way of numerous lectures, books, pamphlets, debates, and weekly newspapers that aimed to reach a wide audience.

My aim in this book is to investigate how ideas about race, atheism, and civilization – all of which reached their peak in many ways in the nineteenth century – were interconnected. In doing so, I hope to shed light on the question of the relationship between secularization and racism.

During this era, white atheists and freethinkers in Europe and the United States imagined themselves as part of the most advanced civilization on the planet. It was widely believed that their nations dominated the globe through a combination of technological innovation, military strength, superior institutions, and, not least, racial superiority. And yet there was a tension: how advanced could these civilizations be, atheists and freethinkers asked themselves, given that the majority of the population believed in Christianity, a doctrine that was not only untrue but also harmful? What right therefore did these white Christian nations have to rule over other societies and races, wiping out whole cultures and civilizations in the process? Might these cultures actually offer their own virtues that were superior in some ways to Christianity? Might it be wrong – indeed, unscientific and irrational – to consider some races as innately inferior to others?

The central argument of the book is that there was, therefore, a profound ambivalence among white atheists and freethinkers about the question of the West's racial and civilizational superiority. On the one hand, they imagined themselves at the pinnacle of the racial and civilization hierarchy. But on the other, the vast majority of their countrymen were Christians who seemed to reject the West's greatest gifts, namely reason and science, which led them to question these same notions of racial and cultural superiority. While white atheists never quite succeeded in resolving this tension, as we will see, their efforts reveal nuanced and often novel attempts to grapple with the problems of race and civilization.

Race, religion, and secularization

Given the ubiquity of Christianity over the course of western history, it is no surprise that, as Colin Kidd contends, "scripture has been for much of the early modern and modern eras the primary cultural influence on the forging of races."[5] Yet, Kidd notes, the Bible is mostly silent on explicit matters of race, except for the verse mentioned above in the book of Acts proclaiming that God created humans of one blood and the verse in the book of Jeremiah (13:23, King James Version) which asked, "Can the Ethiopian change his skin, or the leopard his spots?"[6] This silence has meant that the lessons Christians drew from the Bible about race often needed to be inferred from the text, and, as might be expected, this was not always done in a straightforward way.

Christian anti-Semitism has a long history, and some historians have seen in medieval anti-Semitism the genesis of modern racism. In the Middle Ages, Christians held Jews responsible for the death of Christ and treated them, at best, as second-class citizens. Theories abounded that groups of Jews conspired to kidnap and murder Christian children for blood sacrifices, or to steal and desecrate the Eucharist host – the sacred bread which was, to Christians, literally Christ's body. At numerous times throughout

4

the Middle Ages, such conspiracy theories whipped up whole communities of Christians into frenzies, resulting in mass violence against Jews. Nonetheless, Jews could still, at least theoretically, convert to Christianity and become equals to Christians. This began to change in the early modern period, particularly in Spain during the Christian Reconquista, completed in 1492, when Muslims and Jews were expelled from the Iberian Peninsula. Some Jews, the *conversos*, remained in the country and converted to Christianity to escape the anti-Semitic persecution. But suspicions remained of this group: it was no longer the outward religion of a person that marked them as permanently different, but their potentially tainted blood and lineage. This shift from religion to blood lines, some historians have suggested, was a critical step on the way to modern racism.[7]

Christianity also played an important role in creating racial divisions in colonial America, where Christian European settlers distinguished themselves from supposedly "heathen" Africans. In this period, whiteness became synonymous with Christianity and blackness with heathenism. The perceived lack of religion among Africans allowed Christians to justify their enslavement, but things became more complicated when black slaves converted to Christianity: could fellow Christians still be enslaved? Eventually, in the late seventeenth and early eighteenth centuries, baptism and enslaved status were decoupled, meaning that even if slaves converted to Christianity, they would still remain enslaved. In colonial America there developed the idea of "hereditary heathenism," in Rebecca Goetz's terminology, which saw Africans as essentially and permanently godless heathens who could never truly become Christian – an idea that helped to create modern conceptions of racial divisions.[8]

At the same time, however, many scholars have seen Christianity's universalist message as a bulwark against the division of humanity into distinct races. As noted above, Christianity seemed to suggest that all humans were inherently equal since they all descended from the biblical Adam and were therefore created in the image of God. This is why George Fredrickson argues that "to achieve its full potential as an ideology, racism had to be emancipated from Christian universalism."[9] Such a turning point, some historians have suggested, came in the Enlightenment of the eighteenth century. It was in this period that white European thinkers began to classify humanity into distinct races based on supposedly objective analyses of physical and mental features. An early and influential classification scheme was the Swedish botanist Carl Linnaeus's *Systema naturæ*, first published in 1735 but much expanded in later editions. In this work, humans were grouped into four different races: Europeans, Asians, Americans, and Africans. While his system was not explicitly hierarchical, Linnaeus's views became clear in the descriptions for each race. Europeans, for example, were "acute, inventive," and "[g]*overned* by laws," whereas Africans were "crafty, indolent, negligent," and "[g]*overned* by caprice."[10] Other Enlightenment thinkers followed Linnaeus's lead. Johannes Blumenbach, for example, enlarged the number of races to five and coined the term "Caucasian" for white people, considering them the original type of man from which the other types – Mongolian, Ethiopian, American, and Malay – had degenerated.[11] "Whatever their intentions," Fredrickson notes,

> Linnaeus, Blumenbach, and other eighteenth-century ethnologists opened the way to a secular or scientific racism by considering human beings part of the animal kingdom rather than viewing them in biblical terms as children of God endowed with spiritual capacities denied to other creatures.[12]

This is not to say that the Enlightenment offered straightforward lessons about race. This was a time when, paradoxically, philosophers proclaimed the equality of all men and their common universal nature, even as they developed new and more complex racial classification schemes. This paradox is perhaps best captured in the thought of Thomas Jefferson, the chief author of the Declaration of Independence and the third president of the United States. Jefferson was a man of the secular Enlightenment, although he was fiercely private about his own religious views. He rejected the miraculous claims of the Bible and the doctrine of the Trinity, which he deemed contrary to reason, but he did believe in a creator God and hoped for an afterlife. Despite his rejection of most Christian ideas, Jefferson had a profound admiration for the moral teachings of Jesus, and went about creating his own version of the New Testament – with the aid of scissors and glue – by systematically removing all references to Jesus's miracles, resurrection, and divinity.[13]

The Declaration of Independence proclaimed that "[w]e hold these truths to be self-evident, that all men are created equal," but such high-sounding rhetoric clashed with the reality that millions of Africans and African Americans were then enslaved in the United States, including several hundred at Jefferson's Monticello plantation. In line with other Enlightenment thinkers, Jefferson thought blacks were inferior to whites. He granted that they might be equal in memory, but that "in reason [they are] much inferior, as I think one could scarcely be found capable of tracing and comprehending the investigations of Euclid: and that in imagination they are dull, tasteless, and anomalous."[14] That said, and despite the fact that he owned slaves, he personally abhorred slavery, believing that it harmed both whites and blacks.[15] He recognized the injustice of slavery and feared a future divine reprisal, writing, "I tremble for my country when I reflect that God is just […]."[16] Still, he believed that unconditional freedom for slaves was not a viable solution because of the intractable prejudices and hatreds that had been built up during the time of slavery.[17] He therefore mused on various remedies, including colonizing freed blacks outside the United States, but critics today question the seriousness of Jefferson's commitment to ending slavery given his inaction on that question.[18] Indeed, Jefferson carried on a lengthy relationship and fathered children with his slave Sally Hemings after the death of his wife Martha. These children and a select few others were the only slaves Jefferson freed; the vast majority were sold to other owners on Jefferson's death.[19]

Other Enlightenment luminaries, like David Hume, Voltaire, and Immanuel Kant, expressed similar views to Jefferson that blacks were, in some way or another, inferior to whites.[20] Yet for others, like Thomas Paine, Jefferson's comrade in the revolutionary struggle against Britain and a fellow deist, the lessons of the Enlightenment pointed against racism. In Paine's deist tract *The Age of Reason* (1794–95), he proclaimed his belief in "the equality of man."[21] Before the American Revolution, Paine was an opponent of slavery,[22] and he spoke out against the institution in a 1776 article which urged American independence and, in a footnote, implored the reader to "[f]orget not the hapless African."[23] After independence, Paine was elected a member of the Pennsylvania Society for Promoting the Abolition of Slavery in 1787.[24] Later in life, he continued on the theme of anti-slavery, counseling his friend then-President Jefferson to offer American mediation to support the fledgling state of Haiti, created as a result of a successful slave revolt against France. Paine also encouraged Jefferson to forbid the introduction of slaves into the newly acquired Louisiana territory and to instead support free black labor there.[25]

Secular Enlightenment thought opened new avenues for thinking about race. It offered powerful arguments against inequality and slavery through the rhetoric of the equality of man, but it also served to emphasize the divisions between human races through the guise of rational science. Nineteenth-century atheists and freethinkers were profoundly rooted in the thought of the Enlightenment and therefore also inherited many of these contradictions.

As new speculations about the distinctions between human races came to the fore, Christianity seemed to act, at least theoretically, as a check against such racism. This was through the belief in monogenesis, a theory that posited a single origin for all humans in Adam and Eve. An alternative theory, called polygenesis, began to develop in the sixteenth century. This theory suggested that each human race had arisen independently, such that the races were permanently separate and distinct. As Hannah Franziska Augstein points out, "the very first full-blown racial theories were put forward by men who did not much care for religion. The notion of inherently different races was somewhat alien to the anthropological doctrines of Christian orthodoxy."[26] Owing to new geological and archeological findings that undercut the traditional Genesis creation story, and the techniques of biblical criticism that called into question a single divine authorship for the Bible, "the Christian foundations of theories on man were crumbling. Once natural historians no longer felt obliged to align their tenets to the story of Genesis, the playground for all sorts of racialist speculations was opened."[27] With the Christian framework destabilized, anything was now permitted.

Many polygenists in the nineteenth century were indeed proudly heretical. The innovators in the United States were Samuel Morton, Louis Agassiz, Josiah Nott, and George Gliddon, the so-called American School of Anthropology. While Morton and Agassiz both attempted to square polygenesis with Christianity, Nott and Gliddon delighted in their anticlericalism. Nott and Gliddon wrote the quintessential work of the American School, *Types of Mankind*, in 1854, a massive volume arguing for the distinctiveness of the races. Nott was furthermore a slaveholder and used his poly-genist ideas to bolster the case for black inferiority. In Britain, meanwhile, the Scottish anatomist Robert Knox led the way in polygenist thinking, in turn influencing James Hunt, the leader of the irreligious Anthropological Society of London, and his followers. Historians have typically assigned these mid-nineteenth century irreligious racial theorists a prominent role in the development of racial thought.[28]

The other side of this coin is that the strongest opponents of polygenesis were typically Christians. In the United States, Samuel Stanhope Smith and John Bachman, the two most prominent defenders of monogenesis, were both ordained ministers.[29] In Britain, the chief proponent of monogenesis in the first half of the nineteenth century was James Cowles Prichard, an Anglican with Quaker roots.[30] Quakers and evangelicals dominated anti-slavery and humanitarian groups in the United States and Britain. Hannah Augstein acknowledges that it would be too much to say it was "a general rule" that a belief in monogenesis always accompanied humanitarianism, but in Britain at least, "religious monogenism and anti-slavery agitation went hand-in-hand."[31] This should not be taken too far, however: John Bachman, who argued strenuously against polygenesis and in favor of monogenesis, was completely in agreement with his opponent Josiah Nott about the legitimacy of slavery.

One clearly did not need to be a secular polygenist to support slavery. There were many other ways to defend the institution, and indeed the most common ones were based in Christianity, not secular polygenesis. One could, for example, point to all of the passages in the Old Testament that detailed the conditions under which slavery was allowed for the ancient Hebrews – for example in Leviticus 25:39–55 – or Paul's injunction in the New Testament for slaves to "be obedient to them that are your masters" (Ephesians 6:5, King James Version). The "Curse of Ham" myth likewise was used by some to justify blacks' enslaved status. In the book of Genesis, Noah's son Ham transgressed against his father, who in turn cursed the descendants of Ham's son Canaan to slavery. It was widely held that Ham was therefore the progenitor of the black race, and it became common to suggest that blacks were "the sons of Ham."[32] These Bible-based defenses of slavery were countered by abolitionist Christians who contended that the central message of Jesus was the Golden Rule: to treat others the way one would want to be treated. But these abolitionists were hampered in debates in the nineteenth century by the fact that Jesus never explicitly spoke against slavery, as the defenders of the institution could always point out.[33]

The most outspoken historian on Christianity's links with racism is Forrest G. Wood, whose polemical work *The Arrogance of Faith* makes the case that Christianity "has been fundamentally racist in its ideology, organization, and practice."[34] In every manifestation of racial violence throughout American history Wood finds Christianity involved in some way. This link came from an ethnocentrism that he argues is inherent to the faith, which considered all non-Christian cultures to be inferior or lacking precisely because they were not Christian. This ethnocentrism could easily justify the conquest of other cultures, or the enslavement of Africans, on the grounds of spreading Christianity to godless heathens. Indeed, perceived godlessness was associated with Satan and could open the way for dehumanization of those deemed to be outside the boundaries of Christianity. Those Christian voices of protest against slavery or foreign domination, Wood argues, were too few and often had self-serving motives. Abolitionist Quakers in the United States, for example, appeared more concerned with avoiding the sinful institution of slavery for the sake of their own salvation rather than with the suffering of the enslaved.[35]

Wood, however, does not deny the influence of secular thought – for example the works of Charles Darwin – on the development of racism.[36] Darwin's theory of evolution, put forward in his 1859 *On the Origin of Species*, contended that all species evolved through a gradual process of natural selection that took eons, in contrast to the mainstream Christian view that each species had been created individually by God. Several scholars have seen Darwin's theory as a critical step toward the emergence of scientific racism in the nineteenth and twentieth centuries. By undermining the Genesis account even further, it opened the way to conceiving of races as separately evolved and able to be ranked in a hierarchy.[37] More polemical works, from a clear Christian perspective, have exploited these observations to make a case against Darwinism. Richard Weikart, in his controversial book *From Darwin to Hitler*, notes how the decline of Christianity led to a rejection of its monogenist premise. "Before the nineteenth century,"

Weikart writes, "the intellectual dominance of Christianity militated against some of the worst excesses of racism."[38] In his view, Darwinism introduced a materialistic account of the origins of humanity and ethics, opening the door to moral relativism and the devaluation of human life, which ultimately "smoothed the path for Nazi ideology."[39] For Weikart then, the loss of faith in Christianity and its replacement with a new theory that saw humans as mere animals is bound up with the worst of the Nazis' crimes.

Weikart's account has been strongly criticized by historians,[40] and one can actually identify anti-racist threads running through Darwin's work. This has been done most prominently by Adrian Desmond and James Moore, two of the most important Darwin scholars, who argue convincingly in a recent book that Darwin's evolutionary research was animated by a hatred of polygenesis and the ways in which it could be used to justify slavery or imperial conquest. Darwin's work claimed that all humans, and indeed all life, descended from a common ancestor through evolution by natural selection and that suggestions about the permanent inferiority of certainty races were unfounded.[41] In this respect, Darwin's ideas had an anti-racist core, even if others reworked them to support racial hierarchies.

The ideas of Darwinian evolution provided the basis for the new field of eugenics, developed by Darwin's cousin Francis Galton. Eugenics intended to harness evolution's power by encouraging the "fit" members of society to have more children while discouraging the "unfit" from procreating, sometimes through forcible sterilization. Eugenics programs targeted criminality, alcoholism, "feeble-mindedness," and other traits that seemed, often erroneously, to be inheritable. A race-based eugenics never took off in Britain, but in the United States the link between eugenics and race was clearer since racial minorities were disproportionately targeted for forced sterilization, and eugenicists were some of the most vocal proponents of enacting immigration restrictions on undesirable racial groups.[42] Daniel J. Kevles emphasizes that both Galton and his most prominent follower Karl Pearson were hostile to Christianity and sought to replace it with eugenics. Galton, writes Kevles, "found in eugenics a scientific substitute for church orthodoxies, a secular faith, a defensible religious obligation."[43] But again, the link between secularization and eugenics was not straightforward, as

Kevles admits that the supporters of eugenics in the early twentieth century were "predominantly Protestant."[44]

Another way in which secularization and racism are linked is in the triumph of scientific over religious explanations of natural phenomena that occurred in the nineteenth century. For Douglas Lorimer, scientific racism cannot be explained merely by reference to the emergence of disciplines like anthropology and evolutionary biology, but "needs to be considered as part of the broader cultural and social process of 'secularization.'"[45] Lorimer's argument is that older tropes about racial groups dating from the abolitionist era of the early nineteenth century became secularized in scientific discourses by the end of the century. As he explains, "the racial discourse of the scientists retained the negative attributes of peoples designated as sinners, or savages, and redefined the more positive affirmations of abolitionists and missionaries as pious sentimentality."[46] In conclusion, Lorimer notes:

> This process of secularization may well represent a liberation of reason from the religious and cultural authority of the past. The disturbing question is why the liberation weakened existing forces of resistance to racism and, at the same time, strengthened the forces of colonial oppression.[47]

A related perspective that stresses the continuities between Christian and secular conceptions of race comes from Terence Keel in his book *Divine Variations*. In his view, there was not a sharp break between Christian views of race and secular, modern ones. Rather, he says, "modern scientific theories of race are an extension of Christian intellectual history."[48] This can be seen, for example, in the persistent divisions of races into three on the pattern of ancestry from Noah's three sons. Likewise, Blumenbach's story of an originally perfect white race which subsequently degenerated into non-white races had a biblical parallel in the story of the fall of man in the Garden of Eden. More broadly, the power of a creator God, Keel argues, has been transferred onto nature, biology, and genetics. In short, the process of secularization did not, as others have suggested, open the way for racism, but merely translated previous ideas about race into modern terms.

The relationship between secularization, Christianity, and racism is thus complex. This complexity is perhaps best seen in Colin Kidd's work examining the relationship between Protestantism and racial thought in the previous four centuries. At the outset of the project, he admitted that he "had a suspicion – perhaps verging on a crude hypothesis – that the dethroning of biblical authority was a necessary prelude to the emergence of modern racism." This did not mean that a straight line could be drawn, but "that the liberation of the scriptures opens the *possibility* – no more than that – of a less constrained doctrine of racial difference grounded on a theory of polygenesis." However, Kidd

> came to realise that [...] the historical record [...] is replete with unpredictable and illogical developments. The human imagination is equally capable of interpreting the Christian scriptures in a racialist as in an anti-racialist manner. It often depends less, it seems, on the logic of the scriptures than on the objectives of the interpreter [...].[49]

Thus far, much of the literature on the relationship between race and religion has focused on Christian thought, without addressing atheism specifically. This fact points to the need for an examination of what actual atheists and secular people thought about race during this period. Before beginning this exploration, however, it is necessary to survey the emergence of popular atheist movements in Britain and the United States, since they form the basis of this book.

Transatlantic atheism

The second half of the nineteenth century, aside from seeing a hardening of racial attitudes, also witnessed an efflorescence of outspoken atheists and freethinkers in Britain and the United States. While the context was different in each country, atheists and freethinkers in Britain and the United States formed a transatlantic intellectual community with considerable movement of both ideas and people across the Atlantic, giving the development of freethought in both countries a great deal of unity.[50] Though I use the terms "atheism," "freethought," "nonbelief," and "irreligion" interchangeably, it should be noted that not all of the figures discussed would have accepted the label of "atheist" to describe themselves. As we will see, there was a range of irreligious labels available to nineteenth-century figures.

The development of atheism in both the United States and Britain owed much to late seventeenth- and eighteenth-century deists. Deism held that the universe was created by a god, but one who then stepped back and no longer intervened in the workings of the universe or in human affairs. This meant that revelations supposedly coming from God – such as the Bible – were actually the works of men and that accounts of miracles were contrary to reason. Deists continued to believe, however, that God's existence could be deduced from the design seemingly found in nature and they hoped his existence provided a basis for morality. The deist critique of Christianity nonetheless provided a powerful impetus for atheism since it gave a much reduced role to God. Atheism reduced that role to nothing, arguing that instances where God was seemingly necessary – such as overseeing the forces of gravity in the universe, as Isaac Newton thought – could actually be explained just as well without him. Avowed atheists first appeared in the late eighteenth century and would become increasingly numerous in the nineteenth century.[51]

Probably the most influential figure in the development of freethought on both sides of the Atlantic was the deist Thomas Paine, discussed above.[52] Paine, born in England, first gained fame in the United States, where his republican writings attacking monarchy provided fuel for the American revolutionaries. Paine returned to England in 1787, but his support of the French Revolution led to a hostile reaction that forced him to flee to Paris in 1792. There he wrote *The Age of Reason* (1794–95), a two-part attack on Christianity and the authority of the Bible. Paine argued that all revelations claiming to be from the deity were invalid and that one could discern God's works through a study of nature.

By directing his work toward the masses and not just the educated few, Paine reached a wide audience, even though little in the work was particularly original. In the first half of the nineteenth century, political and religious radicals in Britain and the United States took up Paine's writings and began to form clubs centered on his ideas, while attracting the ire of the law for their controversial views. Many elites – particularly in Britain – feared the links they saw between irreligion and the political radicalism of the French Revolution and wished to prevent similar events from happening in their own countries. For Paine and his followers, irreligion and radical politics were closely interlinked: a hostility to the authority of "priestcraft" and the influence of Christian elites easily fit with a hostility to monarchy and aristocratic elites with inherited wealth and status. A program of increased democracy, which would give greater power to the masses, combined with greater allowance for freedom of conscience and expression was therefore a main feature of nineteenth-century freethought. Paine remained in Paris until 1802, when he returned to the United States, dying in 1809. By the 1820s, American freethinkers had begun to celebrate Paine's birthday, signaling their commitment to both his religious and political radicalism.[53]

Another crucial figure in the early history of popular freethought was the Welsh social reformer Robert Owen, who, like Paine, was influential on both sides of the Atlantic.[54] Owen gained national prominence in the first half of the nineteenth century for his utopian experiments in Britain and America based on his radical view of human nature as being determined almost entirely by circumstances. Owen, disgusted with the condition of the working classes in Britain, wanted to redirect capitalism's productive power to benefit all. He began his experiments in Scotland at New Lanark, a cotton mill purchased from his father-in-law, where he instituted reforms that focused on improving the workers' living conditions and educating their children. Owen wanted to extend his cooperative schemes across the country, but, as Edward Royle explains, "he began to think of communities not only as a solution to the problem of the poor but also as a scheme for promoting the practical happiness and regeneration of all mankind."[55] At the same time, Owen's movement was opposed to Christianity and indeed all religions, since they hampered the adoption of his principles about the malleability of human character. As with Paine, then, Owen's skepticism of religion went hand-in-hand with his reformist politics. In 1824, Owen left for America to begin a utopian community at New Harmony, Indiana. The experiment was, however, a failure, and Owen returned to Britain in 1829, this time to lead several abortive movements aimed at the promotion of his ideas. Nonetheless, his Association of All Classes of All Nations, formed in 1835, soon developed a nationwide organizational presence. Before leaving the United States, Owen gained further publicity when he participated in a public debate on the merits of Christianity with Rev. Alexander Campbell of Virginia in 1829.[56]

In Britain, meanwhile, a number of Owen's followers broke with him in order to focus primarily on religious criticism. Charles Southwell created the newspaper the *Oracle of Reason* along with William Chilton. George

Jacob Holyoake, the son of a tinsmith, became a follower of Owen and later took over the editorship of Southwell's paper after Southwell was imprisoned for blasphemy. Like Southwell and so many other atheists, Holyoake also spent time behind bars for his views. He would later establish his own newspapers, the longest-running of which was the *Reasoner*, published from 1846 to 1861. Through this paper, Holyoake became one of the most prominent irreligious leaders in the country as he built bridges with middle-class intellectuals and liberal theists. He coined the term "secularism" in the 1850s as a replacement for "atheism." In Holyoake's view, a secularist outlook differed from an atheist one in the sense that it was not wholly destructive but sought to establish a framework for ethics that was independent of religion. In other words, Holyoake saw atheism as a purely negative creed, whereas secularism was a positive one.[57]

Holyoake's secularism drew much of its ethics from utilitarianism, a non-Christian system of morals. This philosophy, devised in the late eighteenth century by Jeremy Bentham, held that humans desired the pursuit of pleasure and the avoidance of pain. Pleasure was the only good; pain the only evil. Government policies, Bentham reasoned, should therefore aim to maximize pleasure, minimize pain, and produce the greatest happiness – also called the greatest utility – for the greatest number.[58] Utilitarianism would be further developed by the British liberal philosopher John Stuart Mill in the nineteenth century. For much of his life, Mill was a colonial administrator with the East India Company, and he was elected as a Liberal MP from 1865 to 1868. Mill's philosophy emphasized individual rights and democratic freedoms, including advocacy of women's suffrage. Mill himself was an unbeliever, although assigning a label to his religious views remains challenging. In his autobiography, Mill wrote:

> I am thus one of the very few examples, in this country, of one who has, not thrown off religious belief, but never had it. I grew up in a negative state with relation to it. I looked upon the modern exactly as I did upon the Greek religion, as something which in no way concerned me.[59]

Indeed, according to Mill's friend Alexander Bain, Mill never attended a church service in his life.[60] Many working-class freethinkers revered Mill for his cogent defense of utilitarianism and liberalism – the basis of much of their radical program – and he was friendly with a number of the most prominent figures. For example, he contributed funds to the 1868 election campaign of the leading atheist thinker Charles Bradlaugh.[61] Mill, however, never explicitly joined the popular freethought movement, and in his *Three Essays on Religion*, published posthumously, he seemed to express sympathy for the idea of theistic design in the universe.[62]

Meanwhile, Holyoake began a number of secular societies around Britain, but the leadership of the movement was usurped by Charles Bradlaugh, who adopted a more hardline atheist position than Holyoake. Bradlaugh, the son of a solicitor's clerk, had been a Sunday school teacher as a teenager, but gradually came to doubt the claims of Christianity. Because of his irreligion, he was forced to leave his home and live in poverty before enlisting in the army. After being stationed in Dublin for several years, he returned to London to work as a legal clerk. Bradlaugh gained an increasing reputation in secular circles and consolidated the local secular societies into the National Secular Society in 1866. He was the president of that organization until his death in 1891 and also edited the society's flagship newspaper, the *National Reformer* (1860–93), for much of his life.

Bradlaugh became one of the most prominent atheists of the nineteenth century owing to two major public incidents. In 1877–78, he and his most important secularist ally, Annie Besant, were tried and convicted for publishing a birth control pamphlet, but the conviction was ultimately overturned on a technicality. The other incident that led to national attention was Bradlaugh's election as MP for Northampton in 1880. Because Bradlaugh was an atheist he was unable to swear the oath necessary to take his seat in Parliament. After a long and tortuous legal battle that attracted considerable press coverage, Bradlaugh was finally permitted to take the oath (and his seat) in 1886.[63] With Bradlaugh at the helm, secular societies boomed. The high point was the 1880s, when there were nearly 120 local secular societies, whose message reached an estimated 60,000 people through newspapers or meetings. The number of actual members, however, would have been only several thousand.[64]

The predominantly working-class secularists were not the only irreligious figures in Britain. Agnosticism, a term coined by the British evolutionary scientist T.H. Huxley, was an epistemological position meant to differ from atheism by emphasizing humans' absence of knowledge about

God's existence. The term became influential and was adopted by others, like the scientists Charles Darwin and John Tyndall and the writer and historian Leslie Stephen.[65] Huxley and his fellow scientists were advocates of what has been called "scientific naturalism," which aimed to replace Christian understandings of the natural world with scientific ones, and to ensure scientists assumed a central role as social and cultural leaders, in keeping with their emergent middle-class position.[66] Some working-class atheists, however, rejected what they saw as disingenuous window-dressing on the part of Huxley and the agnostics. In the view of these atheists, the new term "agnostic" did not differ in content from "atheist," but attempted to distance its adherents from the negative associations with the term "atheism" and maintain a respectable status.

Such divisions between atheists and agnostics were not as clear-cut in the United States, and the leading American freethinker, Robert Ingersoll, was popularly known as the "Great Agnostic," even though he admitted that he saw no real difference between the terms "atheist" and "agnostic."[67] Born in Dresden, New York, Ingersoll was raised in a household where both parents were abolitionists. As was the case with many other freethinkers, Ingersoll's father was a preacher, yet as a young man, Ingersoll came to doubt Christianity. At a time when outdoor lectures were a key medium for disseminating political or religious views, Ingersoll became known as one of the greatest orators of the time, and people flocked to hear his lectures – not just atheists and freethinkers but many Christians as well. Ingersoll supported the Republican Party for much of his life, and contemporaries acknowledged that he might have gone on to hold high political office if not for his atheism.[68]

The second half of the nineteenth century saw the growth of the American freethought movement, including a number of freethought newspapers, the most important being the *Boston Investigator* (1831–1904) and the *Truth Seeker* (1873–present).[69] The latter, edited first by D.M. Bennett, who was followed by Eugene Macdonald and later his brother George, was the largest American freethought newspaper and had a national circulation. American freethinkers took up the former Unitarian pastor Francis Ellingwood Abbot's "Nine Demands of Liberalism," which called for further measures ensuring the separation of church and state, and helped to form the

National Liberal League in 1876. Those freethinkers who were more hostile to Christianity, like Bennett, took over the organization from moderates like Abbot in 1878. The organization was renamed the American Secular Union in 1884 and would later merge in 1894 with the Freethought Federation of America, formed by Samuel Porter Putnam.[70]

The influence of Auguste Comte's philosophy of positivism was also strong in both the United States and Britain. In the aftermath of the French Revolution, Comte wrote his six-volume *Cours de philosophie positive* (1830–42), which outlined his theory that western civilization was passing from the theological and metaphysical stages to the final, positive stage, in which a total understanding of the universe through scientific laws would be in reach. Among the many early supporters of his philosophy were major Victorian thinkers like John Stuart Mill, as well as George Holyoake. Following the death of Comte's lover Clotilde de Vaux in 1846, his philosophy took an increasingly religious turn. Named the "Religion of Humanity," Comte's new creed worshipped humanity in the collective and was based on love and altruism. Mill was initially attracted by this approach, but later in life he distanced himself from Comte because of differences both personal and intellectual. Nonetheless, Mill continued his belief that the Religion of Humanity, in some form, was a necessary replacement for Christianity.[71] Richard Congreve, the first of Comte's British converts, established the London Positivist Society in 1867. He broke with other adherents like E.S. Beesly, Frederic Harrison, and J.H. Bridges over his emphasis on the ritualistic aspects of positivism. The latter were more interested in disseminating a positivist philosophy to the masses than in performing rituals. In any case, as Susan Budd notes, the number of committed positivists was small, likely only several hundred at any given time.[72] In America, positivism likewise attracted a small number of adherents, particularly among immigrants from England.[73]

Another variety of unbelief came in the form of ethical societies. The London South Place Chapel had roots as a Unitarian church in late eighteenth-century America. It crossed the Atlantic to London in 1822. Under Moncure Conway, a Virginian who had relocated to London in 1863, the congregation moved away from Christianity entirely, becoming something of an atheist church. After Conway's departure in 1884, leadership of the congregation fell to Stanton Coit, another transplanted American. Coit's theological views were influenced by Felix Adler, a New York rabbi who purged all supernatural elements from Reform Judaism as he began the Society for Ethical Culture in 1876 in New York City. Independent ethical societies sprouted in various cities across the United States soon after. Coit took Adler's ideas with him to London and transformed South Place into an ethical society. He departed after a rupture with the congregation in 1892, but founded the West London Ethical Society and helped to establish similar societies across Britain.[74]

The message of freethinkers was transmitted in books, lectures, and pamphlets, but especially in newspapers. The chief newspapers drawn upon in this book are, from Britain, the *Reasoner*, the *National Reformer*, and the *Freethinker*, and, from the United States, the *Boston Investigator* and the *Truth Seeker*. While there were countless smaller newspapers, these were the longest-running and most important in their respective countries. They represented forums for debate and encompassed a range of perspectives. While they were based in urban centers (London for the British papers, and Boston and New York respectively for the two American ones), they also reprinted articles from smaller newspapers and reported on meetings and events from across each country. In terms of the circulation of the British papers, each might have had about several thousand readers, with the *Reasoner* reaching a peak of 5,000 copies sold per week in the mid-1850s and the *Freethinker* selling over 10,000 copies per week at its height in the 1880s.[75] Albert Post reports that the *Boston Investigator* had a subscription of over 2,000 in 1835, though the number had fallen to 500 in 1850.[76] Sidney Warren meanwhile estimates that freethought works by Ingersoll and others "were read by scores of thousands [...]."[77] Larger newspapers like the *Truth Seeker* had a circulation well into the thousands.[78]

Essential to this book's argument is the fact that atheists' racial views were shaped in large part by their status as a marginalized group in Britain and the United States. In both these countries, atheists and other nonbelievers suffered a variety of penalties, legal or otherwise, for their irreligion. Atheism had long been associated with immorality. If there were no rewards or punishments in the afterlife, the argument went, what reason would people have to act morally in this life? In this sense, then, atheism was a theological sin, but it was also a social one, since it threatened the entire basis of social cohesion.[79]

In Britain, numerous freethinkers spent time in prison for blasphemy, including Richard Carlile, Charles Southwell, George Holyoake, and G.W. Foote.[80] Other penalties could also await those who publicly professed their unbelief. For example, Annie Besant, one of the leading secularists in the second half of the century, lost custody of her daughter to her husband Frank Besant, from whom she was separated, because of her irreligious beliefs and her advocacy of birth control. Laws also hampered the spread of freethought. The post office could seize freethought materials sent through the mail, and some news vendors refused to stock freethought literature, while the popular press routinely painted atheists in a negative light. It was because of the association between atheism and immorality that atheists risked losing their jobs and livelihoods if their irreligious views were discovered.[81] Various by-laws interfered with Sunday freethought lectures or outdoor meetings, while atheists and other nonbelievers had no standing in court because of their inability to swear an oath or affirm.[82]

Atheists in the United States also faced persecution, though unlike their British cousins, they did not have to contend with a legal linkage of religion and state, and were supported by a constitution that, at least in theory, mandated freedom of religion. Still, there were cases of atheists being denied the right to testify in court because of their inability to affirm,[83] or losing their jobs if their irreligious views were discovered.[84] The founder of the *Boston Investigator*, Abner Kneeland, was convicted and jailed for blasphemy in 1838, while the *Truth Seeker*'s D.M. Bennett was targeted by the Comstock Laws, which were devised by the puritanical Anthony Comstock to prevent the sending of "obscene" material through the mail. Comstock despised Bennett's irreligious views and made it his mission to catch him in violation of the law. His chance came in 1879, when Bennett was convicted for mailing a free love pamphlet. Despite being sixty years old, Bennett was sentenced to thirteen months of hard labor in a federal penitentiary.[85] Even for those not directly affected by blasphemy persecutions, the sight of revered figures, and in some cases friends, being hauled off to prison created a sense of being besieged by Christians. Aside from the threat of legal persecution, there was an even greater potential for social ostracism, which further deepened freethinkers' discontent toward their societies.

On top of this religious marginalization, many freethinkers were also economically marginalized. The class background of atheists and other nonreligious people was not uniform, but both Edward Royle and Susan Budd have found that members of the British secularist movement came mainly from the urban working and lower middle classes.[86] In the United States, members of the freethought movement likewise had roots in the working classes before the Civil War, though by the end of the century many members came from the emerging middle classes.[87] The editors of the *Boston Investigator* and the *Truth Seeker* came from humble origins and were sympathetic to the plight of the poor.[88] This is not to say that all nonreligious people were working class. T.H. Huxley, discussed above, came from a poor background, but eventually became one of the most prominent scientists in the country. He was, like his fellow agnostic Charles Darwin, reluctant to associate himself too closely with the working-class freethought and secular movement, even if he continued to prove popular among the working classes through his lectures.[89] Huxley staked out his place in the new scientific establishment, and eventually dominated it with his fellows in the X-Club, a dining club consisting of the leading scientific thinkers in the country.[90] Some of these X-Club scientists, such as John Lubbock, were born into wealthy, aristocratic families; others, such as Huxley or Herbert Spencer, came from more modest backgrounds or from families of Dissenters – those non-Anglican Protestants who were shut out of posts in government or top universities because of their dissent from the Anglican state church. By the second half of the nineteenth century, these men had forced their way into the establishment and many of the barriers to Dissenters had been removed, but they still carried this tradition of being outsiders, and were still aware of the precariousness of their respectable status within a Christian society.

For many atheists and freethinkers, and even the agnostics who moved closest to respectability, there was a sense of being on the outside looking in. Certainly it was true that they considered themselves proud Britons or Americans, and perhaps even the best embodiments of the western, Enlightened tradition, but it was also clear that they were not fully embraced

– to put it mildly – by their Christian countrymen. It was because of their status as outsiders that atheists and nonreligious people found many aspects of their societies unpalatable. This discontent manifested itself in a range of political positions that advocated for reform of their societies. The shape this reform would take was a matter of fierce debate – debates between freethinking socialists and liberals in late nineteenth-century Britain caused a serious split in the freethought movement, for example – but there was no doubt in their minds that reform was required.

The degree to which atheists and freethinkers were outsiders of course varied according to other factors like class or gender, not to mention race. As an independently wealthy gentleman naturalist, Darwin was obviously much more of an insider than someone like the working-class atheist leader Charles Bradlaugh, or indeed an average working-class atheist who might have written only an occasional letter to a freethought newspaper or attended meetings. Women in Britain and the United States were already deprived of equal rights and shut out of many educational and employment opportunities, and this marginalization was compounded in the case of those women who became freethinkers, since they were thought to have violated taboos surrounding women's proper place within the domestic sphere.[91] As a general rule, those who were most marginalized were often the ones who expressed the most subversive views with regard to race.

It should be noted that the focus of the book is mostly on white people. In western countries today, atheists and other nonreligious people are slightly disproportionately white.[92] This has been true historically as well. For example, a 1930 survey of members in the American Association for the Advancement of Atheism (4A) found that all but two of the 350 respondents were white. (The authors of the study did not say which race these two were.[93]) This book is ultimately not, however, an attempt to explain why atheists are or were disproportionately white. There are likely myriad factors for this dynamic – differing economic or educational opportunities might play an important role, for example – but this is not my main focus. I do, though, want to take the "whiteness" of the atheists in the book as an important fact. Some historians have begun to make the creation and maintenance of white racial identities an object of historical study.[94] Their investigations show that we cannot assume that "whiteness" is somehow a neutral or stable category, but rather that what constituted the "white race" has changed over time, and that possessing a white racial identity had implications for one's worldview. While the focus here is mostly on white atheists, I do nonetheless highlight cases of non-white atheists from time to time, although these people were clearly in the minority.

Outline of the book

In the opening chapter, entitled "Were Adam and Eve our first parents? Atheism and polygenesis," I show how a shared hostility to Christianity united white atheists and scientific racists in the nineteenth century. Crucial to this link was the heretical doctrine of polygenesis, the idea that the various races of humanity had multiple origins instead of a single one, as in the Christian doctrine of monogenesis. As has already been suggested, polygenesis was a heretical theory that had both racial and theological implications. If human races had separate origins, atheists pointed out, this would contradict the Genesis account that all humans descended from Adam and Eve and would call into question the veracity of the Bible. The theory of polygenesis had been around for several centuries, but it gained scientific support by the middle of the nineteenth century among racial scientists, who argued that the races were innately different and could be ranked hierarchically. Atheists and freethinkers embraced polygenesis since it seemed to be the most accurate scientific explanation for the diversity of races, in contrast to the quaint theory of monogenesis, which Christians clung to despite seemingly insurmountable scientific evidence. More importantly, the theory seemed to deal a fatal blow to the creation account in Genesis, and with it the entire foundation of Christianity. For this reason, many atheists often aligned themselves with irreligious scientific racists who posited vast differences between the various races.

The monogenist and polygenist division was ostensibly made obsolete by the evolutionary insights of Darwin, who argued that all life evolved from a common ancestor; yet as I show in the second chapter, "Brute men: race and society in evolution," racist ideas persisted within an evolutionary framework. Since evolution challenged the traditional account of creation as found in Genesis, it is unsurprising that many in the atheist movement were interested in these new ideas. The implications for race from evolutionary theory were not, however, straightforward. On the one hand, there were those who argued that evolution showed that all humans were related and any racial differences between them were ultimately superficial in the vast expanse of evolutionary time. On the other hand, there were those who argued that races could be ranked in a hierarchy on the basis of their evolutionary progress or that each race descended from its own unique ape ancestor. Evolution also shed light on the development of civilizations. The eighteenth-century idea that societies followed a linear course on the way to civilization fit well within an evolutionary worldview. Along with accepting the idea that white European civilization represented the apex of progress, other white atheists gave a subversive reading of societal evolution in which religion itself was seen as a product of evolution, formed when humanity was in its "savage" state. In this view, Christians were really no better than their savage counterparts.

An evolutionary perspective seemed to place Europe and the United States at the top of the racial and civilizational pyramid, but, as I demonstrate in the third chapter, "A London Zulu: savagery and civilization," there was considerable ambivalence about this hierarchical approach. An examination of how the so-called savage races – those in Africa, Australasia, and the Americas – appeared in atheists' writing reveals that many white atheists found positives in these societies and seemed, in some cases, to identify with them. The key link was a shared experience, among both atheists and savage groups, of persecution at the hands of more powerful Christians. Atheists recognized their own minority status and saw parallels between their experience of persecution and the missionary and imperial incursions into savage societies. While white atheists and freethinkers were not opposed to imperialism *per se*, they were at least skeptical about the legitimacy of western society running roughshod over these groups. Because western civilization was so tied up with Christianity, atheists were not convinced of its inherent superiority over other cultures. Indeed, there were many positives to be found in these savage societies, including a more egalitarian social structure and a seeming lack of religion and belief in God.

The fourth chapter, "The wise men of the East: India, China, and Japan," carries on in a similar vein by examining these eastern civilizations. Far from constructing the people there as Others, atheists attempted to portray these groups as similar to themselves and to break down the supposed racial and civilizational boundaries between them. In the second half of the nineteenth century, negative stereotypes of Indians and the Chinese dominated western understandings. But atheists for the most part rejected these negative views. India and China, in their eyes, both possessed ancient civilizations and had equally ancient religious traditions that had much wisdom to impart to western audiences. While atheists would not have accepted the supernatural claims of any of these traditions, they nonetheless seemed to present an alternative path to morality. What was more, some aspects of the religions of the East, like Buddhism or Confucianism, seemed to reject the supernatural and be quasi-secularist already, at least in what atheists took to be their uncorrupted forms. It was because of this admiration for the civilizations of the East that so many white atheists and freethinkers opposed western incursions into these societies. The discontent freethinkers felt toward their own societies meant that they were willing to look outside their borders for other ways of living and therefore to express skepticism about imperial and missionary interventions in these countries. This perspective also led many, though not all, atheists and freethinkers to oppose the movement to ban Chinese immigration into the United States. They rejected negative stereotypes of these people and instead found much to admire about these societies.

The fifth chapter, "The best friends the negro ever had: African Americans and white atheists," takes as its starting point that virtually all white Americans in the nineteenth century held a belief in black inferiority – even those who otherwise argued against racist policies. Certainly this was true for white atheists and freethinkers as well. Freethought newspapers often contained one-dimensional caricatures of black people as pious, superstitious, foolish, and immoral – precisely the opposite of the traits that white freethinkers prized in themselves. The image of black Americans therefore often acted as a means by which white freethinkers could clarify their own identities. Despite these negative depictions, however, on the whole white atheists attempted to portray themselves as free from racial prejudice. They claimed that they treated people equally without regard to race and argued that since there existed no innate limitations to black achievement, providing equal opportunities would ensure that the best individuals, regardless of race, would be successful. Yet not all white atheists held such optimistic views. An alternative discourse within freethought circles held that a rational and scientific approach – one that explicitly rejected decision-making based on mere "sentiment" – showed the innate inferiority of blacks. This chapter wrestles once more with the competing demands of scientific rationalism, hostility to Christianity, and a commitment to equality that helped to inform white atheists' racial views.

While earlier chapters note the ambivalence in white atheists' racial views, the sixth chapter, "The curse of race prejudice: rethinking race at the turn of the century," presents the strongest arguments against racism that were rooted in an atheist perspective. Environmentalist ideas that stressed the importance of social circumstances – not biology – for forming character offered ways to attack racial determinism. Atheists and freethinkers also drew upon the Darwinian perspective that showed that all of humanity was one and rejected notions of timeless racial essences. Many atheists challenged "race prejudice" as emotional and irrational and therefore contradictory to the atheist worldview, which prided itself on the use of dispassionate reason. The reaction against "race prejudice" among atheists was not coincidental, but a natural outgrowth of their worldview. The culmination of this chapter's discussion focuses on the 1911 Universal Races Congress, held in London. Atheists and other freethinkers played a crucial role as organizers of the congress and speakers against ideas of scientific racism. The central point of the chapter is to tell an alternative story to the one in which secularization opened the way for racism. In this chapter, I show how an atheist worldview could offer the tools of science and reason as a way to critique ideas of racial prejudice and racial determinism.

The Conclusion summarizes the book's arguments and offers some thoughts on the links between atheism and race in the twentieth and twenty-first centuries. I also put forth some final reflections on the links between atheists' social, economic, and political positions and their views on race in our contemporary society. If nonreligious people become the majority in western societies, as seems to be taking place, will their views on race (and indeed other political questions) become less subversive and instead merely parrot ones that maintain their own power?

1

Were Adam and Eve our first parents? Atheism and polygenesis

For much of the history of Christianity, it was taken as a fact that all humans descended from Adam and Eve about 6,000 years ago. This idea first came under threat upon the European discovery of the Americas and the previously unknown people who lived there. Since the Bible was silent about these mysterious people, various authors – the most important being Isaac La Peyrère (1596–1676) – rejected the orthodox view and instead speculated that there must have been men who existed alongside or before Adam. There were, in other words, multiple Adams, or multiple origins for the various races of mankind.[1] This view, called polygenesis – multiple origins – clashed with the orthodox doctrine of monogenesis – single origin. For the advocates of polygenesis, it seemed implausible that such widely variant races could have descended from only one pair of humans and then differentiated from each other in such a short time span. (The best-known calculation of the age of the earth came in the seventeenth century from the Irish archbishop James Ussher, who dated the creation of the world precisely to October 23, 4004 BCE.) Because polygenesis meant that each human race was permanently separate from every other, it easily allowed for racist readings. As we saw earlier, polygenists emphasized the anatomical and psychological distinctiveness of each race and encouraged the ranking of these races in a hierarchical fashion, with whites inevitably on top. From here, arguments for slavery and against racial mixing often followed, although it should be noted that monogenists often made similar arguments, even if they maintained the theoretical equality of all races.

The fact that polygenesis contrasted with orthodox Christian monogenesis was one reason why historians have sought to link the decline of Christian authority with the rise of scientific racism. The theory of monogenesis, many historians thought, inhibited the racism inherent in polygenesis through its defense of the common ancestry of the entire human race. Once the monogenist creation story fell away, polygenist racism was able to gain a foothold.

Polygenesis was, almost by definition, supportive of a racist viewpoint, but it had theological implications as well, which meant that those advocating it were not only – or even mostly – making a racist argument. Polygenesis had the potential to fatally undermine the creation account in Genesis, and with it, some atheists argued, the whole Christian story. If human races had separate origins, the argument went, this would contradict the Genesis account that all humans descended from Adam and Eve, and this would in turn call into question the veracity of the Bible. Even worse, if all humans did not descend from Adam, then only a subsection of humanity would inherit his Original Sin, meaning that Jesus's atonement would not then apply to the rest of humanity. In short, if polygenesis were true, the entire Christian story would come crashing down.

Some early modern figures were interested in polygenesis as a way to reformulate, not dismantle, the Christian story and to make it better fit new understandings of the diversity of humanity and the discovery of non-western chronologies in Egypt, India, and China that seemed to push the age of the earth back beyond that discerned from the Bible. In the nineteenth century, however, racial scientists in Britain and the United States made the doctrine of polygenesis central to the nascent discipline of anthropology. These thinkers used the language of science as they described, classified, and ranked races. The issue of humanity's origin still had theological implications, but racial scientists insisted that clarifying the nature and origin of various racial groups should fall under the domain of science. Advocates of monogenesis, by far the majority, equally enlisted the help of science to show that the differences between races came about through gradual change and were, at least in theory, ultimately superficial since everyone was related by their descent from Adam and Eve. As a general rule, monogenists were typically motivated by their strong faith in Christianity, while polygenists were comparatively hostile to orthodox Christianity.

Historians have been alert to the theological implications of polygenesis, but have virtually ignored the use of polygenesis by atheists and freethinkers. Given the destabilizing potential of polygenesis to the Christian story, many white atheists seized upon the arguments made by polygenist anthropologists as a way to attack Christianity. Charles Bradlaugh, the leading British atheist in the nineteenth century, particularly drew upon polygenesis as a way to undermine the entire Christian story. One way to do this was through the idea of the "conflict thesis," a narrative developed in the mid-nineteenth century that sought to show that science and religion were inevitably in conflict. Here, Christian opposition to polygenesis was seen as yet another case of Christianity's scientific backwardness in the face of what seemed to be cutting-edge science. While Christians clung to outdated theories of monogenesis, white atheists and freethinkers saw themselves as fearlessly pursuing research that demonstrated the truth of polygenesis, unhindered by theological commitments. Furthermore, as described above, polygenesis had the potential to deal a serious blow to the Genesis creation story and, with it, the entire Christian worldview. It was for these reasons that atheists like Bradlaugh closely followed the work of leading polygenist anthropologists, in particular Josiah Nott from the United States and James Hunt and the Anthropological Society in Britain. Even if these white atheists' intention was primarily to discredit Christianity, their endorsement of polygenist science also found them endorsing racial hierarchy without much question.

The American School of Anthropology

Polygenesis first found a scientific basis in the United States. Samuel Morton, a Philadelphia physician and anatomy professor, played a central role in establishing anthropology in the United States in the first half of the nineteenth century. His work was based chiefly on his collection of crania – the largest in the world – obtained from his many foreign contacts around the globe. Morton carefully classified and measured the skulls to demonstrate, as he saw it, the diversity and permanence of racial types.[2] Morton was raised as a Quaker and was less outspokenly anticlerical than his polygenist colleagues. Still, he frequently clashed with Rev. John Bachman, the chief American monogenist, whom Morton dismissively called his "clerical adversary."[3]

Louis Agassiz, the famous Swiss scientist, proved another valuable contributor to polygenist thought in the United States. Agassiz, known for his work establishing that the world had passed through an ice age, moved to America in 1846 and later became a professor at Harvard University. He declared his support for the polygenist position in three articles published in the Unitarian *Christian Examiner* over the course of 1850–51 – a major coup for the polygenist camp, given Agassiz's reputation as one of the world's leading scientists.[4] Like Morton's, Agassiz's scientific view of the world was pervaded by the divine, but he was an unorthodox believer and was not committed to literalist readings of the Bible.[5] In one article, Agassiz made a case for polygenesis that could be reconciled with Christianity. To him, a diversity of origins for the various human races did not contradict the ultimate unity of mankind – the two were separate questions in his mind – and therefore the universalist ideal of Christianity remained intact.[6] The Bible did not intend to describe the history of mankind, he argued, but only the white race. He was cautious about being perceived as attacking the Bible, and therefore added, "[w]e hope these remarks will not be considered as attacks upon the Mosaic record. We have felt keenly the injustice and unkindness of the charges that have so represented some of our former remarks."[7]

Following the death of Morton in 1851, the torch of polygenism was passed to Josiah Nott, a physician who was born in South Carolina but spent most of his adult life in Mobile, Alabama. Nott, along with George Gliddon, an English-born American consul in Egypt and one of Morton's foreign contacts, produced the "most systematic statement" of American polygenesis, *Types of Mankind* (1854).[8] Both men were alert to the heretical implications of polygenesis, but unlike their mentors Agassiz and Morton, they actually relished tangling with the clergy, an activity they described as "parson skinning."[9] Nott delighted in the idea that his polygenist lectures would "stir up hell among the christians [sic]."[10] Nott's negative attitude toward religion formed while he was a young man. According to Nott's biographer, his father was probably nonreligious, though his mother was a Scots Presbyterian.[11] While a student at South Carolina College (now the

University of South Carolina), Nott was exposed to the views of Thomas Cooper, an English freethinker and the college's president. Cooper frequently clashed with the state's clergy over his unorthodox religious views, but the student body repeatedly rallied behind him.[12] The influence of Cooper's unorthodox religious views coupled with his racial views must have been substantial to the young Nott. As John Bachman, one of Nott's primary monogenist opponents, testified, "[t]he 'heresies' of Dr. Cooper, promulgated at the South-Carolina College, have left deep traces on the minds of the succeeding generation [...]."[13] Nott's brother, Henry, also got into trouble with the state's clergy. He became a professor at South Carolina College and, much like Cooper, attracted its ire for his freethinking views.[14] For much of his early life, then, Nott had considerable exposure to freethought ideas and the ways in which they could lead to conflict with the clergy. Later in life, Nott attended the Episcopal church in Mobile at the urging of his wife, but a fellow physician's wife noted that in fact Nott was "a disbeliever in religion."[15]

Nott began making a name for himself by speaking on racial topics in the 1840s, arguing that the evidence of diverse races dating from the ancient Egyptian monuments, the sterility – or at least reduced fertility – of racial hybrids, and the vast anatomical and mental differences between races all suggested separate origins. But it is too simplistic to say that Nott's primary goal in advancing these views was to justify white superiority, since his works also had theological aims. In his early lectures, Nott took pains to convince the audience that while his scientific views on race seemed to conflict with the Bible, in fact, "[t]he words and works of God, if *properly understood*, can never be opposed to each other – they are two streams which flow the from the same pure fountain, and must at last mingle in the great sea of truth."[16] Nott denied that he wished to generate religious controversy in his lectures about race, but insisted that his goal was to merely ensure the Bible was not used as an authority on mankind's origins.[17] Nott was influenced by the emerging biblical criticism of Germany, most prominently David Strauss, but he also cited leading Unitarian theologians from New England, like William Ellery Channing, Theodore Parker, and Andrews Norton, to make his case that a literal reading of Genesis could not be justified.[18] In these lectures Nott began to form the basis of his arguments about the origins of the human races, but he seemed mostly concerned with stripping away the unjustified claims made by the Scriptures, and thereby "restoring the texts to their original purity [...]."[19]

As Nott's prominence increased, he became acquainted with Gliddon, and together they produced *Types of Mankind*, a work dedicated to their mentor, Morton, and one that quickly became a bestseller. The book's first half, written by Nott, described and classified the various races, while the second, by Gliddon, analyzed the book of Genesis and argued that it referred only to a small group within Palestine, rather than all of humanity. In nearly 800 pages drawing together evidence from archeology, Egyptology, comparative anatomy, biblical exegesis, and other fields, the authors reaffirmed the conclusion that the races did not descend from a single pair, but originated separately and transformed to suit their individual environments.

As in Nott's other works, he and Gliddon were concerned to show that their arguments did not contradict the truths of religion. Indeed, they grounded their whole enterprise on the belief that doing science would help humanity to understand God's laws and that there need not be a contradiction between religion and science. As Nott wrote:

> Man can *invent* nothing in science or religion but falsehood; and all the truths which he *discovers* are but facts or laws which have emanated from the Creator. All science, therefore, may be regarded as revelation from HIM; and although newly-discovered laws, or facts, in nature, may conflict with religious *errors*, which have been written and preached for centuries, they never can conflict with religious truth. There must be harmony between the works and the words of the Almighty, and wherever they *seem* to conflict, the discord has been produced by the ignorance or wickedness of man.[20]

Polygenesis was not anti-religious, then, but rather it was the monogenist account that contradicted Scripture. They wrote that "the Bible really gives no history of all the races of Men, and but a meagre account of one."[21] The one, in this case, was the Caucasian race. Monogenists, Nott and Gliddon argued, knew that their arguments were on their last legs and were consequently becoming desperate and resorting to absurd and unscientific arguments, like "the old hypothesis of a miraculous change of one race into many at the Tower of Babel!"[22] The monogenist account was therefore contradicted both by science and by a close examination of the biblical text.

Yet even common sense seemed to deal a deathblow to the theory that all humans came from a single pair. After all, they asked, would it make sense for "the Almighty" to start with "one seed of grass" as a means of creating all the grass on the whole planet?[23]

While their polygenist arguments might be made compatible with some version of Christianity, ultimately Nott and Gliddon were more interested in constructing an argument that championed the supremacy of scientific explanations over religious ones. This was in line with what historians have called the "conflict thesis," which would receive fuller expression later in the century by John William Draper and Andrew Dickson White. Historians have noted how, in the nineteenth century, a new scientific elite was emerging in Britain and the United States that constructed a narrative in which "religion" and "science" were in perpetual conflict as a way to demarcate themselves from the religious elite.[24] In the view presented by white racial scientists, and endorsed by white atheists and freethinkers, a religious mindset stifled scientific research into racial differences. Opposition to polygenesis was based, in this view, not in science and reason, but in outdated theological commitments. The view that religion must concede much of its domain to science is littered throughout Nott and Gliddon's work. At one point, they wrote, "the diversity of races must be accepted by Science as a *fact*, independently of theology [...]."[25] At another, they complained they while they attempted to make their arguments "in the most respectful manner," their "opinions and motives have been misrepresented and vilified by self-constituted teachers of the Christian religion!"[26] Nott and Gliddon imagined the history of science as a progressive story of science triumphing over religion time and again. In his earlier lectures, Nott had mentioned the persecution that Galileo suffered because of his advocacy of heliocentrism.[27] Nott must have assigned himself, Gliddon, and his fellow polygenists a place in this larger narrative of scientists bravely resisting the bigoted dogma of the religious in the fight for progress.

We have seen that Nott and Gliddon rejected the traditional Christian monogenist theory and wished to radically reform the Bible such that unsupportable portions no longer remained, but what was their actual goal? Historians have rightly included Nott and Gliddon within the story of the development of slavery and white supremacy in the American South.[28]

Indeed, Nott himself was a slave-owner, an 1860 census showing that he owned ten slaves, a large number for someone who lived in the city.[29] But, as Terence Keel notes, it is too simplistic to see Nott's polygenesis as merely a cover for his racist views. If this were true, he could have just as easily – and with less headache – argued for the inferiority of blacks and the necessity of slavery on biblical grounds, as did his main monogenist opponent, Rev. John Bachman.[30] Many of the American School members were indifferent to the political goals of the work. Rather, as William Stanton notes, "[t]he conscious extrascientific bond which linked many of these men together was not sympathy for Southern institutions but anticlericalism and antibiblicism."[31] Since Southern society was so strong in its Christian faith, Stanton points out, the heretical idea of polygenesis was never truly able to gain a foothold. Most white Southerners instead chose to rely, like Bachman, on biblical-based defenses of white supremacy.[32] Nonetheless, George M. Fredrickson contends that given the secular tone of *Types of Mankind*, it is striking that it won as many adherents as it did, gaining support from the leading Southern intellectual journals of the time, like *De Bow's Review* and the *Southern Quarterly Review*, and it was helped along by popularizers like Samuel Cartwright, who tried to square polygenesis with the Bible.[33]

Terence Keel has pointed out the ways in which Christian ideas persisted in Nott's polygenist views, such as his insistence on the short chronology of the Bible.[34] But it is also important to see Nott's work in the context of hostility to revelation and anticlericalism. These commitments are seen throughout his work, but this is also how contemporaries viewed him. John Bachman, for example, argued that a preferable title for *Types of Mankind* might have been "Types of Infidelity."[35] Even though Nott and Gliddon made reference to a deity ("the Almighty" or "the Creator"), they certainly loathed the clergy, especially those who seemed to defend unsubstantiated biblical claims that properly fell under the domain of science.

This was why white atheists and freethinkers considered proponents of the American School of Anthropology as fellow travelers in the war against Christianity. Freethought newspapers claimed Louis Agassiz as a freethinker, despite his professed Christianity. His name was trotted out by atheists and freethinkers when his views seemed to contradict orthodox readings of Genesis.[36] When Agassiz rejected Darwinism,[37] however, they were less charitable: an author in the *Boston Investigator* wrote, "Prof. Agassiz, with all his scientific attainment, is not one of those independent men who have the courage to proclaim new views which differ from those of the majority and from the Bible."[38]

Nott and Gliddon's work also enjoyed a positive reception in the atheist press. The *Reasoner* – edited by the leading British secularist of the time, George Holyoake – gave a favorable review to *Types of Mankind*, a "large and valuable volume." The author of the review, presumably Holyoake, declared that the work "contains passages of great interest to the freethought reader" and "is written with a manly, scientific independence of scripture." The book showed that philanthropists and statesmen must not ignore "the truths of ethnology, which lie at the root of all progress." The reviewer was less convinced, however, about Nott and Gliddon's argument about the inferiority of blacks:

> We are not competent to decide what truth there is in the physical inferiority ascribed to the negro, but we are quite sure there are sufficient moral facts known about the race, to demand that they should have the same chance as the whites, and we have no confidence in any theory which would deny them this full freedom.[39]

The book clearly clashed with the anti-slavery and liberal sentiments of Holyoake and his milieu,[40] yet he hoped nonetheless that the book "will find universal readers."[41] The *Boston Investigator* likewise reprinted a review of the work from the *New York Evening Post*. "This work," the review explained, "is destined to create something of a commotion in the religious world. The idea of the unity of the race of man is totally discarded by the authors, one and all."[42] Additionally, both the *National Reformer* and the *Boston Investigator* published excerpts from the *Types of Mankind* in their pages.[43]

John Watts, an early editor of the *National Reformer*, was similarly influenced by Nott and Gliddon. In one case, he listed them alongside the giants of nineteenth-century science, like Charles Lyell, Charles Darwin, and T.H. Huxley. The contribution of these men, to Watts, was to show that "man existed on this earth many centuries prior to the 6,000 years of Genesis."[44] He even stated that "[m]any of those facts recorded by Sir Charles Lyell [...] were to be found years ago in that excellent volume already alluded to – 'Nott and Gliddon's Types of Mankind.'"[45] Watts also relied upon the American polygenists to refute the idea "that all the various races in existence have proceeded from Mr. Adam and Mrs. Eve."[46] In an earlier article, it seems that for Watts, one of the most important parts of *Types of Mankind* was "a learned and elaborate chapter" written by William Usher, a physician from Mobile like Nott, in which Usher gave a summary of the geological evidence for the antiquity of humans, although rarely mentioning polygenesis.[47]

Even decades after the publication of *Types of Mankind*, the work was still used to support freethought arguments. To show how "the human race has descended from at least five pairs of original progenitors," in contradiction to the biblical story, in 1879 Kersey Graves recommended *Types of Mankind*, which was "compiled from the writings of the ablest naturalists of the age."[48] In 1888, the *Boston Investigator* reprinted an article that disputed the universality of religious belief with reference to *Types of Mankind*.[49] All of this demonstrates the enduring influence of Nott and Gliddon's work even late in the nineteenth century and how freethinkers sought to align themselves with scientific provocateurs who challenged the Genesis story.

The Anthropological Society of London

The American School was not the only source of polygenist thought for atheists; the Anthropological Society of London was similarly influential. Learned societies established to study anthropology – and other nascent disciplines – sprang up in the nineteenth century, the first being the Société d'Anthropologie de Paris formed by Paul Broca in 1859. This group inspired the formation of a similar society, the Anthropological Society of London, in 1863. Led by James Hunt, the Anthropological Society was a breakaway from the Ethnological Society of London, the traditional stronghold of monogenesis and humanitarianism. Hunt instead wished to promote his own polygenist ideas that demonstrated the inferiority of non-white people in an arena free from religious dogma.[50]

Hunt's racial ideas were strongly influenced by Robert Knox, a promising Edinburgh anatomy lecturer who was disgraced by unknowingly accepting bodies of murder victims for his anatomy classes. Knox initially enjoyed a thriving career, but after the scandal – though officially exonerated of any wrongdoing – he became unemployable.[51] This gave him free rein to publish his controversial racial views since he no longer had to worry about potential damage to his career. He produced a polemical tome, *The Races of Men*, in 1850, with an extended second edition in 1862. In the work he argued that race was the key to understanding all of human history. In his oft-quoted phrase: "Race is everything: literature, science, art – in a word, civilization, depends on it."[52] Knox's theories were also deeply pessimistic and bitter, and denied the possibility of progress. Differing from more straightforward racists, Knox had negative things to say about every race, not just the darker ones, even if he did allow that the "fairer races" – Knox insisted there was not a single "white race" – had the sole capacity for civilization. Like other polygenists, Knox believed that racial intermixing was folly since a race of hybrids could never be permanently established. There was an anti-imperialist bent to Knox's work as well. Knox had the chance to see colonialism firsthand, working at the Cape of Good Hope from 1817 to 1820 as an army surgeon, an experience that seemed to spark his interest in ethnology.[53] Races, Knox argued, could survive only in their own environments, and any attempt to transplant them to other climes was doomed to failure. Even the Saxon race could not survive indefinitely in the Americas. The fact that it appeared to be stable there was only the result of continual immigration of new Saxon stock, but if this dried up, the Saxons there would ultimately die out.[54]

Like some of the American racial scientists, Knox was proudly iconoclastic. His nineteenth-century biographer and former pupil, Henry Lonsdale, wrote that Knox "made no religious declaration, and therefore belonged to no Church," but Lonsdale was coy about assigning a label to his views.[55] Knox, in Lonsdale's account, saw all religions as "having their origin in idolatrous credulity and ignorance" and believed that they persisted because of "artful schemers, whose purposes are best served by enslaving humanity and binding it down to the yoke of governmental and priestly tyrannies."[56] The famous series of Bridgewater Treatises, published by leading natural theologians in the 1830s to show the elements of divine design in nature, were scorned by Knox as the "Bilgewater" Treatises.[57] One catches glimpses of this same iconoclasm in *Races of Men*. There he declared the "Jewish chronology" to be "worthless" and the Bible "no more a history than it is a work of science."[58] He also railed against the influence of priests. Knox saw priests, along with a hereditary monopoly on government, as the main obstacles to social progress.[59] Perhaps because of his own circumstances, he complained that "throughout Europe, at the present time, to cease to be orthodox, to cease to conform, is to forfeit all, or most of, the privileges of citizenship."[60] He nevertheless believed that a deity was at work in nature, though he mocked those who held an anthropomorphic conception of God. For example, these people called "fossil remains [...] 'Foot-prints of the Creator,' as if the creative Power had feet and hands."[61]

Because of his radical science and his disregard for orthodoxy, Knox's work appealed to atheists and freethinkers. Autonomos, a pseudonymous contributor to the *National Reformer*, published a number of lengthy excerpts of Knox's work, with his own additional notes. Three excerpts, "respectfully dedicated [by Autonomos] to theologians in general," discussed the racial character of the Jews.[62] In another series of excerpts, eight in total, Autonomos used Knox's racial views as a way to critique colonialism.[63] Rather than providing support for European intervention against non-white people, Knox's racial theories actually intended to discourage these kinds of interventions by noting the inability of white races to survive in tropical climates. Even worse, Knox bemoaned the fact that the white races nonetheless had a natural desire for conquest and plunder, an inclination that was cynically justified in part by the Christian duty to evangelize. Instead the lessons of anthropology seemed to be a kind of racial relativism in which the inequality of the races was accepted. Autonomos argued that if the leaders of British society "could only get a little Anthropology drilled into them [...] there might be some faint rational prospect of the arrival of that millennium when men will form a happy family respecting each others [sic] various physical, mental, and moral distinctions [...]."[64]

Nonetheless, the basic assumption of Knox's followers in the Anthropological Society was that non-white people were inferior, and, while their president James Hunt sought to maintain religious neutrality in public, their work often took on an anti-religious character. In his early speeches to the society, though, Hunt focused on the need to study man dispassionately, while "be[ing] careful never to attack the religious conviction of any one."[65] Several years later, however, he lashed out at the society's opponents, including those "persons suffering from […] the religious mania," an incurable ailment marked by "symptoms of arrested brain-growth."[66] John Beddoe, another member of the Anthropological Society, noted Hunt's "skepticism of religion."[67] Like Josiah Nott, Hunt also drew parallels between himself and Galileo in the fight against religious dogmatism and in defense of science.[68] At a lecture in 1869, the year of his death, Hunt nevertheless reiterated his view that the society was not about transmitting irreligious opinions. One clerical member of the society, Rev. Dr. Kernahan, rose to affirm Hunt's statement and said that in all his years of attendance, "he had never heard a word offensive to Christian faith or life."[69]

The irreligious views of two other leading members of the Anthropological Society, Richard Burton and Winwood Reade, further indicate the group's iconoclastic character. Burton, the African explorer, polyglot, and translator of *One Thousand and One Nights*, was unconvinced of any religion's claim to absolute truth. Perhaps his most definitive religious statement came in his 1880 book-length poem, *The Kasîdah*, which was written in the voice of a Sufi poet and presented criticisms of religious dogma. Burton's biographer Dane Kennedy concludes, "*The Kasîdah*, in short, is the testament of a man who knows there is no God."[70] Reade meanwhile strove to gain fame and recognition by embarking on three exploration missions in West Africa as well as authoring a number of fiction and non-fiction books before an untimely death at age thirty-six. Reade wanted to cultivate an image of himself as a bohemian man of science, attaching himself to the Anthropological Society and later supplying travel data to Charles Darwin that would be used in Darwin's *The Descent of Man*.[71] Reade was a proud iconoclast and, in his masterwork, *The Martyrdom of Man* (1872), pithily summed up his religious views in this way: "Supernatural Christianity is false. God-worship is idolatry. Prayer is useless. The soul is not immortal. There are no rewards and there are no punishments in a future state."[72]

At a meeting of the Anthropological Society in 1865, Reade gave a controversial lecture in which he stated that in Africa, "every Christian negress was a prostitute, and that every Christian negro was a thief."[73] Burton seconded Reade's remarks, noting that the mission settlements that had lasted the longest on the African coast were "the most depraved."[74] This was why Reade (and Burton) believed that Islam was better suited to Africans than Christianity since, in Reade's words, "[t]he Arabs were idolators, gamblers, drunkards, liars, and thieves, as the negroes are: he [Mohammed] made laws against these vices." Mohammed, however, retained polygamy and slavery, things Reade and others saw as vitally important to African societies, yet Christian missionaries tried to stamp these out.[75] The debate enraged a number of Christian members: James Reddie fumed, for example, that Reade's paper was "practically worthless."[76] Following the debate, about twenty members departed the Anthropological Society to form the Christian-friendly Victoria Institute.[77]

It was no surprise then that the Anthropological Society attracted other irreligious thinkers. Several scholars have noted that Charles Bradlaugh moved in circles frequented by members of the Anthropological Society or the Cannibal Club, the society's social club,[78] although he was not formally a member of the Anthropological Society, nor is he listed in the Royal Anthropological Institute's database of individuals involved with the society. Nonetheless, Bradlaugh at least knew James Hunt and referred to him as "my friend."[79] Moncure Conway, minister of the freethought South Place Chapel in London, was a member of the Anthropological Society, however. He was sought out for his knowledge of slavery in the United States, having been born in Virginia, yet he did not remain a member for long, as he quickly "found that it was led by a few ingenious gentlemen whose chief interest was to foster contempt of the negro."[80] Conway hoped to promote his own anti-slavery viewpoint in the society, but without success. "[Thomas Henry] Huxley pointed out to me privately the fallacies of Hunt," Conway explained, "and I made speeches in the Anthropological Society, but it became plain to me that anti-slavery sentiment in England was by no means as deep as I had supposed."[81] The split between the Anthropological Society and the Ethnological Society would ultimately not last, and the death of James Hunt in 1869 smoothed the path for the merger of two societies under the name of the Anthropological Institute of Great Britain and Ireland in 1871.[82] Conway later rejoined the Anthropological Institute, having grown increasingly interested in the cultural anthropology of religion.[83]

Bradlaugh, given his connection with Hunt, was knowledgeable about the development of the polygenist theory. In *Heresy: Its Utility and Morality* (1870), Bradlaugh included the early polygenist Isaac La Peyrère among his list of famous heretics, explaining that while the Catholic Church forced him to recant his polygenist views, "the opinions he recanted are now amongst common truths."[84] Like Nott, Bradlaugh viewed history as the story of science's inevitable triumph over religion in line with the "conflict thesis." While heretics were condemned in their own day, "[w]ith few exceptions, the heretics of one generation become the revered saints of a period less than twenty generations later."[85] The Anthropological Society was, to Bradlaugh, a prominent example of a modern heresy standing up to Christian bigotry in search of the truth. Bradlaugh's inclusion of the society in his history tells us about his view of the importance of anthropology, as well as the society's irreligious character:

> Against the late Anthropological Society charges of Atheism were freely levelled; and although such a charge does not seem justified by any reports of their meetings, or by their printed publications, it is clear that not only out of doors, but even amongst their own circle, it was felt that their researches conflicted seriously with the Hebrew writ. The Society was preached against and prayed against until it collapsed; and yet it was simply a society for discovering everything possible about man, prehistoric as well as modern. It had, however, an unpardonable vice in the eyes of the orthodox – it encouraged the utterance of facts without regard to their effects on faiths.[86]

The influence of the Anthropological and Ethnological Societies extended to other freethinkers. Freethought newspapers regularly gave updates on these societies. Advertisements for the *Ethnological Journal* appeared in the *Reasoner*,[87] and the *Boston Investigator* reported positively on the Anthropological Society, which was formed, in their words, "to prove that all foreign missionary operations not only do no good, but inflict a positive injury on mankind."[88] In another case, the *National Reformer* reported on a speech made in 1865 by John Crawfurd, the president of the Ethnological Society, that demonstrated the "mental inferiority" of blacks.[89] That paper also reprinted, on its front page, the speech that James Hunt gave when he resigned the presidency of the Anthropological Society in 1867.[90] While Bradlaugh was friendly with Hunt, he took issue with Hunt's criticism of the philosopher John Stuart Mill and other utilitarians, who were heroes to most atheists. Such criticisms, Bradlaugh felt, were "utterly unjusti-fiable" and unwise given that the society was itself the target of unfair criticism.[91]

But Hunt's attack on the utilitarians was not enough to sour the rela-tionship with freethinkers. In another edition of the *National Reformer*, J.P. Adams noted that the remarks of Hunt at the 1867 Anthropological Conference in Dundee "comprise so much that recommends itself to the approval of Freethinkers with respect to the mode in which all controversy should be conducted, that we think them entitled to a place in the pages of the *N. R.*" Adams argued that Hunt and the *National Reformer* were equally placed "under a sort of scientific ban" for questioning central dogmas within the society.[92] Another author applauded the Anthropological Society as "truly scientific" and praised its willingness to discuss "every shade of thought relating to the physical and (so-called) moral and mental natures of man [...]."[93] Many freethinkers saw their goals as overlapping with those of the society, since both groups struggled to transmit their views against the protests of the religious.

As further evidence of the influence of anthropology on atheists and free-thinkers, C. Carter Blake, a member of the Anthropological Society, became a frequent writer for the *National Reformer* in the 1870s and 1880s. Here he portrayed himself and his fellow anthropologists as fearless men of science, establishing facts about the world "without any particular assistance from text-clippers."[94] Blake, though a polygenist, believed that both monogenesis and polygenesis appeared bad for orthodoxy: "Monogeny goes with long chronology alone. Polygeny is the logical outcome of the short chronolo-gists."[95] In other words, monogenesis worked only if the earth were much older than 6,000 years, yet if one held to a short chronology, the only pos-sible explanation for the diversity of races was polygenesis. Blake's articles also contained his views on other racial issues that did not directly involve religious criticism, including the futility of racial intermixture,[96] the infe-riority of blacks,[97] and the division of races within Europe.[98] But not every freethinker was favorable to the goals of the Anthropological Society. The English radical and journalist W.E. Adams, a frequent contributor to the *National Reformer*, was one of the chief opponents of slavery in the columns of the paper during the Civil War and routinely attacked members of the society for denying a common humanity, which served to justify slavery and the poor treatment of blacks.[99]

Nonetheless, the leading anthropologists in Britain and the United States found their way into a dictionary of freethinkers compiled by the Scottish freethinker Joseph Mazzini Wheeler in 1889. The dictionary included anyone who "contributed in their generation to the *advance* of Freethought."[100] The entries were brief and in neutral, matter-of-fact language without any editorial comment. Both Hunt and Nott received entries,[101] and although neither Gliddon nor other leaders of the American School of Anthropology received their own entries, the French polygenist and anthropologist Paul Broca was included.[102] Wheeler did not explicitly give his approval or disapproval of the subjects of his dictionary, but he clearly saw Hunt and Nott as belonging within the freethought fold. The freethinker J.N. Morean provided a similar though less exhaustive list to the *Boston Investigator* of "the great and good men who buckled on the armor to defend the principles which your paper advocates, of Universal Mental Liberty [...]." This list included Samuel Morton and George Gliddon, but excluded Nott.[103] J.M. Robertson's history of freethought, from 1929, suggested that while Nott and Gliddon had a reputation for freethinking because of their attacks on biblical monogenism, they "were freethinkers only *ad hoc*."[104] As we will see in Chapter 6, Robertson's dismissal of Nott and Gliddon stemmed from his hostility to their racist polygenism.

The uses of polygenesis

Given the influence of anthropologists on freethinkers, it was no surprise that they were familiar with the arguments of polygenesis and its implications for the Genesis story. A number of atheistic authors around the middle of the century used polygenesis as an example of how Christian doctrines seemed to conflict with the "obvious" facts about reality.[105] John E. Remsburg, an American freethinker, used Christians' defense of monogenesis as a way to demonstrate their unscientific attitude in a 1907 work evaluating the Bible. As Remsburg explained, "[s]cience does not admit that man is the result of a divine creative act, that all the races have descended from a single pair, or that his existence here is confined to the brief period of sixty centuries."[106] Still, the dismissal of monogenesis received only a few lines in Remsburg's larger argument about how Christianity contradicted current scientific knowledge about the world, indicating that it was not central to his case. The issue of unscientific Christian support for monogenesis made no appearance in John William Draper's *History of the Conflict Between Science and Religion* (1874), one of the classic works of the "conflict thesis" that saw science and religion as inevitably in conflict.[107] Indeed, in an earlier work, *Human Physiology*, Draper declared his support for monogenesis, arguing that environmental circumstances accounted for the seeming differences between races.[108] Another of the classics of the "conflict thesis" was Andrew Dickinson White's *A History of the Warfare of Science with Theology in Christendom* (1896), but this contained only a brief mention of La Peyrère.[109]

Charles Bradlaugh, however, was the atheist who most clearly grasped how polygenesis could be used against Christianity. Bradlaugh was no mere demagogue, but was an autodidact interested in many topics, including republicanism, biblical criticism, metaphysics, imperial reform, and science, as well as anthropology. As we have already seen, Bradlaugh was linked with James Hunt and the Anthropological Society. His library furthermore contained a copy of the eighth edition of *Types of Mankind*, as well as journals from the Anthropological Society, the Ethnological Society, and the Anthropological Institute.[110] His interest in anthropology was such that in the fall of 1881, he gave four lectures at the London Hall of Science on the subject, which were subsequently published in an 1882 pamphlet. Again, Bradlaugh gave Nott, Gliddon, Agassiz, and Hunt an important place in the development of anthropology.[111]

Nonetheless, biographers of Bradlaugh and historians of nineteenth-century freethought have paid no attention to Bradlaugh's racial thinking.[112] Three of Bradlaugh's works dealt with polygenesis: *Were Adam and Eve Our First Parents?* (c. 1865), *The Freethinker's Text-Book, Part I. Man; Whence and How? Or, Revealed and Real Science in Conflict* (1876), and *Genesis: Its Authorship and Authenticity* – revised from his previous work *The Bible: What It Is!* (c. 1857) and re-issued in several later editions (1865, 1870, and 1882).

Bradlaugh saw the story of Adam as central to the biblical narrative.

As he explained, "[t]he account of the Creation and Fall of Man" was "the foundation-stone of the Christian Church," and "if this stone be rotten, the superstructure cannot be stable." It was here that polygenesis played a part in disrupting the biblical story. If all humans did not trace their descent from Adam, but rather were members of separately created races, they would not share in his Original Sin. But then, Bradlaugh asked, "what becomes of the doctrine that Jesus came to redeem mankind from a sin committed by one who was not the common father of all humanity?" In other words, if one could cast doubt on the story of Adam, all of Christianity would come tumbling down as well. As Bradlaugh put it: "Reject Adam, and you cannot accept Jesus."[113] Central to Bradlaugh's argument was the existence of diverse and permanent races. If one assumed that the world was 6,000 years old, as the orthodox Christian view did, it seemed inconceivable that the kind of human diversity seen in the world could have come about in such a short time. With such vast differences among humanity, Bradlaugh argued that these distinct races did not descend from Adam and Eve but were "indigenous to their native soils, and climates."[114]

Bradlaugh looked to Nott and Gliddon to supply evidence about the durability of racial types in contrast to the monogenist idea that there was gradual change, citing both *Types of Mankind* (1854) and their later work *Indigenous Races of the Earth* (1857). The existence of ancient Egyptian statues that predated the biblical flood revealed that racial types within Egypt had been stable for at least 5,000 years. In addition, Bradlaugh, on Nott's authority, argued that climate could not change one's physical features like skin color. Sunburns, for example, could not be passed down to one's offspring, and skin color could not therefore change upon moving from one climate to another. Indeed, such a change of natural climates was harmful to individuals, as Bradlaugh argued: "The fact is, that while you don't bleach the colour out of the dark-skinned African by placing him in London, you bleach the life out of him; and vice versa with the Englishman."[115]

In something of a contradiction, Bradlaugh also highlighted new research that indicated the extended chronology of the earth as another weapon against Adam's existence. Bradlaugh cited the research of Baron Bunsen, the Egyptologist, who argued that the Egyptians' own history extended the age of the earth to at least 22,000 years. In addition, geological and archeological evidence put the earth at tens or even hundreds of thousands of years old.[116] The theory of monogenesis became much more plausible as the age of the earth was extended, allowing more time for the races to differentiate from their original source. But Bradlaugh nonetheless continued to assert that even if the age of the earth were extended back beyond 6,000 years, evidence from the Egyptian monuments of the permanency of racial types shows that the races were distinct well into the distant past.[117] While Bradlaugh said that he was reluctant to weigh in on the controversy over whether man had one origin or many, he did give his own preference: "I am inclined to the opinion that the doctrine of a plurality of sources for the various types of the human race is a correct one."[118]

Bradlaugh presented a condensed version of this argument for polygenesis in an 1864 article in the *National Reformer*.[119] The article, however, was met by a stern rebuke from one reader named R. Newstead, who noted that Bradlaugh's arguments were "quite at variance with the great principles taught by Darwin in his work on the 'Origin of Species.'" This was because "[i]f it is difficult to believe 'that climate, mode of life, and congenital or accidental' divergencies [sic] are capable of producing the different varieties of mankind, then how much more difficult to believe the same effects capable of developing man from the animal next in order to him[?]" In other words, if Bradlaugh could not imagine how humans could diversify, how could he imagine whole new species arising through natural means, as Darwin suggested? Newstead insisted that "the probabilities are, that mankind is descended from a single pair." But Newstead's defense of monogenesis was based purely on atheistic grounds. He rejected appeals to divine creation in favor of explanations in terms of natural laws.[120] To Newstead, then, Bradlaugh's arguments were contrary to Darwin's work and indeed to science. Rather than confronting Bradlaugh's naive racial views from a religious perspective, Newstead used his interpretation of Darwinism to refute Bradlaugh's polygenesis.

Bradlaugh never appeared to respond to Newstead's arguments directly, but his later discussions of polygenesis, particularly in *The Freethinker's Text-Book* (1876), touched on Darwin's theories. He admitted that his point was not to prove the polygenist account true, but rather to "render impossible the hypothesis of a common origin in one pair less than 6,000 years ago."[121] But Bradlaugh did wade into a brief discussion of the scientific hypotheses for man's existence, even as he acknowledged that "[t]here is no burden on the Freethinker, who finds evidence to reject the Bible story of man, that he should adopt therefore without reservation the views of Mr. Charles Darwin or of Mr. Herbert Spencer."[122] Unsurprisingly, then, Bradlaugh took a non-committal approach to recent evolutionary science:

> The evolution of man from lower forms of life scarcely, as yet, takes rank as a scientific truth; it is rather a grand hypothesis, which, if verified, may throw light on many problems of existence, and is, at least, in analogy with the workings of nature, so far as we know them. When we first catch a glimpse of man, he is [...] but a half-human animal dwelling in caves, disputing with his co-brutes for existence; we can trace him thence upwards to the civilised European; it seems reasonable, then, to trace him downwards also to the unintelligent life in its lowest forms, halting only when organic and inorganic blend together in the far-off yesterday.[123]

In *Genesis: Its Authorship and Authenticity*, Bradlaugh was even more positive about Darwinism, but conflated it with Lamarckianism by arguing that Darwin simply expanded on Lamarck's work.[124] Here he seemed to highlight how Darwinism could be a way to refute a short biblical chronology, but even then his Darwinism coexisted side-by-side with polygenesis in the same work.

Bradlaugh's acceptance of polygenesis, or at least racial hierarchy, appeared elsewhere as well. In an 1881 debate with Rev. James McCann, the two sparred over, among other things, determinism versus free will. When asked by McCann whether the doctrine of determinism applied equally to humans as it did to vegetable life, Bradlaugh replied that he knew no breaks within life and therefore it applied to all. But there was a difference between them,

> as is there a large difference between the Englishman and the Negro; between the Andaman and the Caucasian; and you have no right to talk of man as though man meant the same everywhere. You have no right to put it as though they were all on one level, on one plain. There are marked degrees of differing ability, and that which is possible in volition for the Negro on given conditions, and that which is possible for me on like conditions, are possibilities which are not the same, are possibilities which differ largely from each other.[125]

In this case, whites, with their presumably higher mental capacity, had a greater ability for volition – though Bradlaugh would not say free will – than blacks. McCann stood up for the monogenist viewpoint and countered that "there is the same consciousness in the Negro as in the European."[126] While Bradlaugh again asserted the difference between the mental capacities of the races, the conversation moved on to other topics.[127] Nonetheless, the example demonstrates that Bradlaugh's polygenist racial thought was not merely or totally instrumental in its use against the Genesis story. In other words, he accepted the reality of racial hierarchy even when this did not immediately suit his irreligious polemics.

Bradlaugh was not the only freethinker to exploit polygenist arguments. Both B.F. Underwood and Robert Ingersoll mentioned the evidence from the Egyptian monuments as ways to suggest the permanency of racial types and therefore to show the flaws of the Bible.[128] Less serious was W.P. Ball, who poked fun at the racial ambiguity of the Bible. Accompanying his article was a drawing of Noah's supposed family, with each son representing a different race (see Figure 1.1). He explained that since the popular belief was that Noah's three sons spawned the three races of humanity, perhaps the cartoon should have shown Noah "with a parti-colored face in squares or patches like a chess-board [...]." The traditional view was, Ball noted, that the white race was the original, and the others were offshoots, but then, since the name Adam "signifies red earth, the Red Indians might fairly claim to be the representatives of the original stock made by God in his own image. In this case the white and black and yellow and brown races would alike be offshoots."[129] In a similar vein, Arthur Moss raised questions about the kind of man Adam was: "Was he Jew? Then I am not his descendant. Was he Chinese? Then I am not his descendant. Was he Hindoo? Then I am not his descendant. Of what color and type was Adam?"[130] A cartoon by the *Truth Seeker* cartoonist Watson Heston, titled "A Question for Theological Ethnologists," similarly illustrated the problem of polygenesis. It showed a variety of exaggerated racial caricatures and asked, since "God created man in his own image," "[w]hich is the image? After what images were the other fellows fashioned[?]" (see Figure 1.2). Even late in the century, then, atheists and freethinkers were still drawing upon arguments inspired by polygenesis to cast doubt upon the biblical creation story.

1.1 "The Noah Family," *Freethinker*, October 19, 1884, 335

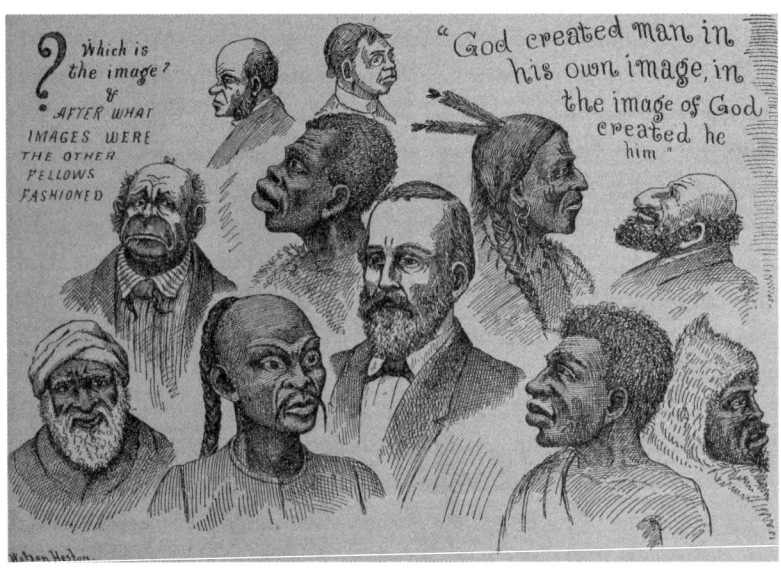

1.2 "A Question for Theological Ethnologists," in Watson Heston, *The Freethinkers' Pictorial Text-Book* (New York: Truth Seeker Company, 1890), 123

Conclusion

This chapter has shown how atheists harnessed polygenist arguments as a weapon against Christianity. Polygenesis could show how Christians' belief in monogenesis was unscientific and stifled further research out of fear that it might contradict the Bible. Even worse for Christians, if polygenesis were true, this would mean the entire narrative of Original Sin and the redemption of Jesus would collapse, as Bradlaugh argued. This was why freethinkers were so interested in the evidence presented by polygenist scientists like Josiah Nott, Robert Knox, and James Hunt. By drawing on these figures, freethinkers further demonstrated their own scientific credentials and allowed themselves to construct a story of religion and science in perpetual conflict, with the latter triumphing in the end.

But by using the polygenist argument, atheists and freethinkers put themselves in the awkward position of accepting the short chronology of the Bible. Monogenesis became much more plausible if the age of the earth was pushed back thousands or millions of years. By the middle of the nineteenth century, developments in archeology and geology had begun to demonstrate just how old the earth was.[131] This research was naturally accepted by atheists since it, too, seemed to contradict the Genesis creation story. But this meant that atheists' polygenist arguments were often disingenuous because they made sense only if the earth was a few thousand years old. Indeed, Josiah Nott stated years after publishing *Types of Mankind* that he would not have published it had he known about the research that was to push back the age of the earth, rendering evidence from several-thousand-year-old Egyptian monuments trivial.[132] The story of descent from Adam could be countered both by recent geologic research and by polygenist arguments. Atheists often used both arguments, but the two contradicted one another. By the 1880s, many Anglicans and other Christian denominations had begun to take on board the insights from geology as well as from German biblical criticism,[133] which meant that after this time, freethinkers' polygenist arguments would have been even more superfluous. This is not to say that atheists' main argument against the story of Adam was polygenesis – most often their case was a logical or moral one – yet this strand of argument still cropped up frequently, even late in the century.

White atheists and freethinkers' use of polygenesis was chiefly instrumental. Still, it was no coincidence that they assented to the idea that science judged their own race and civilization to be superior. For much of the nineteenth century, these atheists were content to accept the findings of racial science since it confirmed their own place at the top of the racial and civilizational pyramid. However, it is another question whether this acceptance of polygenesis influenced atheists' views on racial issues in practice. In other words, would an acceptance of polygenesis lead to support for discriminatory policies or colonial domination of non-white people? As we will see, there is reason to answer "no" to that question, but there was clearly a tension between white atheists' racial views in theory and practice. Before addressing these issues, it is necessary to consider the ways in which the emergence of Darwinism contributed to the growth of racism in the second half of the nineteenth century, the subject of the following chapter.

2

Brute men: race and society in evolution

Evolution is, and was, popularly associated with atheism or deism. The gist of the theory of evolution, put forward by Charles Darwin in his *Origin of Species* (1859), was that humans, and indeed all species, had not been individually created by God, but had evolved in a gradual process over eons, in particular through natural selection. Darwin's theory posited that as individual organisms competed for sparse resources, those with the most beneficial traits would produce more offspring, which would subsequently propagate these traits to future generations. Over the course of many generations, this process would give rise to new species. This theory could explain how life developed from the most basic life forms into complex ones without recourse to divine intervention.

Despite the seemingly godless lessons of evolution and Darwin's own agnosticism, he was reluctant to see infidelity spread to the masses and remained close with many liberal clergymen. He went out of his way to avoid religious controversy and largely remained in the good graces of respectable society, shown, for example, by his interment in the hallowed shrine of Westminster Abbey, burial place of kings and queens.[1] Indeed, many nineteenth-century Christians were actually quick to endorse Darwinism. Evolution, it was reasoned, did not diminish God's power, but rather exalted it, since God designed the process by which all species were produced. One example of this line of reasoning is Asa Gray, the Harvard botanist and evangelical Christian, who was one of Darwin's most important defenders in the United States.[2]

Still, it is no surprise that atheists and other freethinkers, from the late eighteenth century onward, were often leaders in developing and advocating for the idea of evolution since it supplied a plausible alternative to the creation account described in the Bible. Evolutionary theories existed before Darwin, although they lacked the mechanism of natural selection to explain how new species were produced, as well as the mass of evidence that Darwin compiled. Even so, before Darwin, evolutionary ideas attempted to explain the diversity of life forms without the need for direct intervention from a deity, or without the need for a deity at all. Additionally, since so many atheists in the early nineteenth century held radical political views, evolution also offered a dynamic conception of society in which change was possible. In other words, supposedly fixed natural hierarchies between classes need not be natural or fixed at all, but instead were open to change. Such radical arguments could then be deployed in the service of democracy and other social reforms that challenged the entrenched power of elites.[3]

This is not to say, however, that Darwin himself, who came from a wealthy Dissenting family, wanted radical reforms. Darwin's own politics contained optimistic liberal tendencies that argued for an extension of the franchise and greater religious toleration, but he was reluctant to see his theories put toward truly radical politics that would dramatically upend the privileges from which he and his family and friends benefited so much. When Darwin finally published his ideas, after twenty years of tinkering, his theory of evolution could be safely deployed to justify ascendant middle-class values of free trade, open competition, progress, and an industrial-capitalist economy.[4] Indeed, Karl Marx pointed out that "[i]t is remarkable how Darwin recognises among beasts and plants his English society with its division of labour, competition, opening up of new markets, inventions, and the Malthusian 'struggle for existence.'"[5]

It has sometimes been held that Darwinism helped open the path to racism by devaluing humans' uniqueness and conceiving of them as just another species of animal.[6] The lessons of Darwinian evolution were often in the eye of the beholder, but Darwin himself abhorred racism. Some of his writings on race might well be seen as racist today, but to do so would be to view him anachronistically and to ignore the context in which his arguments made sense. Indeed two of the most prominent Darwin scholars, James Moore and Adrian Desmond, have argued that Darwin's evolutionary research was actually driven by a hatred of slavery and the polygenist theories that helped to justify it.[7] Darwin's ideas showed that all species, including humanity and its constituent races, were not timeless and unchangeable, but were perpetually in flux. That said, Darwin did admit the seemingly vast gulf between civilized and savage races.

White atheists and freethinkers drew different interpretations about race from Darwin's work. In vast evolutionary time, the differences between the races of humanity were theoretically insignificant, yet from some vantage points in the nineteenth century, the differences were nonetheless stark and meaningful. While races could be modified through gradual changes to their environments, this did not prevent evolutionary thinkers from accepting racial divisions in their present reality. Furthermore, while the Darwinian scheme supported monogenesis (but not the biblical version), a polygenist interpretation, or at least one that preserved a racial hierarchy, could be maintained within the Darwinian framework. Rather than descending from separate Adams, the individual offshoots of the human race might each have been formed in an ancient period of evolution or descended from its own ape. Even if one retained a monogenist view of evolution, racial divisions still had their place. Since a common argument against evolution was based on the wide gap between apes and humans, the so-called lower races could be slotted in as necessary rungs on the evolutionary ladder from apes on the way to civilized whites. In this argument, the lower races were portrayed as animalistic and degraded in biological and civilizational terms. They were anatomically inferior and lacked many of the defining features of civilized humans.

The links between racial biology and civilization did not stop there. Ideas about the progress of civilizations had dated to the eighteenth century, but in the nineteenth century speculations about social evolution were tinged with racism since the most primitive stage of civilization, savagery, was invariably seen to be occupied by non-white people. These savages were seen as living fossils, frozen in evolutionary time. The study of these savages could therefore offer a glimpse of what the ancestors of civilized Europeans might have been like, but white atheists were particularly interested in using savage religions as a way to shed light on the origins of religion. By providing a naturalistic account of religion, atheist thinkers attempted to show that Christianity was not unique or divine, but was at its core no different from a degraded savage religion. In this picture, then, white Christians were on a similar plane to non-white savages since both shared in a primitive superstition. This begins to point to an ambivalence that will become clearer later on in the book: that while white westerners seemed to occupy the pinnacle of race and civilization, the persistence of religion called this superiority into question.

Evolution before Darwin

Speculations about the evolution, or transmutation, of species dated back to the eighteenth century.[8] These evolutionary theories, up to the early nineteenth century, were typically patterned on the idea of a "great chain of being." Devised in ancient Greece, this idea held that "nature produced living things in a great and continuous ladder, each rung of the ladder separated from the next by almost imperceptible differences."[9] An early example can be seen in the series of articles published in 1842–43 on "the theory of regular gradation" in the *Oracle of Reason*, which demonstrated the gradation of life from simple to complex. Charles Southwell, who co-founded the newspaper with William Chilton, authored the first few articles, but Chilton took over the series following Southwell's imprisonment for blasphemy in 1842. There was little about human evolution or race in these articles, aside from a lengthy quotation from the polygenist – though Christian – Charles White's *Account of the Regular Gradation in Man* (1799), which was modeled on the theory of the great chain of being.[10]

Chilton's evolutionary theory never attracted much interest, but, as James Secord points out, the prominent Edinburgh publisher Robert Chambers's evolutionary arguments – written anonymously – in *Vestiges of the Natural History of Creation* (1844) helped to fill this void: "With its populist emphasis on progress, the book could vindicate freethought upon a scientific basis. Here was a work that summed up the latest science without drowning in details."[11] Chambers was "a moderate deist" strongly influenced by the booming phrenology scene in Edinburgh.[12] He made a point in the work of anticipating theological criticism by insisting that he "take[s] it for granted" that God created the universe and all "animated beings".[13]

God worked through natural laws, yet this meant God's power was "not diminished or reduced in any way [...] but infinitely exalted."[14] Despite Chambers's attempts to pre-emptively rebut charges of atheism, a number of Christian commentators argued that the work might nevertheless lead unsophisticated readers down that path.[15]

Since *Vestiges* charted the development of the entire universe, Chambers devoted only a few pages to the question of the division of races. In his classification scheme, there were five races, each so different "as to give rise to a supposition that they have had distinct or independent origins." But, as Chambers explained, recent research, particularly from the monogenist James Cowles Prichard, showed that humans had a single origin and that the physical differences between the races "are of a more superficial and accidental nature than was at one time supposed."[16] He cited examples of black parents apparently giving birth to white children and vice versa as proof of the mutability of race.[17] At the center of his evolutionary thinking was constant change in which present configurations were ephemeral, with the environment modifying racial groups. Poor environmental and social conditions led to the body becoming ill-formed and ugly, as with, he argued, the Irish. The beauty of the English, by contrast, resulted from the favorable conditions they enjoyed.[18] In opposition to polygenists, then, for whom races existed in the same form since they originated, Chambers held that racial forms were changeable.

Chambers believed that all human races descended from somewhere in India, although he was willing to grant that of all the races, the black race seemed most likely to have had an independent origin. It was more likely, though, that this race was "a deteriorated offshoot of the general stock."[19] That Chambers viewed the races hierarchically – again in the manner of the great chain of being – can be seen in his discussion of the idea of recapitulation, in which a human embryo passed through all the earlier stages of its development, from fish and reptiles to mammals, passing through "the Negro, Malay, American, and Mongolian nations," before finally becoming "Caucasian."[20] The Caucasian, then, to Chambers, represented the highest type, while

> [t]he Negro exhibits permanently the imperfect brain, projecting lower jaw, and slender bent limbs, of a Caucasian child, some considerable time before

the period of its birth. The aboriginal American represents the same child nearer birth. The Mongolian is an arrested infant newly born. And so forth.[21]

Given their superiority, Chambers predicted that "the best examples of the Caucasian type" might one day "supersede the imperfect nations already existing."[22]

A number of freethinkers reported on the evolutionary theories in *Vestiges*. A series of articles in the *Boston Investigator* summarized the contents, including one on Chambers's racial thought.[23] Another freethinker who mentioned Chambers's racial theories was the American John Shertzer Hittell, who drew on the evolutionary arguments from *Vestiges* in his 1856 work *The Evidences Against Christianity*. Like Chambers, Hittell noted that species evolved through organic, gradual processes. This meant that the boundaries between species were blurry, and he cited as proof the apparent fact that "[b]lack parents sometimes have white children [...]."[24] Despite this, Hittell presented the common division of humans into five races, and like Chambers expressed the idea of recapitulation.[25] Hittell returned to the theme of racial divisions in a later work and explained that the "black race" was "in physical organization nearest to the ape, and in mental capacity the lowest [...]."[26] Such discussions reveal that while Chambers's evolutionary theory offered support to a monogenist account of the human races, it still left considerable room for racial hierarchy.

The Darwinians

Chambers's evolutionary ideas were soon superseded following the publication of Darwin's *Origin of Species* in 1859, although *Origin* would actually not overtake *Vestiges* in sales until the end of the century.[27] *Origin* was not an anti-Christian work, but by the time of the book's release, Darwin had long since abandoned the religion. In the 1830s, he began to have doubts about Christianity, in large part because of the moral difficulties raised by the doctrine of eternal punishment for nonbelievers, which included some of his family members. Despite his break with Christianity, Darwin never became affiliated with the popular freethought movement in Britain. He also withdrew an earlier endorsement of the American freethought periodical *The Index* in 1880, possibly because of freethought's growing association with advocacy of birth control. Darwin preferred Huxley's term "agnostic" to describe his own religious position, in contrast to "atheist," which connoted, to Darwin, an unreasonable certainty about the non-existence of God and aggressive proselytizing to the masses.[28]

Adrian Desmond and James Moore have convincingly argued that Darwin's evolutionary research was animated by a hatred of slavery and polygenesis. The context in which Darwin developed his evolutionary theories was shot through with debates on slavery, imperialism, and the origin of human races. These questions, to Darwin, were closely bound together. He had come from an abolitionist family, had seen slavery firsthand while on his famous voyage on the *Beagle* in the 1830s, and closely followed the developments surrounding slavery in the United States. In the 1850s and 1860s, leading anthropologists in Britain and the United States proclaimed victory for polygenesis, a theory that seemed to offer support, directly or indirectly, for the subordination of non-white races. It was in this context that Darwin developed his evolutionary theories that sought to demonstrate the unity of the human family, and indeed all life.[29]

While Darwin wished to include more in *Origin* about human evolution, this was eventually trimmed down to just one line.[30] For Desmond and Moore, the culmination of Darwin's opposition to polygenesis was to be found in *The Descent of Man* (1871).[31] This book made the case for a single origin for humans and accounted for the differences between human races with reference to the theory of sexual selection. Darwin devised sexual selection – an additional mechanism to natural selection – as a way to explain things like the peacock's famously large tail feathers, which had no clear survival benefit and if anything hindered attempts at survival. Darwin posited that such decorations as the peacock's tail were designed to attract mates; those with the most brilliant decorations would produce more offspring and propagate these traits. But sexual selection, Darwin thought, could also help to explain racial differences.

Beginning the section on racial differences, Darwin laid out the arguments for polygenesis and admitted, like Chambers, "[i]f a naturalist, who had never before seen such beings, were to compare a Negro, Hottentot, Australian, or Mongolian," he would undoubtedly rank them as separate species.[32] Upon closer inspection, however, the case for polygenesis and permanently separate races began to unravel. The strongest argument against polygenesis, he believed, was that the different races "graduate into each other," which explained why so many naturalists disagreed on the precise number of races. One naturalist claimed there were as few as two races, another said there were as many as sixty-three, and many more placed the number somewhere in between. All that this demonstrated was the futility of such efforts.[33] Instead, Darwin believed that anyone who accepted evolution "will feel no doubt that all the races of man are descended from a single primitive stock [...]."[34] Darwin predicted that as more and more people accepted the evidence for evolution, "the dispute between the monogenists and the polygenists will die a silent and unobserved death."[35]

The remainder of the book laid the groundwork for the argument that the majority of the anatomical differences between the races could be accounted for not by natural selection, but by sexual selection. Darwin argued that traits like skin color or amount of body hair did not appear to give any survival advantage to individuals.[36] Rather, these differences emerged arbitrarily in early human history, when humans' reasoning powers had yet to be fully formed and humans were still governed by their instincts. Since these early humans lived in polygamous societies, Darwin reasoned that the powerful males would mate with those females they found the most beautiful and produce the most offspring, therefore perpetuating and amplifying these arbitrary racial traits throughout the rest of the society.[37] Nonetheless, as Nancy Stepan notes, sexual selection as the cause of racial differences was not accepted by many contemporaries, and the idea remains controversial today.[38]

While both Chambers and Darwin believed that their work demonstrated the truth of monogenesis – although not the biblical version – it was clear that racial hierarchies often persisted within an evolutionary framework. One way was through the explanation of human evolution from apes. To many doubters, the gulf between apes and humans appeared far too large to have been bridged without the intervention of God. Despite Darwin's desire to refute the racist implications of polygenesis, he nonetheless employed racial hierarchy as a way to answer this challenge, in particular by bringing in the old idea of the great chain of being. There was, he noted, a great difference "in intellect, between a savage who does not use any abstract terms, and a Newton or Shakspeare [sic]." But the savage and the civilized were "connected by the finest gradations," and therefore a large section of *Descent of Man* was devoted to arguing that "there is no fundamental difference between man and the higher mammals in their mental faculties."[39] In this section, Darwin gave numerous examples of animals possessing familiar humans emotions and the ability to reason and use basic forms of language, while also noting that the lower races possessed a form of that ability that was inferior to that of a civilized person. In this case, he emphasized the primitiveness of the lower races. To take self-consciousness as one example, Darwin noted the difficulty of knowing with certainty if animals were self-conscious, but added "how little can the hard-worked wife of a degraded Australian savage, who uses hardly any abstract words and cannot count above four, exert her self-consciousness, or reflect on the nature of her own existence."[40] In this way, the boundary between humans and animals was blurred – but at the expense of savage races who appeared particularly animalistic. Because of this inferiority, Darwin, while he took no joy in it, grimly predicted that in the future "the civilised races of man will almost certainly exterminate and replace throughout the world the savage races." The great apes would likewise become extinct, he thought, meaning that "[t]he break will then be rendered wider [...]."[41]

Racial hierarchy and polygenist ideas were also found in the work of T.H. Huxley, known as "Darwin's Bulldog" for being one of the earliest champions of Darwinism in Britain. In an 1865 essay, he considered the debate between monogenesis and polygenesis in a Darwinian perspective. As Evelleen Richards argues, this essay came out in the midst of the clash between the Ethnological Society, of which Huxley and other Darwinians were members, and the upstart Anthropological Society, which threatened to overtake the Ethnological Society. Huxley, she suggests, was attempting to bridge the divide between the two societies and to disentangle Darwinism from the old-fashioned monogenesis that was associated with the Ethnological Society.[42]

In the essay, Huxley therefore found value in both the monogenist and polygenist schools. On the one hand, "Rational Monogenists" had rightly pointed out that the earth existed for many eons and that various historical migrations accounted for the spread of the races. On the other hand, Huxley agreed with the polygenists that climatic differences alone could not account for the formation of races, even if he acknowledged that their evidence for an original diversity of races was wanting.[43] Huxley instead saw Darwinism as a third way that combined "all that is good in the Monogenistic and Polygenistic schools."[44] Whether the races had one origin or many, Huxley nevertheless identified in the present "eleven readily distinguishable stocks, or persistent modifications," based on traits including skin color, hair type, and head shape.[45] The ranking was not explicitly hierarchical, but Huxley did write of the two white races (fair- and dark-haired): "With them has originated everything that is highest in science, in art, in law, in politics, and in mechanical inventions. In their hands, at the present moment, lies the order of the social world, and to them its progress is committed."[46] The present racial divisions, Huxley contended, had existed with their present features for up to 4,000 years.[47] In this, he broadly agreed with Darwin, as well as with the co-discoverer of natural selection, Alfred Russel Wallace, who argued that races were formed very early on in human history when humans were still "homogenous," after which time racial differences became mostly fixed as natural selection ceased operating on humans' physical forms.[48] Huxley's own view was that humans arose "probably, though by no means necessarily, in one locality." But the time period in which this took place and "[w]hether [man] arose singly, or a number of examples appeared contemporaneously" were unknown.[49]

Again like Darwin, Huxley drew upon the tactic of using the lower races as a way to bridge the gap between humans and apes, particularly in *Man's Place in Nature* (1863). A great deal of the work was dedicated to describing the "man-like apes," namely, gorillas, chimpanzees, orang-utans, and gibbons. This was meant to show that the real gap was not between humans and the higher apes, but between the higher and lower apes. Here Huxley found it necessary to bring in the lower races as bridges between the higher apes and humans. Measuring cranial capacity, for example, showed that "[...] Men differ more widely from one another than they do from the Apes; while the lowest Apes differ as much, in proportion, from the highest, as the latter does from Man."[50] One could measure other anatomical features – "whatever series of muscles, whatever viscera might be selected for comparison" – and the results would demonstrate that "the lower Apes and the Gorilla would differ more than the Gorilla and the Man."[51] For Darwin and Huxley, the goal of such a strategy was to make evolution seem more plausible, not primarily to denigrate non-white people, even if it had this effect.

Herbert Spencer, a friend of Huxley and member of his X-Club of influential scientists, also dealt with racial theories in his voluminous evolutionary and sociological studies. Spencer had come up with his own evolutionary scheme before Darwin – suggesting that species fit themselves to environmental changes – but he later acknowledged that he did not fully foresee the consequences of this. In any case, Spencer was more interested in understanding the structure and function of organisms than in determining the origin of species.[52] In Spencer's evolutionary worldview, everything moved from homogeneity to heterogeneity, from simplicity to complexity; this applied to everything from individual organisms to whole societies to the cosmos. After Darwin, he blended Darwinian natural selection – indeed, he suggested the term "survival of the fittest" to Darwin[53] – with the mechanism of the inheritance of acquired characteristics, also called use inheritance, pioneered by the French naturalist Jean-Baptiste Lamarck. This latter idea meant that the experiences and improvements acquired throughout one's life would then be passed on to future generations.

This had implications for race, even if Spencer rarely talked explicitly about racial differences in his work. Spencer accepted that all races had a common ancestor,[54] but saw the differences between them as resulting not from natural selection, but from the inheritance of acquired characteristics. In particular, this could be seen in the mental differences between races. The gradual accumulation of mental improvements, generation after generation, meant

> that the European inherits from twenty to thirty cubic inches more brain than the Papuan. Thus it happens that faculties, as of music, which scarcely exist in some inferior human races, become congenital in superior ones. Thus it happens that out of savages unable to count up to the number of their fingers, and speaking a language containing only nouns and verbs, arise at length our Newtons and Shakspeares [sic].[55]

The different evolutionary paths of different races also constituted one reason why Spencer recommended to the Japanese diplomat Baron Kentaro Kaneko at the end of the century that the Japanese forbid marriages between Japanese and whites. In general, Spencer argued against introducing rapid changes to modernize Japan, but particularly in this case he reasoned, "if you mix the constitutions of two widely divergent varieties which have severally been adapted to widely divergent modes of life, you get a constitution which is adapted to the mode of life of neither – a constitution which will not work properly, because it is not fitted for any set of conditions whatever."[56] The Japanese ultimately ignored this advice and allowed intermarriage.[57]

Darwin, as we saw, was reluctant to turn his evolutionary theories toward irreligious ends. This was true to a lesser extent for Spencer, who criticized the foundations of religion, but rarely explicitly. One thinker, though, who applied Darwinian evolution more forthrightly in the service of freethought was the British explorer Winwood Reade. This is especially apparent in his universal history, *The Martyrdom of Man* (1872), which became a classic among freethinkers even if Reade himself was mostly uninvolved in the freethought movement before his untimely death in 1875.[58] As a testament to the work's longevity and influence, in 1910, the American freethinker James Morton reflected that "[t]he history of Freethought would be incomplete without the name of Winwood Reade."[59] Reade initially intended to write a history of Africa in a global context, but the project soon expanded to one that charted the history of the world from a Darwinian perspective, emphasizing the role of conquest and struggle in the evolution of societies. Reade drew a direct analogy between the progress of all life and the progress of human civilizations. Both occurred when conditions necessitated a struggle for life. In the case of humanity, this meant war, invasion, and famine. Without such catalysts, life stagnated, as seen in the comfortable life of the savage, which "is one long torpor, with spasms of activity. Century follows century, but he does not change."[60] Reade was, however, quick to note that "[t]he intellectual capacities of such men are by no means to be despised, as those who have lived among them are aware."[61] Indeed, wealthy and comparatively civilized societies could similarly fall into stagnation without external pressures. In this way, dramatic social upheavals, while painful in the short term, were nonetheless necessary events in the gradual march of progress.

Reade rejected the idea of biological race as an explanatory factor in history, since civilizational progress was dependent on contingent and external factors, not innate racial ones.[62] Chinese attitudes, for example, were to blame for their society's stagnation, "not the heat of the climate, or the inherent qualities of the race."[63] Likewise, while the differing patterns of interbreeding between Indo-European people and the indigenous inhabitants of Europe might explain the character differences between, for example, the English and the Irish, race could not explain the genius of the ancient Greeks, which Reade attributed to geographical factors.[64] Furthermore, Reade argued that racial differences were ultimately ephemeral. The idea that there existed permanent, primordial racial essences contradicted Reade's materialist conception of the universe. In the great evolutionary time span,

> the distinctions which exist between the races of men [are] unimportant and external. Such as they are, they have been produced by differences of climate and food acting indirectly upon the races throughout geological periods; and it is also possible that these distinctions of hair and skin were chiefly acquired at a time when man's intelligence being imperfectly developed, his physical organisation was more easily moulded by external conditions than was afterwards the case.[65]

That said, he did allow that external forces continued to work on and enlarge humans' brains, although he did not specifically suggest that some races had more developed brains than others.

This progressive view of life and of humanity can be seen in Reade's optimism that Africans might advance to a higher level of civilization, even if he believed in their present inferiority. Progress was not guaranteed, but from his travels in Africa, Reade was optimistic about black people's ability to become civilized. He continued,

> Whether the negroes are equal in average capacity to the white man, whether they will ever produce a man of genius, is an idle and unimportant question; they can at least gain their livelihood as labourers and artisans; they are therefore of service to their country; let them have fair play, and they will find their right place whatever it may be.[66]

Reade still expected blacks and whites to remain naturally separate, preferring to marry within their own races, but he did not assume that this meant the two races would be hostile to one another.[67] Still, the idea that races could progress struck at the heart of the notion of permanent racial types, though some of Reade's other statements made clear that even if racial characteristics were transitory, they were still meaningful in the present.

Darwinism and the freethought movement

Retrospectively we realize the considerable influence of Darwinism, but as Edward Royle explains, British atheists were actually slow to incorporate Darwin's ideas into their arguments against Christianity. It was not until Edward Aveling became a leading figure in the freethought movement that Darwinism became central in their arguments.[68] Aveling, an anatomy lecturer at the London Hospital and King's College London, was one of the leading atheists in the late 1870s and early 1880s, and served several years as the vice president of the National Secular Society. He also taught various adult science classes at the secularists' Hall of Science in London and was linked romantically with Annie Besant. Aveling's support for socialism and his relationship with Karl Marx's daughter Eleanor, beginning in 1884, coupled with his perpetual reliance on Bradlaugh for financial support, strained his association with the secularists, who were more inclined to liberalism, and he resigned his membership that year.[69]

Further indicative of the ambiguous adoption of Darwin by freethinkers was that a 1905 list in the British newspaper the *Freethinker* on "The Hundred Best Books" of freethought contained no works by Darwin in the section on evolution, even as Aveling's *Darwin Made Easy* was included, as were other works by Huxley, Reade, and Spencer.[70] This indicates that nineteenth-century atheists' understanding of Darwin was second-hand and jumbled with the ideas of other evolutionary thinkers, meaning that Darwin's central message about the unity of the human species was lost.

Still, leading freethinkers drew upon many of the threads running through Darwin and other evolutionists' thought. One of these was the incorporation of polygenesis into an evolutionary framework.[71] As we saw in the previous chapter, Charles Bradlaugh tentatively accepted Darwinism, although his Darwinian ideas sat uneasily alongside polygenist ones. In Bradlaugh's 1881 lectures on anthropology, he spoke positively about Darwinism but saw it as an extension of the ideas of Lamarck on the inheritance of acquired characteristics. Bradlaugh saw no conflict between Lamarckism and Darwinism; in fact, he believed that the latter was simply a restatement of the former, since Bradlaugh saw them as both concerning evolution rather than their differing mechanisms. While "Lamarck's doctrine" was mocked in its own time, Bradlaugh explained, it was now "triumphant in Darwinism [...]."[72] It was for this reason that Bradlaugh sounded like a Lamarckian when he wrote that poor nutrition would lead to the individual to become "short in stature," and "[i]f this be repeated through many generations it will become habit, and then a regularly transmissible character."[73] Darwin himself allowed room for the inheritance of acquired characteristics within his evolutionary scheme, although he gave priority to natural selection. Furthermore, as Peter Bowler explains, while evolution was accepted fairly rapidly following Darwin, the idea of natural selection as the mechanism of evolution was not fully accepted until the early twentieth century.[74]

Even if he ostensibly accepted Darwinism, Bradlaugh still retained many of the central points of polygenesis, particularly that certain races were suited for corresponding environments. Indeed, the study of anthropology could have practical consequences for colonial policy given the diffusion of whites throughout the world. Anthropological research showed that "[o]ne race has a tendency to die out in a country where another thrives easily"; while in time all humans could become adapted to any climate, this was "only after great struggling."[75] In another lecture, Bradlaugh recommended a "slight crossing with native races, or with settled races with greater power of acclimatisation" as a way to ease the transition process. For example, "a small shade of negro blood lessens the tendency of the European to contract yellow fever."[76]

Bradlaugh's discussion of evolution also used anthropological measurements to construct a gradation from the apes to humans, harking back to earlier notions of the great chain of being. Bradlaugh cited Huxley's research from *Man's Place in Nature* about the differing cranial capacity between the lower and higher apes, and between the higher apes and man.[77] He also used the French physician Jules Cloquet's facial angle, measuring "an European, a Negro, an infant chimpanzee, a full grown chimpanzee, a male gorilla, and a Newfoundland dog" to show that the facial angle was highest for a European and gradually became lower as one moved down to the lower races and non-human animals.[78] By studying anatomical differences, and especially cranial measurements, Bradlaugh believed one could best determine how to categorize the various races. On cranial capacity, Bradlaugh reported that Australians had the smallest capacity, but "[t]he capacity increases in the yellow races, and attains its maximum in the white."[79] The rest of the skeleton also yielded clues to help classify races. The arm of "the Negro" was longer than that of the European and was nearly indistinguishable, proportionally, from a gorilla's.[80] These anatomical differences could have consequences for various races' intellects, though Bradlaugh held out the possibility of improvement among lower races.[81]

While Bradlaugh dabbled in the latest anthropological thought, the leading scientific mind among the British secularists was, as noted above, Edward Aveling. He was a student of Darwin and wrote about him frequently.[82] He did, however, break with his idol over monogenesis, instead favoring a polygenist stance, influenced by German evolutionary thought. Before being forced out of the secularist movement for his financial negligence, Aveling wrote a series of articles for the *National Reformer* describing the polygenist evolutionary thought of Carl (also spelled Karl) Vogt, one of the early German supporters of evolution.[83] As Aveling explained, Vogt's measurement of skulls showed "that in brain capacity as in every other anatomical and physiological point, there is more difference between man and man than between man and ape." Aveling noted how a ranking of cranial capacity placed indigenous Australians at the bottom and the English at the top.[84] Analysis of other bones revealed similar hierarchies. Vogt's work on pelvis shapes, for example, showed differences between the races. The "wedge-shaped" pelvis of the black races was, to Vogt, most similar to that of apes, showing the evolutionary closeness between the two.[85] These facts meant that the races of man needed to be considered separate species, or the entire system of classification was untenable.[86] Even though Aveling described Darwin as "our master," he chided him for his hasty approval of monogenesis.[87] Elsewhere, Aveling accepted a classification of the human races into ten species, following the scheme of the German evolutionist Ernst Haeckel.[88]

Despite his socialist politics, one cannot obviously map Aveling's racial views onto his political ones, other than to say that he wrote and lectured primarily with a working-class audience in mind. One might suggest that even if white working men sat at the bottom of their own societies' class hierarchies, they could nonetheless take comfort in the fact that their whiteness made them part of the superior race. While Aveling's socialism seemed concerned mostly with fellow white people, in an account of the working classes in the United States, based on a trip he and his wife Eleanor took there, they commented happily that "the immense coloured population of Kansas is beginning to understand the wage-slavery question."[89] Otherwise, the book is entirely about white people and makes no mention of racist conditions suffered by non-white workers.

Other evolutionary polygenist ideas found their way into freethought newspapers, indicating a continued interest in the most recent anthropological research among white atheists. A 1903 article in the *Truth Seeker* discussed a recent theory that "the yellow race" originated somewhere in Asia, while "the black race" and "the white race" both originated in separate locations outside that continent.[90] Another article, from 1910, speculated on the descent of various races from corresponding gorillas, chimpanzees, orang-utans, and gibbons.[91] The *Freethinker* carried a series of articles in 1915 that rejected the idea that each race descended from a different ape species, but nonetheless argued there were three distinct races, each branching off from a common ancestor during the Paleolithic period.[92] These cases demonstrate that the newspaper editors did not hold to any particular stance on the question of polygenist or monogenist evolution, but instead sought simply to report the latest findings as a way to show their own scientific credentials.

Further demonstrating the persistence of polygenist beliefs in freethought circles was that some white freethinkers highlighted the dangers of racial intermarriage. A main tenet of polygenesis was that interbreeding among distant species produced infertile or degraded offspring, although as we saw above, even someone like Spencer, who supported monogenesis, did not believe in the wisdom of crossings between different races. In one case, Edward Aveling used the curious example that "the Egyptian women and the white are almost universally infertile."[93] In another, a correspondent from

South Carolina asked the editor of the *Truth Seeker,* George Macdonald, if "it is right or wrong for the white people to intermarry with colored?" Macdonald prefaced his remark by noting that "[i]t is a question not of right or wrong, [...] but of biology, or ethnology," and that he was not an authority on the subject, but

> [o]rdinary common sense would dictate the answer that intermarriage might be a good thing for the negro, but not for the white – the one race would be made better, but the other would be worsened. All should seek in marriage qualities calculated to better the stock, and it is not our opinion that for white persons those qualities reside in the negro or any other non-Caucasian race.[94]

In other words, Macdonald would not support intermarriage since it tended to degrade the better partner, in this case the white, although he thought this should be left up to individuals and did not suggest it should be illegal. Someone like Macdonald did not think much about racial issues, but this seemingly commonsensical opposition to racial interbreeding showed how ideas about racial hierarchy could be called upon without much reflection.

Eugenics

Questions about racial intermixing also bring to mind eugenics, which contended that a large number of traits were inheritable and that therefore individuals' reproduction should be carefully managed, either by the state or by society. This could take many forms, ranging from relatively benign encouragement of supposedly superior individuals to breed, to sterilization and euthanasia of those deemed unfit. Eugenics reached its height in Nazi Germany, but it should be noted that other countries, like the United States, also had legal sterilization programs for many decades in the twentieth century and that the sterilization laws in the United States actually served as models for the ones adopted by the Nazis.[95]

The founder of eugenics was Darwin's cousin Francis Galton. The historian of eugenics Daniel Kevles has suggested that for Galton and his followers, eugenics acted as a kind of a replacement "faith" for Christianity – though "often a cruel and always a problematic" one.[96] Indeed, Galton wrote, "I see no impossibility in Eugenics becoming a religious dogma among mankind, but its details must first be worked out sedulously in the study."[97] Race did not feature largely in Galton's theorizing, though he did believe that non-white races produced proportionally fewer exceptional individuals than the white race.[98]

For Karl Pearson, a freethinking socialist and Galton's closest follower, race played a greater role. Like Winwood Reade, Pearson believed in the necessity of struggle for evolutionary (and racial) progress. While this could be painful at times – for example, the near-elimination of the Indians in North America – on the whole, the good results balanced out the bad. "In place of the red man, contributing practically nothing to the work and thought of the world," Pearson explained, "we have a great nation, mistress of many arts, and able, with its youthful imagination and fresh, untrammelled impulses, to contribute much to the common stock of civilized man."[99] Despite this triumphalist note, Pearson was less optimistic about the prospects for racial progress than Reade. For Pearson, inferior "stock" would always persist: "You cannot change the leopard's spots, and you cannot change bad stock to good; you may dilute it, possibly spread it over a wider area, spoiling good stock, but until it ceases to multiply it will not cease to be."[100] This was why superior races could not live in a society with their inferiors, as in the Southern United States. The bad stock would inevitably degrade the good and not vice versa.[101]

Pearson's socialist views fit easily with eugenics. The fear of overpopulation in a socialist system without the natural check of poverty was a common charge by socialists' opponents. To Pearson, however, socialism offered the best response to such a problem: "the Socialistic seems the only form of community which can morally demand, and, if necessary, legally enforce, restraint of some kind upon its members."[102] Other freethinkers who came to accept socialism were likewise interested in the ideas of eugenics, although these questions rarely overlapped with race. Annie Besant, one of the leading secularists in Britain in the late nineteenth century and a convert to socialism, discussed the importance of heredity. One example she used to demonstrate its effects was the case of black parents giving birth to a white child, which suggested a distant white ancestor somewhere in their family tree.[103] It was because of heredity's importance that Besant called for careful consideration of marriage partners, although this was not in any way tied to race in her worldview. This should not, she believed, be brought about by the state but by a common social sense of duty to the human race. Besant thought that such practices, if followed by the middle classes, would eventually trickle down to the working classes.[104] Besant echoed these remarks in a debate over the validity of socialism with her fellow freethinker G.W. Foote. Foote warned that a socialist regime, without natural selection pressures, would take away parental responsibility and would allow the "unfit" to "flourish."[105] Besant countered that under a socialist system, as living standards and comfort increased, the people would better understand the dangers of overpopulation and would naturally work against them. Public opinion should prevent the parents' transmission of diseases to their offspring, and educating women would give them greater control of their reproduction.[106] Besant was of course long interested in birth control education, and she and Charles Bradlaugh faced trial in 1877 for publishing Charles Knowlton's *The Fruits of Philosophy*, a pamphlet on birth control aimed at the working classes.

Evolution and civilization

While evolutionary thought applied most readily to biology, it was also relevant to understanding the progress of civilization by analogy. As species evolve, it was thought, so too do societies. The belief in a transition from savagery to civilization dated back to the eighteenth century, but the Darwinian breakthrough transformed these ideas by presenting savage life as the first step in social evolution. This was in contrast to the long-held Christian idea that savages were the degraded offshoots of humans who had originally been created at a high level of civilization. As new chronologies pushed the age of humans back tens of thousands of years, an answer was needed for how human culture had evolved from a primitive state. Anthropologists used studies of modern savages, invariably one and the same as the lowest races, as a way to understand the distant ancestors of civilized people. There were two ways freethinkers could use such ideas. First, given the huge evolutionary hurdle from apes to humans, savages were called upon to act as a midway point between the two, in terms not just of biology, but of society and culture as well. Second, white freethinkers used social evolution to explain away religion as nothing more than a survival of crude savage superstition. In this way, the primitiveness and backwardness of savage races were emphasized, but there was also subversive content to such an assertion: white Christians could hardly claim superiority over non-white savages when both were held in sway by the same essential superstitions.

As we saw above, both Darwin and Huxley had grasped the utility of considering savages as a midpoint in the evolutionary timeline. Even before these two had fully sketched out their theories of human evolution, John Watts bluntly made a similar point in 1861 when he wrote that "the lowest race of the human species will stand near midway between the highest and the ourang-outang [sic]."[107] Edward Aveling likewise contended that "the interval between the highest man and the lowest man in regard to any anatomical or physiological point is greater than it is between the lowest man and the highest ape."[108] Aveling developed this theme in a series of 1884 articles in the *National Reformer* on "brute men": "those races or individuals whose mental powers are of a nature so low that the possessors would be regarded as non-human, were it not that their bodily structure is that of man." While "[t]he idiots, the insane or criminals, met with in any community" were also brute men, Aveling's primary concern was with those "distinct tribes" that lived in the Americas, Australasia, or Africa.[109] The "distinctive marks" of man were cultural, not biological: they included spoken and written language, self-consciousness, the use of clothing, tools, fire, and shelter, and, somewhat curiously coming from a freethinker, religious belief. As a way to blur the division between man and animals, Aveling argued that these things were either lacking in brute men or were present in animals. On language, for example, he admitted that all savage tribes appeared to have some form of language, albeit sometimes non-written,

> [b]ut it may be fairly contended that the interval between the grunting speech of the Bushman or the clicking dialect of the Kaffir below, and the refined and musical language of a great European orator or singer above, is as great as that between the language of the South African brute-men and the language of the anthropoid apes.[110]

Aveling also contended that animals made progress. Birds, for example, would in time learn to avoid telegraph wires, while travelers' accounts of "the African negro" lamented that this race appeared incapable of progress.[111]

In a later work, Aveling went even further, contending that savage races possessed an inferior memory even to dogs or horses.[112] Love was not a uniquely human trait and could be found in animals, yet appeared to be absent among savage races. "[A]mong the Bosjesmans and Australian blacks," Aveling wrote,

> the father is as likely as not to murder his child as soon as it is born. Even the mother treats her child no better than a cow treats her calf, leaving it to shift for itself at a very early age. On the other hand, the love and respect of children to their parents is almost, or quite, unknown in savage races.[113]

To Aveling, the lower races were not just inferior to the higher ones, but they were even inferior in mental capacity to apes in some respects.[114] As with Darwin and Huxley, Aveling's argument here was not one primarily for white supremacy: it was to make the case for evolution. Still, this defense of evolution clearly relied on a racial hierarchy which placed his own white race on top.

Another freethinker, W.H. Utley, wrote a similar series of articles for Bradlaugh's *National Reformer* in 1886. The influence of Aveling – who actually introduced Utley to his future wife – is clear in these discussions.[115] In his articles, Utley presented the linear evolution of mankind, "a gradual transition from the gibbon, the lowest of the anthropoids, to the European, the highest type of man."[116] Utley, borrowing from Bradlaugh's anthropology lectures, used Cloquet's facial angle to explain the gradation from backward races to civilized ones.[117] Aside from anatomical features, things like language showed how the lower races acted as a bridge between man and apes. Utley described how the "Bosjesmans" (Bushmen or San people) could not talk in the dark since the gestures necessary to supplement their "simple language of clicks and croaks" could not be seen. Indigenous Australians meanwhile did not know how to make fire, while the Fuegians did not wear clothing even in the coldest weather and possessed only "a few branches stuck into the ground" for shelter.[118] These "brute men" arguments continued to appear into the early twentieth century. Numerous articles by a variety of authors in both Britain and the United States made the same arguments, stressing the animalistic nature of savage races while also adding that various animal species possessed characteristics thought to be uniquely human.[119]

One of the more bizarre arguments came from Elmina Drake Slenker, an advocate of birth control and free love as well as a children's author.[120] Slenker spent several months in jail in 1887 on charges of sending sexually obscene material through the mail. She clearly rejected notions of self-censorship with regard to sexual matters and even inquired into bestiality and animal-human hybrids, something deeply shocking even to most free-thinkers.[121] In an article in the *Boston Investigator*, she suggested that blacks and apes could interbreed successfully, "proving a 'kinship' of ancestry."[122] In a subsequent article she explained that the idea came from Frederick Hollick, a nineteenth-century physician and sex educator. Hollick in turn heard this from a traveler in Africa, who reported that the locals believed in the possibility of crosses between chimpanzees and humans and who had apparently seen the "monkeyfied" children who resulted from such unions. These hybrids, however, could be sterile, as Slenker explained was the case with "[m]ulattoes here in the South," harking back to the old polygenist view.[123] In an article intended for children, she again referenced the animal nature of blacks as she explained that "[t]he negro does not seem to be so sensitive to pain as white people are [...]."[124] As further evidence of blacks' inferiority, she explained in a children's book that while "[n]egro dolls are sometimes made for colored children," they still prefer white dolls, "just as the black parents prefer pictures of white people to hang up in their houses." This was because "[w]e all like to imitate those we think better and higher than we are, and so the blacks, being an inferior race, look up to and imitate white people."[125]

Primitive religion

Studying savage societies also threw light on the primitive origins of religion and served to demonstrate that true civilization came from the abandon-ment of religion altogether. While eighteenth-century thinkers drew partly upon travel accounts of savage life to account for the natural origins of reli-gion,[126] after Darwin, the idea that religion itself was a product of evolution became prominent. Studies of savages revealed the origins of religion, but also invited comparisons between savages and Christians, demonstrating, to freethinkers, that the two differed in degree, not kind. These discussions played upon the notion of the savage as "the Other," in terms of race and civilization, from white Europeans and Americans. It was for this reason that comparisons between Christian and savage customs had so much force. Such comparisons were meant to embarrass and shame Christians into re-evaluating their beliefs. To freethinkers, true social progress meant giving up religious ideas altogether.

A major goal of cultural anthropology in the second half of the nineteenth century was uncovering the origins of religion. E.B. Tylor – the preeminent figure of late nineteenth-century British anthropology – paid particular attention to the development of religion among primitive communities. Tylor was born and raised as a Quaker and kept his faith until 1864, when he and his wife resigned their Quaker membership. The precise reasons for the break are unknown, but Timothy Larsen suggests it may have been prompted by the findings of his anthropological research, which he was beginning around the same time.[127]

One of Tylor's innovations was the idea of "survivals": customs and ideas that made sense within earlier forms of society, but that had since lost their original meanings as society progressed and the context changed. The study of survivals had the benefit of highlighting the origins of superstition and therefore making it vulnerable "to the attack of its deadliest enemy, a reasonable explanation."[128] Religion was, in short, a bundle of survivals that had rational explanations in a primitive context, but had outlived their purpose in civilized society. Religious ideas persisted even as people forgot their original meanings, but anthropological study would help to root out and dispose of these bad ideas. For Tylor, religion's origins were to be found in a mistaken belief in individual souls pervading the natural world, a view he described as animism. From this belief in souls, savages reasoned "to a yet wider doctrine of spiritual beings animated and controlling the universe in all its parts [...]." Finally the original idea became increasingly sophisticated as "a general philosophy of man and nature."[129] While Tylor's work had strong implications for the truth of Christianity, these were not stated explicitly but instead were left for "[e]ducated readers [...] to work out [...]."[130] Nonetheless, his discussion of religion revealed that there was "an unbroken line of mental connexion" between "the savage fetish-worshipper and the civilized Christian."[131] Tylor was, however, more forthright about the irreligious goals of anthropology in 1883, when he contributed the following stanza to a poem by Andrew Lang: "Theologians all to expose, – 'Tis the *mission* of Primitive Man."[132]

Herbert Spencer, too, located the origins of religion in primitive life. His "ghost theory," like Tylor's theory, saw religion beginning from a basic error. Primitive man thought that he possessed a double, which was the person apparently active while asleep. This double was thought, after death, to become a ghost that must be propitiated. From there, numerous developments, from ancestor worship, to worship of images or figures representing the dead, to the deification of dead leaders, steadily evolved to produce the various phenomena then described as religion. Like Tylor, Spencer was subtle about the implications of this for Christianity: "While among all races in all regions the conceptions of deities have been naturally evolved in the way shown; must we conclude that a small clan of the Semitic race had given to it supernaturally, a conception which, though superficially like the rest, was in substance absolutely unlike them?"[133] For Spencer, the answer was clearly no. Indeed, to suggest otherwise was to admit a morally "repugnant" implication: "that a complete simulation of the natural by the supernatural has been deliberately devised to deceive those who examine critically what they are taught. Appearances have been arranged for the purpose of misleading sincere inquirers, that they may be eternally damned for seeking the truth."[134]

While much of this theorizing was based on the concept of differing levels of civilization, not race, these levels of culture closely aligned with contemporary understandings of racial hierarchies. As Tylor said, "[f]ew would dispute that the following races are arranged rightly in order of culture: – Australian, Tahitian, Aztec, Chinese, Italian."[135] Furthermore, despite his monogenism, his 1881 work *Anthropology* contained a chapter detailing the various anatomical differences between races.[136] In this sense then, Tylor's and others' location of the origins of religion in savage life also meant, although this was not stated explicitly, that the essence of religion was to be found among Europeans' racial inferiors.[137]

Many other freethinkers drew upon such anthropological theorizing to construct naturalistic explanations of religion, in which religion was seen as an increasingly complex version of savage superstition. John Shertzer

Hittell was an early freethinker to present a naturalistic explanation of religious belief in *Evidences Against Christianity* (1857). In Hittell's view, the doctrines of Christianity did not come "from the brain of Jehovah, but grew by slow, gradual, and natural processes, from the low instincts which lead savages to worship stocks and stones."[138] Robert Ingersoll likewise saw religion as an early and feeble attempt by humans to make sense of their world. In one of Ingersoll's earliest lectures, entitled "The Gods," delivered in 1872, he explained the development of religious ideas by a climatic theory. He argued that savages, terrified of nature's inexplicable power, saw it as "malevolent," which made them "[resort] to prayer, to flattery, to worship and to sacrifice."[139]

In *The Martyrdom of Man*, Winwood Reade too delved into the origins of religion among savages.[140] A religion corresponded to a society's level of civilization and made sense within that context. As Reade said, "There is a kind of Natural Selection in religion; the creed which is best adapted to the mental world will invariably prevail; and the mental world is being gradually prepared for the reception of higher and higher forms of religious life."[141] For example, Africans' religion, "whether pagan or moslem, is suited to their intellects, and is therefore a true religion; and the same may be said of Christianity amongst uneducated people." Reade thought, however, that Christianity was now no longer "in accordance with the cultivated mind," and therefore it "ought to be destroyed."[142] At one stage in civilization, Christianity was useful, but that time had now passed: western society had simply outgrown Christianity, and true progress required throwing off its last vestiges in favor of a religion of virtue, even if, Reade admitted, the process would be painful.

While freethinkers were interested in studying savage religion as a way to uncover the natural origins of religion, the image of the savage "Other" also served to shame or embarrass Christians by equating them with the lowest African or Native American savages. Such an equation, to be effective, relied upon the view that these groups were at the bottom of the civilizational and evolutionary hierarchy. In one case, Robert Ingersoll drew parallels between the supposed Native American custom of placing "the heads of their children between pieces of bark until the form of the skull is permanently changed" and Christians putting their children "in the strait-jacket

Driving Away the Comet.   Driving Away the Eclipse.

2.1 "Parallel Cases," *Truth Seeker*, March 22, 1890, 177

of a creed."[143] This comparison is also seen in a cartoon by Watson Heston, the *Truth Seeker* cartoonist. This showed a side-by-side comparison of a white priest driving away a comet, in reference to the apocryphal story that Pope Calixtus III excommunicated Halley's Comet in 1456, and an African savage banging a drum as a way to drive away an eclipse (see Figure 2.1). The main target of these critiques was Christianity, but depended on portraying savages as especially ignorant and degraded.

Similarly, white freethinkers drew comparisons between modern savages and the ancient Hebrews. Ingersoll said that the ancient Jews were "as ignorant as the inhabitants of Central Africa" and the God of the Old Testament was "a poor, ignorant, superstitious savage."[144] This point was made in another Watson Heston cartoon, which contained a quote from the book of Psalms ("But God shall wound the head of his enemies, and the hairy scalp of such a one as goeth on still in his trespasses") and showed God's hand reaching down from the clouds to cut off the scalp of a man – in reference to the practice of scalping frequently associated with Native Americans (see Figure 2.2). The message was that the Old Testament was

2.2 "Does God Scalp His Enemies?," *Truth Seeker*, January 30, 1892, 80

not a guide to morality or metaphysics for enlightened westerners, but a creation of people no better than contemporary savages. These kinds of arguments, whether consciously or not, reflected Tylor's notion of survivals. Superstitious and savage ideas had survived among civilized people long after they were meaningful. But these arguments also had racial implications. Readers could not miss the fact that modern Christians and ancient Jews were being compared with non-white savages who sat at the lowest rung of the racial and evolutionary hierarchy.

This criticism of the ancient Hebrews could occasionally turn into prejudice against Jews in the present. Watson Heston's cartoons poking fun at the Bible occasionally relied on stereotypes of present-day Jews for comedy and often depicted them with pronounced Jewish features. One such cartoon depicted a scene from the book of Ezekiel in which God had destroyed the hordes of Gog of Magog, which threatened the Jews, and encouraged his followers to put signs next to their bones so others would bury them. In Heston's take, Ezekiel puts up signs about money-lending and pawn shops, drawing on old anti-Jewish stereotypes (see Figure 2.3).

2.3 "Setting Up Signs," *Truth Seeker,* May 26, 1894, 336

Other freethinkers critiqued the Jews for their provincialism and their clinging to outdated faiths. Horace Seaver, in the *Boston Investigator*, wrote in 1863 that the Jews "were about the worst people of whom we have any account, and the poorest guides to follow."[145] He continued that the Jewish sect "is bigoted, narrow, exclusive, and totally unfit for a progressive people like the other Americans […]."[146] Still, in the following issue, he clarified that "[o]f course we were speaking of them as a religious sect. We have nothing against a Jew personally."[147] Nonetheless, Seaver's editorial drew a response from the Polish-born Ernestine Rose, a prominent nineteenth-century freethinker and abolitionist who was of Jewish descent (although she rejected any identification with her Jewish background).[148] In the editorial, she wrote that she "almost smelt brimstone, genuine Christian brimstone" in the characterization of the Jews and encouraged Seaver and the readers to "not add to the prejudice existing towards the Jews, or any other sect."[149]

Other freethinkers were more careful to nuance their views on the character of Jews. While Hittell argued that the ancient Hebrews were as savage as various primitive tribes,[150] he rushed to disassociate himself from crude anti-Jewish prejudice. He stated, "I trust that no one will understand my language, in this chapter or elsewhere, as countenancing the vulgar prejudices against the blood or faith of the modern Jews. […] I know many of them to be enlightened, liberal-minded, good men, and feel honored by their friendship."[151] This was hardly unique to Hittell. While freethinkers had few qualms about condemning the ancient Hebrews in the harshest terms, they were alert to the dangers of contemporary persecution of Jews and spoke out against it.[152]

Conclusion

Like the prior chapter on polygenesis, this chapter has shown how evolutionary doctrines – devised and supported by atheists and other freethinkers – allowed for racist interpretations. While pioneers of evolutionary thought like Darwin and Chambers both believed that their theories gave support to monogenesis, it is clear that polygenesis – or at least a persisting belief in the importance of racial differences – could continue to flourish within this new framework. This stance could come in the direct support of a polygenist conception of evolution, as seen in the work of Edward Aveling, or more subtly by the insertion of a racial hierarchy as a way to explain how humans made the seemingly impossible evolutionary jump from apes, a tactic that Darwin and Huxley both employed. As seen in the previous chapter, it is clear that in the various shades of evolutionary theorizing white people emerged on the top. The white identity of the theorists therefore cannot be just a coincidence, nor should it be overlooked. As these ideas spread, both authors and audience no doubt flattered themselves by counting their own race and civilization among the most evolved.

Evolutionary thought also had implications for understanding the development of societies. In this case, racial hierarchies easily aligned with civilizational and evolutionary ones. Freethinkers' use of sociocultural evolution was particularly directed toward investigating religion's origins. By studying the religion of savages, one could glimpse religion in its primitive form. While Christianity was undoubtedly a more sophisticated version of this basic religion, it remained in essence the same. This tactic then demonstrated that Christianity was not, as its proponents contended, a divine revelation, but was instead a dressed-up version of savage superstition. This comparison was designed to shame white Christians by equating them with their supposed civilizational and racial inferiors.

In these discussions, it was useful to portray savage races as especially degraded, either as ignorant and frightened thinkers who first conceived religious ideas, or as midway points on the evolutionary path between apes and civilized Europeans. In other words, these so-called lower races often came out badly in evolutionary theorizing. But the fact that white Christians appeared to share this savage belief in superstition begins to highlight the ambivalence present in white atheists' thinking on race. The next chapter makes that ambivalence even starker as it traces atheists' views of the savage races. When considered in a social, rather than a theoretical perspective, the so-called lower races actually appeared quite favorable in the eyes of white atheists and freethinkers.

3

A London Zulu:
savagery and civilization

In the eighteenth and nineteenth centuries, it was commonly held that societies passed through a linear progression from the stage of "savagery" (the hunter-gatherer stage) to "barbarism" (the agricultural stage) and finally to "civilization" (the stage at which western industrialized countries found themselves). These stages often corresponded to racial hierarchies as well, with the lowest races thought to occupy the lowest rung on the ladder to civilization. The previous two chapters showed how white atheists and freethinkers often accepted that non-white people were racially inferior to and less evolved than Europeans. This sometimes appeared as part of their anti-Christian polemics, but was not wholly instrumental. Their worldviews assumed a hierarchical conception of races and civilizations, with themselves at the top. In the previous chapter, though, we began to see glimpses of the ways this superiority could be undermined through anthropological speculations on the origins of religion. While British and American societies might represent the apex of civilization, this did not erase the fact that Christianity – a creed little different from the primitive superstition of savages – was still dominant.

This ambivalence of white atheists and freethinkers toward their own societies' superiority becomes much starker as we begin to consider their racial views in a social and cultural perspective. In particular, this chapter looks at so-called savage races: those in Africa, Australasia, and the Americas.[1] Polygenist and evolutionary views occurred within the context of a growing imperial presence in these regions by Britain and other European nations (and to a lesser extent the United States). While in some cases, an imperial presence had existed for centuries, the latter half of the nineteenth century saw indigenous people in Australia and New Zealand subdued and dispossessed of their land, the westward expansion of white settlers in the United States and accompanying violence against Native Americans, and the parceling-up of nearly all of Africa among European powers. Racist attitudes helped in part to justify these conquests, and the successful conquests in turn reinforced a belief in white racial and civilizational superiority.

Paradoxically, however, this chapter will show that many white atheists and freethinkers found positives in the societies of savage people and even seemed, in some cases, to identify with them. Although the analogy should not be stretched too far, both atheists and savages were marginalized groups who faced persecution at the hands of more powerful Christians. White atheists recognized their minority status, and this may have been part of the reason why they opposed missionary incursions into savage societies. They were not opposed to imperialism *per se*, but they did at least doubt the wisdom of western nations completely trampling over these cultures. Their criticism of imperialism, it should be noted, was part of a wider trend among liberal radicals and socialists who were skeptical of empire variously because of the ways it violated the rights of the colonized, diverted resources needed at home to far-flung regions, hindered the fair development of international trade, threatened the rights of those at home by increasing the power of the government and the military, and encouraged militarism through its never-ending quest for new markets.[2] Aside from the political and economic case against imperialism, atheists and freethinkers had further reason to be skeptical of the inherent superiority of the West because of the close links they saw between western civilization and Christianity.

But freethinkers' discussions of savage life often said more about their own societies than about savage ones. Indeed, whether their portrayal of savages was positive or negative depended in large part on how such a portrayal would assist in their wider arguments against Christianity. In the previous chapter we saw that portraying non-white savages as especially degraded provided a useful tool in evolutionary narratives as a way to bridge the gap between civilized whites and apes. The contradictory view of savages was highlighted by E.B. Tylor, who noted the tendency of his fellow anthropologists "to treat the savage mind according to the needs of our argument, sometimes as extremely ignorant and inconsequent, at other times, as extremely observant and logical."[3] George Stocking has labeled this the "double image of savagery," and it will be seen throughout the chapter in freethinkers' discussions of savage life.[4]

A clear example of this comes in the first part of the chapter, which shows that some atheists used the alleged godlessness of savages as a way to refute the notion that belief in God was universal. This absence of religion was sometimes turned against savage people as a way to demonstrate their primitiveness; in other words, they were so primitive as to lack even religion. But freethinkers also believed that savages possessed a naive rationality that immunized them against Christian proselytizing and allowed them to see through Christianity's absurdity. Furthermore, savage life seemed in many ways preferable to British and American societies since it offered an apparent alternative to the harsh inequalities of industrial capitalism.

On practical questions of the treatment of savage people, atheists and freethinkers were critical of unwanted Christian missionary incursions into savage societies. Attempts to force civilization – a concept closely bound up with Christianity – on savages seemed to freethinkers to have had disastrous consequences. Freethinkers were likewise critical of imperial military adventures. Again, since these actions were either directly or indirectly bound up with Christianity, freethinkers opposed them. In their discussions of their own societies' military actions, they adopted a relativist position as they turned the dichotomy of civilized and savage on its head by questioning which side in the conflict was truly civilized. The often brutal behavior of the British and American forces seemed to suggest that these so-called civilized societies might better deserve the label of savage.

As Michael Adas cautions, however, "sympathy for subjugated peoples, and even considerable understanding of their cultures, cannot necessarily be taken as proof that an individual was free of racial prejudice."[5] Indeed, it seems unlikely that white atheists completely rejected their belief in the superiority of white, western civilization over that of the savages. Yet any sense of superiority they might have felt was tempered by the unavoidable fact that their own societies and cultures were so intertwined with Christianity, a harmful and hypocritical creed from their perspective. This made atheists and freethinkers at least ambivalent about the wisdom of bringing civilization to foreign people.

Godless savages

As we saw in the previous chapter, savage religion appeared primitive and, since savages were seen as living fossils through which the early history of mankind could be glimpsed, the study of their religion allowed one to understand the origins of religion. Other thinkers, however, contended that savages lacked religion altogether. This presented a paradox: either their lack of religion demonstrated that their minds were so primitive as to be unable even to comprehend the notion of a deity, or it indicated that these people possessed superior minds in comparison to white Christians.

Many nineteenth-century authors noted that savages appeared to be entirely devoid of religion.[6] It should, however, be noted that "religion" is not a straightforward term, and its meaning is rooted in western modernity. In other words, "religion" is not a universal category, but one that was created in the West and modeled on Christianity. The "religions" of other cultures were judged therefore by the extent to which they possessed similar criteria to Christianity, like a system of belief in God or gods, a holy text, an ecclesiastical structure, and a central place of worship.[7] Furthermore, the data of nineteenth-century anthropologists were not based upon systematic study of their subjects, but on second-hand information taken from the writings of colonial officials, explorers, missionaries, and naturalists.[8] This meant that the views of savage culture were filtered through a number of different conceptual, political, and religious lenses, which inevitably obscured what these westerners were seeing. Needless to say, the beliefs of so-called savage groups were eclectic and are not easily summarized. These ranged from traditional animistic understandings, in which all of nature is pervaded by gods and spirits, to monotheistic religions; indeed, Islam and Christianity had existed for centuries in Africa.[9] It is also fair to speculate that there existed instances of skepticism toward supernatural beliefs and the authority of spiritual leaders in these cultures as well.[10]

John Lubbock was one of the most prominent figures to hold the view that savages did not possess religion. An archeologist and gentleman in

Darwin and Huxley's circle, in his 1865 *Pre-Historic Times* Lubbock discussed ancient humans and used modern savages to throw light on early humanity. He saw savages as intellectually, as well as morally, inferior to civilized Europeans. He cited numerous travelers on the question of savage religion and concluded:

> in the state of their religious conceptions, or rather in the absence of religious conceptions, we get another proof of extreme mental inferiority. It has been asserted over and over again that there is no race of men so degraded as to be entirely without a religion – without some idea of a deity. So far from this being true, the very reverse is the case. Many, we might almost say all, of the most savage races are, according to the nearly universal testimony of travellers, in this condition.[11]

Lubbock dismissed travelers' reports that savages possessed ideas of God: "How, for instance, can a people who are unable to count their own fingers, possibly raise their mind so far as to admit even the rudiments of a religion[?]"[12] In a later work, he further argued that "[s]ailors, traders, and philosophers, Roman Catholic priests and Protestant missionaries, in ancient and in modern times, in every part of the globe, have concurred in stating that there are races of men altogether devoid of religion."[13]

While Lubbock presented a gradualist and naturalistic account of religion that accorded with the theories of E.B. Tylor, his belief that savages were without religion altogether was disputed. Tylor picked apart Lubbock's examples and noted that many were the result of travelers misunderstanding, intentionally or not, savage religious practice.[14] Darwin too argued against the idea that savages lacked religion. Matthew Day has convincingly shown that for centuries, authors had speculated that religious belief was a uniquely human trait and therefore that to call savages godless was also to say they were somehow less than human. By providing a naturalistic account of religion in *Descent of Man* that saw rudimentary superstitions present in animals, Darwin wished, in Day's words, "to sever the traditional association between the moral status of being human and the anthropological status of having a religion."[15]

Lubbock and others did not posit godless savages explicitly as a way to criticize Christianity. Atheists, however, drew upon such accounts to refute the long-held Christian "argument from universal consent" – namely that all people in all times and places believed in some kind of deity and that this therefore offered evidence for the truth of God's existence. In *The Freethinker's Text-Book* (1876), for example, Charles Bradlaugh cited Lubbock's *Pre-Historic Times* and *Origin of Civilisation* on the existence of races who had no belief in God and mined Lubbock's work for travelers' testimony on this account.[16] W. Mann similarly wrote two series of articles for the *Freethinker* on the question of the universality of religion or belief in God. One facet of the argument was the use of travelers' accounts and anthropological works, again drawing from Lubbock, to demonstrate that many tribes were indeed without a belief in God and that these beliefs were therefore not innate, but had to be taught.[17]

Some freethinkers used savages' lack of belief as proof of their low status, however. E.R. Woodward, writing in the *Freethinker*, admitted that "it is a strange reflection for the Freethinker" to ponder "that there are people existing at the present day who are too degenerate to be even religious."[18] But such a view was not the norm; more often the irreligion of savages was seen favorably. Savages, to white atheists and freethinkers, were untainted by Christianity and possessed a simple, even child-like, rationality that allowed them to see through the claims of foreign missionaries. Freethinkers therefore routinely cast savages as foils to missionary attempts at proselytizing. A standard of nineteenth-century thought was to portray savages as having the minds of children,[19] but this child-like naivety seemed to allow them, in freethinkers' narratives, to successfully resist Christian dogma. The sentiment behind Thomas Paine's famous quip that "any system of religion that has anything in it that shocks the mind of a child cannot be a true system" seems to be what freethinkers had in mind as they trotted out numerous examples, real and imagined, of savages successfully exposing the absurdities of Christianity.[20]

One example of this came from a confrontation between Samuel Baker, a Christian explorer, and an East African chief named Comorro (also rendered Commora or Comoro). Baker recorded the conversation in a travel memoir in which he tried to convince Comorro of the reality of an afterlife, but Comorro repeatedly rebutted Baker's arguments.[21] The story was described multiple times in the freethought press, intending to show the superior wisdom of the African and more importantly the absurdity of the

Christian.[22] The most famous case of this kind of confrontation, however, was Bishop John Colenso's "conversion" at the hands of the Zulu. The British-born Colenso, who became the first bishop of Natal in South Africa from 1854, serving to his death in 1883, was already theologically unorthodox, but was put on the path to further skepticism in 1861 by questions from his Zulu assistant, William Ngidi, about the truth of the story of Noah's Ark. In 1862, Colenso began working on his seven-part tome *The Pentateuch and the Book of Joshua Critically Examined* (1862–79), which argued that the Pentateuch – the collective name for the first five books of the Bible – could not be considered inspired or historical given its many inconsistencies and contradictions. In 1863, the Bishop of Cape Town, Robert Gray, convicted Colenso for "false teaching," though the ruling was overturned two years later on the grounds that Gray had no such authority.[23]

While many contemporaries mocked Colenso as a fool for his "conversion" at the hands of the Zulu,[24] the incident became a staple of freethought lore throughout the nineteenth century and into the twentieth. As George Macdonald described it, "[t]he criticisms of the intelligent African were so shrewd that the bishop himself became convinced that the theory of the inspiration of the Bible was untenable, and he wrote his famous work on the Pentateuch, which has never been answered."[25] While freethinkers praised Colenso for his open-mindedness toward the Zulu criticisms of the Bible, one writer in the *Freethinker* urged that "we should not forget 'the intelligent native'" who sparked Colenso's inquiry.[26] Indeed, J.M. Robertson, in his history of freethought, expressed optimism about the progress of freethinking in Africa, citing the example of Colenso's conversion.[27] Freethinkers were, however, perhaps too quick to look to Colenso as one of their own, since his own views remained on the liberal wing of Christianity and he never accepted their atheism.

Nonetheless, these confrontations between Christians and savages allowed white atheists to find common cause with their non-white brothers. The persona of a savage or barbarian offered an ideal guise for religious and social criticism since their outsider status permitted an analysis free from initial biases. European writers in the eighteenth century occasionally adopted a foreign guise for their critiques – a trope Anthony Pagden describes as the "savage critic."[28] Montesquieu adopted an outsider's perspective in *Persian Letters* (1721), which described the fictional voyage of two Persian travelers through France. Prominent French freethinkers in the eighteenth century also used this tactic: Voltaire's *L'ingénu* (from 1767, set in North America) and Denis Diderot's *Supplément au voyage de Bougainville* (from 1772, set in Tahiti) both used savage protagonists as a way to make social and religious criticisms. Nineteenth-century freethinkers also found this literary technique useful. By draping themselves in a foreign garb, they could view routine cultural practices through unfamiliar eyes and therefore point out their absurdity or hypocrisy. This kind of criticism sometimes found humor in the strangeness of the foreigner or their confusion about aspects of western culture. More importantly, however, was that the satires directly challenged notions of western superiority. Indeed, the fact that atheists were so willing to imagine themselves as non-white foreigners indicates how they saw themselves as outsiders within their own societies.

An example of this is an 1863 book on the Colenso controversy by George Holyoake. Here Holyoake adopted the persona of a "London Zulu" as he defended Colenso against one of the many refutations published against him – this by the Scottish clergyman John Cumming.[29] There was no doubt that Holyoake intended to link the cause of freethinkers and the Zulu, as he noted that their former ethnographical name, "Kaffirs," came from the Arabic for "infidel."[30] Aside from defending Colenso's arguments on the Pentateuch, Holyoake, through his Zulu character, also challenged assumptions about the supposed savagery of the Zulu. This was a matter of perspective: westerners saw the Zulu as savages for "venerat[ing] the bloody and ferocious memory" of their leader Shaka Zulu, whereas the civilized French venerated Napoleon "who deluged Europe in blood, and his own country too [...]." Given this, Holyoake mischievously noted, "the Zulus are not so much behind European civilization."[31] But the Zulu possessed an excellent moral sense, one which clearly did not come from the Bible: "trustiness as noble, devotion as honest, and fidelity as unswerving, and incorruptible as ever the world saw, dwells in the Zulu – ignorant of Moses and all his Hebrew wonders."[32]

Even before that, an 1853 article in Holyoake's *Reasoner* favorably discussed the "Kaffirs" of South Africa.[33] While the "sad, wild, and untameable race [...] are sometimes spoken of with contempt," the author – perhaps

Holyoake himself – believed "that strong speculative faculty lies at the bottom of their character." Some commentators had also suggested they were the ancestors of "a race who refused to accept the Mahomedan tenets in the seventh century […]." Indeed, "[t]he very name of Kaffir signifies the rejection of a faith."[34] Robert Ryder, also writing in the *Reasoner*, explained in an 1856 article that the Zulu "are a shrewd race of men, very powerful, and very rich, logical and witty, real orators. When the missionary has told his story, they laugh and tell him that their grandmothers told them such tales," while "they themselves believe nothing, and care for nothing, except oxen and wives."[35] Others were less charitable. While acknowledging the "incisive logic" of the Zulu which led Colenso to begin questioning the Pentateuch, Douglas Blackburn noted that in his twenty-year experience in South Africa the people were unable to comprehend spiritual topics, and the individual "Kaffir" "has no perception of humor apart from physical buffonry [sic], and sarcasm or irony are lost on him."[36] The lack of religious understanding was, as we have seen, a double-edged sword for savage people: were they irreligious because they possessed formidable intellects, or were their minds too primitive to even comprehend such ideas?

On the whole, most freethinkers favored the first explanation, at least in so far as it suited their arguments against Christianity. Playing on the theme of the wise Zulu, an article from 1882 in the *National Reformer* purportedly came from "an unconverted Zulu" living in Britain and writing back to a friend in South Africa. The author attempted to render a pidgin dialect in his discussion of the Colenso encounter:

> English nation once sent very big mystery-man to convert poor Zulu to English religion; but poor Zulu and intelligent bishop talked together, and so Zulu converted bishop instead. So Bishop Colenso became a good man and kind friend to Zulus, and not like Christians, who shoot us and steal our women and children and cattle.

The author mocked Christians over their hypocrisy toward the Ten Commandments and wondered why the commandments against killing and stealing were not obeyed. Perhaps, the author speculated, these commandments did not apply to foreigners, "[e]lse why do Christians covet and steal our land and make black people slaves? […] Why they kill thousands of Zulus who never did them harm except in defending fatherland?"[37] When the author was asked by a clergyman in England about sending more missionaries to South Africa, the author declined, suggesting, "it much better if Zulu chiefs come over to English land to change the hearts of English people, so that they grow just and good, and love their black brothers in distant lands, and no longer do them wrong and unkindness."[38] Certainly the author found humor in the juxtaposition of an African savage claiming superiority over white westerners, but there was a serious and subversive point in the article as well. The dichotomy of civilization and savagery could be turned on its head by viewing Christian society from an outsider's perspective.

A similar case came from Autonomos, an already-pseudonymous author in the *National Reformer*, who adopted a further guise, purporting to have translated a letter from "Gelele, King of Dahome" to "Soapy Sam" – Bishop Samuel Wilberforce, the foe of Thomas Huxley in their famed debate on Darwinism in 1860. In his letter, Gelele addressed Wilberforce as "the most cunning of the chief fetish-men of England" and repeatedly referred to priests as "mystery-men." He complained that he was "called a savage in England" even though he had forbidden his countrymen to eat missionaries, a difficult task since they were "very nice eating" and "most quarrelsome when alive."[39] Gelele pointed out the hypocrisy of Christians denouncing the superstitious practices of Africans. He asked, for example, "[h]ow can you taunt the African races with their local Gods, when the English believe in three Gods who favour *them* above all other Christians?"[40] He also favorably contrasted his people's relatively peaceful behavior with that of the English by referring to the Morant Bay rebellion of 1865 in Jamaica, and the subsequent crackdown, which was "far more bloody than those of Dahome."[41] In this way, the barbarity of the English was meant to have shocked even the most savage African.[42]

Savages and the good life

Studies of savage life appeared to show that many savage groups lacked religion, a fact that struck at the Christian argument of the universality of a belief in God. But since Christians held that morality and religion were inextricably linked, freethinkers had to further demonstrate that a lack of religion did not inhibit morality but in fact allowed for a purer form, untainted by the hypocrisies of Christian society. White atheists and freethinkers found that savage societies offered alternative ways of living that were particularly appealing in light of freethinkers' own economic and social marginalization. Of course it is unlikely that freethinkers would have actually preferred living in a savage society. But they did find positives in it that offered alternatives to the problems in their own societies, particularly the excesses of industrial capitalism which left many impoverished.

Within an evolutionary framework, however, freethinkers might consider savage morality as a rudimentary form of that of civilized Europeans. Darwin believed that while savages possessed morality, it was chiefly practiced between members of the tribe.[43] Winwood Reade took a similar view to his idol Darwin, saying that "savages within their own communion do live according to the golden rule," but "they are not in reality good men."[44] This was because their moral code extended only to those within their own society. This was not true morality, but "only a kind of honour among thieves." Nonetheless, savage morality gradually extended beyond their own families and tribes to eventually encompass all people.[45] E.B. Tylor was more positive than these thinkers and argued that any kind of social life necessitated morality: "Without a code of morals, the very existence of the rudest tribe would be impossible; and indeed the moral standards of even savage races are to no small extent well-defined and praiseworthy."[46] Morals, then, had a natural origin: they were not divinely inspired, but had evolved.

This is a clear example of the "double image of savagery." When savage life was considered in terms of social evolution, savage morality seemed inferior in comparison to that of civilized people. Yet when using savage life as a way to critique the problems of western society, many atheists and freethinkers found that savage life actually had much to teach westerners. As I noted in the Introduction, nineteenth-century freethought was descended in large part from the political radicalism of the late eighteenth and early nineteenth centuries that advocated for greater political rights and social reforms to end concentrations of wealth and to ease the plight of the poor. It was no surprise therefore that many freethinkers looked to savage societies as an alternative to the inequalities that were inherent in western society. As one author in the *Boston Investigator* explained with regard to Native

Americans, "[i]n the forest, virtue is native, and hospitality impulsive; the hand is open to receive the wretched, not as in Christendom, like a beggar, but as a brother." A hypocritical disregard for the poor pervaded Christian society, he suggested, but equality and fair treatment formed the basis of Native American society. The article further quoted George Catlin, known for his artistic depictions of Native Americans during his travels in the American West: "They possess everything that they want or regard as a luxury. They have no inequality, no confinement to business hours; no debts, notes in bank, credit system, no competition!"[47]

Other authors made similar observations. Emily G. Taylor in the *Truth Seeker* explained that the so-called Hottentots of South Africa, "in the excellence of their morals, surpassed all nations of the earth" despite lacking ideas of God or future rewards or punishments. She also noted that this society had not succumbed to the problems of wealth inequality in modern life: "Peace and prosperity reigned; no wealthy class was supported in idleness by the toiling poor; no dens of infamy, no saloons, and – no churches."[48] Robert Ryder, who lived in Pietermaritzburg (in Natal), similarly noted the many virtues of the irreligious Zulu, including their honesty, faithfulness, and hospitality. The Zulu were "Epicureans to the back bone" who lived only for "freedom and pleasure." Ryder questioned the use, therefore, that Christianity – and the capitalist system that went along with it – would have for such a people who lived a simple but plentiful life.[49] The Zulu had "[p]lenty of wives, plenty of cattle, plenty of land, plenty of corn," and Ryder encouraged the predominantly working-class readers of the *Reasoner* to "contrast that with your condition."[50] In other words, a simple savage life provided all one could want for happiness, while Christianity and capitalism seemed to leave people destitute.

The highly moral savage became a common figure in freethought journals. Reports abounded about the superior morality of various groups in Africa,[51] the "Arafuras" of the Aru Islands,[52] the Dyaks of Borneo,[53] the Samoyedic people of Siberia,[54] Australian aborigines,[55] and the indigenous people of the Philippines.[56] In particular, white American freethinkers were keen to stand up for Native Americans. An 1861 meeting convened to build support for the plight of Native Americans was composed of "about half Spiritualists" and half "Infidels and doubtful Christians" and featured the editor of the *Boston Investigator*, Horace Seaver, as one of the speakers.[57] A.L. Posey, a Native American student from the Indian Territory (in present-day Oklahoma), wrote to the *Boston Investigator* in 1890 to sing the praises of the paper, which was "the grandest and the most scientific paper published within the bounds of America." He spoke in glowing terms of the paper's virtues such as its "exhaustless intellectual brilliancy," which would "unveil the fretful heavens of human superstition to brightness." L.K. Washburn, the editor, added a note at the bottom of the letter that read:

> The glowing words of our Indian friend are appreciated by the publisher of this paper. The Investigator has stood for the rights of man, white, black, or red, and has always been devoted to the best interests of the whole human race, of whatever land or color. We are pleased to know of one emancipated red brother and extend to him the cordial fellowship of Liberalism.[58]

Another "Indian," named George Freeman, wrote to Charles Chilton Moore's the *Blue-Grass Blade* asking for some copies of the freethought paper. Freeman explained that he had known Moore while the two were imprisoned (Moore for blasphemy and Freeman for robbery – although he claimed his innocence). Moore agreed to send some copies and wrote of his admiration for Indians since "Tecumsey [sic] saved my father from the British at the battle of the River Raisin [...]." He added, "I like red men, black men and yellow men – Indians, Negroes and Chinamen, and I like white women, but I ain't much stuck on white men."[59]

Freethinkers also sought to refute negative stereotypes of savage people. In the *National Reformer*, Charles Bradlaugh's daughter Hypatia favorably reviewed Helen Hunt Jackson's *A Century of Dishonor*, an 1881 work that offered a sympathetic account of the history of indigenous people in America. The book, Hypatia believed, would help to dispel "the false impressions that we have so long harbored concerning the North American Indians."[60] George C. Bartlett meanwhile wrote an article that refuted the idea that aboriginal people in Fiji engaged in cannibalism. In fact, he claimed, "[a] more gentle, loving, peaceable race of people I never met."[61] In another case, a correspondent from New Zealand, Charles Rae, wrote to the *National Reformer* in 1879 to chide Annie Besant for her quip that some Maori, "desiring to thoroughly digest Christianity," had killed and ate five missionaries. Rae insisted that such a stereotype was no longer valid: "to the credit of the Maori be it said, that cannibalism no longer exists."[62]

This is not to say all freethinkers avoided the temptation of making jokes about the alleged cannibalism practiced by savages. The butt of the jokes, however, was usually naive missionaries, but the humor depended on savages appearing especially degraded. For example, one news item in 1867 in the *National Reformer* noted the death of a West African king, who – in a play on the popular abolitionist phrase from earlier in the century – "was a man and a brother, and lunched off cold missionary, when in season, with great regularity."[63] These kinds of jokes were frequently inserted as short paragraphs in the news sections of freethought newspapers or at the bottoms of columns to fill space. While they demonstrated the persistence of crude stereotypes, they also existed side-by-side in the freethought press with more favorable and thoughtful views of savage life.

Criticism of missionaries

It may be too much to say that atheists and freethinkers genuinely admired savage cultures, but they nonetheless viewed them with enough respect that they did not want to see those societies trampled over by Christian missionaries. Concepts of civilization were closely bound up with Christianity, and civilizing heathens often included converting them to Christianity. Freethinkers' true targets, as usual, were Christian missionaries, yet freethinkers certainly sympathized with the people whose societies were destabilized by the introduction of Christianity.

While humanitarian opinion in the mid-nineteenth century worried about the dangers of white contact with indigenous people, many Christian humanitarians thought that white missionaries would actually serve as protective buffers between indigenous people and white settlers.[64] Freethinkers naturally disagreed with this since they did not distinguish between settlers and missionaries: all were agents of imperialism, in their eyes. Some historians have argued that missionaries assisted with the spread of imperialism, but Andrew Porter has convincingly argued that in fact there was frequent tension between missionaries and colonial officials. Missionaries were as likely to push against colonial rule as they were to harmonize with it. Their relationship with empire ebbed and flowed over the course of the century, and they always evaluated this relationship according to how it helped to achieve their own goals.[65]

One common narrative held throughout this period was that indigenous people were dying out in the face of white settlement.[66] This was, to atheists and freethinkers, connected with the introduction of Christianity into these societies. Freethinkers saw themselves as powerless to slow the incursion of Christian missionaries into foreign lands, where the missionaries would unintentionally bring on the demise of the local races. As George Macdonald put it when writing about a group in Tierra del Fuego, "[t]he remnant is being Christianized off the face of the earth."[67] Historically this had been true as well, particularly in the case of the European colonization of the Americas. Samuel Porter Putnam, in his *400 Years of Freethought*, discussed the consequences of Columbus's voyage: "The discovery of Columbus was followed by destruction and cruelty unparalleled in the history of the world. [...] Bloody wars annihilated a happy people. The cross which Columbus bore and in whose name he took possession of the continent, gilded the blackest flag of piracy and murder that ever cursed humanity."[68] A similar idea can be glimpsed in an 1893 cartoon by Watson Heston. On one side stood a Native American figure who received only death, slavery, and violence, while on the other stood a European figure reaped wealth and dominion over the New World (see Figure 3.1).

Part of the reason for the devastation wrought by foreign invaders was that Christianity demanded a drastic change of lifestyle among native people: not only did the people need to change their religion, but they also needed to adopt an alien lifestyle. J.M. Wheeler cited the work of H.R. Fox Bourne, the leader of the Aborigines Protection Society, on the negative impact of Christian civilization on indigenous people. These people were forced to wear western dress, which made them "susceptible to cold and disease."[69] The reason why wearing clothes was harmful was explained by W. Mann in reference to the South Sea Islanders: "In the native state the body, being saturated with cocoanut [sic] oil, sheds the water like a duck's back, and in a few minutes after the shower, in a tropical sun, he is perfectly warm and comfortable. On the other hand, when clothed, he sits cowering in his drenched garments," which led to various illnesses.[70] While these

3.1 "Some Providential Gifts," *Truth Seeker*, June 3, 1893, 337

were pleas for compassion toward native people, in the case of Mann, the discussions sometimes also relied partly upon the peculiar racial character-istics of indigenous people: the ability to shed water "like a duck's back" for example.

White freethinkers believed that missionaries disrupted local economies by attempting to import a western capitalist lifestyle to savage societies. This can be seen in Robert Ryder's discussion of Zulu society. There, everyone's basic needs were met, yet "[i]f he [the Zulu] turns Christian, he becomes melancholy and desponding, begins to wear clothes, and soon goes ragged and tattered; he loses caste with his tribe; he is alone in the world – and ultimately becomes the poor day labourer!"[71] A cartoon by Watson Heston played upon the idea of the "White Man's Burden" being brought to the Philippines, a territory recently acquired by the Americans. The burden in this case included the trappings of modernity – taxes, debts, litigation, along with religion – that the white Americans would unload upon the simple Filipinos (see Figure 3.2). Chapman Cohen, a prominent secular-ist who became the president of the National Secular Society after G.W.

3.2 "The White Man's Burden," *Truth Seeker*, April 8, 1899, 209

Foote's death in 1915, also discussed how missionaries' encouragement of local industries damaged societies – in his example, Eskimo society – by redirecting resources away from traditional methods of gathering food. The introduction of firearms further disrupted traditional hunting techniques and led to the depopulation of the reindeer. While the Eskimos' lifestyle required frequent migration, this was hindered by missionary attempts to force them to remain in one location.[72] "[I]f it is necessary to bring the natives [...] under Western influences," Cohen said in another article, "then the trader is a much better civiliser than the missionary [...]."[73] But given the emphasis on "if" in the sentence, Cohen seemed unconvinced of the necessity of making these people "civilized." This emphasis on free trade as a natural civilizer, in contrast to direct interventions by missionaries or colonial administrators, mirrored the arguments of late nineteenth- and early twentieth-century critics of empire.[74]

Many of these themes are captured in a satirical dialogue reprinted in the *Freethinker*, which contrasted "civilized" life with that of the savage. The dialogue occurs between "a large, strong man dressed in a uniform, and armed to the teeth," representing Christian civilization, and a native African. The white Christian explains to the African that he wants to "make a reasonable human being out of [him] if it is possible." This involves wearing clothes "like a white man," but the African protests that it is too hot to wear those clothes and, since he is unaccustomed to them, he "shall perish from the heat." But the Christian replies, "[w]ell if you do die, you will have the satisfaction of being a martyr to civilisation." The African, despite his pleas that food is plentiful and he therefore has no need to work, is told that "[y]ou must settle down to some occupation, my friend. If you don't, I shall have to lock you up a vagrant." The African suggests that he can start a coffeehouse since he has so much coffee and sugar, but the Christian demands payment for setting up the shop. When the African asks why, the white man replies, "[a]s an occupation tax, you ignorant heathen. Do you expect to get all the blessings of civilisation for nothing?" When the African explains that he has no money, the Christian says he will take payment in sugar and coffee, and if not, he will put the African in jail. The African mutters, "[w]hat a great thing Christian civilisation is," and the story ends with his disappearance into the woods, never to be heard from again.[75] Although the sketch was meant to be comedic, it also highlighted again how Christianity and a commercial lifestyle seemed to go hand-in-hand, causing a disruption to savage societies. It was also a critique of the logic of capitalism itself, particularly the notion that the government should coerce all people into employment, even when resources were otherwise plentiful.

In the eyes of freethinkers, missionaries also inadvertently brought along vices like alcoholism. According to Robert Ingersoll, "when a superior race meets an inferior, the inferior imitates only the vices of the superior, and the superior those of the inferior."[76] A cartoon in the *Freethinker* depicted a degraded African convert, smoking while holding an empty bottle of rum (see Figure 3.3).[77] A series of cartoons by Watson Heston likewise demonstrated that while civilization might bring technological benefits to savage societies, more insidious things also came with Christianity, like "Christian Rum" (see Figures 3.4 and 3.5). Given that so many freethinkers were teetotalers, the introduction of alcohol into previously uncorrupted societies would have been particularly appalling.[78]

Even if Christianity were not innately harmful, to atheists and

3.3 "An African Convert," *Freethinker*, November 29, 1887, 377

3.4 "A Yankee Way to Make Converts," *Truth Seeker,* May 17, 1890, 305

3.5 "A Few Other Christian Tools for the Consideration of the Heathen," *Truth Seeker*, May 24, 1890, 321

freethinkers it was, at best, a useless doctrine. Great amounts of resources and time were expended teaching nonsensical doctrines when these same resources might be better used helping people at home or at least teaching useful skills to foreign savages.[79] From the 1860s to the 1890s, criticism of missionaries in general, not just from freethinkers, concerned the high costs of supporting missions and the lavish expenditures of the missionaries.[80] In some cases, freethinkers' discussions about the wastefulness of missionaries were vindictive toward savages. This was true of Eugene Macdonald, who had no doubt about the need to civilize Native Americans, but questioned the missionaries' method. To achieve this required a "tough love" approach. As he argued, "the way to civilize them is to place them among civilized surroundings. As long as Indians are allowed to hav [sic] guns, ponies, and practically unlimited range, they will remain nomads. Surroundings, climate, and habits of life are all-powerful influences to mold [sic] the character of races." In the same conditions, even "[i]ndustrious, intelligent white men […] would degenerate into vagabonds in a few decades […]." Since Native Americans were simply too lazy to work on their own, they should be given vacant land and then left to their own devices, "for, until hunger drives him, an Indian will not work." On the other hand, "they never will become civilized by learning the miraculous birth of Jesus Christ."[81] On the whole, however, Macdonald's hostility to Native Americans was out of step with most other white freethinkers, who looked favorably upon savage society and were reluctant to see it become westernized.

Racial and cultural relativism

Some historians, like Douglas Lorimer, have noted that the premise of white and western superiority in Britain "[was] not subject to dispute but rather had become […] [a matter] of common sense."[82] While such a characterization no doubt applies to most of British society, it overlooks the rare dissenting voices. In atheists and freethinkers' discussions of savage societies, we have already seen their belief that savage societies had many virtues in contrast to their own flawed societies. Even if freethinkers did not completely disown their belief in progress and the racial and civilizational superiority that we saw in the first two chapters, the skepticism inherent in an atheist worldview made them constantly question their own societies' orthodoxies, including the notion that white, western civilization was superior. There appeared to be no common standard by which to measure the worth of a society, indicating a kind of cultural relativism on the part of atheists. In fact, in discussions of imperialism, freethinkers asserted that the conduct of western nations revealed the backward state of western civilization.

One exception to this was Charles Southwell, who edited the freethought journal the *Oracle of Reason* but left Britain in 1855 after a stint in jail for blasphemy and a failure to find success through his publications. He moved to Australia and finally settled in New Zealand. There, Southwell opposed the white Anglican clergy and Maori converts to Christianity not only on religious grounds, but also because they defended the rights of the Maori against the encroaching white settlers, whom Southwell supported. In this way, Southwell's religious and political views led him to dismiss the Maori as irredeemable savages. As John Stenhouse writes, "[t]hroughout his almost five-year colonial career, England's most militant atheist expressed probably the most extreme, systematic, and inflammatory racism in colonial New Zealand. It cannot be understood apart from the militant secularism he brought with him from Britain."[83] An article by Bill Cooke, written partly in response to Stenhouse's article, has cast doubt on Stenhouse's conclusions about Southwell, however.[84] Cooke argues that Stenhouse overstates the racism in Southwell's thought and instead points to Southwell's denunciation of American slavery and his approving citation of one Maori leader's speech, both things that, Cooke argues, would contradict a racist mindset.[85] Further, Cooke argues that many settlers, the vast majority of them Christian, supported Southwell's views toward the Maori, which undermines a clear link between atheism and racist thought.[86] Cooke offers some useful corrections to Stenhouse's argument, but on the whole they are not fatal to Stenhouse's interpretation that Southwell's atheism informed his racial views in the colonial context of New Zealand.

While Stenhouse has used Charles Southwell as a case study of atheist attitudes toward race, we have already seen above many examples that demonstrate that Southwell's views were not the norm for most white atheists and freethinkers. Furthermore, other freethinkers' views on the conflict between settlers and the Maori show again that Southwell was an outlier. Instead, the activities of the New Zealand government only called into question their claims to be called civilized. During a particular brutal period in the 1860s of the protracted war between the New Zealand government and the Maori resistance, one commentator in the *National Reformer* denounced the government's actions and linked them to Christianity: "The war against the Maori is a Christian war – instigated by a Christian governor, who is the servant of a Christian Government, which boasts of its Anglican Church and its Christian humility."[87] As white immigration increased and the Maori were forced off their land, non-violent Maori protesters in the village of Parihaka called for the retention of their land. An 1879 news report in the *National Reformer* described the arrest and imprisonment, without trial, of several of these Maori protesters. One of the prisoners died after being held for eleven months, and the author of the report ironically remarked, "[t]hese Maories are savages – we English who hold them are civilised."[88] The atheist leader Charles Bradlaugh took up the prisoners' cause once he was elected to Parliament in 1880. He described their continued imprisonment as "exceedingly cruel" and noted, "[t]hey are the savage Pagan subjects of a civilised Christian Government."[89] In another case, W.P. Ball, a writer for the *Freethinker*, drew explicit parallels between the Maori and British atheists in their struggle against Christians. As he said, "[t]he 'Infidel' can do little in the matter except stir up the Christian by his reproaches, *for he himself, like the Maori*, is fighting the Christian for the common rights of humanity stolen from him by self-complacent bigotry."[90] In this case, Ball saw the Maori and freethinkers as common allies together facing off against the more powerful Christians. While the oppression in each case was different, the enemy was the same. Here, then, a white atheist like Ball imagined himself united with his non-white brethren in a common struggle for rights against Christians.

This inversion of the language of superiority and civilization can be seen in other critiques of western interventions of Africa and Asia.[91] When Britain went to war against the Zulu in 1879, one author echoed the positive views of the Zulu and mentioned their role in Colenso's "conversion" as proof of their intelligence, but he grimly (and correctly) predicted that the British would defeat them and annex their lands: "And so one more wrong will have been done, and once more we shall teach the 'inferior' races our superior cunning and honesty."[92] A notice in the *Freethinker* condemned the British campaign in Matabeleland (1893–94) and noted sarcastically that in the conflict "the African 'savages' had a beautiful experience of the virtues of 'civilisation.'"[93] Elizabeth E. Evans, in her discussion of the American war in the Philippines (1899–1902), likewise noted: "Now more than ever before the phrase 'Christian civilization' implies a scathing satire upon Christian conduct."[94] In these cases, the authors made a specific point of enclosing the terms "inferior," "savages," and "civilization" in quotation marks, indicating that they were using them ironically and did not accept the validity of such labels.[95] This relativist strategy meant casting doubt upon the entire notion of inherent western racial or civilizational superiority that served to justify imperial conquest.

Like other freethinkers, the American novelist Mark Twain was skeptical about the wisdom of imperial policies.[96] In his 1895 trip around the British Empire, documented in his book *Following the Equator*, Twain lamented British policies that decimated indigenous groups like the Tasmanians. This is not to say, however, that he was wholly sympathetic to indigenous people. On indigenous Australians, Twain admitted that they must have possessed some intelligence, given their skills at tracking and their invention of the boomerang, but for all that, "[t]hey were lazy – always lazy," which perhaps accounted for their failure to build houses or develop agriculture.[97] Generally, though, he saw attempts to bring civilization as disastrous failures of empathy:

[A civilized man] cannot turn the situation around and imagine how he would like it to have a well-meaning savage transfer him from his house and his church and his clothes and his books and his choice food to a hideous wilderness of sand and rocks and snow, and ice and sleet and storm and blistering sun, with no shelter, no bed, no covering for his and his family's naked bodies, and nothing to eat but snakes and grubs and offal. This would be a hell to him; and if he had any wisdom he would know that his own civilization is a hell to the savage – but he hasn't any, and has never had any; and for lack of it he shut up those poor natives in the unimaginable perdition of his civilization, committing his crime with the very best intentions, and saw those poor creatures waste away under his tortures; and gazed at it, vaguely troubled and sorrowful, and wondered what could be the matter with them. One is almost betrayed into respecting those criminals, they were so sincerely kind, and tender, and humane, and well-meaning.[98]

This led Twain to a kind of civilizational relativism: so-called civilized people had no right to claim superiority over others. As he wrote, "There are many humorous things in the world; among them the white man's notion that he is less savage than the other savages."[99]

Upon his return home to the United States, Twain became an outspoken critic of his own nation's war against the Philippines.[100] In his essay "To the Person Sitting in Darkness," Twain denounced the notion of bringing "civilization" as a mere cover for greed and exploitation. In the past, this had been entirely a European preoccupation, but he lamented that the United States had recently become involved in this too in taking over the Philippines. This cynical mission made the people abroad worse off and also debased those at home. Ultimately Twain asked, "*[s]hall we?* That is, shall we go on conferring our Civilization upon the peoples that sit in darkness, or shall we give those poor things a rest? Shall we bang right ahead in our old-time, loud, pious way, and commit the new century to the game [of bringing civilization]; or shall we sober up and sit down and think it over first?"[101]

Herbert Spencer likewise was not convinced about the supposed moral superiority of civilized people to savages. As he said, "[c]haracters are to be found among rude peoples which compare well with those of the best among cultivated peoples. With little knowledge and but rudimentary arts, there in some cases go virtues which might shame those among ourselves whose education and polish are of the highest."[102] Here, Spencer had in mind particularly the primitive hill tribes in India, who were superior in their virtues to the more settled "Hindoos" as well as to Europeans. In contrast to the virtues of these supposedly uncivilized people, when considering the bloody history of European conquests abroad, "we must admit that between the types of men classed as uncivilized and civilized, the differences are not necessarily of the kinds commonly supposed."[103] Indeed, Spencer disagreed with the application of the label "savage" – with its connotations of ferociousness – to so-called primitive peoples: "Were it not that men are blinded by the theological bias and the bias of patriotism," they would see that the violence of Europeans "has been carried to extremes beyond those reached by inferior peoples whom we think of as ferocious."[104] Spencer lamented that the process of civilization seemed to necessitate a warlike disposition in order to build complex social structures, but he did look forward to a time in the future when societies progressed even further so that the need for such warlike characteristics would fall away: "While the benefits achieved during the predatory period remain a permanent inheritance, the evils entailed by it will decrease and slowly die out."[105]

Spencer had long been opposed to colonization, in part on account of his liberal philosophy. In his early work *Social Statics* (1851), Spencer defended a very limited role for government, which included rejecting its involvement in functions like education or sanitation. It followed from this that Spencer also saw colonization as an example of gross government overreach. It was, he thought, a violation of the rights of people in the parent colony as well as those who settled in the colony, but "[g]reat, however, as are the evils entailed by government colonization upon both parent state and settlers, they look insignificant when compared with those it inflicts upon the aborigines of the conquered countries."[106] Spencer listed numerous examples of cruelties committed by the British and other European powers that he saw not as aberrations but as central features of colonization. In 1879, Spencer mused to friends about "the possibility of doing something towards checking the aggressive tendencies displayed by us all over the world – sending, as pioneers, missionaries of 'the religion of love,' and then picking quarrels with native races and taking possession of their lands."[107] He, along with Frederic Harrison and others, formed a group opposing foreign aggression, but there was ultimately not enough popular support for this movement to get off the ground.[108]

One of the most outspoken arguments for upsetting notions of western superiority came from Chapman Cohen. A series of articles by Cohen in the *Freethinker* in 1912 considered the question of what it meant to be civilized. For him, superficial technological achievements did not themselves equal civilization. Neither did virtues like kindness or sympathy, which he argued were common to all humans: "Savages get born, grow up, get married, become parents, and die just as do civilised people. And the feelings that accompany these states and conditions are with both more or less alike." For Cohen, what really mattered was individual "mental outlook" to determine if a person were civilized or savage. With this in mind, "[t]here are people belonging to what would be called [...] a comparatively primitive social state who would be really less primitive than some belonging to a comparatively advanced social state."[109] The primitive mindset could be seen not just in so-called savage tribes, but in modern Britain: "It may be discerned as clearly in our own House of Commons or in a modern church as in a primitive pow-wow or savage witch-dance. The method of reasoning is often substantially the same; the outlook on life often identical."[110]

Cohen was even more scathing in his second article, saying, "[f]rom the throne – that stronghold of primitive ideas and barbaric ceremonial – downward, we meet with frequent reminders that our veneer of civilisation is of the thinnest possible kind." He mocked "the sheep-like, sanctimonious manner" in which the British public received the national anthem and adored the monarch. For Cohen, patriotism was a primitive devotion to one's tribe that had been useful in humanity's evolutionary past, but was no longer.[111] Patriotism was something that would in time be evolved away in favor of greater unity among humanity: "For what is the one dominant lesson of social evolution? It is, in a word, the growing interdependence of the whole human race." War was therefore a true example of uncivilized behavior, no matter what the technology used: "In what ways is a fight between modern gunboats more civilised than a fight between canoes?"[112] Cohen's skepticism about religion seemed to lead him to question established orthodoxies about the superiority of western civilization. While not completely giving up a belief in progress, Cohen's relativistic view contended that there were multiple ways to be civilized and that the West could not therefore assume it had a monopoly on the concept of civilization.

A similar article in the *Blue-Grass Blade* also questioned civilization. The author noted the frequent claims "that we are now enjoying a superlatively Christian civilization" that was built upon Christian teachings. But, the author continued, "[d]uring the same period of time the advocate of Freethought persistently urged that our present civilization is little more than a sham, almost a fraud, practiced upon mankind [...]." Possessing the latest technology like telegraphy or "death-dealing motor cars" did not necessarily imply that "we are living in the greatest and best of all the ages known to the cycles of time." Indeed, all these new technologies might not necessarily make us happy. The author quoted from a Native American woman, identified as Princess Chinquilla, who explained that while she had become educated, she nonetheless "long[ed] for the old life [...]."[113]

This relativist approach to questions of civilizational difference and imperialism was to some extent compatible with a polygenist viewpoint. As we saw in the previous chapter, Charles Bradlaugh suggested in his anthropology lectures that whites simply could not colonize some regions given the inhospitable climate that was unsuited for their race.[114] G.W. Foote struck a similar note to Bradlaugh when he cited the Australian politician Charles Henry Pearson's *National Life and Character* (1893), which "laughed at the exaggerated pretensions of the white race" and "proved that they can only flourish in certain latitudes, and that outside these they cannot compete in population with the indigenous inhabitants." Foote predicted that "the brown, black, and yellow races will at least hold their own in the future" and that they would maintain their dominant position in their own continents, though whether they would threaten the white race in Europe, as Pearson suggested, was an open question.[115]

The clearest example of using polygenesis to oppose imperialism came earlier in the century in a lengthy series of articles excerpting the polygenist Robert Knox's *Races of Mankind* (1850). Knox's work was filled with anti-imperialist passages, and this had been a theme of his thought since early in his career. Knox's biographer recounted that in Knox's early anatomy lectures in the 1820s, he might hold up the skull of a South African "Caffre" and ask his students provocatively: "Are we to be told that the Caffre of this cerebral stamp is a savage because he lives in the 'wilde,' and that John Bull is the happy creature of civilization because he wears breeches, learns catechisms, and does his best to cheat his neighbours – always, of course, on Christian principles!"[116]

Autonomos, who authored the satire on the African king seen above, provided eight excerpts of Knox's work, with his own commentary, in the *National Reformer*. The series, from 1867, took a grim and fatalistic view of Christian imperialism and offered a defense of polygenist anthropological thought with regard to colonial policy. In Knox and Autonomos's view, the white races had an irrepressible desire for conquest and plunder that inevitably led them into conflict with non-white races. While temporary conquest was possible, the forces of climate meant that whites could not survive permanently in Africa or other foreign continents. Christianity often justified these conquests, and Autonomos argued it that was "the nature of English Christians to exterminate the dark races under the lying pretense of civilising and Christianising them [...]."[117] Much of the colonial violence, Autonomos pointed out, was ironically committed by those "who are indignant with Anthropologists for hinting that all races cannot come from Adam."[118] The monogenist view was unreasonably sentimental, and Autonomos was shocked that "[s]ecularists, lovers of appeals to reason alone on theology, should follow the example of Exeter Hall [the center of British humanitarian thought] in being led entirely by the feelings, and virtually refusing the trial of Freethought on this important anthropological and social question."[119] An anti-imperial polygenist attitude therefore could be seen in Knox's writing, as quoted by Autonomos:

> Would it not be better to accept of the races of men as Nature made them; study their history, trace their social history when congregated into nations, and the modifications it undergoes by civilisation; show them, by good example, the advantages of modern European civilisation, and leave them to govern themselves?[120]

While Knox and Autonomos argued for a conception of the world that was made up of distinct and unequal races, such a view could actually be turned to a kind of cultural relativism. If such a view took for granted whites' racial superiority, it did not follow that whites possessed superior morality or that they would use their superiority wisely. In fact, the fatalistic lessons of racial science seemed to show that whites were biologically determined for bloody conquests.

The use of polygenesis as a way to critique imperialism was also seen at the turn of the nineteenth century, primarily in the work of Mary Kingsley and E.D. Morel. These authors encouraged a relativist conception of racial difference that decried attempts to impose western standards upon African people.[121] The secularist and ethicist F.J. Gould drew upon the work of one of their allies, the colonial administrator and African explorer Harry Johnston, as he lamented the fate of native African populations. In particular, Gould discussed "the Mandingo woman" of Liberia, with whom "[a]t first glance [he] fell in love [...]." In his description of the women's bodies, he emphasized their distinctive racial features: "the lips of African amplitude, yet feminine; the eyes mild and sociable; the skin a mellow brown; the bust shapely, the left breast – the only one exposed, – full without obtrusiveness;

the hands long and slender." Gould came across "these charming dusky brethren" in Johnston's work on Liberia, which included photographs of the people as well as sketches. While Gould enjoyed the photographs of Africans in a natural environment, he recoiled at a photograph of black Liberian students at college dressed in western clothes: "All these negro striplings wear mortar-boards! Africa apes Oxford, or, for that matter, the fifth-rate boarding-schools of our unæsthetic kingdom."[122] Gould followed Johnston in his view that Africans should retain their distinctive culture, rather than try to mimic the West.

This aligns with a polygenist viewpoint that regarded individual races not as inherently superior or inferior, but as simply different. This difference should be accentuated, argued Gould, not covered over: "the Mandingo form [should] be draped in those vestures that the negro taste has gradually selected as the most congruous with the complexion and habits of the Liberian tribes." He lamented the failed attempts of "Liberian negresses" to look feminine in western garb, and even worse were the men, who were "a far more dismal failure." Despite Gould's patronizing tone, he pleaded for Europeans to respect Africans' culture: "The White People would lose nothing by manly recognition of what is valuable in the negro world; and the negro would all the more gratefully and intelligently absorb the wisdom of the West."[123]

Conclusion

While a polygenist framework could be harnessed to question racial hierarchy, it is not true to say that white atheists' and freethinkers' views of savage people were based entirely or even mostly on a belief in polygenesis. Despite the influence of polygenist thought, when discussing savages in a social context, freethinkers rarely used explicitly racial language. Rather than emphasizing their racial and civilizational difference with savages, white freethinkers often highlighted their commonalities. The clearest way was to note that many savages had no religion. While some took this to mean that savages were intellectually deficient, a more common route was to show savages – real or imagined – as the heroic and logical resisters of Christian proselytizing. In this way, freethinkers drew parallels between themselves and the savages: both were outcasts fighting the absurd religion of Christians.

In order to understand why freethinkers found savage life desirable, it is necessary to consider their context of social and economic marginalization. Savage life seemed to offer a favorable alternative to the harsh realities of Christian capitalism, which left many destitute. Given that so many free-thinkers in both Britain and the United States came from the working classes and had radical political views, the image of a bountiful savage life that provided for every want was no doubt appealing. It was because of this idealization of savage societies that so many atheists and freethinkers looked with dismay upon foreign incursion into these societies. In their discussions of imperial conflict, freethinkers routinely inverted the idea of civilizational superiority by suggesting that it was the Christians who were the true savages. While not completely abandoning ideas of progress, this relativistic approach instead questioned what it meant to be civilized and found that common societal definitions of civilization were deficient.

One can, however, question how much these positive depictions of sav-agery were simply rhetorical devices in freethinkers' larger arguments. It seems unlikely that these white freethinkers were really ready to abandon their western lifestyle or their belief in the superiority of their civilization. Certainly white freethinkers imagined themselves to be at the pinnacle of civilization, yet this perspective sat uneasily with the fact that many of their compatriots were Christians. Nonetheless, it would be unfair to dismiss their views of savages as simply posturing. Their sympathies with subju-gated savage peoples were real enough, even if their idealistic depictions of their societies were at times exaggerated. This same theme will be continued in the next chapter, which investigates how atheists imagined India, China, and Japan.

4

The wise men of the East: India, China, and Japan

Any discussion of western views of the East inevitably needs to confront the issue of "Orientalism." In the nineteenth and early twentieth centuries, the term referred to the scholarly study of the East by the West. An Orientalist was therefore a scholar of the East and, in contrast to today, there were no negative connotations that went with the term; indeed, many prestigious scholars were proud to consider themselves Orientalists.

The meaning of "Orientalist" now, however, is dramatically different, owing in large part to Edward Said's *Orientalism* (1978), which argued that there was a link between the production of knowledge about eastern societies and imperial conquest. Scholarship of the East was not a neutral activity, in his view, but was directly implicated in the growing western imperial presence in these regions. Said put it bluntly when he wrote that "every European, in what he could say about the Orient, was consequently a racist, an imperialist, and almost totally ethnocentric."[1]

Despite its enduring influence, a number of scholars have found fault with the book.[2] One of the most pertinent criticisms of Said and his followers was that, through their criticism of westerners essentializing the East, Said and others actually essentialized the West. In other words, Said painted the West with such a broad brush as to miss out on important differences within western society. Sadik Jalal Al-'Azm explains that because Said attributed essentialist views of the Middle East to figures throughout western history, he "seems to be saying that the 'European mind' [...] is inherently bent on distorting all human realities other than its own and for the sake of its own aggrandisement." But, he continues, "this manner of construing the origins of Orientalism simply lends strength to the essen-tialistic categories of 'Orient' and 'Occident,' representing the ineradicable distinction between East and West [...]."[3] This broad criticism applies more generally to histories of racial thought and western perceptions of foreign societies, which run the risk of treating their subject societies as monolithic and ignoring potential places of dissent.

While Said critiqued all Orientalists, his work limited itself to studies of the Middle East and the Islamic world. Other scholars have extended the scope of Said's work to other societies in "the Orient." Indeed, China and India might be a better fit for the kind of "Othering" undertaken by Europeans of foreign societies, since, as Ronald Inden notes,

> [t]he Ottoman was a potentially dangerous Alter Ego of the European. His religion, Islam, was a false, fanatical cousin of Christianity and he continued to rule over parts of eastern Europe. But the Chinaman and Hindoo were the true Others. Both China and India were, thus, the opposites of the West.[4]

Western views of the East were about constructing these people as Others and in turn constructing oneself. The Orientalist discourse, as Inden explains, "speaks of Asian Others in ways that contrast rather sharply with the way in which it speaks of itself."[5]

While not disputing the main thrust of these thinkers' analyses – that knowledge production and representations often went hand-in-hand with imperialism and power relations, and that on the whole Europeans saw those in the East as inferior to themselves – I want to point out that such works often overlook opposing voices to the dominant discourses. The aim of this chapter is to show instead that atheists and freethinkers' views of the East often did not correspond to the negative, imperial discourse discerned by Said and others. In the previous chapter, we saw that athe-ists and freethinkers found many positive aspects of savage life, and the same conclusion applies to those looking upon India, China, and Japan. Far from constructing them as Others, freethinkers attempted to portray these people as similar to themselves and to break down the supposed racial and civilizational boundaries between them. This is not to say, however, that all freethinkers were without prejudice or that these positive portrayals were necessarily more objective or accurate, since positive portrayals had their own polemical uses just as negative ones did. Atheists and freethinkers still saw those "Orientals" through their own lenses, even if they were often rose-colored.

In the second half of the nineteenth century, negative stereotypes of Indians and the Chinese dominated western understandings. The fact that India had been under British rule for over a century and that China was gradually being picked apart by western colonial powers only strengthened the idea that these societies were backward, inferior, and in need of the West's tutelage on the road to civilization. But white atheists and freethinkers for the most part rejected these negative views. India and China, in their eyes, both possessed ancient civilizations with equally ancient religious traditions that had much wisdom to impart to western audiences.

As noted in the previous chapter, however, "religion" itself is a modern, western category, and this was imperfectly grafted onto various eastern cultural phenomena. The idea that there were coherent eastern "religions" – like Hinduism, Buddhism, or Shintoism – really only came about in the eighteenth and nineteenth centuries in the context of increased western penetration into these areas and the attempts by westerners to make sense of what they found there.[6] White freethinkers likewise attempted to make these traditions familiar by assuming they were "religions" like Christianity, though they invariably found them to be superior to Christianity. For example, the *Truth Seeker*, in its early issues, published a column called "Words of the Wise," which featured quotations from contemporary and historical freethinkers as well as from canonical religious texts, like the Analects of Confucius or the Vedas.[7] Furthermore, the moral teachings of these religions, particularly the Golden Rule, seemed to have been reached independently from the teachings of Christianity and indeed often pre-dated them.[8] Both D.M. Bennett and Moncure Conway undertook voyages through India (and in Bennett's case, China and Japan as well), where they visited temples and discussed religion with the local populations.[9] Other authors spent much time attempting to uncover the common links held between Christianity and eastern religions, albeit sometimes with the goal of discrediting Christianity as a mere re-telling of eastern myths.[10]

Of course, atheists for the most part would not have accepted the truth claims of any of these religions, but the religions were important because they presented an alternative path to morality. Often, freethinkers favorably contrasted the morality of the Chinese or Indians with that of their fellow citizens. What was more, some aspects of the religions of the East, like Buddhism or Confucianism, seemed to reject the supernatural and to be quasi-secularist already, at least in what freethinkers took to be their uncorrupted forms. Freethinkers also routinely reported on the apparently positive reception of freethought literature in these countries.

This chapter will first discuss India, and then China and Japan. While each country had its own context, the broad themes that emerge are similar for all. As described in the previous chapter, the discontent that atheists and freethinkers felt toward their own societies made them willing to look outside their borders for other ways of living and to therefore express skepticism about imperial and missionary interventions in these countries. Furthermore, they rejected negative stereotypes of these people, and this is particularly clear in debates surrounding Chinese immigration. Freethinkers' outlooks were based on anti-Christian views and ostensibly framed through rationalist or scientific perspectives.

India

The antiquity of the religious traditions in India impressed freethinkers. The region contained two ancient religions, Hinduism and Buddhism. Hinduism began to be described in the second half of the eighteenth century and was impressive primarily to Europeans for its literary output, particularly the Vedas.[11] As Tony Ballantyne explains, a common view in the eighteenth and nineteenth centuries, dating back to the Sanskrit scholar William Jones, was a "Sanskritocentric" vision of India "that celebrated Sanskrit and the Vedic texts, but decried contemporary culture as debased and backward."[12] This meant there was "a stronger interest in India's past than its present."[13] White atheists and freethinkers also shared this disproportionate interest in India's history, although their interests were not identical to those of their Christian counterparts. For one thing, eighteenth- and nineteenth-century debates were waged over which of Noah's sons originally peopled India: some claimed Ham while others claimed Japhet. Furthermore, Jones's and others' philological research linking Sanskrit with Greek and Latin was meant to demonstrate the truth of monogenesis and therefore to make history accord with the Genesis accounts.[14] Of course, to atheists, such debates were completely wrong-headed, since they were premised on the idea that the Genesis accounts were factual.

Another thing working in Indians' favor from the European perspective was their "Aryan" heritage. Today the term "Aryan" is associated with Nazi racism, but it was originally a benign linguistic category devised by Friedrich Max Müller in the mid-nineteenth century to describe the common language of Indians and Europeans. Müller was reluctant to see the term take on racial implications, but many scholars nonetheless extrapolated that a common language implied a common racial ancestry.[15] As Thomas Trautmann explains, the "deep and lasting consensus" in nineteenth-century Britain with regard to the Aryans was "that India's civilization was produced by the clash and subsequent mixture of light-skinned civilizing invaders (the Aryans) and dark-skinned barbarian aborigines (often identified as Dravidians)."[16] While the racial theory of Aryanism was rarely referenced by freethinkers, one author who did discuss the Aryans was John Shertzer Hittell in his multi-volume *A History of the Mental Growth of Mankind in Ancient Times* (1893). He explained that the descendants of the superior Aryans became

> the nations that in the past have played the greatest parts in the history of the world; that in the present century occupy or dominate over most of the temperate regions of the globe; and that, for many centuries to come, will continue to lead all other branches of the human family in industry, social refinement, wise government, enlightened religion, and polished literature.[17]

Hittell accepted the common view that the Aryans entered India and imposed their "laws, customs, language, and religion" on the original inhabitants, "the Dravidians, a dark-skinned people, apparently of the black race […]."[18] Hittell ranked the Aryans' Sanskrit literature above the Greeks and all other contemporary nations, save those, perhaps, in Mesopotamia.[19] While freethinkers and others looked fondly upon the religion of the ancient Aryans, contemporary Hinduism was seen as a corruption. D.M. Bennett noted that numerous deities were imposed upon the simple Aryan religion by the priestly classes, as well as practices of the caste system and widow burning (sati).[20]

Buddhism was likewise of great interest in the Victorian period. While there were hardly widespread conversions, as Philip Almond notes, Buddhism appealed to those who could not accept Christianity but who nonetheless wished to retain a sense of spirituality.[21] Christian critics charged that disagreeable aspects of Buddhism were the result of the "Oriental mind," which was superstitious and child-like. Furthermore, they contended that doctrines of contemplation and Nirvana were rooted in the indolence of these people, which contributed to the stagnant quality of their societies.[22] In contrast, most atheists praised Buddhism as a highly rational religion. Hittell noted that the Buddha did not incorporate "deity, immortality, or ceremonial worship" into his system, although – in what was a standard view of the time – he conceded that Buddhism became corrupted with superstitious beliefs as it spread.[23] Other freethinkers offered similar praise. Bennett described the Buddha as "one of the best and most wonderful men that ever lived" who founded a religion "the influence of which has been kindly, peaceful, and beneficent," while Robert Ingersoll asked, "[i]s there anything in our Bible as lofty and loving as the prayer of the Buddhist?"[24]

Observers of Buddhism had long held that it was atheistical. This was corroborated in several reports in the *Boston Investigator* which described Buddhism as an atheistic or agnostic system and also one with exemplary moral teachings.[25] During his travels through Ceylon (present-day Sri Lanka), Bennett gave a speech at a Buddhist temple and said that despite their small disagreements, "we recognize you as comparative Freethinkers, while we are comparative Buddhists."[26] Authors generally suggested that Buddhism contained either the same moral teachings as Christianity or superior ones, indicating that the creeds derived from a common aspect of human nature, not from something divine.[27]

Perhaps because of the legacy of these quasi-atheistic religions, India seemed receptive to the influence of freethought and secular literature, at least among the educated classes. In contrast to other nineteenth-century accounts that took Hinduism as the essence of Indian civilization,[28] atheists and freethinkers de-emphasized this religion, instead opting to note the rapid advance of science and freethought in the country. British and American newspapers reported on the distribution of freethought works in India and on how major figures in freethought, like Charles Bradlaugh,

Charles Darwin, and John Stuart Mill, were all well known among educated Indians. This influx of foreign freethought literature led to the development of indigenous movements and newspapers dedicated to freethought.[29] When D.M. Bennett toured India, he was able to observe this firsthand, noting that "I have had interviews with several of the Brahman [sic] class, and I find them cultured, deeply read men" who were familiar with the leading British thinkers like Mill, Spencer, Huxley, and Darwin.[30] The National Secular Society also had a presence in India: two branches opened, one in Fyzabad in 1883 and one in Madras in 1884, although it is not clear whether the members were predominantly white British or Indians.[31] The converse of this picture was that Indian converts to Christianity were described in the harshest terms. They were "the scum of native society, unworthy of trust and with no idea of honesty or integrity" and came only from "the savage hill tribes and devil worshippers."[32]

Freethought newspapers likewise featured Indian authors who complained about Christian missionaries in their homeland and explained how the introduction of western freethought works helped to combat Christianity.[33] One author, C.V. Varadacharia, wrote in the *Truth Seeker* of the positive influence of western thought in the country, yet also explained that India had its own tradition of freethinkers:

> there were many Mills, Bains, Spencers, Darwins, and Paines and Ingersolls in ancient India. Buddha, the prince of reformers, was the founder of that scientific system called Buddhism, which means the religion of enlightenment, *i.e.*, Freethought.

Varadacharia closed the letter by explaining to the editor, Eugene Macdonald, that all freethinkers were united in this common tradition: "I belong to such band of men, and you, too, belong to them."[34] Because of the tradition of freethought in India, the image of the clever Indian – though appearing less frequently than that of the savage in the previous chapter – was deployed in fictional dialogues with missionaries, in which the "Hindu" inevitably bested the Christian.[35] This view that Indians represented potential or actual atheists strikes at the notion of Indians as the racial or civilizational Others to white freethinkers. Instead, these discussions show how white atheists and freethinkers found common cause with their Indian counterparts through their shared belief in rationality and freethought.

Freethinkers found many positives in Indian culture, and these led them to support reforming imperial governance there. The British secularist leader George Holyoake was one exception to this, however: he contemplated a British withdrawal from India – not out of reverence for Indian culture, but because the poor character of Indians made the country ungovernable. In an article from 1856, Holyoake denounced the excessive religiosity of Indians. "The Hindoo," explained Holyoake, "is the most religious being in existence. Not an action he performs, not a step he takes, not a word he utters, not a breath he draws, but he does all agreeably to the institution of his religion."[36] Holyoake's views hardened following the Indian Mutiny of 1857–58, a massive but ultimately unsuccessful revolt against British rule. After the mutiny, as Christine Bolt explains, "the romance of India" ended among the British when they reacted to what they saw as "a gross ingratitude on the part of the Indian people."[37] In a speech from 1858, written in the midst of the mutiny, Holyoake railed against the untrustworthy and disloyal character of Indians. In the speech – although it was not reported verbatim – he argued that

> [t]he Oriental character was totally different from the English. The Hindoo or the Mahomedan, in the very moment that he was prostrate before you, professing the highest esteem for you, kissing the soles of your feet as the "Light of the World," at that very moment he probably had sharpened his knife to cut your throat in your first ungarded [sic] moment. Treat these people with kindness, they despise you; treat them justly, make a bargain, observe it yourself and compel them to fulfil it, and they will respect you, but relax your strictness and treat them with what we should call generosity, and they will despise you and poison you the first opportunity. This was the general characteristic of the Indian people.[38]

It would have been best had Britain never become involved in India, Holyoake reasoned, although he accepted that, on the whole, the rule of the East India Company had been better for Indians than their own rule. Before considering withdrawal from India, Holyoake stated that Britain must first suppress the mutinies, for otherwise "not the throat of an Englishman would be safe in any part of the world."[39]

Nonetheless, Holyoake, as he did in his work on the Zulu described in the previous chapter, drew parallels between the lot of non-Christians in India and that of atheists and secularists in Britain. There existed in Britain "a modified sepoyism of opinion" – a reference to the sepoys, the Indian soldiers who mutinied – because atheists were unable to take oaths in court.[40] Furthermore, in India, British missionaries told inhabitants "to abandon the religion of their forefathers" yet they condemned freethinkers in Britain who themselves had abandoned their Christian religion: "Here, they denounce Atheism, not merely because it is wrong, but on the ground that it is wicked – there they preach and advise the Atheism of the people of India towards the gods of their forefathers."[41] Even though Holyoake's negative portrayal of Indians was an exception among freethinkers, he nonetheless recognized that they faced similar Christian foes. In his criticism of British imperialism, particularly missionaries, Holyoake was in step with the views of his fellow freethinkers.

Richard Congreve, a convert to Auguste Comte's positivist creed, produced one of the strongest statements against British rule in India in his 1857 book *India*. In the aftermath of the mutiny, Congreve called for "justice" for both whites and Indians. This was the clear course for those "not blinded by an overweening sentiment of outraged pride – outraged in its feeling of national superiority, or the still intenser feeling of superiority of race."[42] Congreve called for withdrawal as quickly as possible, yet with an agreement between the other European powers that they would not attempt to intervene in India upon the British departure.[43] He pointed to India's ancient civilization – much older than Britain's – as proof that it would not revert to barbarism in the wake of a British withdrawal, but he clearly saw India as an inferior partner since he described it as "older, and yet younger" in terms of civilization.[44] That said, Congreve admitted that it took many centuries after the Norman Conquest for the invaders to become integrated with the original inhabitants, "and in that case there was no difference of race, of colour, of religion."[45]

Most freethinkers saw the British presence in India as harmful since it disrupted ancient systems of local government and economic organization, which had produced a thriving, pluralistic, and peaceful society. The British, they thought, plundered the country, committed countless atrocities in the name of expansion, and looked on as their exploitative policies caused impoverishment and left the people vulnerable to famine. In view of this, these freethinkers wanted to see a transition, albeit a very gradual one, to Indian self-government, a position likewise held by Indian liberals throughout the nineteenth and early twentieth centuries.[46]

This perspective is exemplified by Annie Besant, the most forceful, and indeed likely the most knowledgeable, commentator on Indian affairs among secularists. In 1878, she wrote a pamphlet entitled "England, India, and Afghanistan," which was also printed over the course of several issues of the *National Reformer*.[47] There she traced the history of British relations with India since 1600. She painted a promising picture of Indian society before India's subjugation by the British: "The Hindus are of the aristocracy of the East: learned, acute, subtle, dignified, courteous, they dwelt in their own land, with no more disturbance among the varying races which inhabited India than was to be found at the same period among the varying peoples of the Continent of Europe."[48] She therefore rejected common notions about the inferiority of Indians, chastising those "who think of all nations as barbarous which are not European" and disputing that the Indians "were rude and savage peoples, rightly subjugated by the English [...]." While Indian civilization differed from the West, it "is not less polished, not less dignified, not less luxurious, and far more ancient than our own."[49] She also punctured delusions that somehow the British had become involved in India for altruistic reasons: "let us drop our hypocritical mask, and acknowledge that we seized India from lust of conquest, from greed of gain, from the lowest and paltriest of desires."[50] Given Britain's responsibility for dramatically disrupting Indian society, Besant felt it would be wrong for Britain simply to "fling it aside."[51] The answer for Besant was to gradually introduce measures for self-government, including greater roles for Indians within the government, civil service, and justice system: "In the old days Indian institutions were representative; let the old genius of native rule be revivified, and let a system of representative government gradually replace the centralised despotism of our present sway."[52]

Besant's interest in Indian culture dated to the late 1870s, but it became even more apparent in her conversion in 1889 to theosophy, a new religion composed of elements taken from eastern creeds and western science and mysticism. Besant was particularly attracted to the Hindu elements within theosophy. The conversion finally severed her links with the rest of the secularist movement, already tenuous because of her unpopular commitment to socialism. After the death in 1891 of theosophy's founder, Helena Blavatsky, Besant became one of the leaders of the international theosophy movement.[53] In this position, she visited India numerous times, and while she initially eschewed involvement with politics, on future visits she grew closer to the movement for Indian home rule. She helped to found the Home Rule League in 1916 and in 1917 was elected for a one-year term as president of the Indian National Congress.[54]

As noted at the outset, scholars like Edward Said have implicated western representations of the East in the entrenchment of colonialism. But, as Mark Bevir notes, "by taking the themes of this indology out of their usual Christian context and putting them in one developed by secularists, spiritualists and socialists, [Besant] promoted the cause of Indian nationalism."[55] In other words, while Besant's secularist and later theosophist worldview drew on Orientalist themes that often idealized the East, it could actually be deployed against imperialism since it rejected Christianity – which helped to legitimize British rule in India – and promoted eastern religion and culture as valid and in many cases superior alternatives to those of the West. Indeed, Besant saw, in Bevir's words, "a spiritual and organic India contrasted with a materialistic and individualistic West [...]."[56] Rather than accepting the colonial logic of Indian inferiority, Besant actually felt that the West had much to learn from the East.

Besant's closest ally and friend, before her conversion to theosophy, was Charles Bradlaugh. As an MP, Bradlaugh took up the unofficial mantle of the "Member for India," the member who expressed the greatest interest in Indian affairs. In Parliamentary and other public speeches, Bradlaugh repeatedly addressed Indian issues. He defended the controversial 1883 Ilbert Bill, which proposed that British whites in the country could be tried by Indian judges. In a speech, he countered arguments that insisted on the right of whites to be judged by those of their own race. The proposed bill was not unfair in Bradlaugh's eyes: "[i]f you go to a foreign country for your own benefit, why should you have a superior position to the people who belong to that country and to whom that country belongs? You are an intruder there."[57] He also refuted opposition to the bill coming from the High Court judge, James Fitzjames Stephen, who said that it was "the privilege of the European not to be tried by a Hindu." But Bradlaugh rejected that "privilege": "If any Englishman puts himself in contact with the Hindu, knowingly beforehand, he is bound to submit himself to the law and he has no right to privilege which prevents his crime from punishment."[58]

Bradlaugh also advocated for gradual Indian home rule. Indians had to be patient, but they would in time be granted "the fullest right of self-government [...]."[59] In another article, Bradlaugh suggested that if the British governed well and "if we win the heart and brain of India gradually to the higher standard of Western civilisation," then the Indians might wish to remain within the empire.[60] J.M. Robertson, his successor as editor of the *National Reformer*, summarized Bradlaugh's views of imperialism in India in his 1895 biography of him (co-written with Bradlaugh's daughter Hypatia):

> Bradlaugh, it may suffice to say, was under no delusions as to the present political capacity of the Indian races. He perfectly recognised their bias to rhetoric and their immaturity of character, as well as the enormous difficulties in the way of their political amalgamation. Hence his programme for them was an extremely gradual introduction of the principle of self-rule.[61]

Bradlaugh's anti-imperialsim came in part from his republican ideology. As David Nash explains, for republicans like Bradlaugh, the despotic actions of the British monarchy in India seemed to offer a grim warning for what might happen if Britain's precarious democracy were ever rolled back. Further to this, many republicans produced idealized visions of pre-Raj India in which Indian communities were self-governing quasi-republics made up of independent farmers. To republicans like Bradlaugh, the rule of the British changed all that, in a parallel to the fate of equally idealized Saxon communities after the Norman invasion.[62] In this sense, then, Bradlaugh's advocacy for India was an extension of his republican politics at home.

Bradlaugh's support for Indian home rule, even if gradual, put him outside the mainstream of British imperial thought and made him a hero in India, where he traveled in the winter of 1889–90. An 1889 report from the newspaper *Hindu*, reprinted in the *National Reformer* and written in advance of his visit, predicted "a scene of genuine and excited enthusiasm" when he visited the country to attend the Indian National Congress meeting in Bombay, since he "has won for himself a home in the hearts of thousands of Indians who have never seen him, but who recognise his fearless advocacy of justice and truth."[63] Bradlaugh gave a rousing speech to the Congress on December 29, 1889 and said, "I feel proud to be fellow-subject with you, in the hope that the phrase fellow-citizen may grow into reality even before my life is ended."[64] The speech drew to a crescendo as he declared, "[b]orn of the people, trusted by the people, I hope to die of the people. (Renewed cheering.) And I know no geographic or race limitations to this word 'people.'"[65] Bradlaugh's visit to India was a great success, and reports from Indian newspapers described the large crowds that gathered to see him off.[66]

His impact was also felt among Indians then living in Britain: his funeral was attended by a large contingent of Indians living in London, among them a young Mohandas Gandhi, then training as a lawyer in the city.[67] Even long after his death, he was lauded by Indian independence activists. One of the most prominent at the turn of the century was Lala Lajpat Rai, who in a 1905 speech in London said, "[i]f ever any Englishman won the hearts of the people of India by his fearless and disinterested championship of the rights and interests of the downtrodden millions that inhabit that land and fully established a claim to be called 'the Member for India' it was the late lamented Charles Bradlaugh."[68] Additionally, a public hall, constructed in 1900 in the city of Lahore (in modern-day Pakistan), was named Bradlaugh Hall. The hall remained a site of anti-colonial activity for the first half of the twentieth century.

The phrasing in Bradlaugh's speech in India, that he knew no "race limitations" to the word "people," and his advocacy of non-white people's rights in the British Empire more generally, are of interest because, as we saw in the first chapter, Bradlaugh championed anthropological research that showed the division and hierarchy of racial groups. Also telling is that Bradlaugh never framed his admiration of India in terms of a perceived common Aryan ancestry. It seems unlikely that Bradlaugh's racial views had changed by the end of his life, but more likely is that his thinking on racial science was somewhat compartmentalized from his thinking on more concrete questions of imperial governance. Considerations of abstract races led to different conclusions when these people were considered as individuals in a social and political context. This was also true when he championed the cause of the Maori prisoners, as seen in the previous chapter. That said, as we saw in Chapter 2, Bradlaugh believed that certain climates were inhospitable to certain races, meaning that imperialism was bound to fail. This was a view inherited from mid-nineteenth-century polygenist thought. Indeed, the American polygenist Josiah Nott made the argument that whites died off in India.[69] In any case, this leads one to question a direct correlation between holding seemingly racist views and supporting policies that oppressed non-white colonial subjects.

China and Japan

Anti-Chinese (and to a lesser extent anti-Japanese) sentiment reached a high point in the latter half of the nineteenth century. An array of negative stereotypes concerning the Chinese was widespread: they smoked opium, ate an unusual diet, lived in filthy conditions, and practiced a strange religion. They had no desire to assimilate into their host culture and stole jobs from white workers because they could live on a smaller income than whites. They also represented an inferior race from a stagnant civilization.[70] Despite these widely held views about the Chinese, white atheists and freethinkers' own opinions of China and Japan, like their views of India, went against the grain of popular opinion.

One positive that they saw in China was Confucianism, which was to many freethinkers an entirely rational religion that seemed to reject the supernatural, deities, and the idea of an afterlife. A typical view came from John Shertzer Hittell, who wrote of Confucius: "Alone among the founders of religions, he neither claimed a divine character or commission, nor taught men to do anything to influence the fate of their souls after the death of their bodies."[71] China was seen in an even more favorable light when its people seemed to be not just adherents of Confucius, but full-blown agnostics or secularists. A report in the *Truth Seeker* claimed that "[e]very true Confucian [...] is an Agnostic. He believes only in the seen; the unseen he regards as unknown and unknowable. As an Agnostic the Confucianist is tolerant of other creeds."[72] An article by J.M. Wheeler meanwhile described Confucius as a "Chinese Secularist" who taught morality without recourse to supernatural invocations or divine judgment.[73] Like Indian ones, Chinese converts to Christianity appeared to come from the lowest ranks of society according to freethinkers. They were, to Eugene Macdonald, "weakminded" or sought an easy life by "being allies of the missionaries."[74]

Despite these positive views of Chinese culture, some freethinkers – though rarely – found humor in mocking the Chinese accent or their alleged diet of dogs and cats.[75] On the whole, however, most freethinkers challenged these negative stereotypes of the Chinese rather than reinforced them. D.M. Bennett acknowledged that on his travels through China he found that people did eat these animals, but he explained that "cats and dogs, when nicely dressed, look as well as pigs and rabbits" and dismissed taboos against eating certain animals as purely arbitrary.[76] Likewise, he thought that concerns about the Chinese habit of opium-smoking were exaggerated and that the use of alcohol in Christian countries posed a far greater problem.[77]

Freethinkers were similarly interested in Japan. An early source was a mid-nineteenth-century work, *Japan and the Japanese* (1852), about the Russian Captain Golownin's captivity in Japan. In that work, as quoted in the *Boston Investigator*, Golownin noted the presence of "atheists and sceptics" in Japan, although he believed that the majority of people there were "not only extremely bigoted but very superstitious."[78] Other reports were more positive. One explained that the Japanese, "according to all accounts, are much better behaved and more moral than Christians."[79] Freethinkers believed Japan, like China and India, was rapidly adopting rationalism and secularism. Eugene Macdonald reported that "the doctrines of Darwin, Spencer, and Huxley have secured a firm hold upon the minds of the educated Japanese," meaning that Christianity had dim prospects for taking root in the country.[80] In another article, Macdonald cited a survey of Japanese university students in 1898 which apparently found that the vast majority identified themselves as either atheists or agnostics.[81] Chapman Cohen likewise stated that, in Japan, "the educated classes became imbued with Agnosticism, or Atheism; and this enabled them to *understand* Christianity, which is really the surest guarantee of one's not believing in it."[82]

Discussions of the Japanese religion of Shintoism – though occurring less frequently than those of Chinese or Indian religions – were favorable since Shintoism was, as J.M. Wheeler explained, not a supernatural religion, but "a creed of jollity, a system of health and happiness for life here and now."[83] Elsewhere, Wheeler drew parallels between Japanese and British freethinkers. The Japanese maintained their religious customs without believing in their literal truth, "just as even Freethinkers still keep up some of the old Pagan observances at Christmas."[84] As was so often the case, then, white atheists and freethinkers highlighted commonalities between those who would be considered as racial and civilizational Others.

Because of their perceived rationality, Chinese figures were ideal vehicles from which to make social criticism. As we saw in the previous chapter, using fictional characters from savage societies allowed for cutting satire of one's own society. Autonomos, noted in the previous chapter as author of a piece from a fictional African king, wrote another series of articles from the perspective of "Whang Chang Bang," a fictional Chinese envoy visiting Britain. In his letters, Whang mimicked the discourse of westerners toward supposedly less advanced societies as he stated he would call "the English simply, *the barbarians*," who, he concluded, "had neither morals, manners, nor religion."[85] Since Chinese civilization was much older than Europe's, the Chinese "can afford to regard these Western nations with a tolerant sympathy akin to that which a venerable sage bestows on the first attempts of a child to walk alone."[86] Whang noted the irony of the English having "stolen India, invaded China, and extirpated whole races of men," while at the same time "there is actually a society for the prevention of cruelty to animals, and another for the protection of the Aborigines." This was proof, to his delight, that "there is even humanity among the English!"[87] Yet Whang concluded with a damning view of English hypocrisy: while there were pretenses of religion and morality, "the characteristics of the average English Christian barbarian" in reality included "a slavish adoration of rank and wealth, a selfish courtesy towards equals in social degree, and contempt for poverty [...]."[88] Like the "savage critics" of the previous chapter, this satire ostensibly found humor in Whang's strangeness and his inability to understand aspects of British society, yet the true target of the article was western society's hypocrisy, more clearly revealed through the lens of an outsider. The shared critique of Christian society emphasized the similarity between white freethinkers and their Chinese counterparts, even if fictitious.

Another fictional perspective came from "Hsiang-Ti-Foo." Like Whang's article, this article derived humor from the inability of the author to understand western culture precisely, but also from his accent: he called Christians "Clistians" for example. But the author also pointed out the hypocrisy behind western condemnation of Chinese customs as backward or degraded: "They forget that we were civilized ages ago, when they were still savages." Hsiang-Ti-Foo also highlighted the contradiction between Christians venerating Jesus as "the Prince of Peace" yet "spend[ing] so much of their wealth on ironclads, cannons, and other munitions of war."[89] A similar example came from a book containing letters from Ah Sin that first appeared in the *Freethinker*. The name Ah Sin was a frequent moniker for Chinese characters and came from the popular 1870 poem "The Heathen Chinee" by the American Bret Harte.[90] Like the other writers, Ah Sin critiqued the irrationality of Christianity through an outsider perspective. Furthermore, he also repeated common beliefs that the Chinese eagerly read the works of scientists like Darwin and Huxley, and that Christian converts came only from the lowest strata of Chinese society.[91] The image of the wise Chinese critiquing western society was also evident in a Watson Heston cartoon of a white American berating a Chinese man over violence against missionaries then occurring in China. The Chinese man retorts that white Americans attacked blacks in "[c]ruelties which would make barbarians blush" (see Figure 4.1).

But freethinkers also featured writings from Chinese and Japanese people – not just fictional characters – especially when they critiqued Christianity or western societies more broadly.[92] Wu Tingfang, the Chinese Minister to the United States from 1896 to 1902 and from 1907 to 1909, was cited by a variety of freethinkers for his criticisms of biblical absurdities while promoting the doctrines of Confucius, who, in Wu's words, "would be called an Agnostic now."[93] Wu was also used as an example to refute negative portrayals of Chinese immigrants and to contest the notion that only people from Christian civilizations could be moral. To John F. Clark, Wu was "a brilliant, versatile, and profound scholar and statesman as well as a well-bred gentleman," while George Macdonald said he was "a man who intellectually as well as morally stands on a plane unapproachable" by many leading Americans. [94]

4.1 "The Heathen and the Hypocrite," *Truth Seeker*, September 14, 1895, 577

Baron Kaneko, a Harvard-educated Japanese envoy to the United States tasked with improving relations between the two countries, was likewise quoted in several articles in the *Truth Seeker*. In the articles, Kaneko rejected the idea of Japan as a "yellow peril" and argued that it was mutually beneficial for the Americans and Japanese to interact.[95] Freethought newspapers also showcased explicitly atheistic Japanese authors. Yoshiro Oyama founded the Japanese Rationalist Association after visiting the United States in 1908, when he "received the true light and became a Freethinker" after reading the *Truth Seeker* and other freethought literature.[96] Oyama insisted "that Japanese educated classes are all Freethinkers and strong opposers of Christian mythology and false doctrines."[97]

Probably the most prominent Chinese freethinker was Wong Chin Foo, an immigrant to the United States. Wong was a forceful advocate for the rights of Chinese immigrants and clashed in public debate with Denis Kearney, an Irish American leader of the anti-Chinese movement. Born in China, Wong lived with an American missionary family from a young age and became a Christian. When he moved to the United States, his Christian faith was gradually eroded. He attended the National Liberal

League convention, organized by the leading American freethinker Robert Ingersoll, in 1879. It is possible that Wong met Ingersoll there, since Wong raved about the convention in a subsequent interview and said Ingersoll was "doing nearly as much good for America as Confucius had done for China, though the identical truths of his philosophy were preached by Confucius over 2,400 years ago."[98] Wong's New York City office, where he ran his newspaper, the *Chinese American*, contained works by Ingersoll and Thomas Paine, and Wong was once advertised on a lecture tour as "The Bob Ingersoll of China."[99]

Wong happily adopted the label of "heathen" and dubbed himself the first Chinese missionary to the United States. In 1886 and 1887, the *North American Review* ran a series of articles on religion with titles like "Why Am I a Jew?" or "Why Am I a Free Religionist?" Wong penned his own, entitled "Why Am I a Heathen?" In this article, Wong described how he gradually lost his faith in Christianity and favorably contrasted Chinese civilization with that of the United States. He criticized American Christians for what he saw as their obsession with money and their self-aggrandizement. Furthermore, Wong wrote that China had advanced beyond the primitive racial prejudice of the United States: "we are so far heathenish as to no longer persecute men simply on account of race, color, or previous condition of servitude, but treat them all according to their individual worth."[100] Whether Wong embraced the agnosticism of Ingersoll is not entirely clear since he also wrote, "[w]e heathen are a God-fearing race. Aye, we believe the whole Universe-creation – whatever exists and has existed – is of God and in God [...]."[101] Nonetheless, he certainly embraced Ingersoll's rationalism. He echoed many other freethinkers' depictions of Confucius as a forerunner of secularism, calling him "our great Reasoner:"[102] In Wong's view, Confucianism represented a rational religion that espoused all the good parts of Christianity, with none of the bad. Indeed, unlike Christians, Confucians actually followed through on their ethical commitments, and for this reason he "earnestly invite[d] the Christians of America to come to Confucius."[103] As Wong's biographer, Scott D. Seligman, points out, however, this kind of writing is better seen as "a device to get Americans to do some self-examination than as a serious gambit to attract converts."[104]

Wong's article was reprinted in both the *Truth Seeker* and the *Freethinker.*[105] The *Truth Seeker* also reprinted a report about an 1877 speech Wong gave in New York. In this speech, Wong expressed his disapproval of missionaries in general and dispelled some of the misconceptions about his country, particularly that China was a backward nation that dined on rats and dogs.[106] Wong also addressed the Freethought Congress of the American Secular Union and the Freethought Federation, held in Chicago in 1896 (two years before his death in 1898). In a report from the *Truth Seeker*, he was described as a "Freethinking Chinaman" (although he was not identified by name). Wong called himself a "Freethought missionary" and explained the common moral values among the different religious traditions and that God had given each nation their own prophet: "To the Chinaman he gave a Confucius, to the Jews a Jesus, and to the Americans he had given an Ingersoll." The report concluded by noting, "[t]he Chinaman got a rousing lot of applause, and promised to tell the Freethinkers of Chicago more about his views at some other time."[107]

As with India, these positive views led to criticism of western intervention in China by freethinkers.[108] In one case, a report in the *National Reformer* described how Harriet Law, a popular secularist lecturer, spoke out against British imperialism in China at a public lecture in 1869. She condemned how both missionaries and opium were pushed into China, often through military means. After an uproar over her remarks at the public meeting, the report noted that Law criticized some members of the audience for their disorderly behavior: "The followers of Confucius would blush to behave in the way the meeting did." Indeed, she noted that it would be beneficial to "have some missionaries who believed in the doctrine of Confucius to come here and civilise them. Talk of going to civilise the heathen! Why, we wanted civilising ourselves."[109] J.M. Wheeler also noticed the tendency of missionaries to wear out their welcome in China. The Chinese "are a peaceful, not easily stirred people, and [...] they accord perfect toleration to all religions," but the missionaries' patronizing attitude toward the Chinese eventually made them hostile to the missionaries.[110]

At the turn of the century, the Boxer Rebellion (1899–1901) in China and the victory of Japan against Russia in 1905 stoked fears of a "yellow peril" that would throw off western influence in Asia and eventually conquer the entire world.[111] White freethinkers, however, did not buy into these fears. Instead, they pinned much of the blame for the violence of the Boxer Rebellion on western interference in China.[112] As described in the previous chapter, freethinkers used the language of savagery to describe the actions of western governments. To Frederick Ryan, the violence of western governments was an "outburst of savagery," and he lamented that "we are really so little removed from maniacal brutes [...]."[113] Mark Twain was also strongly critical of missionaries in China in the wake of the Boxer Rebellion. In his essay "To the Person Sitting in Darkness," he recounted how, after the rebellion, Rev. William Ament had forcibly collected indemnities from the Chinese population, at thirteen times the value of the property damage. This, Twain said, "condemn[ed] them and their women and innocent children to inevitable starvation and lingering death, in order that the blood-money so acquired might be '*used for the propagation of the Gospel*' [...]."[114] To Twain, this was Christian hypocrisy at work.

Freethinkers also unanimously supported Japan in the Russo-Japanese War. One reason for this was that, to Eugene Macdonald, Russia was a religious and reclusive society, but "Japan, on the contrary, is a wide open country, and the Japanese have advanced wonderfully in modern civilization because of such open communications with the world."[115] Macdonald also favorably contrasted the humane conduct of the Japanese toward Russian prisoners and wounded soldiers with the American record in the Philippines.[116] G.W. Foote likewise supported the Japanese and denounced prejudiced talk toward them and the Chinese. "If the Japs and the Chinese together are able to dominate this planet," he wrote, "Nature will not exclude them from the front position because they are yellow. And the white man should really try to rid himself of the silly egotism connected with the color of his epidermis." He continued, "[f]or our part, we have no belief whatever in this Yellow Peril." He predicted that Asian countries would rise up against western governments to become independent – a good thing in his view – "[b]ut it is a fantastic idea that the Yellow races will wage a war of extermination against the White races."[117] Elsewhere, Foote wrote that "the Yellow Peril is merely a symptom of the uneasy conscience of the Western Powers" resulting from their imperial record.[118]

White atheists and freethinkers were also interested in the treatment of Chinese immigrants to the United States. Agitation against Chinese immigration began in the 1850s on the west coast, yet did not become a national movement until after 1869, when the transcontinental railroad was completed. This drove the Chinese immigrants who had come to work on the railroad into other industries and also facilitated greater trade across the continent, worrying white workers around the country that the Chinese would drive down wages everywhere. The anti-Chinese movement scored a victory with the passage of the Chinese Exclusion Act in 1882, which restricted Chinese immigration for a period of ten years. The Geary Act of 1892 closed loopholes within the previous legislation and extended the ban on Chinese immigration for another ten years. Meanwhile, the Chinese who were already in the United States faced violence from disgruntled whites.[119]

Robert Ingersoll was one of the most vocal supporters of Chinese immigrants among freethinkers (and indeed all Americans), and it is possible that Wong Chin Foo awakened him to the issue; as mentioned above, the two may have met at the National Liberal League convention in 1879. In an interview in 1880, Ingersoll explained that he opposed "contracts that amount to slavery" in which Chinese were forcibly sent to the United States by Chinese owners, but did not oppose "voluntary immigration."[120] Nonetheless, Ingersoll noted sardonically that given the history of United States–Chinese relations, "there is very little danger of any Chinaman voluntarily coming here. By this time China must have an exceedingly exalted opinion of our religion, and of the justice and hospitality born of our most holy faith."[121] This criticism of Christian hypocrisy was a theme for Ingersoll when he discussed the treatment of immigrants. Rather than having missionaries travel to China to convert the Chinese, "[w]ould it not be a good thing for the Methodists to civilize our own Christians to such a degree that they would not murder a man simply because he belongs to another race and worships other gods?"[122]

In 1893, a year after the passage of the Geary Act, which extended the prohibition on Chinese immigration, Ingersoll wrote an article in the *North American Review* (alongside a counter-article by Congressman Thomas Geary, the architect of the Act) on the question of Chinese exclusion. In his article, Ingersoll appealed to his fellow Americans to reject xenophobia. Fear of outsiders seemed to be human nature, but the negative influence

of nationalism and religion exacerbated this natural tendency by shrink-
ing people's minds and decreasing tolerance for difference. "The average
American," Ingersoll contended,

> like the average man of any country, has but little imagination. People who
> speak a different language, worship some other god, or wear clothing unlike
> his own, are beyond the horizon of his sympathy. He cares but little or nothing
> for the sufferings or misfortunes of those who are of a different complexion
> or of another race. His imagination is not powerful enough to recognize the
> human being, in spite of peculiarities. Instead of this he looks upon every
> difference as an evidence of inferiority, and for the inferior he has but little if
> any feeling. If these inferior people claim equal rights he feels insulted, and for
> the purpose of establishing his own superiority tramples on the rights of the
> so-called inferior.[123]

He added that American history was marked with incidents of hostility
to various immigrant groups, including the Irish, the Germans, and the
Italians. In time, however, these groups were gradually accepted by their
host nation and eventually thrived. The Chinese, Ingersoll predicted, were
no different in their potential to succeed and integrate. There was no reason
for Americans to dislike the Chinese, since they "are inoffensive, peaceable
and law-abiding."[124]

Ingersoll also discussed how the prejudice toward Chinese immigrants
translated to violence in America. Again, Ingersoll seized upon the disjunc-
tion between the United States' supposed Christian charity and its practices:
"All this [violence] was done in a country that sends missionaries to China
to tell the benighted savages of the blessed religion of the United States."[125]
Ingersoll appealed to Americans to look objectively at their situation to see
how they would respond if the same sort of racial violence were occurring
in a foreign country, in particular the violence against Jews occurring in
Russia.[126] Ingersoll's freethought allowed him to transcend the widespread
anti-Chinese sentiment and instead advocate for a more inclusive approach.

Ingersoll was not the only freethinker to defend the Chinese against
xenophobic sentiments. A common argument from other supporters of
Chinese immigration was to emphasize the positive qualities of the Chinese.
Commentators regularly pointed to Chinese immigrants' frugality, their
diligence, their respect for laws, their peacefulness, and their abstention

from alcohol.[127] For some, the Chinese even seemed superior to other white immigrants. Eugene Macdonald, although perhaps not enthusiastic about Chinese immigration, explained that the Chinese immigrants were in many respects superior to the Catholic Irish, Italians, and Germans, who lived in the same areas as the Chinese, yet were "more in need of civilization" than them.[128]

As we will see in more detail in the sixth chapter, regarding racial prejudice, freethinking defenders of Chinese immigration cast their opponents as motivated by irrational prejudice and racial hatred. For George C. Bartlett, the entire issue was the old problem of "hatred of race," dating to the times of clan warfare.[129] John F. Clark believed that the opposition to Chinese immigration "surely must be founded upon race prejudice, fostered by religious intolerance."[130] Writers also expressed optimism that this racial prejudice would disappear in the future. Bartlett hoped that "each race [would] soon give up its peculiar egotism and conceit and with mutal [sic] humility and respect be willing to learn one of another."[131] J.E. Roberts imagined a day when barriers of race would disappear, "when the map of the world is changed, when the lines of demarcation that separate peoples are less and less observed, [and] when caste and race prejudice have been overcome [...]."[132] In this way, racial prejudice was contested from a uniquely freethought perspective.

Nonetheless, some freethinkers did oppose Chinese immigration, primarily on the grounds that the Chinese could live more cheaply than their white counterparts, and therefore would drive down living conditions for everyone. One correspondent in the *National Reformer*, the English economist Joseph Hiam Levy, writing under the name D.,[133] was particularly opposed to Chinese immigration because of a concern for the lower classes of Britain. Greedy capitalists, forever looking for cheaper labor, encouraged immigration from among "the lower races of mankind" who could live on less. "Our sole desire," he explained, "is to save our working-classes from extinction or degradation to a lower standard of living." Despite Levy's talk of higher and lower races, he attempted to show that he was not motivated by racial antipathy. He claimed opponents of immigration cared for both races, but he drew parallels between the Chinese and "men afflicted with small-pox." There was no "dislike" for either, but the immigration of "a race with a low standard of living" could not be accepted, just as one would not allow "persons suffering from infectious disease 'freedom' to carry that disease among healthy people [...]."[134] In another article, Levy further insisted, "[h]e is no true Liberal to whom the happiness of the Chinese is not as dear as that of any other portion of the human race."[135] Whether or not his protests were convincing, Levy recognized that there seemed to be a contradiction between being a freethinker (or a "Liberal") and possessing racial prejudice. This was why he went to such lengths to make the case that he was not motivated by irrational prejudice, but by a rational concern for workers in Britain.

Understandably, most of the opposition among atheists and freethinkers came from Americans, particularly those on the west coast, who protested that those on the east coast could not comprehend the problem posed by the Chinese. One argument was that the Chinese would never integrate into American society; they wanted only to earn money to send back home to China. As one correspondent from Los Angeles explained, "this is not his home; he says he 'no like Melican man,' 'me go home when me makee some money.'"[136] Clarke Irvine, based in Portland, echoed Levy when he painted an unsettling picture of millions of Chinese coming to the country, where they would "fill every occupation" and be stuffed "from garret to cellar" in tenement buildings.[137]

Atheists and freethinkers in British Columbia, Canada – a disproportionately secular province – were also sometimes critical of Chinese immigration and particularly of the way white Christian ministers seemed to encourage it in hopes of winning more converts to Christianity. Robert Thornton Lowery, a provocative freethinking journalist in British Columbia, condemned these ministers for wanting to "flood this fair land with hordes of yellow boys in order to pump Christ in them."[138] Another journalist and freethinker from British Columbia, John Houston, castigated a Presbyterian missionary for his "sentimental talk about the brotherhood of man" and his defense of Chinese immigration.[139]

Part of the debate simply concerned geographical location: atheists and freethinkers in the western United States (and western Canada), who ostensibly had the most experience with Chinese immigration, tended to oppose it, whereas those in the eastern part of the country, for whom the debate was more abstract, tended to support it. But there was something more going on than this. Numerous freethinkers defending immigration made their arguments specifically on the ground that racial prejudice was completely alien to freethought, since freethinkers prided themselves on their adherence to evidence and rationality. Even the opponents of Chinese immigration, like Levy above, recognized this contradiction and attempted to claim that their views were not based in irrational prejudice but rather in solidarity with the working classes.

Conclusion

This chapter began with a discussion of Edward Said's influential critique of western views of the Orient. To Said and his followers, those in the West imagined those in the East as the Other in terms of race and civilization. This chapter has shown, however, that for white atheists and freethinkers, those in India, China, and Japan were not in fact the Other, but were in many ways comparable to themselves. While negative stereotypes of these people abounded in Britain and the United States, white freethinkers for the most part rejected these characterizations.

Although India, China, and Japan had their own particular contexts, familiar patterns emerge in all of them. These countries seemed to possess ancient religions and civilizations that provided favorable alternatives to Christianity. Furthermore, the religions seemed quasi-secular already, and the people there, at least the educated ones, appeared eager to embrace atheism and freethought. It seems likely that white atheists exaggerated the extent of these societies' irreligiosity, but whether or not their characterizations were accurate, the more important point for my overall argument is that in seeing Indians, Chinese, and Japanese as being like themselves, white freethinkers broke down the idea that these people represented a racial or civilizational Other.

Here, the freethought worldview provided a link between freethinkers in Britain and the United States and those in India, China, or Japan. Atheism, freethought, and rationality therefore worked against attitudes of racial and civilizational hierarchy in this case. In the final section on attitudes to Chinese immigration, we saw how white atheists and freethinkers rejected racial prejudice on the grounds that it was opposed to their own principles. This theme will emerge again in the next two chapters, the first of which considers white freethinkers' views of African Americans.

The best friends the negro ever had: African Americans and white atheists

Before the outbreak of the Civil War, many freethinkers were involved in the anti-slavery cause. Samuel Porter Putnam, in his history of free-thought, includes a lengthy list of biographies of individual freethink-ers, and the number of them involved in the abolitionist movement is striking.[1] Among the more prominent freethinking abolitionists were those like Elizur Wright, Elizabeth Cady Stanton, Ernestine Rose, and Moncure Conway, but even those abolitionists who remained Christians, like William Lloyd Garrison or Parker Pillsbury, were highly unorthodox thinkers and were strongly anticlerical.[2] Francis Wright, the Scottish-born follower of Robert Owen, even started a commune in 1825 in Nashoba, Tennessee, that intended to educate and eventually emancipate slaves (although the experiment was ultimately a failure and collapsed after only a few years).[3] In Britain as well, freethinkers supported the abolitionist cause in the Civil War, in line with other radical intellectuals.[4] George Holyoake, the foremost secularist of the time, supported the North, as did Charles Bradlaugh.[5] Liberals like John Stuart Mill likewise supported abolition and the efforts of the North in the Civil War.[6] Charles Darwin, meanwhile, wrote in a letter to his ally in evolution, the American scientist Asa Gray: "Great God how I sh^d like to see that greatest curse on Earth Slavery abolished," and hoped, presciently as it turned out, that Lincoln and the Republicans would declare the slaves free as a tactic in the war.[7] While we have already examined white atheists' and freethinkers' views of racial issues beyond the theoretical abstractions of racial science with regard to those non-white races outside their own borders, this chapter looks at how these same atheists responded to debates about the fate of blacks in the post-Civil War United States.

After the North's victory in 1865, the period known as Reconstruction saw attempts to enfranchise and uplift the newly freed slaves and to rebuild the South. The optimism of the Reconstruction period began to fade in 1877 as Northern soldiers withdrew from the South in a compromise to allow Republicans to take control of the presidency after a disputed election. In the following years, the Supreme Court rolled back civil rights legislation, Jim Crow laws enforced segregation and discrimination in the South, and lynchings and large-scale white attacks against blacks – called "race riots" – became common. Furthermore, there was a sense among many whites in both the North and the South that Reconstruction had failed and was proof of the futility of trying to create a biracial society.

The historian George Fredrickson has argued that the nineteenth-century debate among whites over the fate of black Americans was typically constrained by a belief in black inferiority – in physical, intellectual, and societal terms – that was either innate or subject to very slow change. Only "a tiny (and often uncertain) minority of white spokesmen" rejected these premises.[8] Many white atheists and freethinkers were part of this skeptical minority, although this is not to say that all of them resisted stereotypical conceptions of black people. One-dimensional tropes of black people often featured in freethought newspapers. These included the suffering slave, the black criminal, and the superstitious black Christian. While these images had an instrumental purpose in attacking Christianity, they showed blacks in a negative light as well. Furthermore, white freethinkers seemed to use these images of blacks as a means to define their own identity. The alleged traits of blacks – pious, superstitious, foolish, immoral – were precisely the opposite of the traits that white freethinkers prized in themselves.

Despite the common images of blacks as innately religious, there were nonetheless a small number of black freethinkers in the nineteenth century. Aside from W.E.B. Du Bois, whom I discuss more in the next chapter, Frederick Douglass – the ex-slave and abolitionist – seems to have been the most prominent, although his precise religious orientation is not known with certainty. While some white freethinkers were happy to tacitly accept racial caricatures of blacks, many more were eager to link themselves with Douglass as a way to demonstrate their own rejection of racial prejudice. The clearest case of this was when Douglass found refuge at the home of the "Great Agnostic" Robert Ingersoll. This story of Ingersoll and Douglass's meeting entered into freethought lore and was repeatedly called upon to demonstrate Ingersoll's morality and, by extension, that of all freethinkers.

Douglass was also held up as an example to show how blacks could rise to high levels of achievement and were not constrained by any innate inferiority. This is part of what might be called the discourse of racial optimism. White atheists and freethinkers spoke up in favor of suffrage and civil rights for blacks by appealing to a sense of justice and equal treatment without regard to race. Since there existed no innate limitations to black achievement, racial optimists believed that providing equal opportunities would ensure that the best individuals, regardless of race, would be successful. Robert Ingersoll was one of the most vocal racial optimists, as we saw in the discussion of his opposition to anti-Chinese prejudice in the previous chapter. He was regarded in his own time as a humanitarian whose racial views should be models for other freethinkers. Yet not all freethinkers were racial optimists. An alternative discourse within freethought circles held that a rational approach – one that explicitly rejected decision-making based on mere "sentiment" – showed the innate inferiority of blacks. While these freethinkers contended that they harbored no ill will toward blacks, they argued, for example, that granting voting rights to uneducated blacks had been folly. This chapter again points to the tensions within atheist and freethought circles between an ostensible commitment to racial equality and the persistence of scientific racism.

Racial caricatures of African Americans

As was the case for so many of the images of non-white people in white freethinkers' works, images of black people said more about the creators and audience for the works than about the subjects of the images. A host of caricatures of black people pervaded freethought newspapers, often contributing directly or indirectly to white atheists' and freethinkers' critiques of Christianity. One of the most prominent was the stereotype of blacks as helpless and pitiable slaves. In this argument, freethinkers highlighted how Christians had justified slavery through the Bible and showed how other freethinkers often played a leading role in the abolitionist movement.[9] To create maximum effect for this argument, freethinkers often painted a simplistic portrait of passive black slaves. As Douglas Lorimer explains, the images of blacks as helpless and degraded dated from Christian abolitionist propaganda, and over the course of the nineteenth century these images gradually lost their religious connotations.[10]

One example of this is *Christianity and the Slave Trade*, written in the early 1880s by the Scottish agnostic William Stewart Ross, under the pen name Saladin. Ross drew a contrast between Christian rhetoric and the realities of slavery by quoting the Anglican cleric Frederic Farrar's *Life of Christ* (1874), which said of Christianity: "It elevated the woman; it shrouded as with a halo of sacred innocence the tender years of the child."[11] Ross returned to this quotation throughout the book, and specifically criticized the violation of femininity resulting from slavery by emphasizing the suffering of the mother and her child. The figure of an African woman seems to have been chosen specifically to arouse sympathy from Ross's readers. Such a figure was portrayed as passive and therefore much less threatening than the figure of an African man. Ross said, for example, in allusion to Farrar's quotation: "The Christian slave-owner elevated woman by tearing her away from her husband and children and father and mother and native land to toil for his profit, with the lash of the whip ever liable to descend upon her naked back and limbs."[12] In further depictions of the way Christianity led to the degradation of women and children, he described how "some huge negro" would at times be "let in among the negresses, that he might impregnate them, and thus provide a new relay of slaves [...]."[13] Such discussions relied on a notion of black feminine innocence and purity, corrupted by white Christians. Images of the suffering slave appeared numerous times in other freethought works as a way to show the link between Christianity and support for slavery (see Figures 5.1 and 5.2).

Portrayals of blacks as sympathetic yet foolish figures were also common. The *National Reformer*, for example, republished a story which recounted a black preacher talking about the story of Adam and Eve's fall. It supposedly came directly "from the thick lips of the reverend orator himself." The

5.1 "A Biblical Custom," *Truth Seeker*, December 24, 1892, 817

5.2 "Inspired Slavery," *Freethinker*, May 3, 1885, 137

excerpt undoubtedly intended to amuse readers through its reproduction of a black dialect and its simple religiosity:

> My tex', breden and sister, will be found in de fus chapter Genesis and twenty-sebenth werse; "And de Lord make Adam." I tole you how he make him. He make him out of clay, and when he git dry he breathed into him de bref ob life. He put him in de garden of Eden, and he set him in de korner ob de lot, and he told him to eat all de apples ceptin' dem in de middle ob de orchard; dem he want for he winter apples.[14]

Such reports occurred frequently in freethought newspapers, often appearing in sections that contained serious news or at the bottom of columns to fill space, indicating that little thought was put into them; rather, the stereotype was produced almost reflexively.[15]

This use of blacks as figures of amusement might also be used to build cohesion among white freethought groups. One report in 1846 in the *Reasoner* described the opening of the Finsbury Mechanics' Institute, a place for adult education supported by secularists and freethinkers. A report of the meeting noted that someone apparently performed a minstrel song in blackface: "An Indian gentleman gave a 'Nigger song.'" Later at the meeting, George Holyoake, who was attending, applauded the opening of the institute and said:

> The "Nigger song" had been heard by some with surprise, by some with pleasure [...]. Let Mechanics' Institutions flourish, and their influence would reach the negro, and he would contribute one day to our instruction as now his eccentricities do to our amusement. Let Mechanics' Institutions flourish, and their influence would travel across the Atlantic, strike the fetters from the American slave, and rescue, by the force of public opinion, that glorious republic from the odium now attached to it by the existence of slavery within its territory.[16]

Yet the intention of the "Nigger song" was not obviously to demean or mock blacks. Holyoake remarked in his speech and in a later article that Thomas D. Rice, the famous minstrel performer, had intended to get audiences accustomed to seeing black performers on stage, in the same way, in Holyoake's view, as Shakespeare hoped to win acceptance for Jews on stage in his depiction of Shylock.[17] In this way, then, Holyoake and presumably his fellow secularists did not feel their enjoyment of the minstrel show was based on mockery, but on an admiration for black culture – especially given Holyoake's own sympathies for abolition. As Eric Lott argues, black minstrelsy was about more than white domination; it harmonized contradictory and ambivalent white male feelings of both attraction and repulsion toward black men.[18]

Freethinkers also portrayed blacks as criminals in their newspapers as a way to show the degrading influence of Christianity. In the view of freethinkers, the Christian doctrine of forgiveness encouraged blacks to commit crimes, safe in the belief that they would ultimately be forgiven. A cartoon in the *Truth Seeker* by Watson Heston demonstrated this point. Based on events in 1894 in Alabama, the cartoon shows three black men ("The Believing Saints") at the gallows as a white priest points to heaven, where the three men are shown dancing with angels. Below the cartoon was a report that reprinted the speeches of the three men. One, for example, said, "Brethren, in fifteen minutes I'll be in Paradise with a long white robe on and golden slippers a walking de golden streets" (see Figure 5.3).[19] The same attitude can also be seen in some portrayals of lynching, which held that Christianity was the cause both of the initial crime of the black person and of the violent reprisal by the white mob (see Figures 5.4 and 5.5).

Another trope about blacks was that they were deeply superstitious and so especially prone to the negative influence of Christianity. In some cases, authors highlighted non-Christian folk beliefs as a way to emphasize the irrationality of blacks. An article written in the *Truth Seeker* in 1907 by "A Country Doctor" in Maryland discussed various superstitions he had come across, particularly "hoodoo," in which "[t]he Negro, as a race, is a firm believer [...]."[20] Such reports seemed to emphasize the backwardness and innate difference of blacks.[21] Eugene Macdonald agreed that blacks were, as a race, naturally religious. As he explained, "[t]here is no class of people in the world more religious than the negroes. Their fervent African temperament makes them peculiarly susceptible to religious sentiment and at the same time leads them into licentious lives."[22] While such statements suggested that blacks had a natural tendency toward superstition, the influence of Christianity only exacerbated this tendency and drove them further away from more productive pursuits. Various discussions of black churches showed that the mix of Christianity with innate black religiosity produced

5.3 "Sickening Talk on the Gallows," *Truth Seeker*, September 1, 1894, 545

5.4 "A Christian Endeavor," *Truth Seeker*, November 16, 1895, 721

5.5 "About Evenly Balanced," *Truth Seeker*, May 13, 1899, 289

5.6 "The Infallible Judgment of the Majority," *Truth Seeker*, July 12, 1890, 433

a harmful combination.[23] But an article in the *Boston Investigator*, while not denying the irrationality of black churches, also noted that white churches were equally irrational.[24]

This discussion of black superstition and religiosity could be used as a contrast to the cool rationality of white freethinkers. Cartoons by Watson Heston in the *Truth Seeker* invariably portrayed freethinkers in the abstract as white men. One example from 1890 showed this clearly: it depicted a white man and boy – representing the brave freethought minority – facing off against a large mob of irrational people, among them white priests, Puritans, and children, but also a stereotypical black man and a Native American (see Figure 5.6).[25] Such an image showed how freethinkers understood themselves. In contrast to blacks, who embodied many of the characteristics freethinkers despised, white freethinkers were composed and rational in the face of the superstitious hordes that threatened their freedom. It was for this reason that an 1857 meeting of the Infidel Association of the United States debated a resolution that religious beliefs were held only by "negroes and a few white fanatics" – though the reference to "negroes" was eventually deleted.[26] Portrayals of the negative and undesirable traits of blacks therefore offered a lesson to clarify and strengthen the key values held by white atheists.

The negative stereotypes of blacks led some white freethinkers to mockingly suggest that God or Jesus was actually black. While there is a tradition in black theology of this kind of speculation,[27] such comparisons were hardly meant to be flattering in this context. Kersey Graves wrote in 1876 that there was as much evidence that Jesus was black as there was that he was born of a virgin. Early Christian portraits of Jesus apparently depicted him as a black man, and

> the only text in the Christian bible quoted by orthodox Christians, as describing his complexion, represents it as being black. Solomon's declaration, "I am black, but comely, O ye daughters of Jerusalem" (Sol. i. 5), is often cited as referring to Christ. According to the bible itself, then, Jesus Christ was a black man.[28]

Graves also mused about whether white Christians would accept a black Jesus if he returned to earth and went to their churches: "What a ludicrous series of ideas is thus suggested by the thought that Jesus Christ was a 'darky.'"[29] Elmina Slenker also penned an article on this topic and cited Graves, who in her words had discovered "the dark, ugly, hateful, repulsive, forbidding features of the negro" in Jesus's family tree.[30] In another article, W.P. Ball also followed Graves in suggesting that Jesus was black. He also proposed "that the God of the Bible is a negro" because in the book of Jeremiah (8:21), God said, "I am black" – although Ball omitted to say that in context "black" was meant as a synonym for "hurt."[31] While there were hints in these articles of criticism of white Christians' own racial hypocrisy, the main goal was to find humor at the expense of white Christians and black people more generally.

Black freethinkers

These negative caricatures of blacks could be a result of white freethinkers' lack of actual interaction with real black people. In 1903, George Macdonald reported positively on the behavior of a black neighbor who secretly fed a hungry dog belonging to another white neighbor. Macdonald had lived for decades in New York, a city in which blacks lived largely apart from whites,[32] and therefore this was "the first colored man whose conduct [he had] been able to observe [...]."[33] When an inquirer wrote to the editors of the *Boston Investigator* in 1889 to ask "whether there are many Freethinkers or Infidels among the colored people," the editors replied: "We are not acquainted with many of the colored people who are Infidels. They are generally either Protestants or Catholics, for they are apt to be credulous, and easily imposed upon [...]."[34] This physical separation of blacks and whites meant that white freethinkers' mental image of blacks would come primarily from second-hand accounts like the caricatured descriptions provided in the pages of freethought papers.

But as the above questioner suspected, there were black freethinkers, who are charted by Christopher Cameron in his forthcoming book on the subject.[35] The historian Evelyn Kirkley is right, however, to point out that the involvement of non-white people in the popular freethought movement was rare enough to be considered "newsworthy."[36] Susan Jacoby, in her history of American freethought, suggests some reasons for the dearth of black freethinkers in the nineteenth century. One reason was that black slaves had long looked to Christianity as a source of inspiration and hope for a future liberation in this world or the next. After emancipation, the black church offered a stable institution that bound the community together. On the other hand, freethought, with its emphasis on individuality, would have threatened the community that membership in the black church supplied. Furthermore, in the latter half of the nineteenth century, as blacks saw their civil rights eroded and their physical safety under threat, debates about the authenticity of the Bible or the merits of evolution, for example, would have seemed unimportant in the face of these more pressing issues. Finally, Jacoby argues that many blacks simply would not have had the educational and social opportunities to be exposed to freethought.[37] Additionally, Kirkley notes that white freethinkers "made no effort to enlist African Americans."[38]

Nonetheless, some white freethinkers reacted angrily to segregated organizations and expressed their commitment to open membership for all regardless of race. In one case in 1847, the *Boston Investigator* cited an incident in which the Newburyport Branch of the Sons of Temperance rejected a member "on account of his color." The editor, Horace Seaver, disagreed with the move, arguing that "[a] man's color, being nothing that he had the slightest concern in producing, should never create a prejudice against him; but to deprive him of rights and privileges on that account, is peculiarly unjust [...]." In the Boston Infidel Relief Society, a group formed in 1845 to assist freethinkers suffering hardship, Seaver gladly noted, "the whole human race stand on an equality, and a black man is as eligible to membership as a white man. So it should be in all Societies."[39] Will S. Andrews, from Portsmouth, Oregon, made a similar point in an 1890 letter to the *Boston Investigator* in which he criticized the Assembly of Progress, a whites-only progressive organization. Andrews asked, "Why white persons solely? [...] Do they hold that in order to be progressive and liberal your skin must be white?" He recommended they remove that clause, since "[i]f a human is progressive, liberal, of good moral character, and socially accept-able, no matter what color the skin, he is my brother and should be yours." The idea of segregation accorded with Christianity, he argued, but it "is too foreign to Free Thought and Secular ideas to deserve serious attention and consideration."[40]

Despite white freethinkers' ostensible commitment to openness – though given the stereotypical rendering of blacks seen above, it is fair to question how widespread that commitment was – there were black freethinkers. There had long been a skeptical tradition among African Americans, including those who were enslaved. As Cameron shows, the "problem of evil" – namely, how an all-powerful and all-good God could allow suffering and evil – made many slaves question Christianity. This kind of questioning – even if it did not necessarily lead to full-blown atheism – was apparent in slave narratives and accounts of travelers in the South.[41]

An early example of this black skeptical tradition is William Wells Brown, a former slave who later moved to London to publish *Clotel, or the President's Daughter* (1853), the first novel to be published by an African American. Brown's biographer Ezra Greenspan notes the difficulty of deter-mining his religion with certainty. As Greenspan says, it is easier to rule out the many forms of Christianity that Brown despised because of their association with slavery than to come up with a definitive statement of his actual views.[42] Brown was strongly critical of Christianity's complicity in slavery, in both his autobiographical account of his life under slavery and in his novel *Clotel*. In the former work, Brown recounted that slave women were sometimes advertised as "having got religion." This was, as Brown explained, because Christian teaching counseled slaves to passively accept their condition, which benefitted the slaveholders.[43] Brown could also be cavalier about religion. At one plantation, he described how during the whites' prayer services, he would help himself to some of their mint julep, and "[b]y the time prayer was over, I was about as happy as any of them."[44] But he may not have been an atheist. On his escape from slavery, Brown ran out of food on his way to Canada, but eventually found some corn to eat, "thanking God that I was so well provided for."[45]

In *Clotel*, he criticized those in "high places" who owned slaves, and "especially professed Christians," for allowing slavery to persist.[46] He cited one source that suggested that over 660,000 Christians owned slaves in the United States.[47] Christian characters in the book often support slavery and justify it on biblical grounds. Rev. John Peck, who owns a large plantation with dozens of slaves in Mississippi, argues that any natural rights possessed by man were squandered in the Fall. Peck sees slavery as a way to Christianize heathen Africans and employs a missionary to preach sermons to the slaves, arguing that blacks should be grateful for their condition: "Your fathers were poor[,] ignorant and barbarous creatures in Africa, and the white fitted out ships at great trouble and expense and brought from that benighted land to Christian America [...]."[48]

However, Peck's daughter Georgiana is an equally committed Christian, but unlike her father supports abolition and gives an impassioned defense of the rights of blacks in a debate with him. She eventually emancipates his slaves following his death. Georgiana also converts and marries a freethinker named Miles Carlton. He initially thought that Christianity and support for slavery went hand-in-hand, yet hearing Georgiana argue against it leads him to "[view] Christianity in its true light" for the first time.[49] While he was already sympathetic to abolition, the conversion sparks a deeper support for it: "She had converted him from infidelity to Christianity; from the mere theory of liberty to practical freedom. He had looked upon the negro as an ill-treated distant link of the human family; he now regarded them as a part of God's children."[50] This seems to suggest that while Brown was critical of Christian hypocrisy, he nonetheless accepted that it held anti-slavery potential.

A similar case is that of Frederick Douglass, the escaped slave and leading abolitionist, who was probably the most famous black man in nineteenth-century America. Historians have seen Douglass as a Christian, if a conflicted one.[51] A recent article by Zachary McLeod Hutchins, however, suggests that a close reading of Douglass's *Narrative of the Life of Frederick Douglass* (1845) reveals a wholesale rejection of Christianity, though one shrouded in metaphor that present-day readers of Douglass have overlooked. For example, Douglass speaks of a fellow slave telling him that carrying a certain "root" would protect him from his overseer's violence. This was not a literal root: a common metaphor for Jesus in the Bible was a root – something with which Douglass was doubtlessly familiar – and when Douglass continued to suffer violence at the hands of his overseer, he realized that this root offered no protection, in turn giving up his faith in it and instead success-fully resisting his master in violent confrontation.[52] Christopher Cameron offers further evidence for Douglass's religious skepticism. Douglass regu-larly criticized the Christian endorsement of slavery and stated that even atheism or infidelity was better than that dishonest and hypocritical creed. Douglass also saw problems with black Christianity. In his view, it was too focused on other-worldly matters, distracting from more pressing issues in the present and hindering their resolution. Indeed, Douglass insisted that it was men – not God – who should be thanked for the abolition of slavery. Further indicating his commitment to the principles of religious liberty, in 1889 Douglass became a vice president of the Free Religious Association, a hub for liberal Christians and freethinkers.[53]

Freethought newspapers – without claiming him as one of their own – sometimes quoted Douglass on Christianity and its relationship to slavery.[54] Douglass's national prominence meant that white freethinkers praised his achievements and sought to highlight their associations with him. Such a strategy had two goals. For one, Douglass's accomplishments lent support for the argument that blacks were capable of full citizenship. Secondly, by linking themselves with Douglass, white freethinkers also demonstrated their own tolerance and humanity in contrast to the supposed bigotry of white Christians. A typical description of Douglass came from an 1890 news item in the *Truth Seeker*, which stated, "Frederick Douglass states the true wisdom for both parties on the negro question in the terse saying: 'Let us alone and giv [sic] us fair play.'"[55] John E. Remsburg described Douglass as "the greatest of his race," while Sara A. Underwood said he was as "a born orator, and a noble pleader for his despised race."[56] Another freethinker defended Douglass against criticism for marrying a white woman. Such criticism, he believed, came from those "who are presumably Christians," yet he pointed to the example of Moses marrying an Ethiopian woman in the Bible.[57]

The clearest way in which atheists linked their cause to Douglass was through the famous story of his meeting with the leading American free-thinker, Robert Ingersoll. The incident entered freethought lore and would be re-told multiple times. Douglass narrated the story in his final autobiography, *The Life and Times of Frederick Douglass* (1881). After stopping in Elmwood, Illinois, on a lecture tour in the late 1860s or early 1870s, Douglass needed to spend the night in nearby Peoria after the lecture in order to reach his next speaking engagement on the following day. When Douglass worried that he would be unable to find accommodation there, a companion suggested that he look up Ingersoll, who would gladly welcome any visitor. As it happened, Douglass found accommodation at a hotel in Peoria that night, but was curious about Ingersoll and "resolved to know more of this now famous and noted 'infidel.'"[58] On calling at his door, Douglass found Ingersoll just as advertised: "I received a welcome from Mr. Ingersoll and his family which would have been a cordial to the bruised heart of any proscribed and storm-beaten stranger, and one which I can never forget or fail to appreciate." Douglass concluded that his view of "infidels" had changed as a result of the meeting:

> Incidents of this character have greatly tended to liberalize my views as to the value of creeds in estimating the character of men. They have brought me to the conclusion that genuine goodness is the same, whether found inside or outside the church, and that to be an "infidel" no more proves a man to be selfish, mean, and wicked, than to be evangelical proves him to be honest, just, and humane.[59]

While Ingersoll appears never to have spoken about the encounter during his life, the British secularist George Holyoake recounted the story in his autobiography, written in 1892, and claimed that on his trip to the United States in 1879, he visited Ingersoll's house and also met Douglass there.[60] In another article in the *Freethinker*, an author named H.J. criticized the black preacher Celestine Edwards for his criticism of atheists. With segregation and discrimination in view, H.J. cautioned that Edwards should think twice about his views of atheists. While Frederick Douglass faced discrimination from white Christians, he was, as H.J. explained, "a personal friend of Col. Ingersoll, at whose house I believe he is a welcome guest. Let Mr. Celestine Edwards, who is never tired of holding Atheists up to public execration, make a note of this."[61] Again, the story was brought up as proof of Ingersoll's – and by extension all atheists' – superior morality. The story would appear several more times in the *Freethinker* before the end of the century.[62]

Douglass's encounter with Ingersoll was again brought up when a group of "colored Freethinkers" met in 1901 in Washington, DC, to celebrate the life of Ingersoll, who had passed away in 1899. The hall was decorated with portraits of Douglass and Ingersoll on either side of the stage. Many speakers discussed Ingersoll's achievements and emphasized his great humanity. One speaker, Reverdy C. Ransom, brought up the story about Douglass and was reported to have praised Ingersoll "particularly for his championship of human rights regardless of race or color."[63] In his speech, Ransom stated:

> Ingersoll was one of the first fruits of the evolution of humanity away from tribe and clan and race into a manhood bounded only by humanity. He saw no black peril in America, or yellow peril on the other side of the world. He saw only man, and believed that all should walk by the light of reason under the sway of the sceptre of liberty and justice.[64]

At the meeting a resolution was passed, proposed by William Calvin Chase, editor of the black newspaper the *Washington Bee*, which said in part, "[Ingersoll's] sympathies were boundless, they were confined by no narrow limitations of race, class, or sex. All men who suffered wrong found in Ingersoll an advocate and champion."[65] Eva Ingersoll, Robert's wife, could not attend the meeting but wrote a letter that was read aloud and in which she expressed her regrets and support for the meeting. "Since his death," she said, "I have received innumerable expressions of affection for him and sympathy for me and mine from the colored people throughout the entire country, for which I am deeply grateful."[66] Such words, while given at a celebratory event, suggest that Ingersoll was regarded in his own time as a champion of civil rights for blacks.

Aside from Douglass's association with Ingersoll and his vice presidency of the Free Religious Association, Douglass remained mostly uninvolved in the American freethought movement. Other blacks were, however, more active. David S. Cincore (also sometimes spelled Cincose), a former slave and former preacher, attended various freethought conventions in the 1880s and 1890s.[67] He spoke at the International Congress of Freethinkers, held in 1893 in Chicago, where he was billed as "the Colored Bob Ingersoll."[68] By the end of the nineteenth century, however, Cincore became a stage actor and actually returned to the church. Other black freethinkers, like Lord A. Nelson and R.S. King, remained active around the turn of the century.[69]

Another prominent example was Hubert Harrison, who was born in the West Indies in 1883 but settled in New York in 1900. Like so many other freethinkers, Harrison was an autodidact. He became one of the leading black intellectuals in New York – advocating for greater class and race consciousness – and was dubbed by contemporaries the "father of Harlem radicalism." Harrison's work helped to spark the Harlem Renaissance, a black cultural and artistic movement in Harlem during the 1920s.[70]

Harrison, influenced by Paine, Huxley, and Darwin, lost his faith in 1901 and became an agnostic.[71] He was involved in the New York freethought scene at least from 1903 and contributed a number of articles to the *Truth Seeker* on a range of topics from Thomas Paine's legacy to arguments for taxing church property.[72] In a 1914 article, Harrison took his fellow blacks to task for what he saw as their political and religious conservatism. Harrison blamed the legacy of Christianity for this and noted, "it should seem that negroes, of all Americans, would be found in the Freethought fold, since they have suffered more than any other class of Americans from the dubious blessings of Christianity." Yet Harrison sympathized with those who remained Christians; after all, he understood the burden of leaving behind the religion of one's community. For this reason he believed it would take years before there were large numbers of black freethinkers, although he noted that there were some in New York and Boston, especially those who were immigrants from the Caribbean.[73] Of course, Harrison was equally critical of white Christianity. In one article, for example, he called for a distinction between Christianity and the creed preached by Jesus. The latter, he thought, was preferable, but clearly differed from the religion practiced by supposed Christians: "It is in Christian Europe and America that we find most hatred and race prejudice, greed, obscenity, drunkenness and organized bloodshed and banditry."[74]

Criticism of black churches by black freethinkers was a familiar theme. In a 1910 article in the *Truth Seeker*, W.S.T. Harris pleaded with his fellow blacks to recognize the harmful effects of religion. "Negroes," he wrote, "you are asleep. Wake up. We are too religious for our own good." He recommended putting church buildings to better use by turning them into workshops, schools, banks, and theaters. The money spent on churches and especially the money spent on foreign missions could be better used "to civilize our own race out of superstition, fears, and ignorance."[75] This negative view about black religion was not unanimous, however. The *Truth Seeker* reprinted an article (written by W.E.B. Du Bois) from the *Crisis*, the official journal of the National Association for the Advancement of Colored People. The article argued that black Christianity was no more superstitious than its white counterpart. Specifically, the author of the article pointed to Billy Sunday, the former baseball star and popular evangelical preacher. Sunday's exaggerated and charismatic preaching style led the author to note parallels with "the whirling dervish, the snake dancer and devotee of 'Mumbo Jumbo.'" With the example of Billy Sunday in view, "let no white man sneer at the medicine men of West Africa or the howling of the Negro revival. The Negro church is at least democratic. It welcomes everybody. It draws no color line."[76]

Racial optimists

Given his prominence as the leading freethinker in the United States, Ingersoll has attracted attention from historians. Some have argued that he did little to protest against racial injustice in the United States. David Anderson says that "he was almost silent as second-class citizenship became a reality" and that, while Ingersoll was "[a] strong supporter of civil rights, particularly for Negroes, he did not make the emergence of Jim Crow and segregation, for which his party [the Republicans] bore much responsibility, a political issue as he might have done."[77] Jeremy Rich, citing Anderson, states that Ingersoll "rarely touched on racial themes, even as he expounded on practically every other intellectual topic. [...] Although Ingersoll attacked slavery and supported Republican civil rights legislation after the late 1860s, he did nothing to decry the rise of Jim Crow in the 1880s and 1890s."[78] More generally, Evelyn Kirkley says that white American freethinkers as a group "held paternalistic, racist attitudes prevalent among postbellum Euro-Americans. Although many of them and their parents had supported abolition, they were reluctant to endorse African American civil rights."[79]

These accounts give Ingersoll and his colleagues far too little credit. Of course, as we have seen, racial stereotypes persisted in freethought newspapers, but white atheists and freethinkers – and particularly Ingersoll – were often outspoken on the issue of racial equality. Indeed, as we saw in the previous chapter, Ingersoll was a strong defender of Chinese immigrants. Of course one must also be careful to avoid the assumption that Ingersoll held racial views that would fit comfortably in our contemporary society, and there is a risk of overlooking some of the limitations of his racial views. Ingersoll was not exceptional among freethinkers in his criticisms against racism, but he was not the norm either. Sidney Warren rightly points out that "freethinkers were sometimes radical and other times reactionary" about racial issues.[80] There was a range of views among white freethinkers, from optimistic support of racial justice, egalitarianism, and a belief in blacks' capacity for progress, to pessimistic, racial determinist views, which held that innate black inferiority made true racial equality impossible. Even those on the egalitarian side, like Ingersoll, held a lingering belief in black inferiority.

Robert Ingersoll was certainly the leading racial optimist among white freethinkers. This was not the case, however, in his early political career, when he ran for Congress as a Democrat in 1860 and opposed Abraham Lincoln's leadership for the first half of the Civil War. (Ingersoll himself was a colonel during the conflict, and would retain the title throughout his life.) One point of contention with Lincoln was the Emancipation Proclamation, which Ingersoll worried would make the South more intractable and bring a massive influx of emancipated slaves into Northern states.[81] This would be a recurring worry for Ingersoll, who said in an 1863 speech that these ex-slaves were "a dangerous element" and were "too ignorant and degraded." Therefore, he wanted "the negro to be put in a territory by himself."[82] By the middle of 1863, however, he was thoroughly behind Lincoln and supported his brother Ebon's successful run for Congress as a Republican in 1864. After the war was over, Ingersoll encouraged Ebon to oppose leniency and pursue a radical policy toward the South.[83]

At the start of the Civil War, however, Ingersoll was, in the words of his biographer Orvin Larson, "not as yet a godless man."[84] It was not until the 1860s that Ingersoll's anti-religious views really took shape: in 1862 he married Eva Parker, who came from a freethinking family, and in the mid-1860s he began to read canonical anti-religious works.[85] It is not unreasonable, therefore, to suggest that Ingersoll's growing hostility to religion might have influenced his evolving racial politics. Soon after the war, in 1867, Ingersoll gave a speech in Galesburg, Illinois, to a group of blacks, who requested that Ingersoll, then Attorney General of Illinois and an increasingly prominent orator, address them. In the talk, Ingersoll explained to his audience how the Bible helped justify slavery. He also stated that blacks should have the same rights as white people and encouraged them to use their voting rights with sophistication by making the two political parties fight for their votes.[86]

Ingersoll was an active Republican for much of his life. He campaigned for the Republicans in the 1876 and 1880 presidential elections and made racial issues a prominent theme during these campaigns. In campaign speeches, he painted the Democrats as untrustworthy and conniving given their historical support for slavery.[87] While his campaign speeches in these years mainly slung mud at the Democrats, he also used these speeches to make a broader point about racial injustice. Ingersoll gave the example of a horse race, "free to every horse in the world, and to all the mules, and all the scrubs, and all the donkeys." Why, Ingersoll asked, would the superior "blooded horse" care about the mules and donkeys on the track? On the other hand,

> the Democratic scrub, with his chuckle-head and lop-ears, with his tail full of cockle-burrs, jumping high and short, and digging in the ground when he feels the breath of the coming mule on his cockle-burr tail, he is the chap that jumps the track and says, "I am down on mule equality."[88]

Here, however, Ingersoll seemed to accept the notion of inherent white superiority: whites represented "the blooded horse" and therefore had no reason to restrict the rights of their inferiors since, in a fair competition, whites would come out ahead anyway. In another speech, he noted, in a similar vein, "[i]f I belong to the superior race, I will be so superior that I can make my living without stealing from the inferior."[89] Ingersoll seemed to take whites' superiority as a given, which meant that laws infringing upon blacks' freedoms were simply gratuitous and were used to help those whites who could not succeed on their own.

Ingersoll also protested against the curtailment of civil rights for blacks. In 1883, the Supreme Court struck down the Civil Rights Act of 1875, which ensured equal access for blacks and whites to various services, like hotels, trains, and theaters, a decision that was, to Ingersoll, "a disgrace to the age in which we live."[90] Far from being silent on the scaling back of civil rights, Ingersoll criticized his own party, the Republicans, for failing to make this a major issue in their unsuccessful 1884 presidential campaign – a decision that he believed led blacks to lose faith in the party.[91] In a speech delivered on October 22, 1883, only a few days after the Supreme Court's decision, Ingersoll gave an impassioned critique of the ruling:

> I am the inferior of any man whose rights I trample under foot. Men are not superior by reason of the accidents of race or color. They are superior who have the best heart – the best brain. Superiority is born of honesty, of virtue, of charity, and above all, of the love of liberty. The superior man is the providence of the inferior. He is eyes for the blind, strength for the weak, and a shield for the defenceless. He stands erect by bending above the fallen. He rises by lifting others.[92]

In arguing against the decision, Ingersoll used the example of Frederick Douglass to show the injustice. It was "simply absurd" that "a man like Frederick Douglass" could be denied entrance to a hotel, theater, or train on account of his race.[93] While such an argument was no doubt powerful, the implication was that unequal treatment was wrong because it would provide unequal treatment not to just any average black man, but to someone of Douglass's status. Equal rights therefore seemed contingent upon sufficient black achievement. This is what Ibram X. Kendi has called "uplift suasion": the idea that one could convince racist whites of the falsity of their views by pointing out examples of high-achieving blacks. Such an argument, Kendi points out, could backfire since it seemed to unintentionally emphasize the fact that black achievement was an aberration.[94]

This use of black success stories was a common tactic for racial optimists. Another example was Booker T. Washington.[95] Washington, born into slavery in 1856, went on to become the inaugural leader of the Tuskegee Institute in Alabama, an agricultural and industrial training center for blacks. Washington recommended that blacks focus on self-improvement as a way to earn the respect of white people, rather than challenging segregation and disfranchisement directly.[96] Many whites, including freethinkers – North and South – found in Washington a relatively uncontroversial figure on whom they could count to express moderate and agreeable views on the race question. One news report in the *Truth Seeker* from 1890 described Washington as "one of the most competent and cultivated colored men in the country," while Eugene Macdonald said he was "probably the brainiest colored man in the country today."[97] Charles Chilton Moore was so enthusiastic about Washington that he invited to host him at his home when he visited Kentucky (although it is not clear if Washington took him up on the offer).[98] When arguing against racial prejudice, Washington could be called upon as an exemplar of black progress. Hugh O. Pentecost, in a speech from 1907, criticized the notion of the innate inferiority of blacks and said, "[l]ook at Booker T. Washington himself; he contradicts that statement."[99] Another exemplar was Clement G. Morgan, who was voted the speaker of his 1890 graduating class at Harvard, the first black man to receive the honor. Ingersoll invoked Morgan as an example of the extent of black progress following emancipation.[100] A report in the *Boston Investigator* likewise sang the praises of Morgan, while denouncing the negative reactions against him, which "spring from prejudice, or are dictated by foolish sentiments unworthy the age in which we live."[101] This was part of a wider strand of the optimist argument holding that blacks needed to be given a fair opportunity before one could decide on the merits of their race.

In Britain too, there was hope among white freethinkers about the prospects of African Americans, but also condemnation of white attempts to hinder their progress. The *National Reformer* reported on positive developments among former slaves in the years following the Civil War, but also noted with worry the white backlash in the South.[102] During Charles Bradlaugh's visit to America in 1875, he penned a series of articles on American politics and touched on the condition of former slaves in one section. He noted that while blacks received "a paper political equality" through the Fifteenth Amendment allowing equal voting rights, it would take "several generations" of education and training "to even give the coloured race the possible chance of making the best of the organisation they inherit." But Bradlaugh also acknowledged the role of white supremacist groups in the South, which "represent an element which will never cease to oppose the recognition of the equality before the law of the negro race."[103]

Black freethinkers most obviously spoke out against racial injustice. One speech by James D. Carr, a former district attorney, was given to the Manhattan Liberal Club in 1903. As a preface to the speech, Carr expressed his belief that the "liberal" in the name of the club meant those who have "minds that are open to reason, and that from the discussions the element of prejudice is eliminated." The thread that ran through Carr's speech was the idea of justice. Whites, in his view, needed to be prepared to accept blacks if they became educated and acquired property. Voting laws also needed to be just. He accepted "educational and property qualifications" so long as they were applied equally to whites and blacks.[104] George E. Wibecan Jr. struck a similar note to Carr in his lecture to the Brooklyn Philosophical Association in 1909. He stressed that when blacks had similar opportunities to whites, they flourished. He pointed to the example of Alain Locke, who in 1907 became the first black man to be awarded a Rhodes Scholarship to Oxford. Like Carr and others, Wibecan argued for the importance of judging someone "according to his worth as a man and not by the shade of his skin."[105]

The issue of lynching was another flashpoint in the debate about blacks at the turn of the nineteenth century. Ingersoll addressed the subject in the final speech before his death in 1899. In the speech, he questioned the idea that Christianity improved morality by pointing to lynching as one example: "Has the Bible made the people of Georgia kind and merciful? Would the lynchers be more ferocious if they worshipped gods of wood and stone?"[106] In an 1899 interview, Ingersoll responded angrily to a lynching in Georgia, in which Sam Hose, a black man, killed his white employer – probably in self-defense – and was subsequently captured by a mob, mutilated, and burned alive. Of the incident, Ingersoll said, "I know of no words strong enough, bitter enough, to express my indignation and horror."[107] He called the perpetrators "savages" and said, "[t]hey are a disgrace to our country, our century and the human race."[108] Finally, Ingersoll wondered, "Are white people insane? Has mercy fled to beasts?"[109] Both the *Truth Seeker* and the *Freethinker* reprinted excerpts of Ingersoll's condemnation of the lynching.[110]

Ingersoll's response generated a number of letters to the *Truth Seeker* to defend lynching, or at least to defend the character of the South. No writers defended the barbarity of the practice, and most said that they would never personally engage in a lynching. As George Fredrickson observes, "the more educated and sophisticated Southern Negrophobes of the period generally condemned the practice in the abstract [...]. But [...] these spokesmen often ended up apologizing for the practice as virtually unavoidable under existing circumstances."[111] This was the case for white Southern freethinkers: various authors stated that while they disapproved of lynching, it was unfair of Ingersoll and the *Truth Seeker*'s readership to judge the South because they could not adequately understand the conditions there.[112] Numerous other authors wrote in to the *Truth Seeker* to condemn those apologists for lynching. Lynch mobs, they argued, often targeted innocent men and had no place in a civilized society.[113]

Ingersoll was not the only white freethinker to speak out against lynching, but the fact that he was the most prominent in the country undoubtedly encouraged others to do so. Eugene Macdonald's younger brother, George, who wrote regularly for the *Truth Seeker* and took over as editor after Eugene's death, also denounced lynching. Macdonald denounced the brutality of the mob violence and dismissed arguments that lynchers were nobly trying to prevent crime through their actions.[114] Similarly, Charles Chilton Moore, a freethinker who edited the *Blue-Grass Blade* in Lexington, Kentucky, condemned lynching and argued that there seemed to be a contradiction between participating in a lynching and being a freethinker. He cited one report that claimed that a recent lynching was perpetrated by numerous church members, yet the report "didn't say that there was any Infidel in the crowd, and I do not believe that there was one, because Infidels do not do things like that, and Christians do." Furthermore, "[a]ny Infidel who was known to have been in that gang would receive the condemnation of all leading Infidels in the world [...]."[115] In this case, Moore explicitly categorized lynching as contrary to the values of freethought.

On a similar note, white freethinkers attacked the hypocrisy of Christians with regard to race. One example is criticism directed at Celestine Edwards, a prominent black lecturer for the Christian Evidence Society and a founding member of the Society for the Furtherance of the Brotherhood of Man. Edwards frequently criticized British atheists in his speeches, and styled himself "BC," the "Black Champion," while labeling opponents like Bradlaugh or J.M. Robertson "WC" or the "White Champion."[116] In response, an article in the *Freethinker* by an author identified as H.J. sought to remind Edwards "about the way in which his white fellow-Christians in the United States treat the black man." While the British were happy to "shake hands with their 'black brother,'" white Americans refused to worship in the same church as blacks "and hold the 'nigger' in undisguised contempt."[117] White freethinkers had no such prejudices, and H.J. said they would always be willing to meet a black man in public debate "as if he were a 'white man' in a figurative as well as in a literal sense." Furthermore, the author brought up the abolitionist history of atheists and infidels as he encouraged Edwards to

> remember that some of the best friends the negro ever had were infidels and Atheists. Let him remember it, to his shame, when he is trying to paint the characters of great and good men to his ignorant Christian audiences in colors as black as his own skin.[118]

In this instance, H.J. used historical and contemporary examples to demonstrate the hypocrisy of Christians' proclaimed commitment to racial equality. At the same time, H.J. argued that atheists were truly the ones who consistently opposed racism.

Racial pessimists

This is not to suggest that all white atheists possessed optimistic views with regard to the potential for black progress. As we have already seen, negative stereotypes of blacks were littered throughout their writings. The British evolutionist T.H. Huxley, as we saw in the second chapter, regarded the lower races as intermediaries between apes and men on the evolutionary ladder. Not surprisingly, then, he was skeptical about the progress of African Americans following the Civil War, even if he opposed slavery. He conceded in an 1865 essay that some blacks might be better than some whites, "but no rational man, cognisant of the facts, believes that the average negro is the equal, still less the superior, of the average white man."[119] Furthermore, it was "simply incredible" to think that on a level playing field "our prognathous relative [...] will be able to compete successfully with his bigger-brained and smaller-jawed rival, in a contest which is to be carried on by thought and not by bites."[120]

This is not to say that Huxley was a supporter of slavery, however. He brushed aside what he saw as the unscientific claims of abolitionists with regard to the capacity for black progress in an 1864 lecture, "[b]ut I must freely admit that the aberrations from scientific fact or fair speculation, on the anti-slavery side, are as nothing compared with the preposterous ignorance, exaggeration, and misstatement in which the slave-holding interest indulges." Here Huxley had in mind the polygenist racism of James Hunt, and the remainder of the lecture was devoted to exposing the absurdities of his *The Negro's Place in Nature* (the title of which was a play on Huxley's own work *Man's Place in Nature*).[121] His ambivalence was likewise displayed in an 1864 letter to his sister Lizzie, who lived in Tennessee. He wrote that, like "most thoughtful Englishmen," "[m]y heart goes with the south, and my head with the north." But he had "not the smallest sentimental sympathy with the negro [...]." Rather, slavery was a concern primarily because of the harm done to whites. It eroded morality and boded ill for "free labour and freedom all over the world." "For the sake of the white man," he continued, "for your children and grandchildren, directly, and for mine, indirectly, I wish to see this system ended."[122]

A similar rationale justified his membership – along with many other leading liberal freethinkers like Charles Darwin and John Stuart Mill – of the Jamaica Committee, which aimed to prosecute Governor Edward John Eyre for his brutal crackdown on black protesters and declaration of martial law in which hundreds were killed, following the Morant Bay rebellion in Jamaica in 1865. The most prominent of those executed in the crackdown was George William Gordon, a mixed-race local politician and critic of the colonial government. But Huxley's support for the committee's goals was, he said, not out of "any particular love for, or admiration of the negro"; rather it was out of a desire to see the rule of law maintained: "Does the killing [of] a man in the way Mr. Gordon was killed constitute murder in the eye of the law, or does it not?"[123]

White freethinking suffragists like Elizabeth Cady Stanton also drew upon these racial pessimist arguments in debates surrounding the prospect of black male enfranchisement in the years following the Civil War. As noted above, Stanton had worked extensively for abolition before the war, but she and fellow leading suffragist Susan B. Anthony opposed the Fifteenth Amendment, which granted the vote to black men, since it did not also enfranchise women. Stanton was angered by the seeming injustice of what she saw as uneducated black men receiving the vote while educated white women like herself did not, even if in general she had long supported black suffrage.[124] This view could easily turn to one that emphasized the racial inferiority of blacks. As Stanton put it,

[...] I would not trust him [the black man] with my rights; degraded, oppressed himself, he would be more despotic with the governing power than ever our Saxon rulers are. If women are still to be represented by men, then I say let only the highest type of manhood stand at the helm of State.[125]

Elsewhere, she wrote, "As long as he [the black man] was lowest in the scale of being, we were willing to press his claims; but now, as the celestial gate to civil rights is slowly moving on its hinges, it becomes a serious question whether we had better stand aside and see 'Sambo' walk into the kingdom first."[126] Stanton's (and other white suffragists') racial views alienated allies like Frederick Douglass, who was also a supporter of women's suffrage, not to mention female black suffragists.[127]

Other white freethinkers possessed an outright disdain for blacks. Such was the case with William Cowper Brann, a freethinker from Texas who published a newspaper called the *Iconoclast* and who was murdered in 1898 by a Christian gunman. In an article reprinted in the *Freethinker*, Brann railed against black preachers with vitriol unmatched by other major white freethinkers. The black preacher, Brann contended, had "even less morals than the usual darkey." It was these men who had been responsible for uprisings in the South, and "[t]he belief in many negro skulls that the black is several degrees better than the white is largely due to the assurances of their preachers." Similarly, assaults against white women were laid at the feet "of these greasy, indolent, vociferous mal-odorous nuisances," and Brann recommended that in addition to lynching the perpetrator, the black preacher who compelled the initial violence should also be lynched.[128] As Susan Jacoby points out, however, the fact that Brann was "a militant racist [...] made him a pariah within the national freethought movement [...]."[129] Indeed, Charles Chilton Moore thought Brann was a Christian. Noting that he received a copy of his *Iconoclast* – and insisting that he would never have paid for it – he said, "[i]t is now, as it has always been, a religious paper, and like all religious papers, is calculated to do harm." He also condemned Brann's racial demagoguery, which included his "proposition to exterminate the whole Negro race in America."[130] Still, the fact that the *Freethinker* reprinted Brann's essay without comment suggests that his language was not completely beyond the pale of freethought discussions.

A lesser-known American freethinker, Richard Lynn Garner, also professed racist views of blacks, as charted by the historian Jeremy Rich. Garner was a self-trained scientist, who researched primate language and studied African religion during his many years of living in Gabon, in West Africa. Influenced by Charles Darwin and Robert Ingersoll, Garner's private writings were filled with skepticism about Christianity. Garner believed that his freethinking attitude shielded him from sentimental religious views that called for political equality between races. This was unacceptable and unscientific, since, to Garner, blacks and whites represented separate species.[131] Garner opposed missionary evangelizing in Africa and in general hated the French colonial system he witnessed in Gabon, espousing instead a kind of cultural and moral relativism.[132] At the same time, he expressed a personal dislike for Africans, emphasizing their inferiority to whites.[133]

Probably the most prominent freethinker to express a racial pessimist position was Eugene Macdonald, the editor of the *Truth Seeker* from 1883 to his death in 1909. His racial views signaled a broader shift in white American opinion around the turn of the nineteenth century. As Fredrickson explains, "[s]pokesmen who claimed to represent an unsentimental and tough-minded perception of racial reality denied the prospect of gradual black 'progress' in an atmosphere of increased mutual accommodation,

projecting instead a future of increasing racial antagonism."[134] One particular editorial by Macdonald in April 1903 exemplified this change as he
launched into a lengthy rant on black character:

> The negro is unquestionably of an inferior race. He is imitative, not initiative,
> and like most imitators imitates the worst, not the best. He is not and can
> never be the equal of the white race, for he is several hundred years behind,
> can never catch up. His customs and manners, otherwise known as morals,
> are widely different from the white man's. He picks up small portable articles
> with the same irresponsibility as a monkey. He chatters away from the truth
> as easily as a minister slanders Infidels. He has the passions of an animal with
> scant intellectual command of them.

Furthermore, he maintained that most blacks were "lazy, lying, shiftless,
immoral, superstitious, and dishonest."[135]

Given blacks' inferiority, according to Macdonald, black suffrage was a
mistake. Northern politicians used the issue of voting as a ploy to gain black
support in the South. Such a tactic was "no way to elevate" blacks from their
inferior condition, and in fact only harmed them since it encouraged them
to think "Nigger good as white man." Furthermore, Macdonald argued that
blacks simply voted for the Republicans out of "gratitude" without understanding what they were voting for. Earlier portrayals of blacks lingering
from earlier "Abolition doctrines" were unrealistic. Abolitionists thought
that "every negro was a persecuted saint" and that a black man "was just
as good if not a little better than a white man […]." But this was only "a
splendid dream." Macdonald also believed that forcing blacks and whites
together in "the same cars and restaurants and other places where physical contact is impossible to avoid, is to violate sociological laws as well as
healthful natural instincts." He called for future policy toward blacks to
come "from the sociologists and not from the politicians." As he argued
further, "[i]t would be as reasonable to enact a statute against the thunder
and lightning as one proclaiming the equality of the white and colored
races. […] Nature knows neither charity nor justice; inexorable law governs
the universe."[136] Macdonald's freethought certainly influenced his view of
blacks: he claimed to base his views of proper race relations on scientific and
rational grounds, without recourse to mere sentimentality.

The editorial attracted both positive and negative feedback. One writer,

S.M. Lewis, disagreed with the "very one-sided and prejudiced" editorial. He contested Macdonald on the grounds of freethought. While Lewis accepted that blacks were presently inferior, this was "because [they had] been crushed by the brutal power of might for centuries [...]." Lewis gave a poignant rejoinder to Macdonald's idea that the black man "would be improved by crushing him" when he asked – in a question sure to wound an atheist priding himself on rationality – "[a]re you a homeopath?" Lewis further took issue with Macdonald's invocation of sociology. There was no "sociological law" that stated whites and blacks could not ride in the same cars or eat at the same tables. Lewis noted that considerable advancement had been made among the black population since 1865 and called for judgment based on "individual merit." He closed his letter by quoting Thomas Paine's famous phrase, "The world is my country, to do good my religion," which had connotations of opposing racial prejudice.[137]

But Macdonald's editorial also attracted some support. A letter from Francis Smith, from Arkansas, stated that Macdonald's opinion was "eminently correct" and in complete harmony with Southern views. He called for giving blacks civil rights and "practical education as far as they are capable of receiving it." While Smith acknowledged that while there were "some good negroes, [...] many others are but little better than savages." Additionally, most blacks did not have "sufficient intelligence" to be able to vote. He believed that those blacks who focused on "honest labor [...] will always be respected by the white people." That said, Southern whites, in Smith's view, did not want to have social interaction or "amalgamation" with blacks.[138]

In other articles, Macdonald continued his attacks on sentimental portrayals of blacks. As he said in one article, "the days of Uncle Tom's Cabin are over. Sentiment, except that of justice, benevolence, and forbearance, should be excluded." Instead, Macdonald looked to "the sociologists who can advance a rational mode of settlement."[139] On the subject of lynching, Macdonald wrote in a brief response to one letter defending lynching that getting vengeance on a criminal or rapist "is to be expected." But the torture, brutality, and festive nature only took away sympathy from the original victim and turned "brutal negroes into heroes and martyrs in the eyes of some Northern sentimentalists."[140] Still, Macdonald denounced Charles

Carroll's book *"The Negro a Beast"* or *"In the Image of God"*, which argued that blacks were beasts, one of whom had married Cain. Such a book, Macdonald contended, was designed "to injure the negro" by misrepresenting the Bible.[141] Here, however, the fact that Carroll was a Christian may have influenced Macdonald's hostility – and this points to the way racial views could vacillate according to the needs of one's argument.

Conclusion

This chapter has traced white atheists' and freethinkers' views of African Americans in the decades following the Civil War. Freethinkers often used unflattering and simplistic portrayals of blacks as an instrumental way to critique Christianity. Additionally, the characteristics attributed to blacks, such as their foolishness, their piety, and their criminality, were all opposites of the ones on which white freethinkers prided themselves. In this way, blacks represented a mirror in which white freethinkers could define their own identities. Part of the reason why so many of these images of blacks were simple caricatures may have been that white freethinkers had such little contact with black people that they could imagine them only through common tropes.

Despite the negative portrayals of blacks, a number of white atheists did assert that the freethought movement was open to anyone regardless of race. Depictions of superstitious blacks were partially refuted by the presence of a number of black freethinkers, some of whom were directly involved in the freethought movement. Frederick Douglass is the most prominent example, and while he was mostly uninvolved with the freethought movement over the course of his life, his connection with Robert Ingersoll was drawn upon time and again by other white freethinkers to demonstrate Ingersoll's superior humanity and by extension their own. Indeed, Ingersoll was the most vocal racial optimist among this group. He argued for equal civil rights for African Americans and protested against lynching and the onset of renewed segregation. Ingersoll and others argued against racial prejudice toward blacks, particularly on the grounds that it clashed with the rationalist principles of freethought. The racial optimist position, however, seemed to take present black inferiority for granted, even while it argued for equal opportunities for all. Likewise, the emphasis on black achievement, seen especially through the use of black exemplars like Douglass, seemed to make equal rights dependent on sufficient progress and, though unintentionally, underscored that figures like Douglass were actually very rare. There was also a more pessimistic position with regard to blacks. This was exemplified by Eugene Macdonald, who argued late in the nineteenth century against the wisdom of having granted blacks the right to vote. True equality could not be legislated into existence, he argued, and pretending away the sociological fact of black inferiority was mere sentiment, unsuited to the rationalist freethinker.

These different perspectives within the white atheist movement show the many factors that pushed and pulled their racial views. On the one hand, arguments against Christianity encouraged these white atheists and freethinkers to see black religiosity as particularly ridiculous. But, on the other hand, Christian justifications for slavery and racial violence led white atheists to take the side of blacks and to protest at racial injustice. This approach, however, ran up against scientific racist ideas that held that blacks were innately inferior. As we have seen, many white atheists did indeed accept this kind of racial science, yet fewer applied these lessons to practical political questions – although some, like Macdonald, obviously did. There was a range of views that a freethought perspective could permit with regard to race. One of these avenues was to oppose racial prejudice. We have seen glimpses of this already in the past few chapters, but it becomes even clearer in the next chapter, which examines how an atheistic perspective offered the tools to critique racism.

6

The curse of race prejudice: rethinking race at the turn of the century

In the previous chapters, we have seen the diverse positions that atheists and freethinkers might take on questions of race and civilization, ranging from scientific racism that argued for the inferiority of non-white people, to skepticism about imperialism and racist policies at home. This chapter, however, offers the starkest cases of atheists and freethinkers explicitly speaking out against racism.

As I noted in the Introduction, some historians have suggested that Christianity could inhibit the growth of racist thinking through its emphasis on ideas of universal brotherhood and a shared humanity resulting from a common ancestry for all humans in Adam and Eve. The flip side of this argument was that as secularization occurred – as the authority of Christianity began to fall away in the nineteenth century – this opened the way for racism.

There is undoubtedly some truth in this picture, but, as we have already seen, it was also possible to challenge racist ideas within an atheist worldview. Scientific racism, with its emphasis on racial classification and ranking, often through purportedly scientific measurements of things like skull shape or evolutionary progress, began to be questioned around the turn of the nineteenth century, and particularly after the First World War.[1] These voices were still few and far between – it would not be until after the Second World War and the civil rights activism of the 1960s that these racist ideas truly became taboo – but this chapter shows how atheists in the late nineteenth and early twentieth centuries were at the forefront of attacking racist ideas about the biological or civilizational inferiority of certain racial groups, and even questioning the idea of "race" itself.

175

Earlier in the century, the environmentalist ideas of Robert Owen and John Stuart Mill offered strong arguments against racial determinism. While not linked intellectually, these ideas contended that social or political circumstances determined (or greatly influenced) character and this often meant the rejection of the importance of innate biological factors. The turn of the century, however, is when we find the clearest cases of prominent atheists opposing racism on rational, secular grounds. This can be seen in the career of J.M. Robertson, a Scottish freethinker and Liberal politician whose work, especially *The Saxon and the Celt* (1897), challenged the idea of race as a guide to history and politics and instead put forth an environmentalist explanation for racial differences. On the other side of the Atlantic, James Morton, an atheist active in the New York freethought scene at the turn of the century, regularly confronted "race prejudice" in the pages of the *Truth Seeker* and in his book *The Curse of Race Prejudice* (1906). Racial prejudice, to Morton, was a primitive superstition that should die out as civilization progressed.

This chapter culminates with a discussion of the Universal Races Congress, held in London in 1911. Organized by Felix Adler and Gustav Spiller, members of the nonreligious Ethical Culture Societies in the United States and Britain, respectively, the congress espoused racial harmony and criticized notions of racial difference that were purportedly based on science. The event had a large freethought presence – hitherto unrecognized – which included Robertson and other leading freethinkers who confronted racist ideas. These included W.E.B. Du Bois, the African American sociologist, and Franz Boas, a German American anthropologist. These two are important figures known more for their anti-racist activities than for their freethought, but one cannot easily separate these strands of their work.

The ambivalence toward ideas of race and civilization among atheists and freethinkers has been the central theme of this book. In this case, however, that ambivalence was virtually absent among the figures discussed: they fell clearly on the side of opposing racism. The central goal of this chapter is therefore to tell an alternative story to the one in which racism thrives as Christianity's authority declines. Rather, the atheist worldview could offer the tools of science and reason as ways to critique racism.

Robert Owen

Owen, as we saw in the Introduction, greatly influenced the development of the freethought movement in both Britain and the United States through his religious criticism and proto-socialist organizations. In his autobiography, he linked his rejection of religion with a greater feeling of openness to all humanity that transcended artificial human constructs like race or nation. As he explained, he adopted "the spirit of universal charity, – not for a sect or a party, or for a country or a colour, – but for the human race, and with a real and ardent desire to do them good."[2] Central to Owen's worldview and political program was that human nature was formed by social or environmental circumstances, not innate faculties.[3] Such an idea theoretically challenged racial determinism, even though Owen rarely applied this environmentalist view to racial issues. When he did discuss perceived racial or civilizational differences, however, he emphasized how they were produced by external circumstances. In a speech in Glasgow in 1812, Owen discussed the apparent differences between the races of mankind: "Man becomes a wild ferocious savage, a cannibal, or a highly civilised and benevolent being, according to the circumstances which he may be placed from his birth."[4] This was why, as he said at a later date, "we ought not to be *displeased* or to *blame* any individuals, tribes, or people; or to be less *friendly* to them, because they have been made to differ from us in *colour, form,* or *features.*"[5]

Since non-white people were not inherently inferior, given this environmentalist theory, they might expect to fare better in Owen's worldview. This was not always the case in practice, however. While in Scotland, Owen could avoid confronting racial issues, but when he visited Jamaica in 1828, he reported that the black slaves there were actually in a better condition than the working classes in Britain and Ireland.[6] Furthermore, when Owen and his followers began a utopian commune at New Harmony in the United States, its constitution, adopted in 1825, explicitly placed non-white people a rung below whites:

> Persons of all ages and descriptions, exclusive of persons of color, may become members of the Preliminary Society. Persons of color may be received as helpers to the society, if necessary; or it may be found useful to prepare and

enable them to become associates in communities in Africa, or in some other country, or in some other part of this country.[7]

It is not clear whether Owen himself drafted this particular passage in the constitution, but it seems difficult to believe that he would have been completely ignorant of it.

On the other hand, the goal of Owen's Association of All Classes of All Nations, founded in 1835, was "to effect peaceably, and by reason alone, an entire change in the character and condition of mankind, by establishing over the world, in principle and practice, the religion of charity for the opinions, feeling, and conduct of all individuals, *without distinction of sex, class, sect, party, country, or colour*, combined with a well-devised, equitable, and natural system of united property [...]."[8] Race, however, rarely entered into Owen's worldview, and later freethinkers almost never discussed his ideas with respect to their bearing on racial issues. The only exception appears to be an 1849 article in the *Reasoner*. The article told a story, possibly apocryphal, about the display of a group of "Bosjesmans" – Bushmen or San people – at a London museum. The narrator recounted how, at the museum, an Anglican bishop mused about "the probability of a child of the Bosjesmans ever attaining the language, manners, and customs, and the intellectuality of Europeans."[9] The narrator, evidently influenced by Owen's ideas, interjected that "any future knowledge that the child might imbibe would be entirely attributable to the circumstances it was placed in in early youth." The narrator then left for a short time, but noticed that another person had been listening intently to their conversation. After the narrator returned to the conversation, he heard this person say: "That is what I have been endeavouring for the last forty years to prove, both in this and in other countries, that a man is guided in the future by the present circumstances, over which we have no control." The narrator noted the surprise on the bishop's face on realizing the man's identity: "it was Robert Owen, the Socialist."[10] At the middle of the century, as racial determinism was beginning to gain greater scientific acceptance, the story of Owen – real or not – arguing for the innate capacities of even the degraded Bosjesman demonstrates the ends to which his environmentalist views might have been put.[11]

John Stuart Mill

The mid-nineteenth-century liberal philosopher John Stuart Mill also held that character was largely determined by circumstances, but did not appear to be directly influenced by Owen in this view. Mill, much more than Owen, applied his philosophy to racial thought. He rejected what he saw as his age's growing fascination with explaning all differences through innate traits, racial or otherwise. To Mill, to regard the differences between "individuals, races, or sexes" as "innate and in the main indelible" ignored the fact that these differences "would be produced by differences in circumstances [...]." Indeed, this biological determinist view "is one of the chief hindrances to the rational treatment of great social questions and one of the greatest stumbling blocks to human improvement."[12]

Mill's environmentalist ideas had practical implications for racial issues, and the condition of recently emancipated slaves in the West Indies provided one such flashpoint for debate. The perceived slow pace of improvement among these freedmen, as they were called, increased anti-black sentiment among white Britons, following the enthusiastic abolitionist sentiment of earlier decades.[13] Thomas Carlyle, the famed Scottish writer, exemplified this pessimistic attitude in his anonymous work "Occasional Discourse on the Negro Question" (1849). In the article, Carlyle lamented the abolition of slavery in the West Indies, which allowed "Quashee" – his generic term for a black person – to wallow in virtual idleness, since his subsistence was provided by a surplus of pumpkins and therefore he never learned the virtues of hard work.[14] Carlyle argued instead that blacks should simply resign themselves to being slaves for those "born wiser" – namely the whites.[15]

Mill responded to Carlyle, his former friend, with an anonymous article of his own. While refuting some of the practical and ethical issues in Carlyle's defense of slavery, Mill also took issue with the racial determinism of Carlyle's assertion that whites had a natural right to rule over blacks. If Carlyle had understood how human character was formed through external forces, Mill argued, "he would have escaped the vulgar error of imputing every difference which he finds among human beings to an original difference of nature." Mill used the example of two trees growing side-by-side, with one taller than the other:

Is nothing to be attributed to soil, nothing to climate, nothing to difference of exposure – has no storm swept over the one and not the other, no lightning scathed it, no beast browsed on it, no passing stranger stript off its leaves or its bark? If the trees grew near together, may not the one which, by whatever accident, grew up first, have retarded the other's development by its shade?[16]

In fact, Mill explained, human beings were subject to far greater external forces than trees and could, unlike trees, actively conspire to prevent the flourishing of another, "since those who begin by being strongest, have almost always hitherto used their strength to keep the others weak."[17] Mill and Carlyle clashed again later in the century, as they found themselves on opposite ends of the debate over Governor Edward John Eyre's harsh response to the Morant Bay rebellion in Jamaica in 1865. Mill led the Jamaica Committee that attempted (unsuccessfully) to have Eyre tried for his conduct, while Carlyle led the Eyre Defence Committee.[18]

Further indicative of the importance of Mill's protests against racism is the fact that Mill drew the ire of James Hunt, the founder of the polygenist Anthropological Society of London, discussed in Chapter 1. Hunt rejected the optimistic doctrines of utilitarians like Mill, who argued for the possibility of social improvement. He believed that the work of his own organization was opposed by two main groups, those "suffering from [...] the religious mania, and the rights-of-man mania." The latter and more serious case was produced by accepting "the one gigantic assumption of absolute human equality, which is generally known under the title of rights of man."[19] To Hunt, Mill was the exemplar of this unfortunate condition; indeed, he "is perhaps the most painful ever recorded."[20] Elsewhere, Hunt chastised Mill because he refused to admit that the inferiority of "the Australian, the Andaman islander, and the Hottentot" was not innate, but "due to a combination of unfavourable circumstances."[21] Mill, however, never referred to Hunt in any correspondence and admitted his unfamiliarity with the Anthropological Society.[22] The historian Georgios Varouxakis, in summing up Mill's racial views, notes that while Mill accepted some of the racial stereotypes of his time, he was "in the forefront of attempts to discredit the deterministic implications of racial theories [...]."[23]

While Mill clearly opposed biological determinism and the worst excesses of imperial rule, he continued to support imperialism in principle, and indeed his political writing was made possible by income he received for his thirty-five years of administrative work with the East India Company. Recent years have seen an intense debate over Mill's relationship with imperialism.[24] Without entering into a detailed discussion of his imperial thought, it is fair to state that for him, a society's level of civilization was far more germane than its racial makeup in the formulation of imperial policy. In *On Liberty*, he argued that "[d]espotism is a legitimate mode of government in dealing with barbarians, provided the end be their improvement, and the means justified by actually effecting that end." Mill drew a parallel between children and uncivilized people. One did not need to respect the liberty of children or "backward states of society in which the race itself may be considered as in its nonage."[25] In "A Few Words on Non-Intervention," Mill counseled that international relations could not follow normal rules if the two parties were of unequal levels of civilization, but nonetheless justified imperial interventions to raise a level of civilization. He pointed to the example of the Roman conquests and asked, "would it have been better for Gaul and Spain, Numidia and Dacia, never to have formed part of the Roman Empire?"[26] Whatever one thinks of Mill's imperialist views, they did not seem to be informed by a belief in innate racial inferiority. Indeed, his belief in the possibility of an effective civilizing mission almost required a belief that races were not inherently inferior and were able to make progress. This is why a racial determinist view, such as the polygenist thought of Robert Knox, could be used to oppose imperialism, since if racial groups were static and could never improve, attempts at bringing civilization would be futile at best. All of this points to the complexity of nineteenth-century views of race and imperialism.

J.M. Robertson

While both Owen and Mill were freethinkers, their racial views were not explicitly atheistical. The turn of the nineteenth century, however, saw a number of other freethinkers begin to oppose racism from a perspective rooted in freethought. One such example is J.M. (John Mackinnon) Robertson.[27] Born in 1856 in Scotland, Robertson gave up religion in his youth and became involved in the small but active Edinburgh Secular

Society in the early 1880s. He eventually moved to London, where he became assistant editor of Charles Bradlaugh's *National Reformer*. Like other secularists – though not Bradlaugh – Robertson was sympathetic to socialism and the aims of the Fabian Society, a turn-of-the-century group that aimed to bring about socialism through gradual reform rather than revolution. Following Bradlaugh's resignation as head of the National Secular Society in 1890, Robertson was passed over for the leadership in favor of G.W. Foote. Disputes with Foote eventually drove Robertson out of the society, yet he was a lecturer with the nonreligious South Place Ethical Society from 1900 until his death in 1933. He also acted as president of the Rationalist Peace Society from its foundation in 1910 until its disbandment in 1921. Robertson was elected as a Liberal MP for the riding of Tyneside in 1906, serving until 1918.

Robertson's intellectual interests varied from literary criticism to ancient mythology to radical politics, but he was also a fierce critic of racism and even the idea of race itself. This is best seen in his 1897 work *The Saxon and the Celt*, which aimed to counter talk of the "peculiarities of character in the Irish race [...]."[28] Both supporters and opponents of Irish nationalism based their political programs on the supposed racial tendencies of the Irish, yet Robertson wanted "to upset such generalisations, and to discredit all claims of innate and unchanging racial peculiarity," and therefore to "take up an independent and non-partisan position [...]."[29] Nonetheless Robertson seemed more sympathetic to the Irish nationalists, for he characterized their opponents as having "a certain psychological compulsion [...] to revert in some way to the attitude of race prejudice."[30]

More generally, talk of races within other European countries seemed absurd to Robertson. On works that discussed, for example, the "Teutonic" characteristics of the British, Robertson could "see no scientific coherence in these generalisations."[31] He likewise took on Josiah Nott and George Gliddon's polygenist *Types of Mankind* – "an ill-made but then-esteemed work of the last generation of ethnology" – in a lengthy footnote and deemed their discussion of the racial basis for recent French history incoherent.[32] Robertson also criticized the work of Frederick Hoffman, a German statistician working in the United States.[33] While Hoffman argued that African Americans' racial "tendencies" accounted for their inferior condition, Robertson countered that the work "not only gives no proof of such primordial 'race tendencies' as it alleges, but on the contrary shews that a race's tendencies are constantly determined by its environment."[34] Robertson contended that differences between nations must be found in institutional, environmental, or political factors – "in anything, in short, rather than in primordial and perpetual qualities of 'race.'"[35]

Robertson returned to this theme in his 1916 work *The Germans*. There he charted much the same ground, this time attacking the "Teutomania" that explained European history and contemporary politics with reference to the unique characteristics of the "Teutonic" race. But, Robertson said, "Teutomania is to be superseded not by Keltomania or any other race-gospel, but by a sociology which sees in all races the varying products of antecedents and environments, conditions and institutions."[36]

Other freethinkers made similar points, such as Joseph Kaines, a member of the Anthropological Institute, who dismissed notions about the coherence of an Aryan race in an 1876 article in the *National Reformer*. When one asked about the precise identity or origins of the supposed Aryan race, "one gets replies remarkable mainly for their variety rather than their intelligibility."[37] World history demonstrated the fallacy of assuming there were discrete races: conquests, migrations, and intermarriage occurred so frequently that no race could be considered pure. Kaines accepted that there were differences between what he identified as the three main races – white, black, and yellow – but asked, like Robertson: "Are not these diversities the result rather of sociological than cosmological influences? The enormous power of the former over the latter as modifiers can hardly be overrated. If it be so, what becomes of race?"[38]

As we saw earlier, evolution could be deployed both to support racism and to oppose it. Robertson, for his part, drew upon Darwinian arguments to explain how racial differences were in fact superficial. These differences, he reasoned, occurred in a long and gradual process of evolution from apes and proto-humans. In this early period of human evolution, there were multiple varieties, some of which quickly went extinct. The surviving groups slowly became dispersed across the globe, leading to, in the vast expanse of time, the differences commonly associated with race, like skin color or language. These differences were not ancient, in Robertson's reading, but actually occurred relatively recently in human history.[39] Within this evolutionary framework, it was absurd to talk, for example, of "primordial, purely blond and dark, long-headed and broad-headed races" since "[i]n no part of the world to-day do we find such definitely marked-off races [...]."[40] The notion of permanent racial essences, central to scientific racist thought, was in fact contrary to an evolutionary worldview, Robertson argued.

Robertson was similarly critical of eugenics. In 1905, he criticized a paper by Francis Galton, Darwin's cousin and the originator of eugenics. Robertson's central criticism was that one could not separate talk of eugenics from talk of politics. Galton assumed that families that were successful over the course of many generations must have simply possessed good stock, but Robertson suggested that their success was better explained by their inherited wealth. This said nothing about their biological fitness, but it did speak to their political and economic circumstances.[41]

Much like other freethinkers, Robertson accepted the idea of civilizational progress. During much of the nineteenth century, this narrative of progress often saw non-white people as backward and inferior. Robertson, however, used the idea of progress to suggest that a belief in racism was actually a sign of a backward society. For him, racial thinking was "an irrational play of instinct" and "an energy of mere animal passion, surviving unpurified from the stage of sheer barbarism [...]."[42] In this way, Robertson harnessed the widespread view of civilizational progress in order to make an argument against racial prejudice. Such an argument had much in common with the view that religion constituted a primitive and irrational superstition, highlighting how atheist thinking informed his argument. Indeed, Robertson cited "rationalist" thinkers like John Stuart Mill and T.H. Huxley as some of the few who spoke with "sanity and righteousness" on racial issues.[43]

Robertson was not the only atheist to express skepticism about supposed Anglo-Saxon superiority. While Anglo-Saxon supremacy was celebrated in the mid-nineteenth century, Irish and other "Celts" often took issue with this ethnocentrism.[44] In one case, an 1850 anonymous writer in the *Boston Investigator* said, "Anglo-Saxon-dom is a rum-drinking, beer-guzzling, monopoly-loving, man-stealing, land-stealing, fighting, trading, cheating, lying race."[45] Another example was a lengthy article in the *National Reformer* by William Maccall, a former Unitarian minister and a Scot like Robertson. Maccall criticized the hysteria around identifying "Anglo-Saxon" lineages and attributing events like the American Revolution or the British conquest of India to the race's supposed virtues. Maccall's investigations into the Anglo-Saxons led him to the conclusion that "the Anglo-Saxon is a wholly fabulous personage"; instead, the repeated migrations into Britain by Celts, Romans, Vikings, and Normans had made the British population highly mixed.[46] Maccall also pointed out the absurdity of hyphenated racial groupings. If the British were called Anglo-Saxons, there would need to be similar names for the Greeks and Romans and other races. Since the Italians were "a mixed race, ought we not to have a compound name for the Romans of a hundred syllables at least?"[47] In conclusion, he recommended jettisoning the term "Anglo-Saxon" and instead "call[ing] ourselves simply and frankly Britons or Englishmen."[48]

This is not to say that all freethinkers eschewed prejudice toward the Irish or other Catholic immigrants in the United States. These people represented a danger to freethought insofar as they were perceived to be slavishly loyal to the papacy, a foreign power that was hostile to the interests of science and reason, but also, it was thought, to American democracy. This is perhaps best reflected in the cartoons of Watson Heston, who drew upon the popular political cartoonist Thomas Nast in his negative portrayals of the Irish, even to the point of near-plagiarism.[49] While the dislike of the Irish was ostensibly about their religion, not their race, Heston's cartoons nonetheless often depicted them as degraded and ape-like, in line with common caricatures of the Irish in Britain and the United States. One cartoon showed a white man and woman, representing ideal Americans, facing off against hordes of European immigrants – poor Catholics from Ireland, Italy, and elsewhere, as well as Jews (see Figure 6.1). Another showed Uncle Sam giving money to a poor Irish family, only for them to hand it out of the back door to a Catholic bishop (see Figure 6.2). In both cases, while the Irish and other immigrants were white, their ape-like facial features, sickly bodies, and shabby dress marked them as racially different from the seemingly upstanding white Anglo-Saxon majority.

Others, like Eugene Macdonald, actually compared Catholic immigrants like the Irish and the Italians unfavorably with the Chinese immigrants:

6.1 "The Emigrant Question," *Truth Seeker*, December 3, 1892, 769

6.2 "A Contribution to the Irish Question," *Truth Seeker*, March 20, 1886, 177

"The Catholic Italians, Germans, and Irish who dwell in the same quarter of the city, are more in need of civilization than the Chinamen. It is from these classes that our prisons are filled, and it is to them that the civilized missionaries should be sent in the shape of school teachers and temperance lecturers."[50] Others were more optimistic, however. Several articles in the *Truth Seeker* by Franklin Giddings described the racial composition of the United States and noted that the common stereotype of Anglo-Saxons as the archetypal Americans was unfounded. Irish, Scottish, Dutch, Germans, and Scandinavians all could lay claim to being "the old American stock," and he predicted that in the future, "it will be impossible to say to what extent an American is an Irishman, a German, or an Italian. Two hundred years from now those elements will be so blended that no one will be able to say to what extent his neighbor is Celtic or Teutonic or Latin or Slav."[51]

Robertson, for his part, thought talk of Celtic or Teutonic races was folly in general, and he criticized the ways these nationalistic impulses could drive imperialism. In particular, he penned two books criticizing the British cause in the South African War (1899–1902).[52] Robertson was skeptical of any talk of patriotism. With his socialist sympathies in mind, Robertson considered patriotism just a tool of the wealthy to whip up enthusiasm for war among the working classes.[53] As a freethinker and rationalist, he described the impulses of patriotism, militarism, and imperialism – like racial prejudice – as all having grown out of "the same animal roots," while imperialism itself was "an insensate superstition" with an economic basis that "belongs to the life of the redskins and its sociology to the civilization of Tamerlane."[54] While Robertson was a critic of imperial conduct and did not want the empire to expand, he felt that in some cases, like India, the subject countries needed to be governed by the British, who would gradually guide them to self-rule.[55] Furthermore, in contrast to his rejection of racial science described above, Robertson noted that "the simple biological fact that Englishmen cannot breed in India for two generations" should weigh against the idea that there could ever be a permanent English imperial presence there.[56]

Throughout Robertson's time in Parliament, he also expressed an interest in Egyptian affairs. He believed that Britain's only justification for being in the country was to help it transition to self-rule. During the

First World War, however, Egypt was made a British protectorate, and its reigning monarch, Abbas Hilmi II, was deposed. After the protectorate was ended, Egypt remained under the influence of Britain. Robertson kept up a lengthy correspondence with Hilmi, whom Robertson believed was the rightful ruler of Egypt.[57] Robertson's anti-imperialist views make a brief appearance in Edward Said's *Orientalism*, which I mentioned at the start of Chapter 4. The first chapter of Said's work opens with a discussion of the 1910 exchange in the House of Commons between Robertson and the Conservative leader Arthur James Balfour. Robertson asked, referring to the Egyptians, "What right have you to take up these airs of superiority with regard to people whom you choose to call Oriental?"[58] Balfour proceeded to explain to Robertson and the rest of the House that the British simply "know" about Egypt and therefore have a right to govern it – the essence of Said's argument throughout the book.[59] Said unfortunately never returns to consider how it was that Robertson asked the question in the first place. To do so would undermine Said's argument about the pervasiveness of Orientalist views within British society, which, as I argued earlier, ignores dissenting voices. Robertson was one such voice, and his skepticism about racial and civilizational superiority was informed – not coincidentally – by his freethought.

James Morton

Like Robertson, James Morton, an American atheist, was one of the most outspoken critics of racial prejudice at the turn of the nineteenth century. Unlike many of the other figures considered, James Morton has attracted virtually no scholarly attention.[60] Morton was born into a well-connected religious family in 1870 in Littleton, Massachusetts.[61] He attended Harvard while still a Christian, learning Hebrew and Greek in order to be able to read the Bible in these languages. Reading Plato and Darwin and studying Christianity at university led to his gradual break with the faith. At the end of the century, Morton made his way west and became the editor of a community newspaper in an anarchist colony in Washington.[62] From there, he went to New York City, where he became active in the freethought movement during the first decade of the twentieth century. In the 1910s, however, Morton became an adherent to the Baha'í faith, which he believed was compatible with all the world's religious and irreligious traditions. Aside from anarchism and freethought, Morton was also involved in a variety of other causes, including the promotion of Esperanto, which, as his friend Edward Cole recollected, "he looked upon [...] as a step toward the universal brotherhood of man."[63] Morton experienced prejudice and teasing on account of his red hair. In a short biographical series from 1907, Morton explained the "unending taunts concerning my red hair, first bred in my boyish mind the germs which were later to fructify into a realization of the extreme fallibility of public opinion."[64] Later in life, Morton spoke out against superstitions about redheads at a meeting of the Thirteen Club, a New York group formed to flout superstitions.[65]

It may have been a result of this teasing at a young age that Morton became one of the most vocal opponents of racial prejudice in the free-thought movement. He was involved in a number of debates over racial issues in the *Truth Seeker*. The first concerned Booker T. Washington's controversial dinner at the White House with Theodore Roosevelt in 1901. Inviting a black man to dine in the White House was simply unacceptable to some whites. This position was exemplified by a letter in the *Truth Seeker* from R. Randolph, writing from Alabama. In the letter Randolph argued in the most hyperbolic terms about the horror of Roosevelt dining with a black man. In Randolph's telling, Roosevelt "has thus early shown the cloven-foot by having a coal black 'nigger' dine with himself and family in the White House, a national mansion hitherto held as negro-proof." Randolph also noted Roosevelt's famous characterization of the freethought hero Thomas Paine as "a filthy little atheist," but continued that even if Roosevelt's characterization of Paine were true, "he could not have been near so filthy" as Roosevelt, who allowed "the splay feet of a negro, for the first time in this country's history, under the dinner table that has been so long honoured by the best company of this and foreign lands." The sight of a black man in the White House, Randolph believed, would make blacks "become so insolent and intolerable as to greatly increase the hatred already existing, and possibly lead them to perpetrate more of those fiendish acts which are almost invariably followed by lynchings."[66]

Randolph attracted a few supporters,[67] but most freethinkers denounced him and his views in the strongest terms. One particular theme among the anti-Randolph letters was that his "race prejudice" was incompatible with his claims to be a freethinker. In these responses to Randolph, the inconsistency between holding prejudiced views and being a freethinker was highlighted. P.F. Shumaker, writing from Mississippi, wrote, "Mr. Randolph has taken his seat in the wrong pew. The readers of The Truth Seeker are mostly *Liberals*, and he is very *illiberal*."[68] Moncure Conway, by this point one of the most respected freethinkers on either side of the Atlantic, likewise noted that "a Freethinker animated by race hatred" was "phenomenal." Conway portrayed Randolph's prejudice as something irrational, even pathological. It was motivated not by clear, reasoned thinking, but by an animalistic, emotional reaction. He likened Randolph's prejudice to a disease, namely, "*negrophobia hysterica*."[69] Another writer, D. Mackay, from Texas, diagnosed Randolph as having "the worst case of ethnical race virus" he had seen in his forty years in the South.[70] James Morton, for his part, stated that Randolph's letter "is enough to make any true Liberal shiver that such a man should have the insolence to class himself among Freethinkers."[71]

Morton also wrote a regular column in the *Truth Seeker*, in which a frequent subject was race prejudice, occasionally connected to Christianity. In one case he noted wryly that "Christian brotherly love" was apparent in Honolulu, where the YMCA (Young Men's Christian Association) had refused membership to the Japanese vice consul because of his race.[72] In another case he observed that the Christian Endeavor Convention, held in Washington, DC, segregated its black delegates, which "demonstrated how little modern Christianity really cares for its pretended recognition of human brotherhood."[73] He also criticized the introduction of voting restrictions against blacks and spoke out against the unjust treatment of blacks in the legal system.[74]

Another debate featuring Morton was touched off in the *Truth Seeker* when A.C. Bowers (self-described as "an Agnostic, with a belief in Theism"[75]) commended Eugene Macdonald's recent book on the Inquisition, except for the brief section on Christianity's relationship with slavery. For Bowers, the book "would have done more good had [Macdonald] left out the negro question."[76] Morton shot back, "[t]hat is to say, you can do more good for humanity by ignoring human rights than by recognizing them! This may be the doctrine of race prejudice, but it is not that of reason, science, or Freethought."[77] The two traded letters back and forth, and during their exchange Bowers admitted his prejudice and said that while he would "give the negro justice," the question of whether blacks could be improved was an open one.[78] Morton for his part called for treatment on the basis of individual merits, and, as other racial optimists did, pointed to the fact that "the colored race has produced not one but at least several examples of refinement, culture and intelligence [...]."[79]

Bowers attracted further support from H.C. Bradford from Nashville, who mostly appealed to dispassionate science to make his case about the inferiority of blacks. "To form any just conception of a race," Bradford believed, one had to study blacks "on their own ground" where there were sufficient numbers. The only place where this could be done was the South, but Bradford doubted whether Morton had ever been there or had met blacks in the South, who, unlike some of the more educated blacks in the North, were "[i]gnorant, poverty-stricken, utterly devoid of all sense of honor, and as full of superstition as the most bigoted Roman Catholic foreigner that ever drew breath." Given blacks' superstition, Bradford remarked, "a Negro Freethinker is a thing totally unknown," although he allowed that there might be some in the North. Bradford also worried that disregarding the importance of racial differences would lead to "the mingling of the two races" and that the South would in turn become "mongrelized." Science, in his view, showed that "admixture of the races would inevitably tend to degrade the higher, and that too without in any corresponding degree elevating the lower."[80]

Morton called Bradford's letter "a candid and courteous argument," although it made "no novel point" and contained no new facts.[81] In his response to Bradford, Morton drew upon the arguments from his 1906 book *The Curse of Race Prejudice*. Morton's work on race prejudice was informed by his freethought as seen in his numerous appeals to science and rationality in contrast to the irrationality and emotion of race prejudice. As he stated at the start of the book, he wanted to make his arguments "entirely on the basis of reason, avoiding mere appeals to passion [...]."[82] Elsewhere, Morton described race prejudice as "an attitude of mind which precludes the exercise of reason" and was "wholly emotional [...]."[83]

Like J.M. Robertson, Morton used the idea of civilizational progress when he wrote that race prejudice dated to the era of "primitive man," though he contended that it would be eradicated in the civilizing process.[84] It was for this reason that Morton likened race prejudice to other outmoded superstitions that were in time rooted out. These included witchcraft, "the old tendency to fetich worship," "medieval science," and fears about the number thirteen.[85] Again like Robertson, Morton called upon Darwinian evolution to explain "that the human race is one in all essential charac- teristics" and that therefore it was impossible to talk about a race being superior or inferior to any other.[86] Morton predicted that those in the future would have difficulty in believing that people in the past had accepted irra- tional superstitions about races, particularly in light of Darwinian science: "'What!' we may suppose them to say, 'Did these crude notions prevail in an age when Darwin's epoch-making scientific achievements had made the common origin of the human race a matter of schoolboy knowledge?'"[87] Morton dismissed "pseudo-scientific expositions of the theory of inferior races" by appealing to current knowledge about biology:

> We are told in elaborate detail, adorned by much semi-scientific verbiage, that there are many vast anatomic and physiological differences between the Caucasian and the Negro. [...] Modern science has shown clearly enough the meaning of all these variations, and the manner in which they have arisen through natural selection and other environing influences. Magnified to the utmost, they in no way contravene a probability of one origin for the entire human race. The differences between races of men are all of degree, not of kind; and not one fact can be adduced in support of the contention that any infrangible barrier exists between any two races. Each, like all the others, pos- sesses practically unlimited capacity for change and growth, wholly depending on environment. The immense flexibility of the Negro race is proved by the total transformation that has taken place in it during the comparatively brief period since the abolition of slavery.[88]

Here Morton was drawing not only on the Darwinian argument for a secular monogenesis, but also, if not explicitly, on the environmentalist doctrines elaborated by Mill and others that emphasized the importance of people's environment in forming their character.

While confronting scientific arguments about racial determinism, Morton was equally critical of race prejudice justified by religion. To Morton, it made sense "that the advocates of race prejudice, hopelessly defeated in the forum of reason, and routed by the evidences of science, should rush to religion, and seek to borrow her white robes to cover their besmirched garments." In particular, Morton dismissed justifications of racial prejudice on the grounds that blacks were "semi-human pre-Adamite[s]" or the cursed offspring of Ham.[89] If anything, the Bible appeared to be against race prejudice, as seen in "the unequivocal utterance that God 'hath made of one blood all nations of men for to dwell on all the face of the earth.'" The theme of the unity of mankind was repeated throughout the Bible, making hypocrites of any Christians who professed race prejudice.[90] "On this point," Morton continued, "religion and science, though for very different reasons, are unreservedly agreed."[91]

Morton nonetheless felt it necessary to distance himself from charges of sentimentality toward blacks. He explained that he "has no extraordinary predilection for this particular race, and is in no way fanatical on the subject. A protest against Negrophobia is by no means a eulogy of Negromania."[92] Morton advocated extending voting rights to blacks, but he resisted calls for total "social equality": it "exists nowhere; and nobody ever dreamed of applying it to the colored race, or to any other race, *taken as a whole*."[93] Individuals needed to be judged on their merits, and not their skin color, but this did not mean that Morton would "associate with every Negro as my equal," since "[m]any of them are my inferiors in education, mental culture, refinement and character [...]." Morton's friends included individuals of all races who were selected "on their personal merits, and not on a mere accident of birth or color."[94] Morton likewise dismissed "the only war cry left to out Negrophobiac friends. '*Do you want your sister to marry a nigger?*'" This was a logical absurdity, Morton argued: just because one would sit with someone on a streetcar did not mean one would necessarily want to have that person as a family member. Fears about racial amalgamation were therefore unwarranted.[95]

Morton's circle of friends included a number of prominent black freethinkers. He knew the black sociologist W.E.B. Du Bois from their student days at Harvard.[96] Du Bois was one of the founders of the National Association for the Advancement of Colored People, and that organization regularly advertised *The Curse of Race Prejudice* in its official periodical, the

Crisis. Additionally, Morton served on various committees of the association during the 1910s.[97] He was also acquainted with the black freethinker and radical Hubert Harrison, mentioned in Chapter 5.[98]

Harrison too critiqued racial prejudice from a freethought perspective. Like Morton, Harrison believed that it was a "superstition" that would, like other superstitions, disappear with the advance of civilization. The failure to root out racial prejudice was, to Harrison, proof that the United States was not yet completely civilized and that the country could therefore "fittingly lead in such savage and primitive superstitions as race prejudice and lynching bees."[99] He did not, however, completely share Morton's optimism that rational argument would alone solve the problem. Harrison's socialist worldview saw racial supremacy as bound up with class supremacy. In other words, white capitalists had an interest in dividing the working classes along ethnic lines. This division could be exploited to keep wages for blacks low, which would in turn allow lower wages for whites, with the carrot that they were at least being paid more than their racial inferiors, and the stick that blacks could be used as strike-breakers in the event of a strike.[100]

Other articles also indicate the way freethought could inform Harrison's arguments against racism. In one article, he protested to the *New York Times* about the notion, put forth by another article in that paper, that all blacks had been thieves "since the days of Ham and Noah's ark." Harrison rejected such an argument, citing T.H. Huxley, who had already shown that "the Noah's ark story, far from being a fact, is an impossible myth [...]."[101] Likewise, in an article criticizing Madison Grant's introduction to Theodore Lothrop Stoddard's *The Rise Tide of Color* (1920), which warned that white people would soon be overtaken by non-white people, Harrison dismissed Grant's ideas as "racial clap-trap whose falsity has been demonstrated again and again" by "coldly critical and scientific scholars" including J.M. Robertson.[102]

Universal Races Congress (1911)

Freethinkers also played a critical role in the Universal Races Congress, held in London on July 26–29, 1911. The event attracted upward of 2,000 statesmen, intellectuals, and activists from around the world, but the idea for such a congress came from leaders in the Ethical Culture movement. Founded in New York in 1876 by Felix Adler, this movement had its roots in Reform Judaism, but moved away from all supernatural elements, instead promoting naturalistic moral values. Racial issues had been discussed in American Ethical Societies around the turn of the century, and many of its leading figures signed a petition supporting the creation of the National Association for the Advancement of Colored People.[103] Adler first suggested the idea for the congress in 1906, while the Hungarian-born Gustav Spiller, active in the Ethical movement in Britain and secretary of the International Ethical Union, carried the idea forward.[104] The goal of the congress was, according to the invitation,

> to discuss, in the light of science and the modern conscience, the general relations subsisting between the peoples of the West and those of the East, between so-called white and so-called coloured peoples, with a view to encouraging between them a fuller understanding, the most friendly feelings, and a heartier co-operation.[105]

As the historian Michael Biddiss notes, the congress contained a number of religious impulses, not least "Christian universalism,"[106] but the importance of freethought has not been explicitly acknowledged by historians. In addition to Adler and Spiller, the chief organizers, the congress welcomed papers from J.M. Robertson, who was a member of the congress's executive council and argued against race-based justifications for imperialism in his talk,[107] and from two of the leading thinkers opposing racialist ideas, Franz Boas and W.E.B. Du Bois, both of whom were freethinkers. Additionally, the British freethinker F.J. Gould prepared an "Inter-Racial Lesson" that was taught in a number of countries and in hundreds of schools in Britain,[108] while the rationalist Joseph McCabe was also involved in translating some of the papers written in foreign languages.[109] The African American freethinker, and later one of the founders of the Harlem Renaissance, Alain Locke, who was studying at Oxford at the time, also attended the congress.[110] Watts & Co., the publishing house of the Rationalist Press Association, printed the preliminary pamphlet in advance of the congress.[111]

The paper that summed up the congress's mission was Gustav Spiller's "The Problem of Race Equality." Spiller, born in Hungary, moved in 1885 to London, where he became active in the Ethical movement, eventually becoming the secretary of the International Ethical Union in 1904.[112] Spiller was also a member of the National Secular Society and was, in his own words, "a great admirer of [Robert] Ingersoll."[113] In his speech to the congress, he encouraged harmony among races and called for equal treatment without regard to racial difference. All races had the capacity to excel under the right conditions, as demonstrated by the fact that members of all races had graduated from European universities. Spiller cited with approval the German anthropologist Friedrich Ratzel, "who says, 'There is only one species of man; the variations are numerous, but do not go deep.'"[114] Like the other authors considered in this chapter, Spiller accepted an environmentalist perspective on culture that rejected biological arguments for racial inequality. While race and culture seemed to be linked, "a Zulu, for instance, taken from his tribe where he appears to possess innumerable rooted and peculiar customs, very soon loses them nearly all."[115] The only reason to admit racial inequality was prejudice, which was "based on callousness, ignorance, misunderstanding, economic rivalry, and, above all, on the fact that our customs are dear to us, but appear ridiculous and perverse to all who do not sympathetically study them."[116] That said, Spiller did grant that certain "insignificant" races, like "the Veddahs or the Andamese, the Hottentots or the Dyaks," might be shown to be inferior, although this did not hinder the equality to be found among the main races of mankind, nor did it "preclude our loving [these lower races] tenderly and doing everything which conduced to their welfare."[117]

Despite Spiller's qualifications to complete racial equality, he continued to make the same general argument that all races had the capacity to excel. In a 1912 article for the *Sociological Review*, Spiller argued that one could not fairly judge a race from one moment in time. The fact that the white race was currently dominant was not evidence of any kind of racial superiority, since this was always subject to change; China, for example, might one day take this position.[118] To determine whether races had the capacity for equality, one needed to approach the issue scientifically, thought Spiller. He proposed a simple scientific test to examine the abilities of individuals of different races who studied at British universities. After examining their results and meeting many students of different races personally, Spiller concluded "that men and women of all races are essentially alike and equal in inherent intellectual capacity and moral insight."[119] In another article, Spiller wrote that "the different races of mankind are for all intents and purposes indefinitely modifiable in their mentality [...]."[120] Beyond questioning ideas of racial inequality, Spiller likewise questioned the idea of race itself. While at times seeming to acquiesce to this idea – again mentioning "such insignificant peoples as the Andamanese, the Australians, the Veddas, or the Bushmen"[121] – elsewhere in the article he seemed much more skeptical of the concept. He noted, for example, that leading scientists like Alfred Haddon and Felix von Luschan held "that the term race is unscientific unless used in relation to the human race or species *per se* [...]."[122] Likewise, at the beginning of the article he cautioned that "the words Caucasian and Aryan are products of the fancy rather than of science [...]."[123] Spiller's work was therefore clearly informed by a scientific perspective that sought evidence from leading scientists and empirical tests of racial capacity, even if his own examination of the success of different racial groups at university lacked the scientific rigor we would expect today.

Following Spiller's paper, the congress turned to more practical themes with a speech by Felix Adler. Here Adler attempted to diminish ideas of racial superiority, something he saw as a potential cause of war. He encouraged a racial and civilizational pluralism in which no one type became dominant.[124] An exchange of ideas among civilizations benefited all participants. European life was richer, he argued, because each nation had exchanged its ideas with every other. Nonetheless, he cautioned against cultural arrogance in this process. While the West had brought much to the East, it had also "inflicted incalculable spiritual harm" by disregarding its sacred religions. "If humanity is ever to become a *corpus organicum spirituale* – and that is the aim," then there needed to be recognition and encouragement of human cultural and spiritual diversity.[125] But Adler accepted that there were "uncivilized races" and even seemed to advocate for a benevolent imperialism. These uncivilized people should be governed for their own benefit, which was "in the long run for the benefit of humanity in general." These races furthermore should be studied in order "to engender in the students a generous appreciation of all that is fine and worthy in the character and culture of the alien people."[126] Even as Adler denounced ethnocentrism and exploitative colonialism, then, he still seemed to accept a hierarchical vision of races.

The Universal Races Congress also welcomed contributions from some of the leading scientific thinkers on racial questions, including Franz Boas. Boas was born to a secular Jewish family in Germany and, after completing his doctoral work there in physics in 1882, took up an interest in geography and anthropology. He completed fieldwork with the indigenous people of northern and western Canada and settled in New York City in 1887, escaping the anti-Semitic climate in Germany and eventually becoming a professor of anthropology at Columbia University in 1896.[127] Boas also became a member of Felix Adler's Ethical Culture Society in New York. Adler, a friend of Boas's relatives, placed Boas on the board of the Ethical Culture Society's Workingman's School, which provided education for the children of poor families.[128] As Leonard Glick explains, while Boas came from a Jewish family, his "personal philosophy compounded of rationalism, cultural relativism, and ethical humanism, and [he] identified himself as an enlightened universalist who had transcended both ethnic provincialism and supernatural religion."[129]

Boas was a leading figure in overturning traditional ideas about civilizational and racial hierarchy. Many of his ideas were summed up in *The Mind of Primitive Man* (1911). In this work he challenged notions of "race and civilization" which he dubbed "the two unproved assumptions."[130] He acknowledged that a superficial examination of western civilization would lead one to assume that whites represented a superior race, yet that when examined more closely, this theory fell apart. Given the hundred thousand years of human existence, the gulf between the Old World and the New would be only a few thousand years – an insignificant gap in the vast sweep of time.[131] Furthermore, societal evolution did not follow a linear process. Instead, Boas pointed to various examples of how technology or language, for example, did not evolve in a straightforward way from simple to complex. Technological advances did not occur in a step-by-step process that was typical of all societies, but occurred in different places at different times.[132] Ultimately, the moral of Boas's work was to "teach us a greater tolerance of forms of civilization different from our own" and to "learn to look upon foreign races with greater sympathy, and with the conviction, that, as all races have contributed in the past to cultural progress in one way or another, so they will be capable of advancing the interests of mankind, if we are only willing to give them a fair opportunity."[133] For Boas, this cultural relativist position allowed one not just to respect foreign cultures, but also to realize that one was conditioned by one's own culture and civilization to accept certain truths.

Aside from critiquing ideas of civilization, Boas also challenged notions of race as a static category. This was the theme of Boas's discussion at the congress, which was based on his recent research on European immigrants to New York and their children.[134] The paper, entitled "Instability of Human Types," argued that although there were some differences between races, "the assumption of an absolute stability of human types is not plausible."[135] Like others seen in this chapter, Boas stressed an environmental explanation for racial differences. In his study, Boas found that anatomical measurements of European immigrants and their American-born children produced different values, indicating that a supposed racial type was not in fact static but was strongly influenced by its environment. In particular, Boas found that children born in America were taller than their parents, and their head shapes were longer and narrower.[136] Such a conclusion showed that racial types were not fixed but were in fact mutable – although he cautioned that the extent of this mutability was not known. Nonetheless, "[t]he old idea of absolute stability of human types" had to be jettisoned, along with the corresponding "belief of the hereditary superiority of certain types over others."[137]

Boas's work in both cultural and physical anthropology had far-reaching implications, and historians have given Boas an important place in the turn against racial thinking. Reflecting on the achievements of Boas's anthropological career, Thomas Gossett states, "[i]t is possible that Boas did more to combat race prejudice than any other person in history."[138] As Vernon J. Williams Jr. points out, however, Boas must be seen in his own context. While it is true that he fought against the dominant racial paradigm of his time, he still accepted that blacks, on average, had smaller brains than whites and were slightly less intelligent. Still, to Boas, "the variability of black intelligence" meant that any discrimination toward blacks on the basis of race was unjustified.[139]

Another critical figure in the turn-of-the-century critique of racism was the sociologist W.E.B. Du Bois, who also presented at the Universal Races

Congress. Born in Massachusetts, Du Bois was raised as a Congregationalist, yet his faith was gradually eroded, particularly while he completed his PhD at Harvard and during his visit to Germany in the 1890s. As he wrote in his autobiography, in Germany "[...] I turned still further from religious dogma and began to grasp the idea of a world of human beings whose actions, like those of the physical world, were subject to law."[140] It was here that Du Bois "became a freethinker [...]."[141] Nonetheless, unlike many of the other figures discussed here, Du Bois rarely stated his irreligious views explicitly.[142]

Du Bois's freethought seemed to inform his scientific approach to studying the condition of blacks. His mindset at the start of his career was that "[t]he world was thinking wrong about race, because it did not know. The ultimate evil was stupidity. The cure for it was knowledge based on scientific investigation."[143] The result of his investigations, undertaken while at the University of Pennsylvania, was *The Philadelphia Negro* (1899), which "revealed the Negro group as a symptom, not a cause; as a striving, palpitating group, and not an inert, sick body of crime; as a long historic development and not a transient occurrence."[144] The striking thing about Du Bois's early work is how it appealed to objective, dispassionate science. One of Du Bois's biographers, Brian L. Johnson, highlights how Du Bois used the metaphor of himself as a black crow flying high above and looking down at the world, interpreting it through his sociological training and dispensing it to the people.[145] Du Bois carried this approach into his 1915 work *The Negro*. Here he challenged racial prejudice through a historical and contemporary study of blacks in Africa and throughout the world. A global history, Du Bois contended, would be incomplete without reference to Africa, and he gave the continent a central role in the development of human civilization. Such a project was not very different from the one the freethinker Winwood Reade had originally conceived in the 1870s,[146] and Du Bois quoted him approvingly later in the work.[147] In a subsequent work, *The World and Africa* (1946), Du Bois even wrote, "[o]ne always turns back to Winwood Reade's *The Martyrdom of Man* for renewal of faith."[148]

It should be noted, however, that later in life Du Bois grew weary of what Ibram X. Kendi has called the strategy of "educational persuasion" – namely the idea that racism is the result of ignorance and the solution is therefore to provide facts to disprove it.[149] In an essay in 1935, Du Bois reflected that black leaders used to think that "white Americans did not know of or realize the continuing plight of the Negro." Therefore, it was simply a matter of educating them about the facts, which would in theory change their minds. But, he continued, "[t]oday there can be no doubt that Americans know the facts; and yet they remain for the most part unmoved."[150] Rather than waiting indefinitely for whites to abandon racism, Du Bois instead counseled blacks that in order to attain equality it would be necessary for some kind of "organized and deliberate self-segregation" to develop their own economic and educational institutions.[151]

In the first part of the twentieth century, however, Du Bois still had faith in educational persuasion. In *The Negro*, he critiqued scientific theories about blacks. Scientific attempts to find the perfect example of "an extreme type of black, ugly, and woolly-haired Negro" had proved futile. The lesson in this was that "no scientific definition of race is possible." There were differences between humans, he acknowledged, "but they fade into each other so insensibly that we can only indicate the main divisions of men in broad outlines." On the futility of a quest to define the races, he quoted the Austrian anthropologist Felix von Luschan, who drew parallels with medieval Christian philosophizing: "It is of no more importance now to know how many humans races there are than to know how many angels can dance on the point of a needle."[152] Such a comparison was, as we have seen, common among other freethinkers, who noted that race prejudice was no different from other forms of religious superstition. Later in the book, Du Bois refuted arguments about black inferiority from a scientific perspective. He deemed the argument that blacks had smaller brains to be "an unproved assumption" that was based on faulty measurements, and stated that even if blacks' brains were on average smaller or lighter, there was no proof that this influenced mental faculties. Finally, he concluded by quoting from Gustav Spiller's paper at the congress, itself quoting Friedrich Ratzel: "We may, therefore, say with Ratzel, 'There is only one species of man. The variations are numerous, but do not go deep.'"[153]

At the congress, Du Bois gave a matter-of-fact, statistical account of the condition of blacks in America. "[A]lthough hard pressed by economic and mental strain," Du Bois argued, the black race "is more than holding its own."[154] Despite worrying signs of race prejudice toward blacks, he was nonetheless optimistic that "[t]here are some signs that the prejudice in the South is not immovable, and now and then voices of protest and signs of liberal thought appear there."[155] In an article in the *Crisis*, Du Bois reflected that there had been other world congresses that did not broach the subject of race, including religious ones. As he said, "[t]he Church has repeatedly dodged and temporized with race prejudice."[156] Looking back in his autobiography, Du Bois believed that the congress "was a great and inspiring occasion bringing together representatives of numerous ethnic and cultural groups and bringing new and frank conceptions of scientific bases of racial and social relations of people."[157]

As I noted above, historians of the Universal Races Congress have largely ignored the role played by atheists and freethinkers. This was noticed at the time as well. The *Freethinker* reported on the congress, noting that it was "a laudable endeavor to bring about a better understanding between people of different races and nations" and wishing it success. However,

> the religious press has been anxious to exploit the gathering in the interests of Christianity. Much has been written about its being an expression of the Christian conscience, etc., etc., and the fact that the Congress was suggested by Freethinkers, has been largely engineered by Freethinkers, and a good proportion of Freethinkers take part in its proceedings, being conveniently ignored. We are too much accustomed to this game to be greatly surprised at its being played on the present occasion.[158]

Such a perspective undoubtedly remains valid, as historical works do not discuss the influence of freethinkers explicitly. Nonetheless, as the article in the *Freethinker* stated, and as I suggested here, the congress could not have taken place without the influence of freethinkers.

Conclusion

Earlier chapters have shown how scientific conceptions of race could be pressed into service to justify racism. Here, however, we have seen that white atheists could use science and reason, the foundations of the freethought worldview, against racist ideas. The criticisms of racism mounted by these figures were not just coincidentally related to their atheism, but rather closely intertwined with it. For these thinkers, racial prejudice was an irrational and unscientific superstition that needed to be outgrown. Such an argument tacitly accepted the notion of civilizational progress – a notion that could be used to reinforce the inferiority of certain races. This narrative of progress was retained here, but was deployed to opposite ends. In this alternative narrative, the eventual demise of racial prejudice, like witchcraft or primitive religious ideas, would occur as civilization progressed. One's own society could not truly be considered civilized, some suggested, until racism had been extinguished.

Darwinian evolution was another tool that freethinkers used against racism. Earlier we saw that evolution offered mixed lessons with regard to race. While Darwin himself supported a monogenist version of evolution, one could also interpret evolution in racist ways that emphasized the innate backwardness of some races or their separate evolutionary paths. In this chapter, however, we have seen how Darwinism could support the belief that all humans were a single species and that there was no basis for ranking races hierarchically. Furthermore, an environmentalist conception of evolution showed that circumstances mattered most in accounting for social and physical differences between populations, not innate and immutable biology. Indeed, such talk of unchanging and primordial racial essences became ludicrous in an evolutionary perspective in which all organisms were constantly in a state of change. Empirical science more generally also served to refute racist ideas. While in the mid-nineteenth century some anthropologists measured skulls as a way to determine racial inferiority, Franz Boas used precisely these same methods to come to opposite conclusions, namely that human biology was much more malleable than had been assumed. Likewise, studies of the achievements of non-white people at universities, as done by Gustav Spiller, again showed that there was no incapacity among certain races to match their white counterparts.

One of the themes of this book has been the importance of atheists' marginalization within their own societies, and how this positioning informed their skepticism of claims about racial or civilizational superiority. While the figures discussed in this chapter were already religiously unorthodox, many of them were further marked as different in some way from the Anglo-Saxon majority.[159] Most obvious was W.E.B. Du Bois, an African

American, yet others were also aware of their difference. James Morton endured taunts about his red hair, while J.M. Robertson's Scottish heritage may have contributed to his disagreement with notions of Celtic peculiarity in comparison with the Saxons. Both Felix Adler and Franz Boas were of German Jewish descent and knew the realities of anti-Semitism, while Gustav Spiller was a Hungarian immigrant living in Britain. It seems likely, then, that all of these individuals felt some kind of marginalization on account of their outsider status, and that this in turn influenced their opposition to racial prejudice. Nonetheless, the language with which they attacked racial prejudice was ultimately informed by their freethought.

Conclusion:
what next for racism
in a godless world?

This book began with a question: did secularization pave the way for racism, as some have thought, or did it actually provide new ways to challenge racism? In this concluding section, I want to take stock of the broader lessons that can be gleaned from the study of nineteenth-century atheists' and freethinkers' racial views and to carry the story, if cursorily, into the present. Doing so will, I hope, shed light on more general questions about the nature of secularization.

The central theme of this book has been ambivalence. I have argued that on the one hand, white atheists and freethinkers accepted the common racial science of the time that argued for the biological superiority of white people and the civilizational supcriority of western societies. On the other hand, these same white atheists and freethinkers were skeptical of the claims of racial and civilizational superiority because of their own marginalization within their societies, on account of their irreligious views but also, often, their class.

At times white atheists and freethinkers put forth views that today we would describe as racist. One thinks, for example, of Charles Bradlaugh's embrace of polygenesis, and of secular scientific racists like Josiah Nott and James Hunt who argued for the vast differences between races. Others, like T.H. Huxley or Edward Aveling, constructed an evolutionary hierarchy in which non-white races acted as a midway point between apes and civilized whites. Crude caricatures also appeared in the writings of freethinkers like Eugene MacDonald or Elmina Drake Slenker, who saw African Americans as degraded, superstitious, and inferior to whites. Other caricatures included the Irish as a dangerous horde of Catholic dupes, as in the Watson Heston cartoons, and Chinese immigrants as an unassimilable foreign menace, as so many west-coast atheists thought. One can also point to depictions of the Maori as violent and primitive savages, as Charles Southwell believed, or to George Holyoake's rants against the ungovernable character of Indians. Here, these atheists and freethinkers broadly followed the trends of their own societies, albeit often with a secular bent.

At other times, however, atheists and freethinkers expressed ideas that went against the racist grain of their times. This is not to say that atheists were the lone voices contesting racism, but it is reasonable to suggest that they were disproportionately in that camp. One thinks here of Horace Seaver, who responded to a Native American freethinker that the freethought movement welcomed all regardless of race, or of Moncure Conway, who argued that racial prejudice was pathological and not in accordance with reason. Annie Besant and Charles Bradlaugh (despite his polygenist racism) championed India's rights against claims of British superiority, and Robert Ingersoll attacked the xenophobia inherent in the anti-Chinese immigration movement and the prejudice of those who would deny equal rights to black Americans. George Holyoake's "London Zulu" character showed how skepticism could bridge racial divides through a shared commitment to freethought, while W.P. Ball contended that both atheists and the Maori suffered at the hands of more powerful Christians. Hubert Harrison and W.E.B. Du Bois both drew upon the language of science and reason to confront ideas about the inferiority of black people, while James Morton and J.M. Robertson believed that the teaching of Darwinism made clear that all humanity was one and that this meant racial prejudice was nothing more than an outdated superstition. These views, of which many more could be cited, were far outside the mainstream of their own societies' thinking on race.

For much of the history of atheism, atheists and other nonreligious people sat at the margins of their society because of their nonreligious views; in the nineteenth century, these same figures were often economically and politically marginalized as well. This combination of a commitment to science and reason with a skepticism toward one's own society often led to constructive outcomes. Mitchell Stephens, in his recent work on the history of atheism, shows that atheists were frequently ahead of their times, questioning social and political taboos and adopting radical positions in favor of democracy, abolition, women's rights, and freedom of speech.[1] We should be wary of being too triumphalist about the achievements of historical atheists or of imagining that they would be completely in step with twenty-first-century values, but it does seem to be true, in general, that atheists adopted positions that were radical in their own times but are commonplace now.

Part of this progressiveness may have come from a commitment to science and reason, and a willingness to follow evidence regardless of social taboos. But also important was the fact that atheists glimpsed their societies from the perspectives of outsiders, which forced them to be skeptical about the status quo and to be willing to imagine new futures. Atheists, one might suggest, have a skeptical disposition in their minds that makes them willing to question all of society's sacred cows. This is obviously the case for religion but also extends to other aspects of social and political life. Whether this pattern will continue in the future is a question I take up below.

The twentieth century

Now, however, I wish to briefly sketch some developments in the twentieth century with regard to atheism and race. Perhaps the starkest of these was the emergence of an increasingly vocal number of black atheists and freethinkers in America. Their story has been well charted already by Christopher Cameron, but it is worth highlighting particularly those involved in the Harlem Renaissance and the push for civil rights in the latter half of the century.

The Harlem Renaissance – also called the New Negro Renaissance – was an efflorescence of black intellectual, cultural, and artistic production in the neighborhood of Harlem, New York, in the 1920s and 1930s. Many of its leaders were freethinkers, and of particular interest is the increased prominence of black atheist women, including Zora Neale Hurston and Nella Larsen. Hurston, a deist and materialist according to Cameron, was an anthropologist of folklore who studied under Franz Boas. She was, however, more sympathetic than some of her fellow black freethinkers to African

American religion, writing for example about the empowerment available through the practice of hoodoo. Meanwhile, Alain Locke, a philosopher educated at Harvard and Oxford, is generally credited as the founder of the Harlem Renaissance because of his 1925 book *The New Negro*, which argued that the path to black emancipation would come through black art and culture, and not religion, which in his view only encouraged tribalism. Locke became a member of the Bahá'í faith because of its emphasis on unity and world peace, even as he rejected its monotheist underpinning. Other authors of the Harlem Renaissance, like the poet Langston Hughes and the novelist Nella Larsen, similarly criticized black Christianity's inability to address racism. The works of both Larsen and Hurston would also take the religion to task for its maintenance of gender inequality.[2]

In black freethought, and in freethought in general for that matter, there is a strong tradition of socialism and other forms of political radicalism. We have already seen examples in earlier chapters, particularly in the work of Hubert Harrison and W.E.B. Du Bois, who took up socialism relatively late in life. Political radicalism among black atheists and freethinkers would continue throughout the twentieth century. Other black socialists and communists included Richard Wright, Claude McKay, Audley Moore, and Grace P. Campbell.[3] The stereotyped view is that the civil rights activism of the 1950s and 1960s was almost entirely religiously based, especially given the towering importance accorded to Martin Luther King Jr. in the popular imagination. There is undoubtedly much truth to this picture of course, since religion did animate much of the civil rights struggle, but to overlook African American atheists in this movement is to do them a great injustice.[4] These activists possessed worldviews that were not grounded in Christianity, but in secular humanist philosophy. They included such diverse individuals as the organizer of the 1963 March on Washington, A. Philip Randolph, the Black Power leader Stokely Carmichael, the Student Nonviolent Coordinating Committee organizer James Forman, and the Black Panther Party co-founder Huey Newton. Numerous African American literary figures, including Lorraine Hansberry, James Baldwin, and Alice Walker, were likewise influenced by freethought.[5]

As we have seen, atheists and freethinkers were at the forefront of critiques of scientific racism at the turn of the century, and this pattern would continue into the twentieth century. In the interwar years and particularly after the Second World War, the biological basis of racism came increasingly under attack. Leading the charge were white British atheist scientists who drew from the emerging field of genetics, which was pioneered in the first part of the twentieth century following the re-discovery of the work of Gregor Mendel from the mid-nineteenth century and its incorporation into Darwinian evolutionary theory. These scientists included J.B.S. Haldane, Lancelot Hogben, and Julian Huxley, who was the grandson of T.H. Huxley and the first president of the British Humanist Association upon its founding in 1963.[6]

Many prominent white atheist activists also took up the fight against racism in the twentieth century. Here I consider two of the most well-known on either side of the Atlantic, Madalyn Murray O'Hair in the United States and Bertrand Russell in Britain. O'Hair gained prominence by launching a successful legal challenge – eventually reaching the Supreme Court – that would lead to the end of compelled Bible reading in schools in the early 1960s, and by founding the organization American Atheists in 1963. She was, however, by many accounts an unpleasant person, and she funneled hundreds of thousands of dollars from American Atheists into her own pocket. She met a gruesome end: she was murdered, along with her son and granddaughter, by an aggrieved former employee.

Before she began her atheist activism, however, she was involved with many other causes, including desegregation. As her biographer writes, during the late 1950s, before she became a public figure, and while living in Baltimore, "[s]he picketed the segregated White Tower restaurants in her area, and lobbied against blacks' exclusion from certain public parks. She participated in 'the Route 40 fight,' getting restaurants on the highway to serve black diplomats traveling from the United Nations to Washington."[7] Politically, O'Hair was a communist and made an application to defect to the USSR, which was ultimately rejected. In her application, she wrote that one of the reasons for applying was that "I have certain convictions regarding eqality [sic] for women, for races, and for minority groups, which are unacceptable by the nation."[8]

Bertrand Russell, although worlds apart from O'Hair, also became one of the most famous atheists of the twentieth century. He was a member of the

British aristocracy, albeit from a radical family, and was actually the godson of John Stuart Mill. Russell made his name as a philosopher and mathematician at Cambridge, and through his work *Why I Am Not a Christian* (1927), originally delivered as a lecture to the National Secular Society. Russell was opposed to imperialism and militarism for the vast majority of his life. He had long been a critic of the British Empire, particularly in India, for which he supported independence. Later in life, he became increasingly worried about American foreign dominance and was therefore deeply critical of the Vietnam War.[9] In his *War Crimes in Vietnam* (1967), Russell wrote,

> The racism of the West, especially that of the United States, has created an atmosphere in which it is extremely difficult to make clear the responsibility of America for problems which are held to be "internal" to the underdeveloped countries. The war in Vietnam is looked upon as the inevitable and tragic product of backwardness, poverty and savagery – supposedly indigenous to South East Asia.[10]

Russell was also a long-term supporter of the rights of African Americans. In a speech in 1942, he said that "[t]he Negroes [...] represent the greatest failure of democracy in the United States, and until some justice is accorded to them it cannot be maintained that democracy exists here."[11] Russell condemned restrictions on black voting rights, segregation (whether by law or custom), and the violence and economic discrimination faced by black people. In that same speech, he also highlighted ludicrous racist practices, for example the American Red Cross's decision to give donated African American blood only to other African Americans: "A population which tolerates or expects such action by the Red Cross has no right to pose as the champion of democracy, or to feel morally superior to Hitler."[12] Russell was fully supportive of the civil rights movement, for example backing the famous March on Washington, which took place in 1963, and corresponding with civil rights activists throughout the 1960s.[13]

But the twentieth century also held some surprising developments with regard to the links between atheism and racial thought. The most shocking is that the *Truth Seeker* – the flagship paper for American freethought in the second half of the nineteenth century – was taken over by genuine white supremacists and anti-Semites in 1937, when George Macdonald relinquished his duties as editor. First Charles Lee Smith and then his successor

James Hervey Johnson continued the publication, combining atheism with racism and anti-Semitism over the remaining decades of the twentieth century. In their view, Jewish schemes for power involved foisting doctrines of equality on whites, who would bring about their own demise because they overlooked the threat of being outbred by non-white races. In one 1961 article, Smith painted a picture of whites, deluded by Jewish doctrines of equality and of helping the needy, unwittingly encouraging black "breeding" by helping to support unwed black mothers and their children: "As their sexual desires direct[,] the Blacks breed. As their Jew-revealed duty, the Whites take care of the results." To remedy the problem, Smith suggested that unwed black women be paid to undergo sterilization.[14] James Hervey Johnson put it even more bluntly in linking anti-Semitism and racism: "The Jews who seek to control the Whites are using the Blacks as shock troops to carry out their own purposes."[15] One reader, the prolific socialist philosopher Corliss Lamont, did, however, write to the paper to express his misgivings about the racist direction the paper had taken. "While finding much useful material in this journal opposing supernaturalism," he wrote, "I must protest vigorously against the fascist attitude which your magazine has been taking in reference to the Jews and Negroes in the United States." He continued, "[...] I am ashamed of you, who profess to be a freethinker, for being as backward and bigoted as any supernaturalist who walks the earth today." Finally, "I urge you and your associates on The Truth Seeker to adopt a policy on racial minorities which is consonant with the great tradition of freethought."[16]

As the century wore on, the magazine became increasingly extreme. In an article from 1975, for example, Johnson praised a leader of a Neo-Nazi party who was killed, apparently in an interparty squabble, as "a man of fearless courage" who "had led whites in a number of marches where he was attacked by negroes and mobs of Jews." Johnson also criticized "Jewish controlled papers" that called the leader an extremist – "a smear directed against anyone who is critical of the U.S. Jewish dictatorship."[17] By this point, however, the *Truth Seeker* was far outside the mainstream of the atheist movement and reached only a few hundred subscribers.[18] Happily, the *Truth Seeker* has come under new management in recent years – now edited by Roderick Bradford – and has excised the previous racism and anti-Semitism from its pages.

What next for atheism and race?

As I have argued, atheists' and other nonreligious people's racial views were based in part upon a commitment to science and reason, but also on a skeptical disposition and a contrarian streak. This "skeptical software" can be a great boon to humanity, as atheists have put forth radical political and social views that would later become commonplace. But it also has the potential to lead in negative directions. In the nineteenth century, racism was accepted with little question by the white majority, yet today it has become taboo and those who advocate it are often rendered pariahs. This newfound taboo status for racism has, however, led some atheists – naturally inclined to question all taboos – to become interested in exploring the merits of racist ideas. This is skepticism gone haywire.

As secularization continues and atheists and nonreligious people move from the periphery to the mainstream, there is therefore a danger that the tools of rationality and science could be deployed once again to re-entrench racist ideas. Of course, one might contend that rationality and science are neutral: the facts are simply the facts, whether we like it or not. I agree that reason and science are the best tools we have to gain knowledge about the world, but these same tools have been misused in the past and could be again. Certainly there is enough evidence of that littered throughout this book. For example, Eugene Macdonald – discussed earlier – argued that it was simply science that dictated the inequality of races. As he said, "[i]t would be as reasonable to enact a statute against the thunder and lightning as one proclaiming the equality of the white and colored races."[19] The fact that so many nineteenth-century whites – atheists and otherwise – confidently proclaimed the inferiority of non-white races on scientific grounds should give us pause about what we take as simply objective, scientific facts today.

Indeed, this caution is particularly important now, as there appears to be a growing section of the contemporary atheist movement which is willing to question the sacred cows of our present liberal consensus, particularly the theoretical equality of all people regardless of race and gender. This is not to say that the majority of atheists question these views, but there is an increasing tendency among some atheists today to entertain arguments about, say, the existence of distinct races and the ways in which they could be ranked hierarchically, particularly with regard to IQ.

Part of this inclination, I think, has to do with the desire to appear as a brave iconoclast who is willing to follow the truth no matter how painful it may be. There was a time when coming out as an atheist was enough to demonstrate one's intellectual fearlessness to others. But as secularization continues and the number of nonreligious people rises, being a nonbeliever no longer carries the shock value it once did. For many who live in religiously conservative communities, this is undoubtedly a welcome development. But for those particularly concerned about demonstrating to others their own intellectual courage, it is now necessary to look further afield. To maintain their image as shocking contrarians, some atheists have gravitated to questioning even more taboo subjects, like racial or gender equality. This, I speculate, begins to explain why some atheists and other nonreligious people are attracted to the "alt-right" movement – a loose network of white supremacists and other far right figures who reject mainstream conservatism and desire the creation of a white "ethno-state."

Stephen LeDrew touches upon the ways in which conservativism has entered into contemporary atheist thought in his work *The Evolution of Atheism*.[20] He has in mind mainstream conservative ideas about the value of free markets, limited government intervention in society, and an aggressive foreign policy, but the links between the far right and atheists are, in my view, even more concerning. The alt-right appears to be growing in the United States (and elsewhere), and while this movement is heterogeneous with regard to religion, there is undoubtedly a sizeable contingent – although it is unclear how big – of atheists and other secular thinkers within it. George Hawley explains in his book *Making Sense of the Alt-Right* that "[t]he Alt-Right is (for the most part) secular in its orientation and hostile to the politicized Christianity that dominated Republican politics since the late 1970s."[21] This hostility to Christianity draws variously from Friedrich Nietzsche's criticism of the religion as fostering a "slave morality," a rejection of the universalist premise of Christianity, and a revulsion for the Jewish roots of Christianity.[22]

Most clearly, the outspoken white supremacist Richard Spencer, who coined the term "alt-right" and was recorded giving a Nazi salute following

Donald Trump's election, identifies himself as an atheist, even as he calls himself a "cultural Christian."[23] In one interview, Spencer links his atheism to his racism, noting that he rejects monotheism because it says that "we are 'all one' [...]."[24] This is clearly an echo of the polygenist freethinkers who rejected Christianity in part because of its commitment to a universalist monogenism. In an interview with Hawley, Spencer says, "[i]f I were to sum up your average Alt-Righter, [...] I would probably say someone who is thirty years old, who is a tech professional, who is an atheist, and who lives on one of the coasts."[25]

This is certainly not to suggest that all or even most atheists and secular people are flocking to the alt-right. Most appear to remain on the left politically, but this should not allow us to become complacent, and we should seek to understand why some atheists have begun to drift in their direction. Chris Stedman perhaps best sums up the appeal of the alt-right to atheists:

> The taboo-confronting ethos of both movements, where irreverence is idealized and often weaponized, enables some of their members to style themselves as oppressed outsiders – despite often being relatively privileged straight white men. Many in the alt-right and atheist movements seem to see themselves as a group under siege, the last defenders of unfettered inquiry and absolute freedom of thought and speech, contrarians and truth-tellers who are unafraid to push back against the norms of polite, liberal society.[26]

As I observed above, this contrarianism has been valuable in the past, but poses serious challenges for the present.

To be alarmed by the movement of atheists into the alt-right is not, however, to buy into the narrative that atheists today are racist because they criticize Islam. Certainly this is true of some: Muslims in western societies are more often than not brown or black people, and we should be aware that seemingly race-neutral criticisms can be based in racial prejudice. But this can also be a cheap way to blunt any and all criticism of Islam. The white atheist thinker and neuroscientist Sam Harris has probably been the biggest victim of this form of criticism. He has written a number of books critiquing religion, but his critiques of Islam have been brushed aside with the charge of racism and bigotry and without any sustained analysis of his actual arguments.

As one example, the journalist Murtaza Hussain suggests that the critiques of Islam made by people like Harris hark back to centuries past, when thinkers sought to give their racial prejudices a scientific cover: "Harris engages in a nuanced version of the same racism which his predecessors in scientific racism practiced in their discussion of the blanket characteristics of 'Negroes.'"[27] This is hyperbolic, and Harris has actually been careful to emphasize that Muslims are not monolithic. This is seen mostly clearly in a recent book, co-authored with Maajid Nawaz, where the two discuss the diversity of perspectives in Islam. They agree that only a small minority are jihadists (those who wish to impose Islam on society through force), while a larger group may be sympathetic to the aims of jihadists but not willing to carry out attacks themselves, and a still larger group is not sympathetic to the aims of jihadism at all, but nonetheless hold illiberal views that might call for the prosecution of blasphemy or the repression of women's rights. They acknowledge that there are, as well, numerous liberal Muslims as well as secular individuals within Muslim societies who have a very limited voice.[28] Whether one accepts their points or not, it is absurd to equate this perspective with the crude racism of centuries past.

Harris has also faced criticism for his decision in April 2017 to have as a guest on his popular podcast Charles Murray, the co-author of the hugely controversial book *The Bell Curve* (1994), which among other things made the case that genetic differences might account for at least some of the IQ gaps between different racial groups.[29] During the interview, Harris appeared to endorse much of Murray's science, yet he also insisted that he had no personal interest in the topic and wanted only to understand the taboo around discussing racial differences. As our understanding of genetics grows by the day, he argues, society should be ready in the event that it is discovered that there are indeed psychological differences between population groups. In his view, the right response to such a discovery would be to continue to treat people as individuals and not on the basis of their group identity.

Critics have, however, charged Harris with treating Murray too uncritically by accepting his scientific conclusions as undisputed fact and failing to deal with Murray's conservative political agenda, which would roll back affirmative action and early childhood interventions to raise IQ. Many of these issues came to a head in a debate between Harris and the journalist

Ezra Klein. There Klein argued that Harris's adopted posture as an unbiased scientist, dealing rationally with the facts, was not tenable, but rather that Harris had his own biases that informed his perspective.[30] Whichever side of the debate one falls on, Harris's foray into race differences in IQ is part of a larger interest in flouting liberal taboos among atheists and other nonreligious people. This is not to suggest that people like Harris are necessarily malicious – although some certainly are – but only to say that we seem to be moving into a new phase in the story of atheism and race.

This book has argued that despite the ambivalence that has historically characterized atheists' views on race, there was an anti-racist perspective within the atheist and freethought tradition that was rooted in science, reason, and skepticism, but that was also encouraged by the social and economic circumstances in which atheists and freethinkers found themselves. There is, however, a danger now that, as atheists and other nonreligious people move into the majority, this skepticism will be redirected and that science and reason will instead be used to buttress the status quo by insisting on the innateness of race and gender differences.

Some historians of race and racism have suggested that Christianity held the tools with which to confront the rising tide of racism – through either the idea that all humans descended from Adam and Eve or the idea that God created humanity in his own image – and that consequently we should lament that secularization has removed these tools from the anti-racist toolkit. From my perspective, such a religious defense was ultimately inadequate, since it rested on unsound premises that sooner or later would be found wanting. By contrast, science and reason – if at times deployed toward unsavory ends – still seem to provide the most reliable grounds on which to confront racism. But this can work only when paired with an unrelenting skeptical attitude, especially to one's own cherished ideas. Atheists, both historically and now, have been especially good at turning their skepticism toward others' ideas. As secularization pushes atheists and other nonreligious people from the periphery to the center, what will be needed most of all is for this same skepticism to be turned inward.

Notes

1 See Phil Zuckerman, "Atheism: Contemporary Numbers and Patterns," in *The Cambridge Companion to Atheism*, ed. Michael Martin (Cambridge: Cambridge University Press, 2007), 47–65.

2 Some case studies of atheism and race are John Stenhouse, "Imperialism, Atheism, and Race: Charles Southwell, Old Corruption, and the Maori," *Journal of British Studies* 44, no. 4 (October 2005): 754–74; Jeremy Rich, "Heresy Is the Only True Religion: Richard Lynch Garner (1848–1920), a Southern Freethinker in Africa and America," *Journal of the Gilded Age and Progressive Era* 12, no. 1 (January 2013): 65–94. Recent works that chart the history of atheism in North America have touched on race, but not in detail: Leigh Eric Schmidt, *Village Atheists: How America's Unbelievers Made Their Way in a Godly Nation* (Princeton and Oxford: Princeton University Press, 2016); Lynne Marks, *Infidels and the Damn Churches: Irreligion and Religion in Settler British Columbia* (Vancouver: University of British Columbia Press, 2017). Some of the links between atheism, race, and science in France have been treated in Jennifer Michael Hecht, *The End of the Soul: Scientific Modernity, Atheism, and Anthropology in France, 1876–1936* (New York: Columbia University Press, 2003). See also Jonathon S. Kahn and Vincent W. Lloyd, eds., *Race and Secularism in America* (New York: Columbia University Press, 2016). In this latter volume, "secularism" refers to the management of religion, usually by the state or some other often nebulous force, but this has very little to do with the secularism I am talking about.

3 For some examples, see Philip D. Curtin, *The Image of Africa: British Ideas and Action, 1780–1850* (London: Macmillan and Co., Limited, 1965); Christine Bolt, *Victorian Attitudes to Race* (London: Routledge & Keegan Paul, 1971); George M. Fredrickson, *The Black Image in the White Mind: The Debate on Afro-American Character and Destiny, 1817–1914* (New York: Harper & Row, 1971); John S. Haller, *Outcasts from Evolution: Scientific Attitudes of Racial*

Inferiority, 1859–1900 (Urbana: University of Illinois Press, 1971); Douglas Lorimer, *Colour, Class, and the Victorians: English Attitudes to the Negro in the Mid-Nineteenth Century* (Leicester: Leicester University Press, 1978); Thomas F. Gossett, *Race: The History of an Idea in America*, New Edition (New York and Oxford: Oxford University Press, 1997 [1963]); Douglas Lorimer, *Science, Race Relations and Resistance: Britain, 1870–1914* (Manchester: Manchester University Press, 2013).

4 I use "freethinker" as an umbrella term to mean all those who specifically rejected revealed religions, even if some may have continued to believe in a creator God. By "atheist," I mean someone who rejects the idea of God altogether. Atheists therefore fit under the larger category of freethinker. Also considered under the category of freethinker are other irreligious identities like agnostics, deists, secularists, and so on.

5 Colin Kidd, *The Forging of Races: Race and Scripture in the Protestant Atlantic World, 1600–2000* (Cambridge: Cambridge University Press, 2006), 19.

6 Ibid., 20; see also Timothy Larsen, "The Book of Acts and the Origin of the Races in Evangelical Thought," *Victorian Review* 37, no. 2 (Fall 2011): 35–39.

7 George M. Fredrickson, *Racism: A Short History* (Princeton: Princeton University Press, 2002), 18–26, 31–35; Francisco Bethencourt, *Racisms: From the Crusades to the Twentieth Century* (Princeton and Oxford: Princeton University Press, 2013), 148–51.

8 Rebecca Anne Goetz, *The Baptism of Early Virginia: How Christianity Created Race* (Baltimore: Johns Hopkins University Press, 2012); see also Paul Harvey, *Christianity and Race in the American South: A History* (Chicago and London: University of Chicago Press, 2016), 19–22.

9 Fredrickson, *Racism*, 47.

10 Carl Linnaeus, *A General System of Nature*, trans. William Turton (London: Printed for Lackington, Allen, and Co., 1802), 1:9.

11 See chapter 15 of Bethencourt, *Racisms*.

12 Fredrickson, *Racism*, 57; see also Richard H. Popkin, "The Philosophical Basis of Eighteenth-Century Racism," *Studies in Eighteenth-Century Culture* 3 (1973): 253–54.

13 On Jefferson's religion, see Paul K. Conkin, "The Religious Pilgrimage of Thomas Jefferson," in *Jeffersonian Legacies*, ed. Peter S. Onuf (Charlottesville: University Press of Virginia, 1993), 19–49; Charles B. Sanford, *The Religious Life of Thomas Jefferson* (Charlottesville: University Press of Virginia, 1984).

14 Thomas Jefferson, *Notes on the State of Virginia* (1785) in Paul Leicester Ford, ed., *The Works of Thomas Jefferson* (New York and London: G.P. Putnam's Sons, 1904), 4:51–52.

15 Ibid., 4:82–83.

16 Ibid., 4:83.

17 Ibid., 4:49.

Notes

18 The literature on Jefferson is massive, but a good analysis of the current scholarship can be found in Paul Finkelman, "Thomas Jefferson and Antislavery: The Myth Goes On," *Virginia Magazine of History and Biography* 102, no. 2 (April 1994): 193–228; see also Cassandra Pybus, "Thomas Jefferson and Slavery," in *A Companion to Thomas Jefferson*, ed. Francis D. Cogliano (Hoboken, NJ: Wiley-Blackwell, 2011), 271–83.

19 See Annette Gordon-Reed, *The Hemingses of Monticello: An American Family* (New York and London: W.W. Norton & Company, 2008).

20 See chapter 4 of Kidd, *Forging of Races*.

21 Thomas Paine, *The Age of Reason*, Part I, in *The Writings of Thomas Paine*, ed. Moncure Conway, vol. 4 (New York and London: G.P. Putnam's Sons, 1896), 21.

22 Though Paine is sometimes credited with anonymously authoring an abolitionist work called "African Slavery in America" in 1775, there is actually no evidence of this. That work is found in *The Writings of Thomas Paine*, ed. Moncure Conway, vol. 1 (New York and London: G.P. Putnam's Sons, 1894), 4–9. Alfred Owen Aldridge disputes that this article was written by Paine: Alfred Owen Aldridge, *Thomas Paine's American Ideology* (Newark: University of Delaware Press, 1984), 289–91.

23 Thomas Paine, "The Forester's Letters" (April–May 1776), in *Writings of Thomas Paine*, ed. Conway, 1:154.

24 Edward Needles, *An Historical Memoir of the Pennsylvania Society for Promoting the Abolition of Slavery* (Philadelphia: Merrihew and Thompson, 1848), 29; see also Mariam Touba, "Paine's Antislavery Legacy: Some Additional Considerations," First International Conference of Thomas Paine Studies, Iona College, 2012, http://thomaspaine.org/front/2016/04/16/paines-antislavery-legacy-by-mariam-touba/, accessed March 9, 2018.

25 Moncure Conway, *The Life of Thomas Paine: With a History of His Literary, Political, and Religious Career in America, France, and England* (New York and London: G.P. Putnam's Sons, 1892), 2:344–48.

26 Hannah Franziska Augstein, ed., *Race: The Origins of an Idea, 1760–1850* (Bristol: Thoemmes Press, 1996), xxv.

27 Ibid., xxxii.

28 For some examples, see chapter 1 of Bolt, *Victorian Attitudes to Race*; Michael Banton, *The Idea of Race* (London: Tavistock Publications, 1977), 46–53; C. Loring Brace, *"Race" is a Four-Letter Word: The Genesis of the Concept* (Oxford: Oxford University Press, 2005), 110–19, 125–43; Bethencourt, *Racisms*, 275–79, 283–88; and chapter 15 of Curtin, *Image of Africa*.

29 William Stanton, *The Leopard's Spots: Scientific Attitudes Toward Race in America, 1815–59* (Chicago and London: University of Chicago Press, 1960), 3–10, 123–36.

30 George W. Stocking Jr., *Victorian Anthropology* (New York: Free Press, 1987), 49.

31 Augstein, *Race*, xxii.

32 For one example of such arguments, see Thornton Stringfellow, *Slavery: Its Origin, Nature, and History, Considered in the Light of Bible Teachings, Moral Justice, and Political Wisdom* (New York: John F. Trow, 1861).

33 On Christian justifications for slavery, see chapter 4 of Harvey, *Christianity and Race*.

34 Forrest G. Wood, *The Arrogance of Faith: Christianity and Race in America from the Colonial Era to the Twentieth Century* (Boston: Northeastern University Press, 1991), xviii.

35 Ibid., 277–87.

36 Ibid., 106, 215.

37 See for example Bolt, *Victorian Attitudes to Race*, 207; Curtin, *Image of Africa*, 363–64.

38 Richard Weikart, *From Darwin to Hitler: Evolutionary Ethics, Eugenics, and Racism in Germany* (New York: Palgrave Macmillan, 2004), 103.

39 Ibid., 6.

40 See for example Robert J. Richards, "Myth 19 – That Darwin and Haeckel Were Complicit in Nazi Biology," in *Galileo Goes to Jail: And Other Myths about Science and Religion*, ed. Ronald L. Numbers (Cambridge, MA: Harvard University Press, 2009), 170–77.

41 Adrian Desmond and James Moore, *Darwin's Sacred Cause: How a Hatred of Slavery Shaped Darwin's Views on Human Evolution* (Boston and New York: Houghton Mifflin Harcourt, 2009).

42 Daniel J. Kevles, *In the Name of Eugenics: Genetics and the Uses of Human Heredity* (New York: Alfred A. Knopf, 1985), 74–75, 96–97, 168.

43 Ibid., 12.

44 Ibid., 64.

45 Douglas Lorimer, "Science and the Secularization of Victorian Images of Race," in *Victorian Science in Context*, ed. Bernard Lightman (Chicago and London: University of Chicago Press, 1997), 212–13.

46 Ibid., 214.

47 Ibid., 215.

48 Terence Keel, *Divine Variations: How Christian Thought Became Racial Science* (Stanford, CA: Stanford University Press, 2018), 20–21.

49 Kidd, *Forging of Races*, 271.

50 A similar approach has been taken by Christine Ferguson in her work on spiritualists and race: Christine Ferguson, *Determined Spirits: Eugenics, Heredity and Racial Regeneration in Anglo-American Spiritualist Writing, 1848–1930* (Edinburgh: Edinburgh University Press, 2012).

51 There is a large literature on the history of atheism. See Michael J. Buckley, *At the Origins of Modern Atheism* (New Haven and London: Yale University Press, 1987); David Berman, *A History of Atheism in Britain: From Hobbes to Russell* (London: Croom Helm, 1988); James Thrower, *Western Atheism: A Short History* (Amherst, NY: Prometheus, 2000 [1971]); Nick Spencer, *Atheists: The Origin of the Species* (London: Bloomsbury, 2014); Mitchell Stephens,

Notes

Imagine There's No Heaven: How Atheism Helped Create the Modern World (New York: Palgrave Macmillan, 2014).

52 Recent biographies of Paine include Jack Fruchtman Jr., *Thomas Paine: Apostle of Freedom* (New York and London: Four Walls Eight Windows, 1994); Craig Nelson, *Thomas Paine: Enlightenment, Revolution, and the Birth of Modern Nations* (New York: Viking, 2006).

53 On Paine and his role in the freethought movement, see Edward Royle, *Victorian Infidels: The Origins of the British Secularist Movement, 1791–1866* (Manchester: Manchester University Press, 1974), 26–43; Albert Post, *Popular Freethought in America, 1825–1850* (New York: Columbia University Press, 1943), 22–26, 155–59; Susan Jacoby, *Freethinkers: A History of American Secularism* (New York: Henry Holt and Company, 2004), 36–65.

54 On Owen's life and influence, see Royle, *Victorian Infidels*, 43–53, 59–74; Ian Donnachie, *Robert Owen: Owen of New Lanark and New Harmony* (East Linton: Tuckwell Press, 2000); Robert Davis and Frank O'Hagan, *Robert Owen* (London and New York: Continuum, 2010).

55 Royle, *Victorian Infidels*, 45.

56 For the full debate, see Alexander Campbell, ed., *Debate on the Evidences of Christianity* (London: R. Groombridge, 1839); for a description of the debate, see Post, *Popular Freethought in America*, 131–37.

57 The best sources for Holyoake's life and career are Royle, *Victorian Infidels*; Edward Royle, *Radicals, Secularists and Republicans: Popular Freethought in Britain, 1866–1915* (Manchester: Manchester University Press, 1980); Michael Rectenwald, *Nineteenth-Century British Secularism: Science, Religion and Literature* (Houndmills, Basingstoke, and New York: Palgrave Macmillan, 2016).

58 On Bentham, see James E. Crimmins, "Bentham and Utilitarianism in the Early Nineteenth Century," in *The Cambridge Companion to Utilitarianism*, ed. Ben Eggleston and Dale E. Miller (Cambridge: Cambridge University Press, 2014), 38–60.

59 John Stuart Mill, *Autobiography*, in *The Collected Works of John Stuart Mill*, ed. John M. Robson (Toronto: University of Toronto Press; London: Routledge and Kegan Paul, 1963–91), 1:44.

60 Robert Carr, "The Religious Thought of John Stuart Mill: A Study in Reluctant Scepticism," *Journal of the History of Ideas* 23, no. 4 (December 1962): 475–76.

61 David Tribe, *President Charles Bradlaugh M.P.* (London: Elek, 1971), 110–11.

62 John Stuart Mill, *Three Essays on Religion*, in *Collected Works of John Stuart Mill*, ed. Robson, 10:369–489.

63 The main biographies of Bradlaugh are Hypatia Bradlaugh Bonner and J.M. Robertson, *Charles Bradlaugh: A Record of His Life and Work*, 2 vols. (London: T. Fisher Unwin, 1895); Tribe, *President Charles Bradlaugh*; Bryan Niblett, *Dare to Stand Alone: The Story of Charles Bradlaugh* (Oxford: Kramedart Press, 2010).

64 Royle, *Radicals, Secularists and Republicans*, 132–36.

Notes

65 See A.O.J. Cockshut, *The Unbelievers: English Agnostic Thought, 1840–1890* (London: Collins, 1964); Bernard Lightman, *The Origins of Agnosticism: Victorian Unbelief and the Limits of Knowledge* (Baltimore and London: Johns Hopkins University Press, 1987).

66 Frank Miller Turner, *Between Science and Religion: The Reaction to Scientific Naturalism in Late Victorian England* (New Haven and London: Yale University Press, 1974), 9.

67 Susan Jacoby, *The Great Agnostic: Robert Ingersoll and American Freethought* (New Haven: Yale University Press, 2013), 17.

68 The main sources for Ingersoll's life are C.H. Cramer, *Royal Bob: The Life of Robert G. Ingersoll* (Indianapolis: Bobbs-Merrill, 1952); Orvin Larson, *American Infidel: Robert G. Ingersoll* (New York: Citadel Press, 1962); David D. Anderson, *Robert Ingersoll* (New York: Twayne Publishers Inc., 1972); Jacoby, *The Great Agnostic*.

69 It should be noted that there was a relatively minor freethought newspaper in Britain also called the *Truth Seeker* (published between 1894 and 1915), but in every case, I refer to the American paper.

70 Sidney Warren, *American Freethought, 1860–1914* (New York: Gordian Press, 1966), 35–36, 156–75.

71 T.R. Wright, *The Religion of Humanity: The Impact of Comtean Positivism on Victorian Britain* (Cambridge: Cambridge University Press, 1986), 40–50.

72 Susan Budd, *Varieties of Unbelief: Atheists and Agnostics in English Society 1850–1960* (London: Heinemann, 1977), 190–99.

73 Gillis J. Harp, *Positivist Republic: Auguste Comte and the Reconstruction of American Liberalism, 1865–1920* (University Park, PA: Pennsylvania State University Press, 1995).

74 On ethical societies in Britain and the United States, see Howard B. Radest, *Toward Common Ground: The Story of the Ethical Societies in the United States* (New York: Ungar Publishing, 1969); Colin Campbell, *Toward a Sociology of Irreligion* (London and Basingstoke: Macmillan, 1971), 71–85; Budd, *Varieties of Unbelief*, 188–214.

75 Royle, *Victorian Infidels*, 302; Royle, *Radicals, Secularists and Republicans*, 157–64.

76 Post, *Popular Freethought in America*, 54–56.

77 Warren, *American Freethought*, 230.

78 Ibid., 22.

79 Berman, *Atheism in Britain*, 153–59.

80 On blasphemy, see David Nash, *Blasphemy in the Christian World: A History* (Oxford: Oxford University Press, 2007).

81 Royle, *Radicals, Secularists and Republicans*, 263–64.

82 Ibid., 265.

83 Warren, *American Freethought*, 180–81.

84 Post, *Popular Freethought in America*, 212–13.

85 See Roderick Bradford, *D.M. Bennett: The Truth Seeker* (Amherst, NY: Prometheus, 2006).

86 Royle, *Victorian Infidels*, 304–5; Budd, *Varieties of Unbelief*, 95–98; Royle, *Radicals, Secularists and Republicans*, 126–28.

87 Evelyn A. Kirkley, *Rational Mothers and Infidel Gentlemen: Gender and American Atheism, 1865–1915* (Syracuse, NY: Syracuse University Press, 2000), 22.

88 Post, *Popular Freethought in America*, 69; Warren, *American Freethought*, 119.

89 Adrian Desmond, *Huxley: From Devil's Disciple to Evolution's High Priest* (Reading, MA: Perseus Books, 1997), 525–29.

90 Ruth Barton, "'An Influential Set of Chaps': The X-Club and Royal Society Politics 1864–85," *British Journal for the History of Science* 23, no. 1 (March 1990): 53–81.

91 On gender and freethought, see Kirkley, *Rational Mothers and Infidel Gentlemen*; Laura Schwartz, *Infidel Feminism: Secularism, Religion and Women's Emancipation, England 1830–1914* (Manchester: Manchester University Press, 2011).

92 For the United States, see, for example, Michael Lipka, "10 Facts about Atheists," Pew Research Center, June 1, 2016, www.pewresearch.org/fact-tank/2016/06/01/10-facts-about-atheists/, accessed December 13, 2017; for Britain, see, for example, Linda Woodhead, "The Rise of 'No Religion' in Britain: The Emergence of a New Cultural Majority," *Journal of the British Academy* 4 (December 2016): 251–52.

93 Schmidt, *Village Atheists*, 253; George Vetter and Marin Green, "Personality and Group Factors in the Making of Atheists," *Journal of Abnormal and Social Psychology* 27, no. 2 (1932): 179–94.

94 See Matthew Frye Jacobson, *Whiteness of a Different Color: European Immigrants and the Alchemy of Race*, First Paperback Edition (Cambridge, MA: Harvard University Press, 1999 [1998]); Nell Irvin Painter, *The History of White People* (New York: W.W. Norton, 2010).

CHAPTER 1: WERE ADAM AND EVE OUR FIRST PARENTS? ATHEISM AND POLYGENESIS

A version of this chapter, along with parts of Chapters 2 and 4, was published as "Atheism and Polygenesis in the Nineteenth Century: Charles Bradlaugh's Racial Anthropology" in *Modern Intellectual History* (2018).

1 On the development of polygenesis in the early modern period, see Richard H. Popkin, *Isaac La Peyrère (1596–1676): His Life, Work, and Influence* (Leiden and New York: Brill, 1987); chapters 3 and 4 of Colin Kidd, *The Forging of Races: Race and Scripture in the Protestant Atlantic World, 1600–2000* (Cambridge: Cambridge University Press, 2006); chapters 1–3 of David N. Livingstone, *Adam's Ancestors: Race, Religion, and the Politics of Human Origins* (Baltimore: Johns Hopkins University Press, 2008).

Notes

2 William Stanton, *The Leopard's Spots: Scientific Attitudes Toward Race in America, 1815–59* (Chicago and London: University of Chicago Press, 1960), 28–33.

3 Ibid., 132.

4 Ibid., 100–12.

5 Christoph Irmscher, *Louis Agassiz: Creator of American Science* (Boston: Houghton Mifflin Harcourt, 2013), 2–3.

6 Louis Agassiz, "The Diversity of Origin of the Human Races," *Christian Examiner* 49 (July 1850): 110–11.

7 Ibid., 138.

8 Michael Banton, *The Idea of Race* (London: Tavistock Publications, 1977), 5.

9 Quoted in Thomas F. Gossett, *Race: The History of an Idea in America*, New Edition (New York and Oxford: Oxford University Press, 1997 [1963]), 64.

10 Quoted in Stanton, *Leopard's Spots*, 122.

11 Reginald Horsman, *Josiah Nott of Mobile: Southerner, Physician, and Racial Theorist* (Baton Rouge and London: Louisiana State University Press, 1987), 17.

12 Ibid., 38–39; on Cooper's involvement in the freethought movement, see Albert Post, *Popular Freethought in America, 1825–1850* (New York: Columbia University Press, 1943), 224–25. It should be noted that there was another Thomas Cooper (1805–1892), who was an English freethinker and radical before later converting to Christianity. He is different from the Thomas Cooper (1759–1839) discussed here.

13 John Bachman, *A Notice of the "Types of Mankind," with an Examination of the Charges Contained in the Biography of Dr. Morton, Published by Nott and Gliddon* (Charleston: James, Williams and Gitsinger, 1854), 35.

14 Horsman, *Josiah Nott*, 39–41.

15 Quoted in ibid., 61.

16 Josiah Nott, *Two Lectures, on the Natural History of the Caucasian and Negro Races* (Mobile: Dade and Thompson, 1844), 5.

17 Josiah Nott, *Two Lectures on the Connection Between the Biblical and Physical History of Man* (New York: Bartlett and Welford, 1849), 7.

18 Ibid., 16.

19 Ibid., 15.

20 Josiah Nott and George Gliddon, *Types of Mankind: Or, Ethnological Researches, Based Upon the Ancient Monuments, Paintings, Sculptures, and Crania of Races, and Upon Their Natural, Geographical, Philological, and Biblical History* (Philadelphia: Lippincort, Grambo & Co., 1854), 61.

21 Ibid., 55.

22 Ibid., 57.

23 Ibid., 73.

24 See chapter 6 of Peter Harrison, *The Territories of Science and Religion* (Chicago: University of Chicago Press, 2015).

25 Nott and Gliddon, *Types of Mankind*, 56.

26 Ibid., 61.

Notes

27 Nott, *Natural History*, 3.

28 See, for example, C. Loring Brace, *"Race" is a Four-Letter Word: The Genesis of the Concept* (Oxford: Oxford University Press, 2005), 110–17, 125–43; Francisco Bethencourt, *Racisms: From the Crusades to the Twentieth Century* (Princeton and Oxford: Princeton University Press, 2013), 285–86.

29 Horsman, *Josiah Nott*, 258.

30 Terence D. Keel, "Religion, Polygenism and the Early Science of Human Origins," *History of the Human Sciences* 26, no. 2 (2013): 25–26.

31 Stanton, *Leopard's Spots*, 193.

32 Ibid., 194–95.

33 George M. Fredrickson, *The Black Image in the White Mind: The Debate on Afro-American Character and Destiny, 1817–1914* (New York: Harper & Row, 1971), 85, 87–90.

34 Keel, "Religion, Polygenism"; chapter 2 of Terence Keel, *Divine Variations: How Christian Thought Became Racial Science* (Stanford, CA: Stanford University Press, 2018).

35 Bachman, *A Notice*, 5; see also Stanton, *Leopard's Spots*, 165–73.

36 "Unity of the Homo Race – An Error," *Boston Investigator*, November 3, 1852, 2; F.H.M., "The True Relations of the Human Races," *Boston Investigator*, May 2, 1860, 1; "Not All from One Pair," *Boston Investigator*, July 31, 1867, 101; P.R.J., "Agassiz," *Truth Seeker*, January 15, 1875, 9.

37 See Paul Jerome Croce, "Probabilistic Darwinism: Louis Agassiz vs. Asa Gray on Science, Religion, and Certainty," *Journal of Religious History* 22, no. 1 (February 1998): 35–58.

38 "Professor Agassiz," *Boston Investigator*, July 16, 1873, 6.

39 "Books of the Day," *Reasoner* 18, no. 450 (1855): 6.

40 See Chapter 5.

41 "Books of the Day," 6.

42 "A Man Before Adam," *Boston Investigator*, May 3, 1854, 2.

43 "Climate Not the Cause of Color," *Boston Investigator*, July 8, 1857, 4; "Ethnology," *National Reformer*, June 3, 1866, 346.

44 John Watts, "The Origin of Man," *National Reformer*, January 15, 1865, 42.

45 Ibid., 43.

46 John Watts, "The Origin of Man II – Conclusion," *National Reformer*, January 22, 1865, 57.

47 John Watts, "Theological Theories of the Origin of Man II," *Reasoner*, February 24, 1861, 120; Usher's chapter is in Nott and Gliddon, *Types of Mankind*, 327–72.

48 Kersey Graves, *The Bible of Bibles; or, Twenty-Seven "Divine Revelations,"* 4th ed. (Boston: Colby & Rich, 1879), 291.

49 "The God Idea," *Boston Investigator*, July 11, 1888, 5.

50 George W. Stocking Jr., *Victorian Anthropology* (New York: Free Press, 1987), 247–54.

51 On Knox's life and thought, see Henry Lonsdale, *A Sketch of the Life and Writings of Robert Knox the Anatomist* (London: Macmillan and Co., 1870);

Notes

Evelleen Richards, "The 'Moral Anatomy' of Robert Knox: The Interplay between Biological and Social Thought in Victorian Scientific Naturalism," *Journal of the History of Biology* 22, no. 3 (Autumn 1989): 373–436.

52 Robert Knox, *The Races of Men: A Philosophical Enquiry into the Influence of Race over the Destinies of Nations*, 2nd ed. (London: Henry Renshaw, 1862 [1850]), v.

53 Lonsdale, *Life and Writings of Robert Knox*, 10–13.

54 See lectures I and II of Knox, *Races of Men*.

55 Lonsdale, *Life and Writings of Robert Knox*, 402.

56 Ibid., 404.

57 Richards, "'Moral Anatomy' of Robert Knox," 404.

58 Knox, *Races of Men*, 384.

59 Ibid., 581.

60 Ibid., 555.

61 Ibid., 477; Lonsdale hinted that Knox was sympathetic to deism: Lonsdale, *Life and Writings of Robert Knox*, 407.

62 Autonomos, "Who Are the Jews? I," *National Reformer*, May 12, 1867, 293–94; Autonomos, "Who Are the Jews? II," *National Reformer*, May 19, 1867, 314–15; Autonomos, "Who Are the Jews? III," *National Reformer*, May 26, 1867, 322–24.

63 This is discussed in greater detail in Chapter 3.

64 Autonomos, "Christian Filibusters in Africa VIII," *National Reformer*, August 4, 1867, 70. The whole series is Autonomos, "Christian Filibusters in Africa I," *National Reformer*, June 9, 1867, 362–63; Autonomos, "Christian Filibusters in Africa II," *National Reformer*, June 16, 1867, 373; Autonomos, "Christian Filibusters in Africa III," *National Reformer*, June 23, 1867, 394–95; Autonomos, "Christian Filibusters in Africa IV," *National Reformer*, June 30, 1867, 407; Autonomos, "Christian Filibusters in Africa V," *National Reformer*, July 7, 1867, 5–7; Autonomos, "Christian Filibusters in Africa VI," *National Reformer*, July 14, 1867, 20–22; Autonomos, "Christian Filibusters in Africa VII," *National Reformer*, July 21, 1867, 37–39; Autonomos, "Christian Filibusters in Africa VIII," 69–71.

65 James Hunt, "Introductory Address on the Study of Anthropology," *Anthropological Review* 1, no. 1 (May 1863): 19.

66 James Hunt, "The President's Address," *Journal of the Anthropological Society of London* 5 (1867): lix.

67 Quoted in Douglas Lorimer, *Colour, Class, and the Victorians: English Attitudes to the Negro in the Mid-Nineteenth Century* (Leicester: Leicester University Press, 1978), 138.

68 Hunt, "The President's Address," lxii.

69 James Hunt, "Anniversary Address, Delivered before the Anthropological Society of London, January 19th, 1869," *Journal of the Anthropological Society of London* 7 (1869): cviii.

70 Dane Kennedy, *The Highly Civilized Man: Richard Burton and the Victorian*

World (Cambridge, MA, and London: Harvard University Press, 2007), 199.

71 On Reade's life, see chapter 5 of Felix Driver, *Geography Militant: Cultures of Exploration and Empire* (Malden, MA: Blackwell Publishers, 2001).

72 Winwood Reade, *The Martyrdom of Man* (London: Trubner & Co., 1872), 523.

73 Winwood Reade, "Effects of Missionaries among Savages," *Journal of the Anthropological Society of London* 3 (1865): clxv.

74 Ibid., clxxxiii.

75 Ibid., clxvii.

76 Ibid., clxxviii.

77 James Hunt, "Anthropological News," *Anthropological Review* 6, no. 23 (October 1868): 454.

78 Driver, *Geography Militant*, 99; Kennedy, *Highly Civilized Man*, 169–70.

79 Charles Bradlaugh, *The Freethinker's Text-Book, Part I* (London: Charles Watts, 1876), 38.

80 Moncure Conway, *Autobiography: Memories and Experiences* (London and Paris: Cassell and Company, 1904), 2:1.

81 Ibid., 2:1–2.

82 Stocking, *Victorian Anthropology*, 254–56.

83 Conway, *Autobiography*, 2:303.

84 Charles Bradlaugh, *Heresy: Its Utility and Morality; A Plea and a Justification* (London: Austin & Co., 1870), 31.

85 Ibid., 1.

86 Ibid., 5.

87 See for example *Reasoner* 5, no. 105 (1848): 16.

88 "Heathen and Civilized," *Boston Investigator*, June 21, 1865, 52.

89 G.E.H., "The Ethnological Society," *National Reformer*, December 24, 1865, 822.

90 "Modern Scientific Theories," *National Reformer*, March 24, 1867, 177.

91 Ibid., 178.

92 J.P. Adams, "The Anthropologists and Their Opponents," *National Reformer*, November 3, 1867, 276.

93 Delta, "Anthropology in England," *National Reformer*, February 9, 1873, 84.

94 C. Carter Blake, "Anthropology," *National Reformer*, October 12, 1879, 659.

95 Ibid., 660.

96 C. Carter Blake, "Anthropology," *National Reformer*, November 2, 1879, 711; C. Carter Blake, "Biblical Negroes," *National Reformer*, December 28, 1879, 837.

97 Blake, "Biblical Negroes," 837.

98 C. Carter Blake, "Races in Western Europe," *National Reformer*, February 1, 1880, 69–70.

99 Caractacus, "Science and Slavery," *National Reformer*, April 9, 1864, 58. Caractacus was Adams's pen name.

100 J.M. Wheeler, *A Biographical Dictionary of Freethinkers of All Ages and Nations* (London: Progressive Publishing Company, 1889), vi.

101 Ibid., 180, 240.

102 Ibid., 54–55.

103 J.N. Morean, "Original Communications," *Boston Investigator*, October 20, 1858, 1.

104 J.M. Robertson, *A History of Freethought in the Nineteenth Century* (London: Dawsons of Pall Mall, 1969 [1929]), 2:352.

105 Examples include "Human Genera and Species," *Boston Investigator*, September 8, 1841, 2; "What Men Believed in the Sixteenth Century, and What They Believe Now," *Reasoner* 9, no. 205 (1850): 44; Robert Cooper, *The Infidel's Text-Book, Being the Substance of Thirteen Lectures on the Bible*, American Edition (Boston: J.P. Mendum, 1858), 209–10; J.S.H., "The Unity of the Human Race," *Boston Investigator*, February 24, 1858, 1; "Adam and Eve," *Boston Investigator*, February 22, 1860, 349.

106 John E. Remsburg, *The Bible: I. Authenticity II. Credibility III. Morality* (New York: Truth Seeker Company, 1907), 283.

107 John William Draper, *The History of the Conflict Between Religion and Science* (New York and London: D. Appleton and Company, 1874).

108 John William Draper, *Human Physiology, Statistical and Dynamical; Or, the Conditions and the Course of the Life of Man* (New York: Harper & Brothers, 1856), 563–71.

109 Andrew Dickson White, *A History of the Warfare of Science with Theology in Christendom* (New York: D. Appleton and Company, 1896), 1:255.

110 Hypatia Bradlaugh Bonner, ed., *Catalogue of the Library of the Late Charles Bradlaugh* (London: Mrs. H. Bradlaugh Bonner, 1891), 69, 115, 116.

111 Charles Bradlaugh, *Anthropology* (London: Freethought Publishing Company, 1882), lecture 1, 1–2, 4.

112 There is no discussion of Bradlaugh's racial thinking in David Tribe, *President Charles Bradlaugh M.P.* (London: Elek, 1971); Bryan Niblett, *Dare to Stand Alone: The Story of Charles Bradlaugh* (Oxford: Kramedart Press, 2010); or Edward Royle, *Radicals, Secularists and Republicans: Popular Freethought in Britain, 1866–1915* (Manchester: Manchester University Press, 1980). The only work which mentions Bradlaugh's use of polygenesis is Timothy Larsen's work on Victorians and the Bible, yet the discussion occupies only a paragraph and does not explore his connections to leading polygenist figures: Timothy Larsen, *A People of One Book: The Bible and the Victorians* (Oxford: Oxford University Press, 2011), 86–87; see also Timothy Larsen, "The Book of Acts and the Origin of the Races in Evangelical Thought," *Victorian Review* 37, no. 2 (Fall 2011): 35–39.

113 Charles Bradlaugh, *Were Adam and Eve Our First Parents?* (London: Freethought Publishing Company, 1865), 8.

114 Ibid., 4; see also Charles Bradlaugh, *Genesis: Its Authorship and Authenticity*, 3rd ed. (London: Freethought Publishing Company, 1882), 238–39.

115 Bradlaugh, *Adam and Eve*, 5.

116 Ibid., 6–7.

117 Ibid., 7.

118 Ibid., 1.

119 Charles Bradlaugh, "Antiquity and Unity of Origin of the Human Race," *National Reformer*, October 29, 1864, 513–14.

120 R. Newstead, "Unity of Origin of the Human Race," *National Reformer*, November 12, 1864, 566.

121 Bradlaugh, *The Freethinker's Text-Book, Part I*, 80.

122 Ibid., 87.

123 Ibid., 92.

124 Bradlaugh, *Genesis*, 292.

125 James McCann and Charles Bradlaugh, *Secularism: Unphilosophical, Immoral, and Anti-Social. Verbatim Report of a Three Nights' Debate Between the Rev. Dr. McCann and Charles Bradlaugh* (London: Freethought Publishing Company, 1881), 20–21.

126 Ibid., 22.

127 Ibid., 25.

128 B.F. Underwood, *The Burgess–Underwood Debate: Commencing June 29, 1875, at Aylmer, Ontario, and Continuing Four Days* (New York: D.M. Bennett, 1876), 91; Robert Ingersoll, "Some Mistakes of Moses," lecture given in 1879, in Robert G. Ingersoll, *The Works of Robert G. Ingersoll* (New York: Dresden Publishing Co., C.P. Farrell, 1902), 2:99–100.

129 W.P. Ball, "Noah's Family; or Bible Evolution," *Freethinker*, October 19, 1884, 335.

130 Arthur B. Moss, "The Age of the Earth and Man," *Truth Seeker*, May 21, 1887, 326.

131 Stocking, *Victorian Anthropology*, 69–74.

132 Stanton, *Leopard's Spots*, 186.

133 Larsen, *People of One Book*, 139.

CHAPTER 2: BRUTE MEN: RACE AND SOCIETY IN EVOLUTION

1 James Moore, "Freethought, Secularism, Agnosticism: The Case of Charles Darwin," in *Religion in Victorian Britain*, vol. 1, *Traditions*, ed. Gerald Parsons (Manchester and New York: Manchester University Press in Association with the Open University, 1988), 274–319.

2 See David N. Livingstone, *Darwin's Forgotten Defenders: The Encounter Between Evangelical Theology and Evolutionary Thought* (Edinburgh: Scottish Academic Press; Grand Rapids, MI, William B. Eerdmans, 1987); Peter Bowler, *Monkey Trials and Gorilla Sermons: Evolution and Christianity from Darwin to Intelligent Design* (Cambridge, MA, and London: Harvard University Press, 2007).

3 See Adrian Desmond, *The Politics of Evolution: Morphology, Medicine, and*

Notes

Reform in Radical London (Chicago and London: University of Chicago Press, 1992).

4 Adrian Desmond and James Moore, *Darwin* (London: Michael Joseph, 1991); see also Janet Browne, *Charles Darwin*, vol. 1, *Voyaging* (New York: Alfred A. Knopf, 1995); Janet Browne, *Charles Darwin*, vol. 2, *The Power of Place* (New York: Alfred A. Knopf, 2002).

5 Quoted in Terence Ball, "Marx and Darwin: A Reconsideration," *Political Theory* 7, no. 4 (November 1979): 473.

6 For an extreme formulation of this view, see Richard Weikart, *From Darwin to Hitler: Evolutionary Ethics, Eugenics, and Racism in Germany* (New York: Palgrave Macmillan, 2004); for a criticism of this argument, see Robert J. Richards, "Myth 19 – That Darwin and Haeckel Were Complicit in Nazi Biology," in *Galileo Goes to Jail: And Other Myths about Science and Religion*, ed. Ronald L. Numbers (Cambridge, MA: Harvard University Press, 2009), 170–77.

7 Adrian Desmond and James Moore, *Darwin's Sacred Cause: How a Hatred of Slavery Shaped Darwin's Views on Human Evolution* (Boston and New York: Houghton Mifflin Harcourt, 2009).

8 See chapter 3 of Peter Bowler, *Evolution: The History of an Idea*, 25th Anniversary Edition (Berkeley and Los Angeles: University of California Press, 2009 [1984]).

9 Nancy Stepan, *The Idea of Race in Science: Great Britain, 1800–1960* (London: Macmillan, 1982), 6.

10 William Chilton, "The Theory of Regular Gradation XL," *Oracle of Reason* 2, no. 84 (1843): 253–54; on White, see Stepan, *Idea of Race in Science*, 8–9; William Stanton, *The Leopard's Spots: Scientific Attitudes Toward Race in America, 1815–59* (Chicago and London: University of Chicago Press, 1960), 16–18.

11 James A. Secord, *Victorian Sensation: The Extraordinary Publication, Reception, and Secret Authorship of Vestiges of the Natural History of Creation* (Chicago and London: University of Chicago Press, 2000), 313.

12 Ibid., 85–86, quotation on 85; on Robert and his brother William's publishing business, see Aileen Fyfe, *Steam-Powered Knowledge: William Chambers and the Business of Publishing, 1820–1860* (Chicago and London: University of Chicago Press, 2012).

13 [Robert Chambers], *Vestiges of the Natural History of Creation* (London: John Churchill, 1844), 152.

14 Ibid., 156.

15 Secord, *Victorian Sensation*, 274, 280, 330–31, 453, 466.

16 [Chambers], *Vestiges*, 278.

17 Ibid., 279.

18 Ibid., 280–81.

19 Ibid., 296.

20 Ibid., 306.

Notes

21 Ibid., 307.

22 Ibid., 310.

23 Montgarnier, "Nature's Law of Development," *Boston Investigator*, July 8, 1845, 1.

24 John Shertzer Hittell, *The Evidences Against Christianity*, 2nd ed. (New York: Calvin Blanchard, 1857 [1856]), 1:147.

25 Ibid., 1:149.

26 John Shertzer Hittell, *A History of the Mental Growth of Mankind in Ancient Times* (New York: Henry Holt and Company, 1893), 1:32.

27 Secord, *Victorian Sensation*, 526.

28 Moore, "Freethought, Secularism, Agnosticism."

29 Desmond and Moore, *Darwin's Sacred Cause*.

30 "Light will be thrown on the origin of man and his history." Charles Darwin, *On the Origin of Species*, 2nd ed. (London: John Murray, 1860 [1859]), 488.

31 See especially chapter 13 of Desmond and Moore, *Darwin's Sacred Cause*.

32 Charles Darwin, *The Descent of Man, and Selection in Relation to Sex* (London: John Murray, 1871), 1:217.

33 Ibid., 1:226.

34 Ibid., 1:229.

35 Ibid., 1:235.

36 Ibid., 1:241–49.

37 Ibid., 2:355–85; see also Stepan, *Idea of Race in Science*, 59–66.

38 Stepan, *Idea of Race in Science*, 65; for a contemporary argument for the role of sexual selection in racial formation, see Jared Diamond, "Race Without Color," *Discover Magazine*, November 1, 1994, http://discovermagazine.com/1994/nov/racewithoutcolor444, accessed October 3, 2017.

39 Darwin, *Descent of Man*, 1:35.

40 Ibid., 1:62.

41 Ibid., 1:201.

42 Evelleen Richards, "The 'Moral Anatomy' of Robert Knox: The Interplay between Biological and Social Thought in Victorian Scientific Naturalism," *Journal of the History of Biology* 22, no. 3 (Autumn 1989): 423–24.

43 Thomas Henry Huxley, "Methods and Results of Ethnology (1865)," in *Collected Essays*, vol. 7, *Man's Place in Nature and Other Anthropological Essays* (New York: D. Appleton and Company, 1896), 242–48, quotation on 244.

44 Ibid., 248.

45 Ibid., 234.

46 Ibid., 232.

47 Ibid., 238.

48 Alfred Russel Wallace, "The Origin of Human Races and the Antiquity of Man Deduced from the Theory of 'Natural Selection,'" *Journal of the Anthropological Society of London* 2 (1864): clviii–clxxxvii.

49 Huxley, "Methods and Results of Ethnology," 249.

Notes

50 Thomas Henry Huxley, "Man's Place in Nature (1863)," in *Collected Essays*, 7:106–8, quotation on 108.

51 Ibid., 116; for a similar argument which draws on Huxley's work, see Edward Clodd, *A Primer of Evolution* (London: Longmans, Green, and Co., 1895), 127.

52 Mark Francis, *Herbert Spencer and the Invention of Modern Life* (Stocksfield: Acumen, 2007), 189–90; Spencer's evolutionary ideas first appeared in Herbert Spencer, "The Development Hypothesis [1852]," in *Essays: Scientific, Political, and Speculative*, Library Edition (London and Edinburgh: Williams and Norgate, 1891), 1:1–7.

53 Francis, *Herbert Spencer*, 3.

54 Herbert Spencer, *The Principles of Biology* (London and Edinburgh: Williams and Norgate, 1864), 1:240.

55 Herbert Spencer, *The Principles of Psychology*, 2nd ed. (London and Edinburgh: Williams and Norgate, 1870 [1855]), 1:471; see also Spencer, *Principles of Biology*, 2:502.

56 Letter to Kentaro Kaneko, August 26, 1892, in David Duncan, ed., *The Life and Letters of Herbert Spencer* (London: Methuen & Co., 1908), 323.

57 G. Clinton Godart, "Herbert Spencer in Japan: Boom and Bust of a Theory," in *Global Spencerism: The Communication and Appropriation of a British Evolutionist*, ed. Bernard Lightman (Leiden: Brill, 2015), 69.

58 Felix Driver, *Geography Militant: Cultures of Exploration and Empire* (Malden, MA: Blackwell Publishers, 2001), 111–13.

59 James F. Morton Jr., "W. Winwood Reade," *Truth Seeker*, October 15, 1910, 658.

60 Winwood Reade, *The Martyrdom of Man* (London: Trubner & Co., 1872), 4–5.

61 Ibid., 5.

62 Ibid., 7.

63 Ibid., 494.

64 Ibid., 64.

65 Ibid., 422.

66 Ibid., 385.

67 Ibid., 386.

68 Edward Royle, *Radicals, Secularists and Republicans: Popular Freethought in Britain, 1866–1915* (Manchester: Manchester University Press, 1980), 171; for an early discussion of Darwin among secularists, see John Watts and Iconoclast, eds., "Charles R. Darwin, F.R.S.," *Half Hours with Freethinkers*, December 1, 1864, 1–8.

69 C.A. Creffield, "Aveling, Edward Bibbens (1849–1898)," *Oxford Dictionary of National Biography* (2004), www.oxforddnb.com/view/article/40929, accessed April 23, 2016; Royle, *Radicals, Secularists and Republicans*, 105–6, 317–19; Arthur H. Nethercot, *The First Five Lives of Annie Besant* (London: Rupert Hart-Davis, 1961), 157–67, 212–22.

70 Royle, *Radicals, Secularists and Republicans*, 173; W. Mann, "The Hundred Best Books," *Freethinker*, November 19, 1905, 740–42; W. Mann, "The Hundred Best Books – II," *Freethinker*, November 26, 1905, 762–63.

Notes

71 On the persistence of polygenist ideas after Darwin, see chapter 3 of George W. Stocking Jr., *Race, Culture, and Evolution: Essays in the History of Anthropology*, New Edition (Chicago and London: University of Chicago Press, 1982 [1968]).

72 Charles Bradlaugh, *Anthropology* (London: Freethought Publishing Company, 1882), lecture 1, 5.

73 Ibid., lecture 4, 4.

74 See chapter 9 of Bowler, *Evolution*.

75 Bradlaugh, *Anthropology*, lecture 1, 8.

76 Ibid., lecture 4, 5.

77 Ibid., lecture 2, 4.

78 Ibid., lecture 2, 3.

79 Ibid., lecture 3, 7.

80 Ibid., lecture 3, 8.

81 Ibid., lecture 4, 6.

82 Edward Aveling, *The Religious Views of Charles Darwin* (London: Freethought Publishing Company, 1883); Edward Aveling, *Darwin Made Easy* (London: Robert Forder, 1893).

83 James Hunt of the Anthropological Society was also a supporter of Vogt and translated one of his works: Carl Vogt, *Lectures on Man*, ed. James Hunt (London: Longman, Green, Longman, and Roberts, 1864).

84 Edward Aveling, "Carl Vogt and His Writings X," *National Reformer*, September 9, 1883, 173.

85 Edward Aveling, "Carl Vogt and His Writings XI," *National Reformer*, September 30, 1883, 211.

86 Edward Aveling, "Carl Vogt and His Writings XII," *National Reformer*, October 21, 1883, 262.

87 Edward Aveling, "Carl Vogt and His Writings XIV," *National Reformer*, November 18, 1883, 325.

88 Edward Aveling, "Monkeys, Apes, Men," in Aveling, *Darwin Made Easy*, 5; see also Ernst Haeckel, *The Pedigree of Man: And Other Essays*, trans. Edward Aveling (London: Freethought Publishing Company, 1883), 77–85.

89 Edward Aveling and Eleanor Marx Aveling, *The Working Class Movement in America* (London: Swan Sonnenschein, Lowrey & Co., 1888), 32.

90 Eugene Macdonald, "The White Man's Origin," *Truth Seeker*, March 28, 1903, 194.

91 George Macdonald, "Tracing Racial Origins," *Truth Seeker*, August 6, 1910, 504.

92 T.F. Palmer, "The Origin and Development of Man," *Freethinker*, April 4, 1915, 212–14; T.F. Palmer, "The Origin and Development of Man – II," *Freethinker*, April 11, 1915, 235–36.

93 Edward Aveling, "The Darwinian Theory," in Aveling, *Darwin Made Easy*, 20.

94 George Macdonald, "Notes at Large," *Truth Seeker*, February 18, 1911, 105.

95   See chapters 13 and 14 of C. Loring Brace, *"Race" is a Four-Letter Word: The Genesis of the Concept* (Oxford: Oxford University Press, 2005).

96   Daniel J. Kevles, *In the Name of Eugenics: Genetics and the Uses of Human Heredity* (New York: Alfred A. Knopf, 1985), 300.

97   Francis Galton, "Eugenics: Its Definition, Scope and Aims," in *Sociological Papers* (London: Macmillan and Co., 1905), 50.

98   Francis Galton, *Hereditary Genius* (London: Macmillan, 1869), 338–39.

99   Karl Pearson, *National Life from the Standpoint of Science*, 2nd ed. (London: Adam and Charles Black, 1905 [1900]), 25.

100 Ibid., 19.

101 Ibid., 22–23.

102 Karl Pearson, *The Moral Basis of Socialism* (London: William Reeves, 1887), 26.

103 Annie Besant, "Heredity as a Factor of Evolution," *National Reformer*, January 15, 1888, 37–38.

104 Annie Besant, "Heredity as a Factor of Evolution," *National Reformer*, February 12, 1888, 100; Royle, *Radicals, Secularists and Republicans*, 227–28; see also J.M. Wheeler, "Heredity and Progress," *Freethinker*, January 15, 1899, 43.

105 Annie Besant and G.W. Foote, *Is Socialism Sound? Verbatim Report of Four Nights' Debate Between Annie Besant and G.W. Foote* (London: Progressive Publishing Company, 1887), 90.

106 Ibid., 96–98.

107 John Watts, "Theological Theories of the Origin of Man II," *Reasoner*, February 24, 1861, 121.

108 Edward Aveling, "The Origin of Man," in Aveling, *Darwin Made Easy*, 3–4.

109 Edward Aveling, "Brute Men," *National Reformer*, May 11, 1884, 322.

110 Ibid., 323; John Watts made a similar point: John Watts, "Theological Theories of the Origin of Man III," *Reasoner*, March 3, 1861, 132.

111 Quoted in Edward Aveling, "Brute Men II," *National Reformer*, May 18, 1884, 339.

112 Edward Aveling, "The Origin of Man," in Aveling, *Darwin Made Easy*, 39.

113 Ibid., 39–40.

114 Edward Aveling, "The Darwinian Theory," in Aveling, *Darwin Made Easy*, 22.

115 Freda Utley, *Odyssey of a Liberal* (Washington: Washington National Press, 1970), 5–7.

116 W.H. Utley, "Man-Like Apes – I," *National Reformer*, August 1, 1886, 74.

117 W.H. Utley, "Man-Like Apes – II," *National Reformer*, August 8, 1886, 91.

118 W.H. Utley, "Man-Like Apes – III," *National Reformer*, August 22, 1886, 123.

119 B.F. Underwood, "Darwinism," *Truth Seeker*, June 15, 1875, 6; William Denton, "The Origin of Man," *Truth Seeker*, February 14, 1880, 98–99; Henry MacDonald, "Origin of Man," *Freethinker*, May 22, 1892, 332; James M. McCann, "Man and Brute," *Truth Seeker*, August 23, 1902, 534–35; James M. McCann, "Man and Brute," *Truth Seeker*, August 31, 1902, 550; George Macdonald, "Brain of the Ape and Man," *Truth Seeker*, March 1, 1913, 136.

120 On Slenker's life, see chapter 4 of Leigh Eric Schmidt, *Village Atheists: How*

Notes

America's Unbelievers Made Their Way in a Godly Nation (Princeton and Oxford: Princeton University Press, 2016).

Ibid., 217–18.

122 Elmina Drake Slenker, "Spontaneous Generation," *Boston Investigator*, July 14, 1886, 1.

123 Elmina Drake Slenker, "Hybrids," *Boston Investigator*, August 11, 1886, 2.

124 Aunt Elmina, "Pain," *Boston Investigator*, April 23, 1884, 8.

125 Elmina Drake Slenker, *Little Lessons for Little Folks* (New York: Truth Seeker Company, 1887), 93. Thanks to Suvi Karila for this reference.

126 See chapter 1 of Marjorie Wheeler-Barclay, *The Science of Religion in Britain, 1860–1915* (Charlottesville: University of Virginia Press, 2010).

127 Timothy Larsen, *The Slain God: Anthropologists and the Christian Faith* (Oxford: Oxford University Press, 2014), 20.

128 E.B. Tylor, *Primitive Culture: Researches into the Development of Mythology, Philosophy, Religion, Art, and Custom* (London: John Murray, 1871), 1:15.

129 Ibid., 2:322.

130 Ibid., 1:386–87.

131 Ibid., 1:453.

132 Quoted in George W. Stocking Jr., *Victorian Anthropology* (New York: Free Press, 1987), 191.

133 Herbert Spencer, *The Principles of Sociology*, 3rd ed. (New York: D. Appleton and Company, 1898 [1876–96]), 1:414–15.

134 Spencer, *Principles of Sociology*, 3:36.

135 Tylor, *Primitive Culture*, 1:24.

136 See chapter 3 of E.B. Tylor, *Anthropology: An Introduction to the Study of Man and Civilization* (New York: D. Appleton and Company, 1881).

137 For a similar example, see Edward Clodd, "Presidential Address," *Folklore* 7, no. 1 (March 1896): 35–60.

138 Hittell, *Evidences*, 2:2.

139 Robert Ingersoll, "The Gods," lecture delivered in 1872, in Robert G. Ingersoll, *The Works of Robert G. Ingersoll* (New York: Dresden Publishing Co., C.P. Farrell, 1902), 1:28; for a similar account, see Samuel Porter Putnam, *400 Years of Freethought* (New York: Truth Seeker Company, 1894), 383–86.

140 Reade, *Martyrdom of Man*, 164–72.

141 Ibid., 211.

142 Ibid., 525.

143 Robert Ingersoll, "Individuality," lecture delivered in 1873, in Ingersoll, *Works*, 1:186.

144 Robert Ingersoll, "About the Holy Bible," lecture delivered in 1894, in Ingersoll, *Works*, 3:455; Robert Ingersoll, "Superstition," lecture delivered in 1898, in Ingersoll, *Works*, 4:314; for other examples, see Robert Ingersoll, "Some Mistakes of Moses," lecture delivered in 1879, in Ingersoll, *Works*, 2:v; and E.J. Bowtell, "Man, God's Creator," *Freethinker*, December 23, 1883, 407.

145 Quoted in Sandra J. Berkowitz and Amy C. Lewis, "Debating Anti-Semitism:

Ernestine Rose vs. Horace Seaver in the *Boston Investigator*, 1863–1864," *Communication Quarterly* 46, no. 4 (1998): 460.

146 Quoted in ibid., 461.
147 Quoted in ibid.
148 On Rose, see Susan Jacoby, *Freethinkers: A History of American Secularism* (New York: Henry Holt and Company, 2004), 97–101.
149 Quoted in Berkowitz and Lewis, "Debating Anti-Semitism," 463.
150 Hittell, *Evidences*, 1:91.
151 Ibid., 1:103.
152 See for example, Robert Ingersoll, "The Jews," undated, in Ingersoll, *Works*, 11:457–60; Edward Aveling, "The Persecution of Jews," *National Reformer*, February 12, 1882, 101–2; Henry Frank, "The Massacre of Russian Jews," *Truth Seeker*, May 30, 1903, 344.

CHAPTER 3: A LONDON ZULU: SAVAGERY AND CIVILIZATION

1 Elsewhere in the chapter, I have opted not to use "so-called" each time as this would become tedious, but it should almost go without saying that this is not an endorsement of the legitimacy of that language.
2 See chapter 1 of Bernard Porter, *Critics of Empire: British Radicals and the Imperial Challenge*, 2nd ed. (London and New York: I.B. Tauris, 2008 [1968]); Miles Taylor, "Imperium et Libertas? Rethinking the Radical Critique of Imperialism during the Nineteenth Century," *Journal of Imperial and Commonwealth History* 19 (1991): 1–23.
3 Quoted in George W. Stocking Jr., *Victorian Anthropology* (New York: Free Press, 1987), 187.
4 Ibid.
5 Michael Adas, *Machines as the Measure of Men: Science, Technology, and Ideologies of Western Dominance* (Ithaca and London: Cornell University Press, 1989), 341.
6 Matthew Day, "Godless Savages and Superstitious Dogs: Charles Darwin, Imperial Ethnography, and the Problem of Human Uniqueness," *Journal of the History of Ideas* 69, no. 1 (2008): 60.
7 On "religion" as a modern and western category, see Brent Nongbri, *Before Religion: A History of a Modern Concept* (New Haven and London: Yale University Press, 2013); Timothy Fitzgerald, *Discourse on Civility and Barbarity: A Critical History of Religion and Related Categories* (Oxford and New York: Oxford University Press, 2007).
8 Stocking, *Victorian Anthropology*, 79–81.
9 Paul Harvey, *Christianity and Race in the American South: A History* (Chicago and London: University of Chicago Press, 2016), 17–19.
10 See chapter 2 of J.M. Robertson, *A History of Freethought Ancient and Modern to the Period of the French Revolution* (London: Dawsons of Pall Mall, 1969 [1929]), vol. 1; see also Mitchell Stephens, *Imagine There's No Heaven: How*

Atheism Helped Create the Modern World (New York: Palgrave Macmillan, 2014), 8–9.

11 John Lubbock, *Pre-Historic Times, as Illustrated by Ancient Remains, and the Manners and Customs of Modern Savages* (London and Edinburgh: Williams and Norgate, 1865), 467–68.

12 Ibid., 470.

13 John Lubbock, *The Origin of Civilisation and the Primitive Condition of Man: Mental and Social Condition of Savages* (London: Longmans, Green, and Co., 1870), 121.

14 E.B. Tylor, *Primitive Culture: Researches into the Development of Mythology, Philosophy, Religion, Art, and Custom* (London: John Murray, 1871), 1:379–84.

15 Day, "Godless Savages," 58.

16 Charles Bradlaugh, *The Freethinker's Text-Book, Part I* (London: Charles Watts, 1876), 97–102.

17 W. Mann, "The Idea of God Not Universal," *Freethinker*, April 19, 1914, 245–46; W. Mann, "The Idea of God Not Universal – II," *Freethinker*, April 26, 1914, 266–67; W. Mann, "The Idea of God Not Universal – III," *Freethinker*, May 3, 1914, 277–78; W. Mann, "Is Religious Belief Universal?," *Freethinker*, June 14, 1914, 380–81; W. Mann, "Is Religious Belief Universal? – 2," *Freethinker*, June 21, 1914, 389–90; W. Mann, "Is Religious Belief Universal? – 3," *Freethinker*, June 28, 1914, 410–11.

18 E.R. Woodward, "The Religion of the Savage," *Freethinker*, November 3, 1901, 693.

19 See for example Lubbock, *Pre-Historic Times*, 465; Tylor, *Primitive Culture*, 1:27.

20 Thomas Paine, *The Age of Reason* (New York: Truth Seeker Company, 1898 [1794–95]), 46.

21 Samuel White Baker, *The Albert N'Yanza, Great Basin of the Nile, and Exploration of the Nile Sources* (London: Macmillan, 1866), 167–70.

22 "Negro Infidelity," *Boston Investigator* March 20, 1872, 3; Sanford M. Clark, "A Savage's Philosophy," *Truth Seeker*, May 1, 1886, 275; see also Stephens, *Imagine There's No Heaven*, 13–15.

23 On Colenso's life, see Jeff Guy, *The Heretic: A Study of the Life of John William Colenso, 1814–1883* (Johannesburg: Ravan Press; Pietermaritzburg: University of Natal Press, 1983).

24 Ibid., 133–34.

25 George Macdonald, "Notes at Large," *Truth Seeker*, November 18, 1916, 745.

26 Rusticus, "'The Intelligent Zulu,'" *Freethinker*, October 8, 1899, 651; see also Henry Lonsdale, *A Sketch of the Life and Writings of Robert Knox the Anatomist* (London: Macmillan and Co., 1870), 410; D.M. Bennett, "Around the World," *Truth Seeker*, June 22, 1878, 393; Kersey Graves, *The Bible of Bibles; or, Twenty-Seven "Divine Revelations,"* 4th ed. (Boston: Colby & Rich, 1879), 306; "The African Zulus," *Boston Investigator*, February 4, 1885, 5.

Notes

27 J.M. Robertson, *A History of Freethought in the Nineteenth Century* (London: Dawsons of Pall Mall, 1969 [1929]), 2:606.

28 Anthony Pagden, "The Savage Critic: Some European Images of the Primitive," *Yearbook of English Studies* 13, "Colonial and Imperial Themes" special number (1983): 32–45.

29 John Cumming, *Moses Right, and Bishop Colenso Wrong* (London: Shaw, 1863).

30 A London Zulu [George Holyoake], *Cumming Wrong; Colenso Right: A Reply to the Rev. Dr. Cumming's "Moses Right Colenso Wrong"* (London: Farrah and Dunbar, undated), 8.

31 Ibid., 19.

32 Ibid., 24.

33 As an ethnological term in the nineteenth century, this was usually used in regard to the Xhosa, but the usage here likely refers to a range of ethnic groups on the East coast of South Africa without distinguishing between them. The term is highly pejorative today.

34 "Free Discussion in Kaffirland," *Reasoner* 14, no. 347 (1853): 35.

35 Robert Ryder, "The Kaffirs and the Missionaries," *Reasoner*, April 27, 1856, 133.

36 Douglas Blackburn, "The Unregenerate Kaffir," *Freethinker*, January 11, 1914, 21.

37 An Unconverted Zulu, "An Unconverted Zulu," *National Reformer*, September 10, 1882, 179.

38 Ibid., 180.

39 Autonomos, "Gelele, King of Dahome, to Soapy Sam," *National Reformer*, December 16, 1866, 387.

40 Ibid., 388.

41 Ibid., 389.

42 White freethinkers were also eager to show real examples of non-white freethinkers as a way to demonstrate the universality of their message. See Chapters 4 and 5 for examples.

43 Charles Darwin, *The Descent of Man, and Selection in Relation to Sex* (London: John Murray, 1871), 1:94–95.

44 Winwood Reade, *The Martyrdom of Man* (London: Trubner & Co., 1872), 446–47.

45 Ibid., 447.

46 Tylor, *Primitive Culture*, 2:326.

47 Horace Seaver, "The Indians, Heathen, &c.," *Boston Investigator*, March 4, 1857, 2.

48 Emily G. Taylor, "The Christian and the Hottentot," *Truth Seeker*, December 14, 1895, 790.

49 Robert Ryder, "Secular Life in Africa," *Reasoner*, June 23, 1858, 194.

50 Ryder, "The Kaffirs and the Missionaries," 133.

51 Graves, *The Bible of Bibles*, 216; "Acid Drops," *Freethinker*, July 13, 1890, 328.

52 Robert Cooper, *The Infidel's Text-Book, Being the Substance of Thirteen*

Lectures on the Bible, American Edition (Boston: J.P. Mendum, 1858), 262–63.

53 "The Dyaks of Borneo," *Truth Seeker*, October 10, 1885, 646.

54 "Acid Drops," *Freethinker*, February 9, 1896, 88.

55 Joseph Symes, "Religion of the 'Black Fellows,'" *Freethinker*, May 5, 1907, 282–83.

56 Eugene Macdonald, "Filipinos who are Moral Without Religion," *Truth Seeker*, September 10, 1898, 584–85; Hyland C. Kirk, "Religions of the Filipinos," *Truth Seeker*, November 24, 1906, 738.

57 "A Meeting in Behalf of Indians," *Boston Investigator*, March 6, 1861, 365; see also "Convention for the Indians," *Boston Investigator*, March 13, 1861, 371.

58 A.L. Posey, "Letter from an Indian Student," *Boston Investigator*, September 17, 1890, 6; for a fictional example, see Big Eagle, "From a Chippewa Indian," *Truth Seeker*, April 20, 1878, 251.

59 George Freeman, "An Indian: Who was in the Penitentiary with Me," *Blue-Grass Blade*, May 11, 1902, 2; see also Charles Chilton Moore, *Behind the Bars; 31498* (Lexington, KY: Blue Grass Printing Co., 1899), 15; "Going to Evangelize the Flathead Indians," *Blue-Grass Blade*, December 20, 1903, 2.

60 Hypatia Bradlaugh, "A Century of Dishonor," *National Reformer*, August 19, 1883, 123.

61 George C. Bartlett, "Is Cannibalism a Myth?," *Truth Seeker*, September 5, 1908, 566.

62 Charles Rae, "Eating Missionaries," *National Reformer*, April 20, 1879, 294.

63 "Summary of News," *National Reformer*, May 26, 1867, 328; for another example see "Vegetarian Preferred," *Truth Seeker*, October 19, 1912, 664.

64 See chapter 6 of Andrew Porter, *Religion Versus Empire? British Protestant Missionaries and Overseas Expansion, 1700–1914* (Manchester and New York: Manchester University Press, 2004).

65 Ibid.

66 Stocking, *Victorian Anthropology*, 275–83.

67 George Macdonald, "'A Disappearing Race,'" *Truth Seeker*, June 12, 1909, 372; see also "Influence of the 'Pale-Faces,'" *Boston Investigator*, June 6, 1860, 52; "Civilization – Negroes, Indians," *Boston Investigator*, November 11, 1874, 4; G.W. Foote, "A Maori Messiah," *National Reformer*, October 26, 1879, 693; Henry Henshaw, "Missions and Mission Indians of Upper and Lower California," *Truth Seeker*, August 9, 1890, 503.

68 Samuel Porter Putnam, *400 Years of Freethought* (New York: Truth Seeker Company, 1894), 21.

69 J.M. Wheeler, "Christians and Heathens," *Freethinker*, November 14, 1897, 722.

70 W. Mann, "The Missionary in the South Seas," *Freethinker*, December 11, 1910, 794.

71 Ryder, "The Kaffirs and the Missionaries," 133.

72 Chapman Cohen, "Civilising the Eskimo," *Freethinker*, February 26, 1911, 130.

73 Chapman Cohen, "Papuans, Limited," *Freethinker*, February 28, 1904, 131.

Notes

74 See especially chapter 8 of Porter, *Critics of Empire.*

75 "Christian Civilisation in Africa," *Freethinker*, August 2, 1885, 247.

76 Robert Ingersoll, "Is Avarice Triumphant?" (1891), in Robert G. Ingersoll, *The Works of Robert G. Ingersoll* (New York: Dresden Publishing Co., C.P. Farrell, 1902), 7:436.

77 See also "News of the Week," *Truth Seeker*, February 11, 1882, 81; John P. Guild, "The Zulu's Belief Proves Neither his Spooks Nor his Gods," *Truth Seeker*, June 18, 1892, 394.

78 On freethinkers' teetotalism, see for example Edward Royle, *Radicals, Secularists and Republicans: Popular Freethought in Britain, 1866–1915* (Manchester: Manchester University Press, 1980), 144–45, 223.

79 See for example John Watts, "Bishop Colenso on Missionaryism," *National Reformer*, June 4, 1865, 361; "Rough Notes," *National Reformer*, March 14, 1869, 169; Index, "Wanted, a Missionary," *National Reformer*, May 15, 1870, 308.

80 Porter, *Religion Versus Empire?*, 191–92.

81 Eugene Macdonald, "The Indian Problem," *Truth Seeker*, February 19, 1887, 120; see also V. Arier, "The Indian Problem Again," *Truth Seeker*, April 14, 1888, 227.

82 Douglas Lorimer, *Science, Race Relations and Resistance: Britain, 1870–1914* (Manchester: Manchester University Press, 2013), 24.

83 John Stenhouse, "Imperialism, Atheism, and Race: Charles Southwell, Old Corruption, and the Maori," *Journal of British Studies* 44, no. 4 (October 2005): 771.

84 Bill Cooke, "Charles Southwell: One of the Romances of Rationalism," *Journal of Freethought* 2, no. 2 (Autumn 2012): 1–41.

85 Ibid., 31, 33.

86 Ibid., 34.

87 B.W.W., "A Christian War," *National Reformer*, July 9, 1864, 258; see also B.W.W., "The Christian War," *National Reformer*, July 30, 1864, 309; B.W.W., "The Christian War in New Zealand," *National Reformer*, February 12, 1865, 97–98; an opposing Christian perspective came from A.C., "The New Zealand War," *National Reformer*, January 29, 1865, 75–76.

88 "Summary of News," *National Reformer*, October 3, 1880, 264.

89 Charles Bradlaugh, "Jottings Out of Session," *National Reformer*, October 10, 1880, 270.

90 W.P. Ball, "Christian and Maori," *Freethinker*, June 15, 1884, 191 (my emphasis).

91 On atheist views of empire, and particularly those of the positivists, see Gregory Claeys, *Imperial Sceptics: British Critics of Empire, 1850–1920* (Cambridge: Cambridge University Press, 2012); for British secularists' reaction to the South African War, see David Nash, "Taming the God of Battles: Secular and Moral Critiques of the South African War," in *Writing a Wider War: Rethinking the South African War, 1899–1902*, ed. Greg Cuthbertson, Albert Grundlingh, and Mary-Lynn Suttie (Athens: Ohio University Press, 2002), 266–86.

Notes

92 Jacques Bonhomme, "Our Little War with the Zulus," *National Reformer*, February 16, 1879, 100.

93 "Acid Drops," *Freethinker*, June 10, 1894, 367.

94 Elizabeth E. Evans, "'Christian Civilization,'" *Truth Seeker*, March 24, 1900, 183.

95 For nineteenth-century American antimodernist views more generally, see Matthew Frye Jacobson, *Barbarian Virtues: The United States Encounters Foreign Peoples at Home and Abroad, 1876–1917* (New York: Hill and Wang, 2000), 127–36.

96 On Twain's connection to freethought, see Thomas D. Schwartz, "Mark Twain and Robert Ingersoll: The Freethought Connection," *American Literature* 48, no. 2 (May 1976): 183–93; William E. Phipps, *Mark Twain's Religion* (Macon, GA: Mercer University Press, 2003); Harold K. Bush Jr., *Mark Twain and the Spiritual Crisis of His Age* (Tuscaloosa: University of Alabama Press, 2007); John Bird, "The Mark Twain and Robert Ingersoll Connection: Freethought, Borrowed Thought, Stolen Thought," *The Mark Twain Annual* 11 (2013): 42–61.

97 Mark Twain, *Following the Equator: A Journey Around the World* (New York: Doubleday & McClure Co., 1897), 207.

98 Ibid., 267.

99 Ibid., 213.

100 Nathan G. Alexander, "Unclasping the Eagle's Talons: Mark Twain, American Freethought, and the Responses to Imperialism," *Journal of the Gilded Age and Progressive Era* 17, no. 3 (2018): 524–45; see also Jim Zwick, ed., *Mark Twain's Weapons of Satire: Anti-Imperialist Writings on the Philippine–American War* (Syracuse: Syracuse University Press, 1992).

101 Mark Twain, "To the Person Sitting in Darkness," *North American Review* 172, no. 531 (February 1901): 164.

102 Herbert Spencer, *The Principles of Sociology*, 3rd ed. (New York: D. Appleton and Company, 1898 [1876–96]), 2:233–34.

103 Ibid., 2:239.

104 Herbert Spencer, *The Principles of Ethics* (New York: D. Appleton and Company, 1896), 1:395.

105 Spencer, *Principles of Sociology*, 2:241.

106 Herbert Spencer, *Social Statics: Or, the Conditions Essential to Human Happiness Specified, and the First of Them Developed* (London: John Chapman, 1851), 366–67.

107 Herbert Spencer, *An Autobiography* (New York: D. Appleton and Company, 1904), 2:443.

108 Ibid., 2:443–47.

109 Chapman Cohen, "The Primitive Mind," *Freethinker*, October 27, 1912, 674.

110 Ibid., 675.

111 Chapman Cohen, "The Primitive Mind – II," *Freethinker*, November 3, 1912, 690.

112 Ibid., 691.
113 "The American Indian and Christianity," *Blue-Grass Blade*, October 20, 1907, 3.
114 Charles Bradlaugh, *Anthropology* (London: Freethought Publishing Company, 1882), lecture 1, 8.
115 G.W. Foote, "Mr. Gladstone and Li Hung Chang," *Freethinker*, August 23, 1896, 529.
116 Lonsdale, *Life and Writings of Robert Knox*, 149.
117 Autonomos, "Christian Filibusters in Africa VIII," *National Reformer*, August 4, 1867, 70.
118 Autonomos, "Christian Filibusters in Africa III," *National Reformer*, June 23, 1867, 394.
119 Autonomos, "Christian Filibusters in Africa VII," *National Reformer*, July 21, 1867, 39.
120 Autonomos, "Christian Filibusters in Africa II," *National Reformer*, June 16, 1867, 373.
121 See Nathan G. Alexander, "E.D. Morel (1873–1924), the Congo Reform Association, and the History of Human Rights," *Britain and the World* 9, no. 2 (2016): 219–24.
122 F.J. Gould, "The Fate of the Red Bush Pig," *Freethinker*, May 24, 1908, 321.
123 Ibid., 322.

CHAPTER 4: THE WISE MEN OF THE EAST: INDIA, CHINA, AND JAPAN

1 Edward Said, *Orientalism* (London: Penguin, 2003 [1978]), 204.
2 For a critical but sympathetic account, see chapter 4 of Richard King, *Orientalism and Religion: Postcolonial Theory, India and the "Mystic East"* (London and New York: Routledge, 1999); less sympathetic but also insightful is chapter 9 of Robert Irwin, *For Lust of Knowing: The Orientalists and Their Enemies* (London: Penguin, 2007).
3 Sadik Jalal Al-ʿAzm, "Orientalism and Orientalism in Reverse," in *Orientalism: A Reader*, ed. A.L. Macfie (Edinburgh: Edinburgh University Press, 2000), 219.
4 Ronald Inden, *Imagining India* (Cambridge, MA, and Oxford: Blackwell, 1990), 54.
5 Ibid., 37.
6 See King, *Orientalism and Religion*; Philip C. Almond, *The British Discovery of Buddhism* (Cambridge: Cambridge University Press, 1988); Jason Ānanda Josephson, *The Invention of Religion in Japan* (Chicago: University of Chicago Press, 2012).
7 "Words of the Wise," *Truth Seeker*, February 1874, 16.
8 "Christian Morality Not Unique," *Freethinker*, April 27, 1890, 201.
9 D.M. Bennett, *A Truth Seeker Around the World* (New York: D.M. Bennett, 1882), vols. 2–3; Roderick Bradford, *D.M. Bennett: The Truth Seeker* (Amherst, NY: Prometheus, 2006), 325–31; Moncure Conway, *My Pilgrimage to the Wise*

Men of the East (Boston and New York: Houghton, Mifflin and Company, 1906).

10 Kersey Graves, *The World's Sixteen Crucified Saviors; Or, Christianity Before Christ*, 4th ed. (Boston: Colby & Rich, 1876); Kersey Graves, *The Bible of Bibles; or, Twenty-Seven "Divine Revelations,"* 4th ed. (Boston: Colby & Rich, 1879); J.M. Robertson, *Pagan Christs: Studies in Comparative Hierology* (London: Watts & Co., 1903); J.M. Robertson, *Christianity and Mythology* (London: Watts & Co., 1900).

11 P.J. Marshall, ed., *The British Discovery of Hinduism in the Eighteenth Century* (Cambridge: Cambridge University Press, 1970).

12 Tony Ballantyne, *Orientalism and Race: Aryanism in the British Empire* (Houndmills, Basingstoke: Palgrave Macmillan, 2002), 31.

13 Ibid., 43.

14 Ibid., 28–29, 42.

15 George W. Stocking Jr., *Victorian Anthropology* (New York: Free Press, 1987), 58–60.

16 Thomas R. Trautmann, *Aryans and British India* (Berkeley and Los Angeles: University of California Press, 1997), 4.

17 John Shertzer Hittell, *A History of the Mental Growth of Mankind in Ancient Times* (New York: Henry Holt and Company, 1893), 2:196.

18 Ibid., 2:199.

19 Ibid., 2:208.

20 Bennett, *Truth Seeker Around the World*, 2:784.

21 Almond, *British Discovery of Buddhism*, 35.

22 Ibid., 41–53.

23 Hittell, *Mental Growth of Mankind*, 2:236–38, quotation on 236; see also "Book Chat," *Freethinker*, January 5, 1896, 13; Almond, *British Discovery of Buddhism*, 96–102.

24 D.M. Bennett, "The Indian Saint, or Buddha and Buddhism," *Truth Seeker*, September 8, 1877, 285; Robert Ingersoll, "Heretics and Heresies," lecture delivered in 1874, in Robert G. Ingersoll, *The Works of Robert G. Ingersoll* (New York: Dresden Publishing Co., C.P. Farrell, 1902), 1:244–45.

25 "Buddhism Atheistical," *Boston Investigator*, July 17, 1867, 82; "Buddhism in America," *Boston Investigator*, May 18, 1887, 3.

26 Bennett, *Truth Seeker Around the World*, 3:397.

27 Paul Carus, "Buddhism and God," *Freethinker*, May 24, 1896, 331; J.M. Wheeler, "Max Müller on Christianity and Buddhism," *Freethinker*, August 2, 1896, 491–92.

28 See chapter 3 of Inden, *Imagining India*.

29 See for example "Special Progress," *Reasoner*, June 3, 1846, 12–13; "Current Facts," *Reasoner* 5, no. 113 (1848): 141; "Reports of Secularism in Calcutta," *Boston Investigator*, June 14, 1854, 2; Bombay Correspondents, "Abdoola Shaw, the Freethinking Lecturer of Bombay," *Reasoner*, June 10, 1860, 189; B.V., "Freethought in India," *National Reformer*, January 24, 1875, 53; "Sugar

Plums," *Freethinker*, January 28, 1883, 29; Remly S. Sidelinger, "India Ahead," *Truth Seeker*, November 22, 1884, 745.

30 Bennett, *Truth Seeker Around the World*, 2:765.

31 Edward Royle, *Radicals, Secularists and Republicans: Popular Freethought in Britain, 1866–1915* (Manchester: Manchester University Press, 1980), 80.

32 C.J., "Indian Notes," *Freethinker*, July 15, 1883, 222; "Sugar Plums," *Freethinker*, March 16, 1884, 86; see also J.M. Wheeler, "Christianity in India," *Freethinker*, September 21, 1884, 303; Staff-Sergeant, "Converts in India," *Freethinker*, May 10, 1903, 301.

33 Kedarnath Basu, "A Letter from India," *Truth Seeker*, September 16, 1882, 588; "Sugar Plums," March 16, 1884, 86; Amrita Lal Roy, "The Missionary and the Heathen," *Truth Seeker*, September 19, 1885, 595.

34 C.V. Varadacharia, "A Letter from India," *Truth Seeker*, November 8, 1902, 713.

35 Lucianus, "A Dialogue Between a Missionary and a Hindu," *Freethinker*, February 25, 1883, 57–58; "A Dialogue Between a Missionary and a Hindu," *Freethinker*, February 28, 1904, 140.

36 "Religious Character of the Hindoo," *Reasoner*, February 3, 1856, 36.

37 Christine Bolt, *Victorian Attitudes to Race* (London: Routledge & Keegan Paul, 1971), 201, 157.

38 "The Bolton (Prohibited) Lecture on India," *Reasoner*, January 13, 1858, 12.

39 Ibid.

40 Ibid., 13.

41 George Jacob Holyoake, "Importance of Secularism to India," *Reasoner*, September 11, 1859, 289.

42 Richard Congreve, *India* (London: John Chapman, 1857), 5.

43 Ibid., 6–7.

44 Ibid., 16–17, quotation on 17.

45 Ibid., 31–32; see also Bernard Porter, *Critics of Empire: British Radicals and the Imperial Challenge*, 2nd ed. (London and New York: I.B. Tauris, 2008 [1968]), 27–28; for another positivist view on India, see E.H. Pember, "England and India," in *International Policy: Essays on the Foreign Relations of England*, ed. Frederic Harrison (London: Chapman and Hall, 1866), 223–326.

46 See C.A. Bayly, *Recovering Liberties: Indian Thought in the Age of Liberalism and Empire* (Cambridge: Cambridge University Press, 2012), 14, 58–60, 197, 265–66.

47 The full series is Annie Besant, "England, India, and Afghanistan," *National Reformer*, November 10, 1878, 292–93; Annie Besant, "England, India, and Afghanistan," *National Reformer*, November 17, 1878, 305–7; Annie Besant, "England, India, and Afghanistan," *National Reformer*, November 24, 1878, 323–26; Annie Besant, "England, India, and Afghanistan," *National Reformer*, December 1, 1878, 337–40; Annie Besant, "England, India, and Afghanistan," *National Reformer*, December 8, 1878, 353–54; Annie Besant, "England, India, and Afghanistan," *National Reformer*, December 15, 1878, 369–71; Annie

Besant, "England, India, and Afghanistan," *National Reformer*, December 22, 1878, 386–88.

48 Annie Besant, *England, India, and Afghanistan, and the Story of Afghanistan* (Madras: Theosophical Publishing House, 1931), 7–8.

49 Ibid., 6.

50 Ibid., 16–17.

51 Ibid., 83.

52 Ibid., 84; for similar sentiments, see S.S., "Home Rule in India," *National Reformer*, August 6, 1882, 102–3; G.W. Foote, "Providence and the British Empire," *Freethinker*, August 8, 1897, 497–98.

53 See part 5 of Arthur H. Nethercot, *The First Five Lives of Annie Besant* (London: Rupert Hart-Davis, 1961).

54 Arthur H. Nethercot, *The Last Four Lives of Annie Besant* (London: Rupert Hart-Davis, 1963).

55 Mark Bevir, "In Opposition to the Raj: Annie Besant and the Dialectic of Empire," *History of Political Thought* 19, no. 1 (1998): 62.

56 Ibid., 77.

57 Speech on India at Town Hall, Northampton, November 19, 1883, in Charles Bradlaugh, *Speeches* (London: Freethought Publishing Company, 1890), 42.

58 Ibid., 43.

59 Ibid., 45.

60 Charles Bradlaugh, "England in Asia," *National Reformer*, June 29, 1890, 402.

61 Hypatia Bradlaugh Bonner and J.M. Robertson, *Charles Bradlaugh: A Record of His Life and Work* (London: T. Fisher Unwin, 1895), 2:200. Robertson wrote the second volume.

62 David Nash, "Charles Bradlaugh, India, and the Many Chameleon Destinations of Republicanism," in *Republicanism in Victorian Society*, ed. David Nash and Anthony Taylor (Stroud, Gloucestershire: Sutton, 2000), 106–24.

63 "Mr. Bradlaugh and India," *National Reformer*, January 5, 1890, 12.

64 Indian National Congress Speech, Bombay, December 29, 1889, in Bradlaugh, *Speeches*, 152.

65 Ibid., 153.

66 "Departure from Bombay," *National Reformer*, February 2, 1890, 76.

67 David Tribe, *President Charles Bradlaugh M.P.* (London: Elek, 1971), 289.

68 Lala Lajpat Rai, speech at a meeting of the Liberal and Radical Associations of England held at Kettering, August 10, 1905, in *The Collected Works of Lala Lajpat Rai*, ed. B.R. Nanda (New Delhi: Manohar, 2003), 2:146. Thanks to Chris Moffat for this citation.

69 George W. Stocking Jr., *Race, Culture, and Evolution: Essays in the History of Anthropology*, New Edition (Chicago and London: University of Chicago Press, 1982), 53–54.

70 On stereotypes of the Chinese, see Robert McClellan, *The Heathen Chinee: A Study of American Attitudes toward China, 1890–1905* (Columbus: Ohio State University Press, 1971).

Notes

71 Hittell, *Mental Growth of Mankind*, 2:123; see also "China – Its Religion, &c.," *Boston Investigator*, February 18, 1863, 333.

72 "Notes and Clippings," *Truth Seeker*, June 16, 1883, 368.

73 J.M. Wheeler, "A Chinese Secularist," *Freethinker*, July 31, 1887, 242.

74 Eugene Macdonald, "Effort Worse Than Wasted," *Truth Seeker*, September 8, 1900, 562; see also "Acid Drops," *Freethinker*, August 24, 1884, 207.

75 See for example "Replies and Notices to Reader," *Reasoner* 16, no. 412 (1854): 270; "Acid Drops," *Freethinker*, January 27, 1884, 28; Alec. Zander, "Ah Ling's Religion," *Freethinker*, September 1, 1901, 549.

76 Bennett, *Truth Seeker Around the World*, 3:790.

77 Ibid., 3:807.

78 "Freethinkers in Japan," *Boston Investigator*, July 26, 1854, 2; see also "Civilization Vs. Heathenism," *Boston Investigator*, January 14, 1852, 2.

79 "The Heathen Japanese," *Boston Investigator*, March 14, 1860, 372; see also "Japan," *Boston Investigator*, January 5, 1859, 3.

80 Eugene Macdonald, "A Composite Religion for Japan," *Truth Seeker*, July 24, 1897, 448.

81 Eugene Macdonald, "Many Japanese Agnostics," *Truth Seeker*, August 2, 1902, 488.

82 Chapman Cohen, "Converting the Japs," *Freethinker*, March 20, 1904, 178.

83 J.M. Wheeler, "A Jolly Japanese Religion," *Freethinker*, May 19, 1895, 305.

84 J.M. Wheeler, "Religion in Japan," *Freethinker*, November 29, 1896, 755.

85 Autonomos, "Whang Chang Bang on the Religion of the English, Letter I," *National Reformer*, October 7, 1866, 229.

86 Ibid., 230.

87 Autonomos, "Whang Chang Bang on the Religion of the English, Letter III," *National Reformer*, November 11, 1866, 311.

88 Autonomos, "Whang Chang Bang on the Religion of the English, Letter IV," *National Reformer*, November 25, 1866, 342.

89 Hsiang-Ti-Foo, "O Clismas!," *Freethinker*, December 27, 1896, 820.

90 McClellan, *Heathen Chinee*, 48.

91 Ah Sin, *Letters of a Chinaman to English Readers on English and Chinese Superstition and the Mischief of Missionaries* (London: Pioneer Press, 1903), 7–8.

92 J.M. Wheeler, "Missions in China," *Freethinker*, August 18, 1895, 514; Tse-Shenk Linn, "Qualities of the Chinese," *Truth Seeker*, March 18, 1911, 166.

93 "The Heathen Has His Say," *Truth Seeker*, December 22, 1900, 455; see also "A Chinese Opinion of Christianity," *Truth Seeker*, July 21, 1900, 455.

94 John F. Clark, "A Word for the Chinese," *Truth Seeker*, June 21, 1902, 393; George Macdonald, "A Heathen Bystander," *Truth Seeker*, June 27, 1914, 401.

95 Eugene Macdonald, "The 'White Peril' in the Far East," *Truth Seeker*, November 26, 1904, 755; Baron Kaneko, "Baron Kaneko on Japan," *Truth Seeker*, September 16, 1905, 583.

96 Yoshiro Oyama, "Freethought Lively in Japan," *Truth Seeker*, October 14, 1911, 642.

97 Y. Oyama, "Our Japanese Recruit," *Truth Seeker*, October 15, 1910, 666.

98 Quoted in Scott D. Seligman, *The First Chinese American: The Remarkable Life of Wong Chin Foo* (Hong Kong: Hong Kong University Press, 2013), 75.

99 Ibid., 91.

100 Wong Chin Foo, "Why Am I a Heathen?," *North American Review* 145, no. 369 (August 1887): 175.

101 Ibid., 179.

102 Ibid., 174.

103 Ibid., 179.

104 Seligman, *First Chinese American*, 294.

105 Wong Chin Foo, "Why Am I a Heathen?," *Truth Seeker*, August 13, 1887, 518–19; Wong Chin Foo, "Why Am I a Heathen?," *Freethinker*, August 28, 1887, 279; Wong Chin Foo, "Why Am I a Heathen? II," *Freethinker*, September 4, 1887, 287; Wong Chin Foo, "Why Am I a Heathen? III," *Freethinker*, September 11, 1887, 295; Wong Chin Foo, "Why Am I a Heathen? IV," *Freethinker*, September 25, 1887, 311.

106 "Ye Unspeakable Heathen," *Truth Seeker* 4, no. 20 (May 19, 1877): 58.

107 "A Countryman of Confucius," *Truth Seeker* 23, no. 48 (November 28, 1896): 761.

108 For some early examples, see T.W. Thornton, "Cannoniers of the Cross," *Reasoner* 3, no. 61 (1847): 411–12; John Watts, "The Session and Secularism," *National Reformer*, August 6, 1864, 329; J.H. Bridges, "England and China," in Harrison, *International Policy*, 327–448; J.H. Bridges, "England and China," *National Reformer*, October 30, 1870, 283.

109 "Mrs. Law on Chinese Missions," *National Reformer*, April 4, 1869, 219; see also Josephine K. Henry, "And Yet: We Send Missionaries to China," *Blue-Grass Blade*, February 23, 1902, 1.

110 J.M. Wheeler, "Christianity in China," *Freethinker*, February 14, 1892, 98.

111 McClellan, *Heathen Chinee*, 228–38.

112 G.W. Foote, "Breaking China," *Freethinker*, June 17, 1900, 367; Eugene Macdonald, "The Crisis in China," *Truth Seeker*, July 28, 1900, 468; G.W. Foote, "Chinese Horrors," *Freethinker*, July 29, 1900, 465; L.D. Crine, "Conspiracy Against China," *Truth Seeker*, August 25, 1900, 534; G.W. Foote, "Christian Beasts in China," *Freethinker*, January 20, 1901, 33–34.

113 Frederick Ryan, "The Chinese Horror and Its Lessons," *Freethinker*, July 21, 1901, 460.

114 Mark Twain, "To the Person Sitting in Darkness," *North American Review* 172, no. 531 (February 1901): 164 (emphasis in original).

115 Eugene Macdonald, "Jap and Muscovite," *Truth Seeker*, February 20, 1904, 116.

116 Eugene Macdonald, "The Source of Japanese Humanity," *Truth Seeker*, February 4, 1905, 69; see also M. Wachter, "As to Christianity in Japan," *Truth Seeker*, June 10, 1905, 361; Eugene Macdonald, "The Peace," *Truth Seeker*, September 9, 1905, 565.

Notes

117 G.W. Foote, "That Horrid Japan," *Freethinker*, September 4, 1904, 561.
118 G.W. Foote, "The Yellow Peril," *Freethinker*, November 19, 1905, 737; see also G.W. Foote, "The Japanese Spirit," *Freethinker*, May 21, 1905, 321–22; Annie Lillian Swett, "After the Russian and Japanese War," *Truth Seeker*, June 23, 1906, 387.
119 Thomas F. Gossett, *Race: The History of an Idea in America*, New Edition (New York and Oxford: Oxford University Press, 1997 [1963]), 289–91; Andrew Gyory, *Closing the Gate: Race, Politics, and the Chinese Exclusion Act* (Chapel Hill and London: University of North Carolina Press, 1998); Matthew Frye Jacobson, *Barbarian Virtues: The United States Encounters Foreign Peoples at Home and Abroad, 1876–1917* (New York: Hill and Wang, 2000), 75–81.
120 Robert Ingersoll, interview with *The Commercial*, Cincinnati, Ohio, December 6, 1880, in Ingersoll, *Works*, 8:59–60, quotation on 59.
121 Ibid., 8:60.
122 Robert Ingersoll, interview with *The Press*, Cleveland, Ohio, November 12, 1891, in Ingersoll, *Works*, 8:485.
123 Robert Ingersoll, "Should the Chinese Be Excluded?," in Ingersoll, *Works*, 11:357.
124 Ibid., 11:359.
125 Ibid., 11:361.
126 Ibid., 11:365.
127 E.D. Strong, "The Chinese Question," *Truth Seeker*, July 20, 1878, 457; Susan H. Wixon, "Several Subjects," *Boston Investigator*, April 19, 1882, 1; Crine, "Conspiracy Against China," 534; Clark, "A Word for the Chinese," 393; George C. Bartlett, "A Letter from China," *Truth Seeker*, July 22, 1905, 458.
128 Eugene Macdonald, "The Chinaman and the Christians," *Truth Seeker*, August 4, 1883, 488; for a similar comparison, see James F. Morton Jr., "Certain Comments," *Truth Seeker*, September 17, 1910, 600.
129 Bartlett, "A Letter from China," 458.
130 Clark, "A Word for the Chinese," 393.
131 Bartlett, "A Letter from China," 458.
132 J.E. Roberts, "The Land of Confucius," *Truth Seeker*, November 10, 1900, 708.
133 Robertson identified him: J.M. Robertson, *A History of Freethought in the Nineteenth Century* (London: Dawsons of Pall Mall, 1969 [1929]), 1:300.
134 D., "Immigration," *National Reformer*, February 24, 1878, 1045.
135 D., "The 'Chinese' Question," *National Reformer*, June 10, 1888, 373.
136 R.B.G., "The Chinese Question," *Boston Investigator*, July 26, 1876, 2; see also F.W. Conn, "From California," *Boston Investigator*, April 7, 1886, 2.
137 Clarke Irvine, "Anti-Mongols," *Truth Seeker*, June 12, 1886, 375.
138 Quoted in Lynne Marks, *Infidels and the Damn Churches: Irreligion and Religion in Settler British Columbia* (Vancouver: University of British Columbia Press, 2017), 67.
139 Quoted in ibid., 75.

Notes

CHAPTER 5: THE BEST FRIENDS THE NEGRO EVER HAD: AFRICAN AMERICANS AND
WHITE ATHEISTS

1 Samuel Porter Putnam, *400 Years of Freethought* (New York: Truth Seeker Company, 1894), 681–829.
2 Ibid., 453–71, 787–88, 828–29; Moncure Conway, *Autobiography: Memories and Experiences*, 2 vols. (London and Paris: Cassell and Company, 1904); Susan Jacoby, *Freethinkers: A History of American Secularism* (New York: Henry Holt and Company, 2004); Henry Mayer, *All on Fire: William Lloyd Garrison and the Abolition of Slavery* (New York: St. Martin's Press, 1998).
3 For a critical analysis of Wright's experiment at Nashoba, see Gail Bederman, "Revisiting Nashoba: Slavery, Utopia, and Frances Wright in America, 1818–1826," *American Literary History* 17, no. 3 (October 2005): 438–59.
4 On British attitudes to the American Civil War, see chapter 2 of Christine Bolt, *Victorian Attitudes to Race* (London: Routledge & Keegan Paul, 1971).
5 "The Days of the Negro," *Secular World*, May 10, 1862, 6; Charles Bradlaugh, *The Autobiography of C. Bradlaugh: A Page of His Life* (London: R. Forder, 1891), 23.
6 John W. Compton, "The Emancipation of the American Mind: J.S. Mill on the Civil War," *Review of Politics* 70, no. 2 (Spring 2008): 221–44.
7 Quoted in Adrian Desmond and James Moore, *Darwin's Sacred Cause: How a Hatred of Slavery Shaped Darwin's Views on Human Evolution* (Boston and New York: Houghton Mifflin Harcourt, 2009), 326.
8 George M. Fredrickson, *The Black Image in the White Mind: The Debate on Afro-American Character and Destiny, 1817–1914* (New York: Harper & Row, 1971), 321–22, quotation on 321.
9 George Jacob Holyoake and Brewin Grant, *Christianity and Secularism: Report of a Public Discussion Between the Rev. Brewin Grant, B.A., and George Jacob Holyoake, Esq.* (London: Ward and Co., 1853), 122, 258; J.M. Wheeler, "Was Slavery Abolished by Christianity?," *Freethinker*, April 3, 1887, 111.
10 Douglas Lorimer, "Science and the Secularization of Victorian Images of Race," in *Victorian Science in Context*, ed. Bernard Lightman (Chicago and London: University of Chicago Press, 1997), 212–35.
11 Saladin, *Christianity and the Slave Trade* (London: W. Stewart & Co., c. 1880s), 1.
12 Ibid., 3.
13 Ibid., 7.
14 "A Coloured Discourse," *National Reformer*, December 31, 1865, 834.
15 For example, see "A Negro Story," *Boston Investigator*, November 26, 1851, 4; Scoffer, "A Negro Sermon," *Freethinker*, February 15, 1885, 52; "Colored Piety," *Freethinker*, October 31, 1897, 700; "Justification," *Freethinker*, March 13, 1910.
16 "Opening of the Finsbury Mechanics' Institute," *Reasoner*, July 29, 1846, 137.
17 George Holyoake, "Two Sides of the Jewish Character," *Reasoner* 6, no. 161 (1849): 403.

Notes

18 Eric Lott, *Love and Theft: Blackface Minstrelsy and the American Working Class* (New York and Oxford: Oxford University Press, 1993).

19 For similar examples, see "Notes and Clippings," *Truth Seeker*, August 31, 1878, 545; "Notes and Clippings," *Truth Seeker*, June 6, 1885, 353.

20 A Country Doctor, "Popular Superstitions," *Truth Seeker*, September 14, 1907, 578.

21 For other examples, see "Negro Superstition," *Boston Investigator*, February 28, 1872, 3; "Items of News," *Boston Investigator*, July 30, 1879, 6; "News of the Week," *Truth Seeker*, December 17, 1887, 816; "News of the Week," *Truth Seeker*, April 7, 1888, 224; "The Nigger Preacher and the Black Cat," *Freethinker*, March 22, 1896, 188.

22 Eugene Macdonald, "Colored Preachers," *Truth Seeker*, June 30, 1883, 409.

23 George Macdonald, "Observations," *Truth Seeker*, September 11, 1897, 585; M.M. Mangasarian, "'Colored' Christians in the South," *Truth Seeker*, February 20, 1915, 115.

24 "Negro Religious Worship," *Boston Investigator*, September 9, 1868, 149.

25 For a similar analysis of race and gender in the cartoons of Watson Heston, see Leigh Eric Schmidt, *Village Atheists: How America's Unbelievers Made Their Way in a Godly Nation* (Princeton and Oxford: Princeton University Press, 2016), 135–42.

26 Sidney Warren, *American Freethought, 1860–1914* (New York: Gordian Press, 1966), 194.

27 Colin Kidd, *The Forging of Races: Race and Scripture in the Protestant Atlantic World, 1600–2000* (Cambridge: Cambridge University Press, 2006), 47–48.

28 Kersey Graves, *The World's Sixteen Crucified Saviors; Or, Christianity Before Christ*, 4th ed. (Boston: Colby & Rich, 1876), 51. The reference is to a character in the poem, not to Jesus.

29 Ibid., 52.

30 Elmina Drake Slenker, "Was Christ a Negro?," *Truth Seeker*, January 8, 1876, 11.

31 W.P. Ball, "God's Complexion," *Freethinker*, June 14, 1885, 190.

32 Gilbert Osofsky, *Harlem: The Making of a Ghetto: Negro New York, 1890–1930* (New York: Harper & Row, 1963).

33 George Macdonald, "Observations," *Truth Seeker*, September 5, 1903, 568.

34 "Colored Freethinkers," *Boston Investigator*, July 17, 1889, 5.

35 Christopher Cameron, *Black Freethinkers: A History of African American Secularism* (Evanston, IL: Northwestern University Press, 2019).

36 Evelyn A. Kirkley, *Rational Mothers and Infidel Gentlemen: Gender and American Atheism, 1865–1915* (Syracuse, NY: Syracuse University Press, 2000), 21.

37 Jacoby, *Freethinkers*, 189–91.

38 Kirkley, *Rational Mothers and Infidel Gentlemen*, 22.

39 "Sons of Temperance," *Boston Investigator*, April 28, 1847, 3.

40 Will S. Andrews, "Impromptu Thoughts," *Boston Investigator*, September 17, 1890, 2.
41 See chapter 1 of Cameron, *Black Freethinkers*; Christopher Cameron, "Slavery and African American Irreligion," *Journal of Southern Religion* 18 (2016), http://jsreligion.org/vol18/cameron/, accessed January 30, 2019.
42 Ezra Greenspan, *William Wells Brown: An African American Life* (New York and London: W.W. Norton & Company, 2014), 174–75.
43 William Wells Brown, *Narrative of William W. Brown, a Fugitive Slave: Written by Himself* (Boston: Anti-Slavery Office, 1847), 83–84.
44 Ibid., 37.
45 Ibid., 97.
46 William Wells Brown, *Clotel; or the President's Daughter: A Narrative of Slave Life* (London: Partridge & Oakey, 1853), iv.
47 Ibid., 244.
48 Ibid., 97.
49 Ibid., 92.
50 Ibid., 188.
51 See for example Scott C. Williamson, *The Narrative Life: The Moral and Religious Thought of Frederick Douglass* (Macon, GA: Mercer University Press, 2002).
52 Zachary McLeod Hutchins, "Rejecting the Root: The Liberating, Anti-Christ Theology of Douglass's Narrative," *Nineteenth-Century Literature* 68, no. 3 (2013): 292–322; Frederick Douglass, *Narrative of the Life of Frederick Douglass, an American Slave* (Boston: Anti-Slavery Office, 1845), 70–73.
53 See chapter 1 of Cameron, *Black Freethinkers*.
54 "Fred. Douglass on the Supernatural," *Boston Investigator*, December 14, 1870, 261; Frederick Douglass, "The American Church and Slavery," *Freethinker*, February 22, 1891, 88.
55 "Notes and Clippings," *Truth Seeker*, September 20, 1890, 593.
56 John E. Remsburg, *The Bible: I. Authenticity II. Credibility III. Morality* (New York: Truth Seeker Company, 1907), 381; Sara A. Underwood, "New York Anniversaries," *Boston Investigator*, May 27, 1868, 26.
57 Adolphe Beckett, "Mixed Marriages," *Boston Investigator*, February 27, 1884, 5.
58 Frederick Douglass, *The Life and Times of Frederick Douglass* (Hartford, CT: Park Publishing Co., 1881), 561.
59 Ibid., 562.
60 George Jacob Holyoake, *Sixty Years of an Agitator's Life*, 3rd ed. (London: T. Fisher Unwin, 1903 [1892]), 1:99.
61 H.J., "How Christians Love the Negro," *Freethinker*, June 12, 1892, 371.
62 "Ingersoll and F. Douglas," *Freethinker*, December 9, 1894, 788; "Frederick Douglass and Ingersoll," *Freethinker*, December 22, 1895, 805.
63 J.J.S., "Colored Liberals," *Truth Seeker*, March 23, 1901, 184.
64 "Negroes Praised Him," *Truth Seeker*, April 20, 1901, 247.
65 J.J.S., "Colored Liberals," 184.

Notes

66   "Negroes Praised Him," 248.

67   On Cincore, see Schmidt, *Village Atheists*, 140–41.

68   Putnam, *400 Years of Freethought*, 661.

69   Chapter 1 of Cameron, *Black Freethinkers*.

70   On Harrison's life, see Jeffrey B. Perry, *Hubert Harrison: The Voice of Harlem Radicalism, 1883–1918* (New York: Columbia University Press, 2009); chapter 3 of Cameron, *Black Freethinkers*.

71   Perry, *Hubert Harrison*, 60–63.

72   Ibid., 114–18, 135–37; Hubert Harrison, "Paine's Place in the Deistical Movement," *Truth Seeker*, February 11, 1911, in *A Hubert Harrison Reader*, ed. Jeffrey B. Perry (Middletown, CT: Wesleyan University Press, 2001), 40–42.

73   Hubert Harrison, "The Negro a Conservative," *Truth Seeker*, September 12, 1914, in *A Hubert Harrison Reader*, ed. Perry, 43–46, quotation on 43.

74   Hubert Harrison, "'Democracy' in America," *Negro World* 11 (October 8, 1921), in *A Hubert Harrison Reader*, ed. Perry, 284.

75   W.S.T. Harris, "A Colored Man's Plea," *Truth Seeker*, October 22, 1910, 683.

76   [W. E. B. Du Bois], "The Christianity of White Christians," *Truth Seeker*, March 6, 1915, 147; the original article is "The White Christ," *Crisis* 9, no. 5 (March 1915): 238. For more on Du Bois, see Chapter 6.

77   David D. Anderson, *Robert Ingersoll* (New York: Twayne Publishers Inc., 1972), 7, 129.

78   Jeremy Rich, "Heresy Is the Only True Religion: Richard Lynch Garner (1848–1920), a Southern Freethinker in Africa and America," *Journal of the Gilded Age and Progressive Era* 12, no. 1 (January 2013): 78–79.

79   Kirkley, *Rational Mothers and Infidel Gentlemen*, 21.

80   Warren, *American Freethought*, 117.

81   Orvin Larson, *American Infidel: Robert G. Ingersoll* (New York: Citadel Press, 1962), 63–64.

82   Quoted in ibid., 70.

83   Ibid., 82.

84   Ibid., 42.

85   Ibid., 51–52, 76–78.

86   Robert Ingersoll, "An Address to the Colored People," speech delivered in Galesburg, Illinois, 1867, in Robert G. Ingersoll, *The Works of Robert G. Ingersoll* (New York: Dresden Publishing Co., C.P. Farrell, 1902), 9:5–17.

87   See for example Robert Ingersoll, "Bangor Speech," speech delivered in Bangor, Maine, August 24, 1876, in Ingersoll, *Works*, 9:97–122.

88   Robert Ingersoll, "Cooper Union Speech, New York," speech delivered in New York, September 10, 1876, in Ingersoll, *Works*, 9:181–82.

89   Robert Ingersoll, "Chicago Speech," speech delivered in Chicago, October 20, 1876, in Ingersoll, *Works*, 9:218.

90   Robert Ingersoll, interview with *The National*, Washington, DC, October 17, 1883, in Ingersoll, *Works*, 8:136.

91 Robert Ingersoll, interview with *The Commercial*, Louisville, Kentucky, October [November] 24, 1884, in Ingersoll, *Works*, 8:219.

92 Robert Ingersoll, "Address on the Civil Rights Act," speech delivered in Washington, DC, October 22, 1883, in Ingersoll, *Works*, 11:48.

93 Robert Ingersoll, interview with the *National Republican*, Washington, DC, October 17, 1883, in Ingersoll, *Works*, 8:136–37; see also "Col. Ingersoll on the Colored Race," *Boston Investigator*, April 20, 1892, 6.

94 Ibram X. Kendi, *Stamped from the Beginning: The Definitive History of Racist Ideas in America* (London: Bodley Head, 2016), 124–25.

95 For the debate surrounding Washington's controversial invitation to the White House in 1901, see Chapter 6.

96 On Washington's life, see Robert J. Norrell, *Up from History: The Life of Booker T. Washington* (Cambridge, MA, and London: Belknap Press of Harvard University Press, 2009).

97 "Notes and Clippings," *Truth Seeker*, August 30, 1890, 545; Eugene Macdonald, "The Negro," *Truth Seeker*, April 25, 1903, 264; see also "Acid Drops," *Freethinker*, August 16, 1896, 519.

98 "Heathen Editor: Offers to Entertain Booker T. Washington at 'Quakeracre,'" *Blue-Grass Blade*, May 25, 1902, 2; see also "Booker T. Washington," *Blue-Grass Blade*, June 15, 1902, 1.

99 Hugh O. Pentecost, "How We Treat the Negroes," *Truth Seeker*, June 6, 1903, 354.

100 Robert Ingersoll, "Fragments," undated, in Ingersoll, *Works*, 12:340.

101 "Harvard's Colored Class-Day Orator," *Boston Investigator*, July 2, 1890, 4.

102 "Summary of News," *National Reformer*, September 29, 1867, 280; "Summary of News," *National Reformer*, September 27, 1868, 200; "Summary of News," *National Reformer*, January 30, 1870, 72.

103 Charles Bradlaugh, "American Politics II," *National Reformer*, April 18, 1875, 443.

104 James D. Carr, "The Negro's Viewpoint of the Negro Question," *Truth Seeker*, May 23, 1903, 326–28, quotation on 326.

105 George E. Wibecan Jr., "The Race Problem at the B.P.A.," *Truth Seeker*, May 8, 1909, 296.

106 Robert Ingersoll, "What is Religion?," speech delivered in Boston, June 2, 1899, in Ingersoll, *Works*, 4:494.

107 Robert Ingersoll, "Fragments," undated, in Ingersoll, *Works*, 12:322.

108 Ibid., 12:323.

109 Ibid., 12:324.

110 "Has Mercy Fled to Beasts?," *Truth Seeker*, May 6, 1899, 277; "Sugar Plums," *Freethinker*, May 21, 1899, 329–30.

111 Fredrickson, *Black Image in the White Mind*, 272.

112 For the defenders of lynching, see S. Rittenburg, "Lynching Excused," *Truth Seeker*, June 17, 1899, 378; S.R. Shepherd, "The Leavenworth Lynching," *Truth Seeker*, February 16, 1901, 106–7; Anonymous, "Punishment for Negro

Fiends," *Truth Seeker*, September 21, 1901, 601; Jno. W. James, "Was Born in Tennessee," *Truth Seeker*, August 8, 1903, 506; W.L. Dolphyn, "Must Lynch Them," *Truth Seeker*, October 3, 1903, 634; J.M. Benjamin, "Negro Question Not a Burning One," *Truth Seeker*, December 12, 1903, 790; R.M. Powell, "Facts About Southern Lynching," *Truth Seeker*, January 12, 1907, 25.

113   Charles D. McBride, "The Hose Murder," *Truth Seeker*, July 29, 1899, 474; H. Sandberg, "The Crime of Lynching," *Truth Seeker*, November 2, 1901, 697; Elizabeth E. Evans, "Black and White," *Truth Seeker*, June 16, 1904, 454; James F. Morton Jr., "Certain Comments," *Truth Seeker*, April 8, 1911, 211.

114   George Macdonald, "Observations," *Truth Seeker*, December 15, 1900, 792; George Macdonald, "Observations," *Truth Seeker*, August 8, 1903, 503.

115   Charles Chilton Moore, "Christian Crime in Kentucky and Ohio," *Freethinker*, January 28, 1900, 53.

116   Douglas Lorimer, *Science, Race Relations and Resistance: Britain, 1870–1914* (Manchester: Manchester University Press, 2013), 280–81.

117   H.J., "How Christians Love the Negro," *Freethinker*, June 12, 1892, 371.

118   H.J., "How Christians Love the Negro," *Freethinker*, June 19, 1892, 388.

119   Thomas Henry Huxley, "Emancipation – Black and White (1865)," in *Collected Essays*, vol. 3, *Science and Education Essays* (New York: D. Appleton and Company, 1897 [1893–94]), 66–67.

120   Ibid., 67.

121   Huxley's remarks came from a series of lectures delivered to the Royal College of Surgeons and were reprinted as a pamphlet by an abolitionist society: Mrs. P. A. Taylor, ed., *Professor Huxley and the Negro Question* (London: Ladies' London Emancipation Society, 1864), quotation on 9.

122   T.H. Huxley to sister Lizzie, May 4, 1864, in Leonard Huxley, ed., *Life and Letters of Thomas Henry Huxley* (New York: D. Appleton and Company, 1901), 1:272; see also Desmond and Moore, *Darwin's Sacred Cause*, 334–36.

123   T.H. Huxley in the *Pall Mall Gazette*, quoted in Huxley, *Life and Letters of Thomas Henry Huxley*, 1:301; on the British reaction to the Morant Bay rebellion, see chapter 9 of Douglas Lorimer, *Colour, Class, and the Victorians: English Attitudes to the Negro in the Mid-Nineteenth Century* (Leicester: Leicester University Press, 1978).

124   Kathi Kern, *Mrs. Stanton's Bible* (Ithaca and London: Cornell University Press, 2002), 106–16.

125   Quoted in Angela Davis, *Women, Race and Class* (London: Women's Press, 1982), 84–85.

126   Quoted in Kern, *Mrs. Stanton's Bible*, 111.

127   Ibid., 112.

128   [William Cowper Brann], "Negro Preachers and Their Work," *Freethinker*, May 27, 1900, 332.

129   Jacoby, *Freethinkers*, 155.

130   "Brann's Iconoclast: A Religious Journal That Will Do No Good in the World," *Blue-Grass Blade*, January 26, 1902, 1.

131 Rich, "Heresy," 79–80.
132 Ibid., 85–87.
133 Ibid., 90–91.
134 Fredrickson, *Black Image in the White Mind*, 228.
135 Eugene Macdonald, "The Negro Problem," *Truth Seeker*, March 7, 1903, 148.
136 Ibid.
137 S.M. Lewis, "The Negro Problem," *Truth Seeker*, April 4, 1903, 218.
138 Francis Smith, "The Negro Problem," *Truth Seeker*, April 4, 1903, 218.
139 Macdonald, "The Negro," 264; see also Eugene Macdonald, "Barbarism in the United States," *Truth Seeker*, January 16, 1904, 36.
140 Dolphyn, "Must Lynch Them," 634.
141 Eugene Macdonald, "Christian Hatred of the Negro," *Truth Seeker*, May 2, 1903, 276; Charles Carroll, *"The Negro a Beast" or "In the Image of God"* (St. Louis: American Book and Bible House, 1900).

CHAPTER 6: THE CURSE OF RACE PREJUDICE: RETHINKING RACE AT THE TURN OF THE CENTURY

1 See Elazar Barkan, *The Retreat of Scientific Racism: Changing Concepts of Race in Britain and the United States Between the World Wars* (Cambridge: Cambridge University Press, 1992).
2 Robert Owen, *The Life of Robert Owen, Written by Himself* (London: Charles Knight & Co., 1971 [1857]), 16.
3 This idea runs throughout Owen's work, but see for example Robert Owen, *A New View of Society, or Essays on the Formation of Human Character* (London: Macmillan, 1972 [1813]), 90–91.
4 Quoted in Frank Podmore, *Robert Owen: A Biography* (London: Hutchinson & Co., 1906), 1:24.
5 Alexander Campbell, ed., *Debate on the Evidences of Christianity* (London: R. Groombridge, 1839), 24.
6 Podmore, *Robert Owen*, 1:339–40.
7 Quoted in George Lockwood, *The New Harmony Movement* (New York: D. Appleton and Company, 1905), 85. The constitution is reprinted in full on 84–90.
8 Quoted in Edward Royle, *Victorian Infidels: The Origins of the British Secularist Movement, 1791–1866* (Manchester: Manchester University Press, 1974), 47.
9 "The Bosjesmans and Mr. Owen," *Reasoner* 7, no. 184 (1849): 362–63.
10 Ibid., 363.
11 Christine Ferguson points out that following Owen's conversion to Spiritualism near the end of his life in 1853, he became increasingly receptive to ideas about hereditary determinism: Christine Ferguson, *Determined Spirits: Eugenics, Heredity and Racial Regeneration in Anglo-American Spiritualist Writing, 1848–1930* (Edinburgh: Edinburgh University Press, 2012), 23–25.
12 John Stuart Mill, *Autobiography*, in John M. Robson, ed., *The Collected Works*

of John Stuart Mill (Toronto: University of Toronto Press; London: Routledge and Kegan Paul, 1963–91), 1:270.

13 See chapter 6 of Douglas Lorimer, *Colour, Class, and the Victorians: English Attitudes to the Negro in the Mid-Nineteenth Century* (Leicester: Leicester University Press, 1978).

14 [Thomas Carlyle], "Occasional Discourse on the Negro Question," *Fraser's Magazine for Town and Country* 40 (December 1849): 670–79.

15 Ibid., 677.

16 John Stuart Mill, "The Negro Question," in *Collected Works of John Stuart Mill*, ed. Robson, 21:93.

17 Ibid.

18 J. Joseph Miller, "Chairing the Jamaica Committee: J.S. Mill and the Limits of Colonial Authority," in *Utilitarianism and Empire*, ed. Bart Schultz and Georgios Varouxakis (Lanham, MD: Lexington Books, 2005), 155–78.

19 James Hunt, "The President's Address," *Journal of the Anthropological Society of London* 5 (1867): lix.

20 Ibid., lx.

21 [James Hunt], "Race in Legislation and Political Economy," *Anthropological Review* 4, no. 13 (1866): 122.

22 Georgios Varouxakis, "John Stuart Mill on Race," *Utilitas* 10, no. 1 (1998): 27–28.

23 Ibid., 18.

24 On this debate, see Uday Singh Mehta, *Liberalism and Empire: A Study in Nineteenth-Century British Liberal Thought* (Chicago: University of Chicago Press, 1999); Beate Jahn, "Barbarian Thoughts: Imperialism in the Philosophy of John Stuart Mill," *Review of International Studies* 31, no. 3 (July 2005): 599–618; Jennifer Pitts, *A Turn to Empire: The Rise of Imperial Liberalism in Britain and France* (Princeton: Princeton University Press, 2005); Mark Tunick, "Tolerant Imperialism: John Stuart Mill's Defense of British Rule in India," *Review of Politics* 68, no. 4 (Fall 2006): 586–611; Duncan Bell, "John Stuart Mill on Colonies," *Political Theory* 38, no. 1 (2010): 34–64; chapter 1 of Gregory Claeys, *Mill and Paternalism* (Cambridge: Cambridge University Press, 2013).

25 John Stuart Mill, *On Liberty*, in *Collected Works of John Stuart Mill*, ed. Robson, 18:224.

26 John Stuart Mill, "A Few Words on Non-Intervention," in *Collected Works of John Stuart Mill*, ed. Robson, 21:118.

27 The following summary of Robertson's life is based upon Odin Dekkers, *J.M. Robertson: Rationalist and Literary Critic* (Aldershot and Brookfield, VT: Ashgate, 1998), 1–50.

28 J.M. Robertson, *The Saxon and the Celt: A Study in Sociology* (London: University Press, Limited, 1897), v.

29 Ibid., vi.

30 Ibid., ix; see also L.P. Curtis Jr., *Anglo-Saxons and Celts: A Study of Anti-*

Irish Prejudice in Victorian England (Bridgeport, CT: Conference on British Studies, 1968), 104–5.

31 Robertson, *The Saxon and the Celt*, xii.

32 Ibid., 27–28, quotation on 27.

33 On Hoffman, see George M. Fredrickson, *The Black Image in the White Mind: The Debate on Afro-American Character and Destiny, 1817–1914* (New York: Harper & Row, 1971), 249–51.

34 Robertson, *The Saxon and the Celt*, xii.

35 Ibid., xiii.

36 J.M. Robertson, *The Germans* (London: William and Norgate, 1916), 78.

37 Joseph Kaines, "Race," *National Reformer*, January 2, 1876, 6.

38 Ibid., 6–7.

39 Robertson, *The Saxon and the Celt*, 30.

40 Ibid., 32–33.

41 See J.M. Robertson's written response to Francis Galton, "Eugenics: Its Definition, Scope and Aims," in *Sociological Papers* (London: Macmillan and Co., 1905), 72–74.

42 Robertson, *The Saxon and the Celt*, 124.

43 Robertson, *The Germans*, 109–10, quotation on 109.

44 Matthew Frye Jacobson, *Whiteness of a Different Color: European Immigrants and the Alchemy of Race*, First Paperback Edition (Cambridge, MA: Harvard University Press, 1999 [1998]), 208.

45 "Anglo-Saxon Glorification," *Boston Investigator*, February 20, 1850, 2; for a more positive view, see "The Anglo-Saxon Race," *Boston Investigator*, December 10, 1851, 1.

46 William Maccall, "The Fabulous Anglo-Saxon," *National Reformer*, February 25, 1866, 122.

47 Ibid., 123.

48 Ibid., 124.

49 Leigh Eric Schmidt, *Village Atheists: How America's Unbelievers Made Their Way in a Godly Nation* (Princeton and Oxford: Princeton University Press, 2016), 98–101; on Nast and his Irish caricatures, see Fiona Deans Halloran, *Thomas Nast: The Father of Modern Political Cartoons* (Chapel Hill: University of North Carolina Press, 2012), 33–36, 203–5.

50 Eugene Macdonald, "The Chinaman and the Christians," *Truth Seeker*, August 4, 1883, 488.

51 Franklin H. Giddings, "Who Are The People?," *Truth Seeker*, December 7, 1907, 770; Franklin H. Giddings, "The Jewish Race in America," *Truth Seeker*, December 28, 1907, 823.

52 J.M. Robertson, *Wrecking the Empire* (London: Grant Richards, 1901); J.M. Robertson, *The Boer War: Open Letter to Dr. Conan Doyle* (Philadelphia: G.H. Buchanan & Co., 1902).

53 J.M. Robertson, *Patriotism and Empire*, 2nd ed. (London: Grant Richards, 1900 [1899]), 9–10.

54 Ibid., 71, 191–92.

55 Ibid., 144.

56 Ibid., 200.

57 Dekkers, *J.M. Robertson*, 44–45.

58 Edward Said, *Orientalism* (London: Penguin, 2003 [1978]), 31; for the entire debate, see *Hansard*, June 13, 1910: 17 Parl. Deb., H.C. (5th ser.) (1909–80) 1103–63, available online at http://hansard.millbanksystems.com/commons/1910/jun/13/consolidated-fund-no-2-bill, accessed October 4, 2015.

59 Said, *Orientalism*, 32.

60 The Wikipedia page for Morton is surprisingly comprehensive and brought to my attention many important sources used in the following paragraphs. "James Ferdinand Morton, Jr.," *Wikipedia: The Free Encyclopedia*, https://en.wikipedia.org/w/index.php?title=James_Ferdinand_Morton,_Jr.&oldid=688715834, accessed November 2, 2015.

61 On Morton's life, see "Introduction," in *H.P. Lovecraft: Letters to James F. Morton*, ed. David E. Schultz and S.T. Joshi (New York: Hippocampus Press, 2011), 7–16; James F. Morton Jr., "Fragments of a Mental Autobigraphy," published in 1907, and James F. Morton Jr., "My Intellectual Evolution," published in 1923, in *H.P. Lovecraft*, ed. Schultz and Joshi, 418–25 and 425–26 respectively.

62 On Morton's activities there, see Charles P. Lewarne, "The Anarchist Colony at Home, Washington, 1901–1902," *Arizona and the West* 14, no. 2 (Summer 1972): 155–68.

63 Edward H. Cole, "James F. Morton, Jr.," in *H.P. Lovecraft*, ed. Schultz and Joshi, 433, 436, quotation on 436.

64 James F. Morton, Jr., "Fragments of a Mental Autobiography," in *H.P. Lovecraft*, ed. Schultz and Joshi, 422.

65 "All Superstitions Defied at Thirteen Club Dinner," *Brooklyn Daily Eagle*, February 14, 1907, 22.

66 R. Randolph, "As It Strikes a Southerner," *Truth Seeker*, November 9, 1901, 714.

67 H.S. Trott, "An Unnecessary Discussion," *Truth Seeker*, January 4, 1902, 9; Francis B. Livesey, "Booker Should Turn Press-Writer," *Truth Seeker*, January 11, 1902, 25.

68 P.F. Shumaker, "A Tempest in a Teapot," *Truth Seeker*, March 15, 1902, 170.

69 Moncure Conway, "Negrophobic Hysteria," *Truth Seeker*, December 21, 1901, 803.

70 D. Mackay, "Concerning Booker T. Washington and Vegetarianism," *Truth Seeker*, March 8, 1902, 153.

71 James F. Morton Jr., "The Negro and the Anarchist," *Truth Seeker*, November 30, 1901, 762.

72 James F. Morton Jr., "Certain Comments," *Truth Seeker*, December 3, 1910, 771.

73 James F. Morton Jr., "Certain Comments," *Truth Seeker*, May 4, 1912, 279.

74 James F. Morton Jr., "Certain Comments," *Truth Seeker*, August 16, 1913, 520; James F. Morton Jr., "Certain Comments," *Truth Seeker*, March 4, 1911, 137.

75 A.C. Bowers, "Race Prejudice," *Truth Seeker*, January 23, 1909, 58.

76 A.C. Bowers, "In Narrow Quarters," *Truth Seeker*, October 10, 1908, 651.

77 James F. Morton Jr., "The Race Question," *Truth Seeker*, October 24, 1908, 683.

78 A.C. Bowers, "The Negro," *Truth Seeker*, December 12, 1908, 795.

79 James F. Morton Jr., "Race Prejudice," *Truth Seeker*, December 26, 1908, 826.

80 H.C. Bradford, "The Race Question," *Truth Seeker*, November 19, 1910, 746.

81 James F. Morton Jr., "The Biological Imperative," *Truth Seeker*, December 3, 1910, 779.

82 James F. Morton Jr., *The Curse of Race Prejudice* (New York: Published by the author, 1906), 4.

83 Ibid., 8.

84 Ibid., 11–12.

85 Ibid., 36, 65, 46, 66.

86 Ibid., 7–8.

87 Ibid., 31; for another example of using Darwin against racial chauvinism, see A Citizen of the World, "The Pride of Race and the Love of Country," *National Reformer*, October 9, 1870, 234–35.

88 Morton, *Curse of Race Prejudice*, 46.

89 Ibid., 47.

90 Ibid., 48.

91 Ibid., 51.

92 Ibid., 3.

93 Ibid., 60.

94 Ibid., 62.

95 Ibid., 64.

96 Ibid., 34.

97 See for example *Crisis* 1, no. 5 (March 1911): 2, 32; *Crisis* 19, no. 6 (April 1915): 308; *Crisis* 21, no. 3 (January 1921): 2.

98 Jeffrey B. Perry, *Hubert Harrison: The Voice of Harlem Radicalism, 1883–1918* (New York: Columbia University Press, 2009), 147.

99 Hubert Harrison, "Race Prejudice – II," *New York Call*, December 4, 1911, in *A Hubert Harrison Reader*, ed. Jeffrey B. Perry (Middletown, CT: Wesleyan University Press, 2001), 57.

100 Ibid., 56.

101 Hubert Harrison, "A Negro on Chicken Stealing," letter to the editor, *New York Times*, December 11, 1904, in *A Hubert Harrison Reader*, ed. Perry, 32.

102 Hubert Harrison, "*The Rising Tide of Color against White World-Supremacy* by Lothrop Stoddard," *Negro World*, May 29, 1920, in *A Hubert Harrison Reader*, ed. Perry, 307.

103 Howard B. Radest, *Toward Common Ground: The Story of the Ethical Societies in the United States* (New York: Ungar Publishing, 1969), 94, 170–71.

104 Michael Biddiss, "The Universal Races Congress of 1911," *Race and Class* 13, no. 1 (July 1971): 37.

105 "Circulars Issued by the Executive Council," in *Papers on Inter-Racial Problems*

Notes

Communicated to the First Universal Races Congress, Held at the University of London July 26–29, 1911, ed. Gustav Spiller (London: P.S. King & Son, 1911), xiii.

106 Biddiss, "Universal Races Congress," 40.

107 J.M. Robertson, "The Rationale of Autonomy," in Spiller, *Papers on Inter-Racial Problems*, 40–49.

108 Biddiss, "Universal Races Congress," 40.

109 Gustav Spiller, "Preface," in Spiller, *Papers on Inter-Racial Problems*, vi.

110 Chapter 2 of Christopher Cameron, *Black Freethinkers: A History of African American Secularism* (Evanston, IL: Northwestern University Press, 2019).

111 *First Universal Races Congress, University of London, July 26–29, 1911* (London: Watts & Co., 1910).

112 Ian MacKillop, *The British Ethical Societies* (Cambridge: Cambridge University Press, 1986), 138.

113 Gustav Spiller, "Ethicists and Secularists," *Freethinker*, July 26, 1908, 477.

114 Gustav Spiller, "The Problem of Race Equality," in Spiller, *Papers on Inter-Racial Problems*, 31.

115 Ibid., 36.

116 Ibid., 35.

117 Ibid., 30.

118 Gustav Spiller, "Science and Race Prejudice," *Sociological Review* 5, no. 4 (1912): 334–35.

119 Ibid., 342.

120 Gustav Spiller, "Darwinism and Sociology," *Sociological Review* 7, no. 3 (1914): 239.

121 Spiller, "Science and Race Prejudice," 346.

122 Ibid., 346–47.

123 Ibid., 331.

124 Felix Adler, "The Fundamental Principle of Inter Racial Ethics, and Some Practical Applications of It," in Spiller, *Papers on Inter-Racial Problems*, 265.

125 Ibid., 266.

126 Ibid., 267.

127 On Boas's early life, see Douglas Cole, *Franz Boas: The Early Years, 1858–1906* (Seattle and London: University of Washington Press, 1999).

128 Leonard B. Glick, "Types Distinct from Our Own: Franz Boas on Jewish Identity and Assimilation," *American Anthropologist* 84, no. 3 (September 1982): 555–56; Cole, *Franz Boas*, 109.

129 Glick, "Types Distinct from Our Own," 546.

130 Franz Boas, *The Mind of Primitive Man* (New York: Macmillan, 1922 [1911]), 4.

131 Ibid., 8–10.

132 Ibid., 182–96.

133 Ibid., 278.

134 Franz Boas, "Changes in the Bodily Form of Descendants of Immigrants," *American Anthropologist* 14, no. 3 (September 1912): 530–62; a summarized

version appears in Franz Boas, "Changes in Bodily Form of Descendants of Immigrants," in *Race, Language, and Culture*, Reprint (Chicago and London: University of Chicago Press, 1982 [1940]), 60–75.

135 Franz Boas, "Instability of Human Types," in Spiller, *Papers on Inter-Racial Problems*, 99.

136 Ibid., 101.

137 Ibid., 103.

138 Thomas F. Gossett, *Race: The History of an Idea in America*, New Edition (New York and Oxford: Oxford University Press, 1997 [1963]), 418.

139 Vernon J. Williams Jr., *Rethinking Race: Franz Boas and His Contemporaries* (Lexington, KY: University Press of Kentucky, 1996), 1.

140 W.E.B. Du Bois, *The Autobiography of W.E.B. Du Bois: A Soliloquy on Viewing My Life from the Last Decade of Its First Century* (New York: International Publishers Co., Inc., 1968), 205.

141 Ibid., 285.

142 On Du Bois's religious views, see Brian L. Johnson, *W.E.B. Du Bois: Toward Agnosticism, 1868–1934* (Lanham and Plymouth: Rowman & Littlefield, 2008).

143 Du Bois, *Autobiography*, 197.

144 Ibid., 198–99.

145 Johnson, *Du Bois*, 72–73.

146 Winwood Reade, *The Martyrdom of Man* (London: Trubner & Co., 1872).

147 W.E.B. Du Bois, *The Negro* (New York: Holt, 1915), 7.

148 Quoted in Robin Law, "Du Bois as a Pioneer of African History: A Reassessment of The Negro (1915)," in *Re-Cognizing W.E.B. Du Bois in the Twenty-First Century: Essays on W.E.B. Du Bois*, ed. Mary Keller and Chester J. Fontenot Jr. (Macon, GA: Mercer University Press, 2007), 28.

149 Ibram X. Kendi, *Stamped from the Beginning: The Definitive History of Racist Ideas in America* (London: The Bodley Head, 2016), 505–7.

150 W.E.B. Du Bois, "A Negro Nation Within the Nation," *Current History* 42, no. 3 (June 1, 1935): 266.

151 Ibid., 270.

152 Du Bois, *The Negro*, 7.

153 Ibid., 63.

154 W.E.B. Du Bois, "The Negro Race in the United States of America," in Spiller, *Papers on Inter-Racial Problems*, 351.

155 Ibid., 364.

156 [W.E.B. Du Bois], "The World in Council," *Crisis* 2, no. 5 (September 1911): 196.

157 Du Bois, *Autobiography*, 263.

158 "Acid Drops," *Freethinker*, August 6, 1911, 503.

159 Elazar Barkan has made a similar observation in the case of interwar scientists who contested racism and the idea of race. See Barkan, *Retreat of Scientific Racism*, 9–10.

CONCLUSION: WHAT NEXT FOR RACISM IN A GODLESS WORLD?

1 Mitchell Stephens, *Imagine There's No Heaven: How Atheism Helped Create the Modern World* (New York: Palgrave Macmillan, 2014).

2 See chapter 2 of Christopher Cameron, *Black Freethinkers: A History of African American Secularism* (Evanston, IL: Northwestern University Press, 2019).

3 See ibid., chapter 3.

4 On religion and the civil rights movement, see chapter 7 of Paul Harvey, *Christianity and Race in the American South: A History* (Chicago and London: University of Chicago Press, 2016). It should be noted that Harvey is careful to give atheists and other nonreligious people their due in the movement.

5 See chapter 4 of Cameron, *Black Freethinkers*; see also Anthony Pinn, "What If God Were One of Us: Humanism and African Americans for Humanism," in *Varieties of African American Religious Experience: Toward a Comparative Black Theology*, 20th Anniversary Edition (Minneapolis: Augsburg Fortress Publishers, 2017 [1998]), 175–212.

6 Daniel J. Kevles, *In the Name of Eugenics: Genetics and the Uses of Human Heredity* (New York: Alfred A. Knopf, 1985), 122–28; chapters 6 and 7 of Nancy Stepan, *The Idea of Race in Science: Great Britain, 1800–1960* (London: Macmillan, 1982).

7 Ann Rowe Seaman, *America's Most Hated Woman: The Life and Gruesome Death of Madalyn Murray O'Hair* (New York and London: Continuum, 2006), 39.

8 Quoted in ibid., 42.

9 Alan Ryan, *Bertrand Russell: A Political Life* (New York: Hill and Wang, 1988), 174–76, 197–99.

10 Bertrand Russell, *War Crimes in Vietnam* (London: George Allen & Unwin Ltd., 1967), 9.

11 Bertrand Russell, "The Problem of Minorities," unpublished lecture delivered to the Rand School of Social Science, New York, between October and December 1942, in Barry Feinberg and Ronald Kasrils, eds., *Bertrand Russell's America: His Transatlantic Travels and Writings*, vol. 1, *1896–1945* (London: George Allen & Unwin Ltd., 1973), 319.

12 Ibid., 320.

13 Barry Feinberg and Ronald Kasrils, eds., *Bertrand Russell's America*, vol. 2, *1945–1970* (Boston: South End Press, 1983), 219–41.

14 Charles Lee Smith, "Negro-Breeding Dooms Newburgh," *Truth Seeker*, August 1961, 115.

15 James Hervey Johnson, "Some Facts Concerning the Negro," *Truth Seeker*, July 1960, 107.

16 Corliss Lamont, "Supports Worldwide Racial Equality," *Truth Seeker*, May 1957, 73.

Notes

17 James Hervey Johnson, "White Leader Assassinated by Fellow White," *Truth Seeker*, September 1975, 181.

18 Tom Flynn, "Smith, Charles Lee," in *The New Encyclopedia of Unbelief*, ed. Tom Flynn (Amherst, NY: Prometheus, 2007), 718–19; Fred Edwords, "Johnson, James Hervey," in Flynn, *The New Encyclopedia of Unbelief*, 451–52.

19 Eugene Macdonald, "The Negro Problem," *Truth Seeker*, March 7, 1903, 148.

20 Stephen LeDrew, *The Evolution of Atheism: The Politics of a Modern Movement* (Oxford: Oxford University Press, 2016).

21 George Hawley, *Making Sense of the Alt-Right* (New York: Columbia University Press, 2017), 100.

22 Ibid., 100–101.

23 David G. McAfee, "White Nationalist Richard Spencer Says He's an Atheist," The Friendly Atheist, January 22, 2017, www.patheos.com/blogs/friendly atheist/2017/01/22/white-nationalist-richard-spencer-says-hes-an-atheist/, accessed February 10, 2018.

24 David G. McAfee, "The 'Alt-Right' and ISIS Agree on More Than You Think," No Sacred Cows, July 1, 2017, www.patheos.com/blogs/nosacredcows/2017/07/alt-right-isis-agree-think/, accessed April 3, 2018.

25 Quoted in Hawley, *Making Sense of the Alt-Right*, 78.

26 Chris Stedman, "Too Many Atheists Are Veering Dangerously Toward the Alt-Right," Vice, April 2, 2018, https://www.vice.com/en_us/article/3k7jx8/too-many-atheists-are-veering-dangerously-toward-the-alt-right, accessed April 3, 2018.

27 Murtaza Hussain, "Scientific Racism, Militarism, and the New Atheists," Al Jazeera, April 2, 2013, www.aljazeera.com/indepth/opinion/2013/04/20134210413618256.html, accessed March 11, 2016; for similar criticisms, see Glenn Greenwald, "Sam Harris, the New Atheists, and Anti-Muslim Animus," *The Guardian*, April 3, 2013, https://www.theguardian.com/commentisfree/2013/apr/03/sam-harris-muslim-animus, accessed February 13, 2018; Nathan Lean, "Dawkins, Harris, Hitchens: New Atheists Flirt with Islamophobia," *Salon*, March 3, 2013, https://www.salon.com/2013/03/30/dawkins_harris_hitchens_new_atheists_flirt_with_islamophobia/, accessed February 14, 2018.

28 Sam Harris and Maajid Nawaz, *Islam and the Future of Tolerance: A Dialogue* (Cambridge, MA, and London: Harvard University Press, 2015), 16–35.

29 "Forbidden Knowledge: A Conversation with Charles Murray," Sam Harris: Waking Up Podcast, April 22, 2017, https://samharris.org/podcasts/forbidden-knowledge/, accessed May 23, 2018; for a review of recent science on race and IQ, see Richard E. Nisbett et al., "Intelligence: New Findings and Theoretical Developments," *American Psychologist* 67, no. 2 (2012): 130–59, especially 146–48.

30 "The Sam Harris Debate," Vox, April 9, 2018, https://www.vox.com/2018/4/9/17210248/sam-harris-ezra-klein-charles-murray-transcript-podcast, accessed May 23, 2018.

Bibliography

Primary sources

Principal freethought newspapers

Boston Investigator
Freethinker
National Reformer
Reasoner
Truth Seeker

Books and articles

Adler, Felix. "The Fundamental Principle of Inter Racial Ethics, and Some Practical Applications of It." In *Papers on Inter-Racial Problems Communicated to the First Universal Races Congress, Held at the University of London July 26–29, 1911*, edited by Gustav Spiller, 261–67. London: P.S. King & Son, 1911.

Agassiz, Louis. "The Diversity of Origin of the Human Races." *Christian Examiner* 49 (July 1850): 110–45.

Ah Sin. *Letters of a Chinaman to English Readers on English and Chinese Superstition and the Mischief of Missionaries*. London: Pioneer Press, 1903.

"All Superstitions Defied at Thirteen Club Dinner." *Brooklyn Daily Eagle*, February 14, 1907, 22

"The American Indian and Christianity." *Blue-Grass Blade*, October 20, 1907, 3.

"And Yet: We Send Missionaries to China," *Blue-Grass Blade*, February 23, 1902, 1.

Aveling, Edward. *Darwin Made Easy*. London: Robert Forder, 1893.

_____. *The Religious Views of Charles Darwin*. London: Freethought Publishing Company, 1883.

_____ and Eleanor Marx Aveling. *The Working Class Movement in America*. London: Swan Sonnenschein, Lowrey & Co., 1888.

Bachman, John. *A Notice of the "Types of Mankind," with an Examination of the Charges Contained in the Biography of Dr. Morton, Published by Nott and Gliddon*. Charleston: James, Williams and Gitsinger, 1854.

Bibliography

Baker, Samuel White. *The Albert N'Yanza, Great Basin of the Nile, and Exploration of the Nile Sources.* London: Macmillan, 1866.

Bennett, D.M. *A Truth Seeker Around the World.* 4 vols. New York: D.M. Bennett, 1882.

Besant, Annie. *England, India, and Afghanistan, and the Story of Afghanistan.* Madras: Theosophical Publishing House, 1931.

_____ and G.W. Foote. *Is Socialism Sound? Verbatim Report of Four Nights' Debate Between Annie Besant and G.W. Foote.* London: Progressive Publishing Company, 1887.

Boas, Franz. "Changes in Bodily Form of Descendants of Immigrants." In *Race, Language, and Culture,* Reprint, 60–75. Chicago and London: University of Chicago Press, 1982 [1940].

_____. "Changes in the Bodily Form of Descendants of Immigrants." *American Anthropologist* 14, no. 3 (September 1912): 530–62.

_____. "Instability of Human Types." In *Papers on Inter-Racial Problems Communicated to the First Universal Races Congress, Held at the University of London July 26–29, 1911,* edited by Gustav Spiller, 99–103. London: P.S. King & Son, 1911.

_____. *The Mind of Primitive Man.* New York: Macmillan, 1922 [1911].

"Booker T. Washington," *Blue-Grass Blade,* June 15, 1902, 1.

Bradlaugh, Charles. *Anthropology.* London: Freethought Publishing Company, 1882.

_____. *The Autobiography of C. Bradlaugh: A Page of His Life.* London: R. Forder, 1891.

_____. *The Freethinker's Text-Book, Part I.* London: Charles Watts, 1876.

_____. *Genesis: Its Authorship and Authenticity.* 3rd ed. London: Freethought Publishing Company, 1882.

_____. *Heresy: Its Utility and Morality; A Plea and a Justification.* London: Austin & Co., 1870.

_____. *Speeches.* London: Freethought Publishing Company, 1890.

_____. *Were Adam and Eve Our First Parents?* London: Freethought Publishing Company, 1865.

Bradlaugh Bonner, Hypatia, ed. *Catalogue of the Library of the Late Charles Bradlaugh.* London: Mrs. H. Bradlaugh Bonner, 1891.

"Brann's Iconoclast: A Religious Journal That Will Do No Good in the World." *Blue-Grass Blade,* January 26, 1902.

Bridges, J.H. "England and China." In *International Policy: Essays on the Foreign Relations of England,* edited by Frederic Harrison, 327–448. London: Chapman and Hall, 1866.

Brown, William Wells. *Clotel; or the President's Daughter: A Narrative of Slave Life.* London: Partridge & Oakey, 1853.

_____. *Narrative of William W. Brown, a Fugitive Slave: Written by Himself.* Boston: The Anti-Slavery Office, 1847.

Bibliography

Campbell, Alexander, ed. *Debate on the Evidences of Christianity*. London: R. Groombridge, 1839.

[Carlyle, Thomas]. "Occasional Discourse on the Negro Question." *Fraser's Magazine for Town and Country* 40 (December 1849): 670–79.

Carroll, Charles. *"The Negro a Beast" or "In the Image of God."* St. Louis: American Book and Bible House, 1900.

[Chambers, Robert]. *Vestiges of the Natural History of Creation*. London: John Churchill, 1844.

Chilton, William. "The Theory of Regular Gradation XL." *Oracle of Reason* 2, no. 84 (1843): 253–54.

"Circulars Issued by the Executive Council." *In Papers on Inter-Racial Problems Communicated to the First Universal Races Congress, Held at the University of London July 26–29, 1911*, edited by Gustav Spiller, xiii–xvi. London: P.S. King & Son, 1911.

Clodd, Edward. "Presidential Address." *Folklore* 7, no. 1 (March 1896): 35–60.

_____. *A Primer of Evolution*. London: Longmans, Green, and Co., 1895.

Congreve, Richard. *India*. London: John Chapman, 1857.

Conway, Moncure. *Autobiography: Memories and Experiences*. 2 vols. London and Paris: Cassell and Company, 1904.

_____. *My Pilgrimage to the Wise Men of the East*. Boston and New York: Houghton, Mifflin and Company, 1906.

Cooper, Robert. *The Infidel's Text-Book, Being the Substance of Thirteen Lectures on the Bible*. American Edition. Boston: J.P. Mendum, 1858.

Cumming, John. *Moses Right, and Bishop Colenso Wrong*. London: Shaw, 1863.

Darwin, Charles. *The Descent of Man, and Selection in Relation to Sex*. 2 vols. London: John Murray, 1871.

_____. *On the Origin of Species*. 2nd ed. London: John Murray, 1860 [1859].

"The Days of the Negro." *Secular World*, May 10, 1862, 6.

Douglass, Frederick. *The Life and Times of Frederick Douglass*. Hartford, CT: Park Publishing Co., 1881.

_____. *Narrative of the Life of Frederick Douglass, an American Slave*. Boston: Anti-Slavery Office, 1845.

Draper, John William. *The History of the Conflict Between Religion and Science*. New York and London: D. Appleton and Company, 1874.

_____. *Human Physiology, Statistical and Dynamical; Or, the Conditions and the Course of the Life of Man*. New York: Harper & Brothers, 1856.

Du Bois, W.E.B. *The Autobiography of W.E.B. Du Bois: A Soliloquy on Viewing My Life from the Last Decade of Its First Century*. New York: International Publishers Co., Inc., 1968.

[_____]. "The Christianity of White Christians." *Truth Seeker*, March 6, 1915, 147.

_____. *The Negro*. New York: Holt, 1915.

_____. "A Negro Nation Within the Nation." *Current History* 42, no. 3 (June 1, 1935): 265–70.

_____. "The Negro Race in the United States of America." In *Papers on Inter-*

Bibliography

Racial Problems Communicated to the First Universal Races Congress, Held at the University of London July 26–29, 1911, edited by Gustav Spiller, 348–64. London: P.S. King & Son, 1911.

[_____]. "The White Christ." *Crisis* 9, no. 5 (March 1915): 238.

[_____]. "The World in Council." *Crisis* 2, no. 5 (September 1911): 196.

Duncan, David, ed. *The Life and Letters of Herbert Spencer.* London: Methuen & Co., 1908.

Feinberg, Barry, and Ronald Kasrils, eds. *Bertrand Russell's America: His Transatlantic Travels and Writings.* Vol. 1, *1896–1945.* London: George Allen & Unwin Ltd., 1973.

_____, eds. *Bertrand Russell's America.* Vol. 2, *1945–1970.* Boston: South End Press, 1983.

First Universal Races Congress, University of London, July 26–29, 1911. London: Watts & Co., 1910.

Ford, Paul Leicester, ed. *The Works of Thomas Jefferson.* 12 vols. New York and London: G.P. Putnam's Sons, 1904.

Freeman, George, "An Indian: Who was in the Penitentiary with Me." *Blue-Grass Blade,* May 11, 1902, 2.

Galton, Francis. "Eugenics: Its Definition, Scope and Aims." In *Sociological Papers,* 43–50. London: Macmillan and Co., 1905.

_____. *Hereditary Genius.* London: Macmillan, 1869.

"Going to Evangelize the Flathead Indians." *Blue-Grass Blade,* December 20, 1903, 2.

Graves, Kersey. *The Bible of Bibles; or, Twenty-Seven "Divine Revelations."* 4th ed. Boston: Colby & Rich, 1879.

_____. *The World's Sixteen Crucified Saviors; Or, Christianity Before Christ.* 4th ed. Boston: Colby & Rich, 1876.

Haeckel, Ernst. *The Pedigree of Man: And Other Essays.* Translated by Edward Aveling. London: Freethought Publishing Company, 1883.

Hansard, June 13, 1910. 17 Parl. Deb., H.C. (5th ser.) (1909–80) 1103–63. http://hansard.millbanksystems.com/commons/1910/jun/13/consolidated-fund-no-2-bill. Accessed October 4, 2015.

Harrison, Frederic, ed. *International Policy: Essays on the Foreign Relations of England.* London: Chapman and Hall, 1866.

Harrison, Hubert. *A Hubert Harrison Reader.* Edited by Jeffrey B. Perry. Middletown, CT: Wesleyan University Press, 2001.

"Heathen Editor: Offers to Entertain Booker T. Washington at 'Quakeracre.'" *Blue-Grass Blade,* May 25, 1902, 2.

Heston, Watson. *The Freethinkers' Pictorial Text-Book.* New York: Truth Seeker Company, 1890.

Hittell, John Shertzer. *The Evidences Against Christianity.* 2nd ed. 2 vols. New York: Calvin Blanchard, 1857 [1856].

_____. *A History of the Mental Growth of Mankind in Ancient Times.* 4 vols. New York: Henry Holt and Company, 1893.

Bibliography

Holyoake, George Jacob. *Sixty Years of an Agitator's Life*. 3rd ed. 2 vols. London: T. Fisher Unwin, 1903 [1892].

_____ and Brewin Grant. *Christianity and Secularism: Report of a Public Discussion Between the Rev. Brewin Grant, B.A., and George Jacob Holyoake, Esq.* London: Ward and Co., 1853.

Hunt, James. "Anniversary Address, Delivered before the Anthropological Society of London, January 19th, 1869." *Journal of the Anthropological Society of London* 7 (1869): civ–cix.

_____. "Anthropological News." *Anthropological Review* 6, no. 23 (October 1868): 442–68.

_____. "Introductory Address on the Study of Anthropology." *Anthropological Review* 1, no. 1 (May 1863): 1–20.

_____. "The President's Address." *Journal of the Anthropological Society of London* 5 (1867): xliv–lxxi.

[_____]. "Race in Legislation and Political Economy." *Anthropological Review* 4, no. 13 (1866): 113–35.

Huxley, Leonard, ed. *Life and Letters of Thomas Henry Huxley*. 2 vols. New York: D. Appleton and Company, 1901.

Huxley, Thomas Henry. *Collected Essays*. Vol. 3, *Science and Education Essays*. New York: D. Appleton and Company, 1897 [1893–94].

_____. *Collected Essays*. Vol. 7, *Man's Place in Nature and Other Anthropological Essays*, New York: D. Appleton and Company, 1896 [1893–94].

Ingersoll, Robert G. *The Works of Robert G. Ingersoll*. 12 vols. New York: Dresden Publishing Co., C.P. Farrell, 1902.

Knox, Robert. *The Races of Men: A Philosophical Enquiry into the Influence of Race over the Destinies of Nations*. 2nd ed. London: Henry Renshaw, 1862 [1850].

Lajpat Rai, Lala. *The Collected Works of Lala Lajpat Rai*. Edited by B.R. Nanda. 10 vols. New Delhi: Manohar, 2003.

Linnaeus, Carl. *A General System of Nature*. Translated by William Turton. 7 vols. London: Printed for Lackington, Allen, and Co., 1802.

A London Zulu [George Holyoake]. *Cumming Wrong; Colenso Right: A Reply to the Rev. Dr. Cumming's "Moses Right Colenso Wrong."* London: Farrah and Dunbar, undated.

Lonsdale, Henry. *A Sketch of the Life and Writings of Robert Knox the Anatomist*. London: Macmillan and Co., 1870.

Lovecraft, H.P. *H.P. Lovecraft: Letters to James F. Morton*. Edited by David E. Schultz and S.T. Joshi. New York: Hippocampus Press, 2011.

Lubbock, John. *The Origin of Civilisation and the Primitive Condition of Man: Mental and Social Condition of Savages*. London: Longmans, Green, and Co., 1870.

_____. *Pre-Historic Times, As Illustrated by Ancient Remains, and the Manners and Customs of Modern Savages*. London and Edinburgh: Williams and Norgate, 1865.

McCann, James, and Charles Bradlaugh. *Secularism: Unphilosophical, Immoral, and*

Bibliography

Anti-Social. Verbatim Report of a Three Nights' Debate between the Rev. Dr. McCann and Charles Bradlaugh. London: Freethought Publishing Company, 1881.

Mill, John Stuart. *The Collected Works of John Stuart Mill*. Edited by John M. Robson. 33 vols. Toronto: University of Toronto Press; London: Routledge and Kegan Paul, 1963–91.

Moore, Charles Chilton. *Behind the Bars; 31498*. Lexington, KY: Blue Grass Printing Co., 1899.

Morton, James F., Jr. *The Curse of Race Prejudice*. New York: Published by the author, 1906.

Needles, Edward. *An Historical Memoir of the Pennsylvania Society for Promoting the Abolition of Slavery*. Philadelphia: Merrihew and Thompson, 1848.

Nott, Josiah. *Two Lectures on the Connection Between the Biblical and Physical History of Man*. New York: Bartlett and Welford, 1849.

_____. *Two Lectures, on the Natural History of the Caucasian and Negro Races*. Mobile: Dade and Thompson, 1844.

_____ and George Gliddon. *Types of Mankind: Or, Ethnological Researches, Based Upon the Ancient Monuments, Paintings, Sculptures, and Crania of Races, and Upon Their Natural, Geographical, Philological, and Biblical History*. Philadelphia: Lippincort, Grambo & Co., 1854.

Owen, Robert. *The Life of Robert Owen, Written by Himself*. London: Charles Knight & Co., 1971 [1857].

_____. *A New View of Society, or Essays on the Formation of Human Character*. London: Macmillan, 1972 [1813].

Paine, Thomas. *The Age of Reason*. New York: Truth Seeker Company, 1898 [1794–95].

_____. *The Writings of Thomas Paine*. Edited by Moncure Conway. 4 vols. New York and London: G.P. Putnam's Sons, 1894–96.

Pearson, Karl. *The Moral Basis of Socialism*. London: William Reeves, 1887.

_____. *National Life from the Standpoint of Science*. 2nd ed. London: Adam and Charles Black, 1905 [1900].

Pember, E.H. "England and India." In *International Policy: Essays on the Foreign Relations of England*, edited by Frederic Harrison, 223–326. London: Chapman and Hall, 1866.

Putnam, Samuel Porter. *400 Years of Freethought*. New York: Truth Seeker Company, 1894.

Reade, Winwood. "Effects of Missionaries among Savages." *Journal of the Anthropological Society of London* 3 (1865): clxiii–clxxxiii.

_____. *The Martyrdom of Man*. London: Trubner & Co., 1872.

Remsburg, John E. *The Bible: I. Authenticity II. Credibility III. Morality*. New York: Truth Seeker Company, 1907.

Robertson, J.M. *The Boer War: Open Letter to Dr. Conan Doyle*. Philadelphia: G.H. Buchanan & Co., 1902.

_____. *Christianity and Mythology*. London: Watts & Co., 1900.

Bibliography

_____. *The Germans*. London: William and Norgate, 1916.

_____. *Pagan Christs: Studies in Comparative Hierology*. London: Watts & Co., 1903.

_____. *Patriotism and Empire*. 2nd ed. London: Grant Richards, 1900 [1899].

_____. "The Rationale of Autonomy." In *Papers on Inter-Racial Problems Communicated to the First Universal Races Congress, Held at the University of London July 26–29, 1911*, edited by Gustav Spiller, pp. 40–49. London: P.S. King & Son, 1911.

_____. *The Saxon and the Celt: A Study in Sociology*. London: University Press, Limited, 1897.

_____. *Wrecking the Empire*. London: Grant Richards, 1901.

Russell, Bertrand. *War Crimes in Vietnam*. London: George Allen & Unwin Ltd., 1967.

Saladin. *Christianity and the Slave Trade*. London: W. Stewart & Co., c. 1880s.

Slenker, Elmina Drake. *Little Lessons for Little Folks*. New York: Truth Seeker Company, 1887.

Spencer, Herbert. *An Autobiography*. 2 vols. New York: D. Appleton and Company, 1904.

_____. *Essays: Scientific, Political, and Speculative*, Library Edition. 3 vols. London and Edinburgh: Williams and Norgate, 1891.

_____. *The Principles of Biology*. 2 vols. London and Edinburgh: Williams and Norgate, 1867.

_____. *The Principles of Ethics*. 2 vols. New York: D. Appleton and Company, 1896.

_____. *The Principles of Psychology*. 2nd ed. 2 vols. London and Edinburgh: Williams and Norgate, 1870 [1855].

_____. *The Principles of Sociology*. 3rd ed. 3 vols. New York: D. Appleton and Company, 1898 [1876–96].

_____. *Social Statics: Or, the Conditions Essential to Human Happiness Specified, and the First of Them Developed*. London: John Chapman, 1851.

Spiller, Gustav. "Darwinism and Sociology." *Sociological Review* 7, no. 3 (1914): 232–53.

_____, ed. *Papers on Inter-Racial Problems Communicated to the First Universal Races Congress, Held at the University of London July 26–29, 1911*. London: P.S. King & Son, 1911.

_____. "The Problem of Race Equality." *In Papers on Inter-Racial Problems Communicated to the First Universal Races Congress, Held at the University of London July 26–29, 1911*, edited by Gustav Spiller, 29–39. London: P.S. King & Son, 1911.

_____. "Science and Race Prejudice." *Sociological Review* 5, no. 4 (1912): 331–48.

Stringfellow, Thornton. *Slavery: Its Origin, Nature, and History, Considered in the Light of Bible Teachings, Moral Justice, and Political Wisdom*. New York: John F. Trow, 1861.

Taylor, Mrs. P.A., ed. *Professor Huxley and the Negro Question*. London: Ladies' London Emancipation Society, 1864.

Bibliography

Twain, Mark. *Following the Equator: A Journey Around the World*. New York: Doubleday & McClure Co., 1897.

_____. "To the Person Sitting in Darkness." *North American Review* 172, no. 531 (February 1901): 161–76.

Tylor, E.B. *Anthropology: An Introduction to the Study of Man and Civilization*. New York: D. Appleton and Company, 1881.

_____. *Primitive Culture: Researches into the Development of Mythology, Philosophy, Religion, Art, and Custom*. 2 vols. London: John Murray, 1871.

Underwood, B.F. *The Burgess–Underwood Debate: Commencing June 29, 1875, at Aylmer, Ontario, and Continuing Four Days*. New York: D.M. Bennett, 1876.

Vogt, Carl. *Lectures on Man*. Edited by James Hunt. London: Longman, Green, Longman, and Roberts, 1864.

Wallace, Alfred Russel. "The Origin of Human Races and the Antiquity of Man Deduced from the Theory of 'Natural Selection.'" *Journal of the Anthropological Society of London* 2 (1864): clviii–clxxxvii.

Watts, John, and Iconoclast, eds. "Charles R. Darwin, F.R.S." *Half Hours with Freethinkers*, December 1, 1864, 1–8.

Wheeler, J.M. *A Biographical Dictionary of Freethinkers of All Ages and Nations*. London: Progressive Publishing Company, 1889.

White, Andrew Dickson. *A History of the Warfare of Science with Theology in Christendom*. 2 vols. New York: D. Appleton and Company, 1896.

Wong Chin Foo. "Why Am I a Heathen?" *North American Review* 145, no. 369 (August 1887): 169–79.

Zwick, Jim, ed. *Mark Twain's Weapons of Satire: Anti-Imperialist Writings on the Philippine–American War*. Syracuse: Syracuse University Press, 1992.

Secondary sources

Adas, Michael. *Machines as the Measure of Men: Science, Technology, and Ideologies of Western Dominance*. Ithaca and London: Cornell University Press, 1989.

Al-'Azm, Sadik Jalal. "Orientalism and Orientalism in Reverse." In *Orientalism: A Reader*, edited by A.L. Macfie, 217–38. Edinburgh: Edinburgh University Press, 2000.

Aldridge, Alfred Owen. *Thomas Paine's American Ideology*. Newark: University of Delaware Press, 1984.

Alexander, Nathan G. "E.D. Morel (1873–1924), the Congo Reform Association, and the History of Human Rights." *Britain and the World* 9, no. 2 (2016): 213–35.

_____. "Unclasping the Eagle's Talons: Mark Twain, American Freethought, and the Responses to Imperialism." *Journal of the Gilded Age and Progressive Era* 17, no. 3 (2018): 524–45.

Almond, Philip C. *The British Discovery of Buddhism*. Cambridge: Cambridge University Press, 1988.

Anderson, David D. *Robert Ingersoll*. New York: Twayne Publishers Inc., 1972.

Bibliography

Augstein, Hannah Franziska, ed. *Race: The Origins of an Idea, 1760–1850*. Bristol: Thoemmes Press, 1996.

Ball, Terence. "Marx and Darwin: A Reconsideration." *Political Theory* 7, no. 4 (November 1979): 469–83.

Ballantyne, Tony. *Orientalism and Race: Aryanism in the British Empire*. Houndmills, Basingstoke: Palgrave Macmillan, 2002.

Banton, Michael. *The Idea of Race*. London: Tavistock Publications, 1977.

Barkan, Elazar. *The Retreat of Scientific Racism: Changing Concepts of Race in Britain and the United States Between the World Wars*. Cambridge: Cambridge University Press, 1992.

Barton, Ruth. "'An Influential Set of Chaps': The X-Club and Royal Society Politics 1864–85." *British Journal for the History of Science* 23, no. 1 (March 1990): 53–81.

Bayly, C.A. *Recovering Liberties: Indian Thought in the Age of Liberalism and Empire*. Cambridge: Cambridge University Press, 2012.

Bederman, Gail. "Revisiting Nashoba: Slavery, Utopia, and Frances Wright in America, 1818–1826." *American Literary History* 17, no. 3 (October 2005): 438–59.

Bell, Duncan. "John Stuart Mill on Colonies." *Political Theory* 38, no. 1 (2010): 34–64.

Berkowitz, Sandra J., and Amy C. Lewis. "Debating Anti-Semitism: Ernestine Rose vs. Horace Seaver in the Boston Investigator, 1863–1864." *Communication Quarterly* 46, no. 4 (1998): 457–71.

Berman, David. *A History of Atheism in Britain: From Hobbes to Russell*. London: Croom Helm, 1988.

Bethencourt, Francisco. *Racisms: From the Crusades to the Twentieth Century*. Princeton and Oxford: Princeton University Press, 2013.

Bevir, Mark. "In Opposition to the Raj: Annie Besant and the Dialectic of Empire." *History of Political Thought* 19, no. 1 (1998): 61–77.

Biddiss, Michael. "The Universal Races Congress of 1911." *Race and Class* 13, no. 1 (July 1971): 37–46.

Bird, John. "The Mark Twain and Robert Ingersoll Connection: Freethought, Borrowed Thought, Stolen Thought." *Mark Twain Annual* 11 (2013): 42–61.

Bolt, Christine. *Victorian Attitudes to Race*. London: Routledge & Keegan Paul, 1971.

Bowler, Peter. *Evolution: The History of an Idea*. 25th Anniversary Edition. Berkeley and Los Angeles: University of California Press, 2009 [1984].

_____. *Monkey Trials and Gorilla Sermons: Evolution and Christianity from Darwin to Intelligent Design*. Cambridge, MA, and London: Harvard University Press, 2007.

Brace, C. Loring. *"Race" is a Four-Letter Word: The Genesis of the Concept*. Oxford: Oxford University Press, 2005.

Bradford, Roderick. *D.M. Bennett: The Truth Seeker*. Amherst, NY: Prometheus, 2006.

Bradlaugh Bonner, Hypatia, and J.M. Robertson. *Charles Bradlaugh: A Record of His Life and Work*. 2 vols. London: T. Fisher Unwin, 1895.

Browne, Janet. *Charles Darwin*. Vol. 1, *Voyaging*. New York: Alfred A. Knopf, 1995.

_____. *Charles Darwin*. Vol. 2, *The Power of Place*. New York: Alfred A. Knopf, 2002.

Buckley, Michael J. *At the Origins of Modern Atheism*. New Haven and London: Yale University Press, 1987.

Budd, Susan. *Varieties of Unbelief: Atheists and Agnostics in English Society 1850–1960*. London: Heinemann, 1977.

Bush, Harold K., Jr. *Mark Twain and the Spiritual Crisis of His Age*. Tuscaloosa: University of Alabama Press, 2007.

Cameron, Christopher. *Black Freethinkers: A History of African American Secularism*. Evanston, IL: Northwestern University Press, 2019.

_____. "Slavery and African American Irreligion." *Journal of Southern Religion* 18 (2016). http://jsreligion.org/vol18/cameron/. Accessed January 30, 2019.

Campbell, Colin. *Toward a Sociology of Irreligion*. London and Basingstoke: Macmillan, 1971.

Carr, Robert. "The Religious Thought of John Stuart Mill: A Study in Reluctant Scepticism." *Journal of the History of Ideas* 23, no. 4 (December 1962): 475–95.

Claeys, Gregory. *Imperial Sceptics: British Critics of Empire, 1850–1920*. Cambridge: Cambridge University Press, 2012.

_____. *Mill and Paternalism*. Cambridge: Cambridge University Press, 2013.

Cockshut, A.O.J. *The Unbelievers: English Agnostic Thought, 1840–1890*. London: Collins, 1964.

Cole, Douglas. *Franz Boas: The Early Years, 1858–1906*. Seattle and London: University of Washington Press, 1999.

Compton, John W. "The Emancipation of the American Mind: J.S. Mill on the Civil War." *Review of Politics* 70, no. 2 (Spring 2008): 221–44.

Conkin, Paul K. "The Religious Pilgrimage of Thomas Jefferson." In *Jeffersonian Legacies*, edited by Peter S. Onuf, 19–49. Charlottesville: University Press of Virginia, 1993.

Conway, Moncure. *The Life of Thomas Paine: With a History of His Literary, Political, and Religious Career in America, France, and England*. 2 vols. New York and London: G.P. Putnam's Sons, 1892.

Cooke, Bill. "Charles Southwell: One of the Romances of Rationalism." *Journal of Freethought* 2, no. 2 (Autumn 2012): 1–41.

Cramer, C.H. *Royal Bob: The Life of Robert G. Ingersoll*. Indianapolis: Bobbs-Merrill, 1952.

Creffield, C.A. "Aveling, Edward Bibbens (1849–1898)." *Oxford Dictionary of National Biography*, 2004. www.oxforddnb.com/view/article/40929. Accessed April 23, 2016.

Crimmins, James E. "Bentham and Utilitarianism in the Early Nineteenth Century." In *The Cambridge Companion to Utilitarianism*, edited by Ben Eggleston and Dale E. Miller, 38–60. Cambridge: Cambridge University Press, 2014.

Croce, Paul Jerome. "Probabilistic Darwinism: Louis Agassiz vs. Asa Gray on Science, Religion, and Certainty." *Journal of Religious History* 22, no. 1 (February 1998): 35–58.

Curtin, Philip D. *The Image of Africa: British Ideas and Action, 1780–1850*. London: Macmillan and Co., Limited, 1965.

Curtis, L.P., Jr. *Anglo-Saxons and Celts: A Study of Anti-Irish Prejudice in Victorian England*. Bridgeport, CT: Conference on British Studies, 1968.

Davis, Angela. *Women, Race and Class*. London: Women's Press, 1982.

Davis, Robert, and Frank O'Hagan. *Robert Owen*. London and New York: Continuum, 2010.

Day, Matthew. "Godless Savages and Superstitious Dogs: Charles Darwin, Imperial Ethnography, and the Problem of Human Uniqueness." *Journal of the History of Ideas* 69, no. 1 (2008): 49–70.

Dekkers, Odin. *J.M. Robertson: Rationalist and Literary Critic*. Aldershot and Brookfield, VT: Ashgate, 1998.

Desmond, Adrian. *Huxley: From Devil's Disciple to Evolution's High Priest*. Reading, MA: Perseus Books, 1997.

_____. *The Politics of Evolution: Morphology, Medicine, and Reform in Radical London*. Chicago and London: University of Chicago Press, 1992.

_____ and James Moore. *Darwin*. London: Michael Joseph, 1991.

_____. *Darwin's Sacred Cause: How a Hatred of Slavery Shaped Darwin's Views on Human Evolution*. Boston and New York: Houghton Mifflin Harcourt, 2009.

Diamond, Jared. "Race Without Color." *Discover Magazine*, November 1, 1994. http://discovermagazine.com/1994/nov/racewithoutcolor444. Accessed October 3, 2017.

Donnachie, Ian. *Robert Owen: Owen of New Lanark and New Harmony*. East Linton: Tuckwell Press, 2000.

Driver, Felix. *Geography Militant: Cultures of Exploration and Empire*. Malden, MA: Blackwell Publishers, 2001.

Edwords, Fred. "Johnson, James Hervey." In *The New Encyclopedia of Unbelief*, edited by Tom Flynn, 451–52. Amherst, NY: Prometheus, 2007.

Ferguson, Christine. *Determined Spirits: Eugenics, Heredity and Racial Regeneration in Anglo-American Spiritualist Writing, 1848–1930*. Edinburgh: Edinburgh University Press, 2012.

Finkelman, Paul. "Thomas Jefferson and Antislavery: The Myth Goes On." *Virginia Magazine of History and Biography* 102, no. 2 (April 1994): 193–228.

Fitzgerald, Timothy. *Discourse on Civility and Barbarity: A Critical History of Religion and Related Categories*. Oxford and New York: Oxford University Press, 2007.

Flynn, Tom. "Smith, Charles Lee." In *The New Encyclopedia of Unbelief*, edited by Tom Flynn, 718–19. Amherst, NY: Prometheus, 2007.

"Forbidden Knowledge: A Conversation with Charles Murray." Sam Harris: Waking Up Podcast, April 22, 2017. https://samharris.org/podcasts/forbidden-knowledge/. Accessed May 23, 2018.

Bibliography

Francis, Mark. *Herbert Spencer and the Invention of Modern Life*. Stocksfield: Acumen, 2007.

Fredrickson, George M. *The Black Image in the White Mind: The Debate on Afro-American Character and Destiny, 1817–1914*. New York: Harper & Row, 1971.

_____. *Racism: A Short History*. Princeton: Princeton University Press, 2002.

Fruchtman, Jack, Jr. *Thomas Paine: Apostle of Freedom*. New York and London: Four Walls Eight Windows, 1994.

Fyfe, Aileen. *Steam-Powered Knowledge: William Chambers and the Business of Publishing, 1820–1860*. Chicago and London: University of Chicago Press, 2012.

Glick, Leonard B. "Types Distinct from Our Own: Franz Boas on Jewish Identity and Assimilation." *American Anthropologist* 84, no. 3 (September 1982): 545–65.

Godart, G. Clinton. "Herbert Spencer in Japan: Boom and Bust of a Theory." In *Global Spencerism: The Communication and Appropriation of a British Evolutionist*, edited by Bernard Lightman, 56–77. Leiden: Brill, 2015.

Goetz, Rebecca Anne. *The Baptism of Early Virginia: How Christianity Created Race*. Baltimore: Johns Hopkins University Press, 2012.

Gordon-Reed, Annette. *The Hemingses of Monticello: An American Family*. New York and London: W.W. Norton & Company, 2008.

Gossett, Thomas F. *Race: The History of an Idea in America*. New Edition. New York and Oxford: Oxford University Press, 1997 [1963].

Greenspan, Ezra. *William Wells Brown: An African American Life*. New York and London: W.W. Norton & Company, 2014.

Greenwald, Glenn. "Sam Harris, the New Atheists, and Anti-Muslim Animus." *The Guardian*, April 3, 2013. https://www.theguardian.com/commentisfree/2013/apr/03/sam-harris-muslim-animus. Accessed February 13, 2018.

Guy, Jeff. *The Heretic: A Study of the Life of John William Colenso, 1814–1883*. Johannesburg: Ravan Press; Pietermaritzburg: University of Natal Press, 1983.

Gyory, Andrew. *Closing the Gate: Race, Politics, and the Chinese Exclusion Act*. Chapel Hill and London: University of North Carolina Press, 1998.

Haller, John S. *Outcasts from Evolution: Scientific Attitudes of Racial Inferiority, 1859–1900*. Urbana: University of Illinois Press, 1971.

Halloran, Fiona Deans. *Thomas Nast: The Father of Modern Political Cartoons*. Chapel Hill: University of North Carolina Press, 2012.

Harp, Gillis J. *Positivist Republic: Auguste Comte and the Reconstruction of American Liberalism, 1865–1920*. University Park, PA: Pennsylvania State University Press, 1995.

Harris, Sam, and Maajid Nawaz. *Islam and the Future of Tolerance: A Dialogue*. Cambridge, MA, and London: Harvard University Press, 2015.

Harrison, Peter. *The Territories of Science and Religion*. Chicago: University of Chicago Press, 2015.

Harvey, Paul. *Christianity and Race in the American South: A History*. Chicago and London: University of Chicago Press, 2016.

Hawley, George. *Making Sense of the Alt-Right*. New York: Columbia University Press, 2017.

Hecht, Jennifer Michael. *The End of the Soul: Scientific Modernity, Atheism, and Anthropology in France, 1876–1936*. New York: Columbia University Press, 2003.

Horsman, Reginald. *Josiah Nott of Mobile: Southerner, Physician, and Racial Theorist*. Baton Rouge and London: Louisiana State University Press, 1987.

Hussain, Murtaza. "Scientific Racism, Militarism, and the New Atheists." Al Jazeera, April 2, 2013. www.aljazeera.com/indepth/opinion/2013/04/2013 4210413618256.html. Accessed March 11, 2016.

Hutchins, Zachary McLeod. "Rejecting the Root: The Liberating, Anti-Christ Theology of Douglass's Narrative." *Nineteenth-Century Literature* 68, no. 3 (2013): 292–322.

Inden, Ronald. *Imagining India*. Cambridge, MA, and Oxford: Blackwell, 1990.

Irmscher, Christoph. *Louis Agassiz: Creator of American Science*. Boston: Houghton Mifflin Harcourt, 2013.

Irwin, Robert. *For Lust of Knowing: The Orientalists and Their Enemies*. London: Penguin, 2007.

Jacobson, Matthew Frye. *Barbarian Virtues: The United States Encounters Foreign Peoples at Home and Abroad, 1876–1917*. New York: Hill and Wang, 2000.

———. *Whiteness of a Different Color: European Immigrants and the Alchemy of Race*. First Paperback Edition. Cambridge, MA: Harvard University Press, 1999 [1998].

Jacoby, Susan. *Freethinkers: A History of American Secularism*. New York: Henry Holt and Company, 2004.

———. *The Great Agnostic: Robert Ingersoll and American Freethought*. New Haven: Yale University Press, 2013.

Jahn, Beate. "Barbarian Thoughts: Imperialism in the Philosophy of John Stuart Mill." *Review of International Studies* 31, no. 3 (July 2005): 599–618.

"James Ferdinand Morton, Jr." *Wikipedia: The Free Encyclopedia*. https://en.wikipedia. org/w/index.php?title=James_Ferdinand_Morton,_Jr.&oldid=688715834. Accessed November 2, 2015.

Johnson, Brian L. *W.E.B. Du Bois: Toward Agnosticism, 1868–1934*. Lanham and Plymouth: Rowman & Littlefield, 2008.

Josephson, Jason Ānanda. *The Invention of Religion in Japan*. Chicago: University of Chicago Press, 2012.

Kahn, Jonathon S., and Vincent W. Lloyd, eds. *Race and Secularism in America*. New York: Columbia University Press, 2016.

Keel, Terence. *Divine Variations: How Christian Thought Became Racial Science*. Stanford, CA: Stanford University Press, 2018.

———. "Religion, Polygenism and the Early Science of Human Origins." *History of the Human Sciences* 26, no. 2 (2013): 3–32.

Kendi, Ibram X. *Stamped from the Beginning: The Definitive History of Racist Ideas in America*. London: Bodley Head, 2016.

Kennedy, Dane. *The Highly Civilized Man: Richard Burton and the Victorian World*. Cambridge, MA, and London: Harvard University Press, 2007.

Kern, Kathi. *Mrs. Stanton's Bible*. Ithaca and London: Cornell University Press, 2002.

Kevles, Daniel J. *In the Name of Eugenics: Genetics and the Uses of Human Heredity*. New York: Alfred A. Knopf, 1985.

Kidd, Colin. *The Forging of Races: Race and Scripture in the Protestant Atlantic World, 1600–2000*. Cambridge: Cambridge University Press, 2006.

King, Richard. *Orientalism and Religion: Postcolonial Theory, India and the "Mystic East."* London and New York: Routledge, 1999.

Kirkley, Evelyn A. *Rational Mothers and Infidel Gentlemen: Gender and American Atheism, 1865–1915*. Syracuse, NY: Syracuse University Press, 2000.

Larsen, Timothy. "The Book of Acts and the Origin of the Races in Evangelical Thought." *Victorian Review* 37, no. 2 (Fall 2011): 35–39.

_____. *A People of One Book: The Bible and the Victorians*. Oxford: Oxford University Press, 2011.

_____. *The Slain God: Anthropologists and the Christian Faith*. Oxford: Oxford University Press, 2014.

Larson, Orvin. *American Infidel: Robert G. Ingersoll*. New York: Citadel Press, 1962.

Law, Robin. "Du Bois as a Pioneer of African History: A Reassessment of The Negro (1915)." In *Re-Cognizing W.E.B. Du Bois in the Twenty-First Century: Essays on W.E.B. Du Bois*, edited by Mary Keller and Chester J. Fontenot Jr., 14–33. Macon, GA: Mercer University Press, 2007.

Lean, Nathan. "Dawkins, Harris, Hitchens: New Atheists Flirt with Islamophobia." *Salon*, March 3, 2013. https://www.salon.com/2013/03/30/dawkins_harris_hitchens_new_atheists_flirt_with_islamophobia/. Accessed February 14, 2018.

LeDrew, Stephen. *The Evolution of Atheism: The Politics of a Modern Movement*. Oxford: Oxford University Press, 2016.

Lewarne, Charles P. "The Anarchist Colony at Home, Washington, 1901–1902." *Arizona and the West* 14, no. 2 (Summer 1972): 155–68.

Lightman, Bernard. *The Origins of Agnosticism: Victorian Unbelief and the Limits of Knowledge*. Baltimore and London: Johns Hopkins University Press, 1987.

Lipka, Michael. "10 Facts about Atheists." Pew Research Center, June 1, 2016. www.pewresearch.org/fact-tank/2016/06/01/10-facts-about-atheists/. Accessed December 13, 2017.

Livingstone, David N. *Adam's Ancestors: Race, Religion, and the Politics of Human Origins*. Baltimore: Johns Hopkins University Press, 2008.

_____. *Darwin's Forgotten Defenders: The Encounter Between Evangelical Theology and Evolutionary Thought*. Edinburgh; Grand Rapids, MI: Scottish Academic Press; William B. Eerdmans, 1987.

Lockwood, George. *The New Harmony Movement*. New York: D. Appleton and Company, 1905.

Lorimer, Douglas. *Colour, Class, and the Victorians: English Attitudes to the Negro in the Mid-Nineteenth Century*. Leicester: Leicester University Press, 1978.

_____. "Science and the Secularization of Victorian Images of Race." In *Victorian Science in Context*, edited by Bernard Lightman, 212–35. Chicago and London: University of Chicago Press, 1997.

_____. *Science, Race Relations and Resistance: Britain, 1870–1914*. Manchester: Manchester University Press, 2013.

Lott, Eric. *Love and Theft: Blackface Minstrelsy and the American Working Class*. New York and Oxford: Oxford University Press, 1993.

MacKillop, Ian. *The British Ethical Societies*. Cambridge: Cambridge University Press, 1986.

Marks, Lynne. *Infidels and the Damn Churches: Irreligion and Religion in Settler British Columbia*. Vancouver: University of British Columbia Press, 2017.

Marshall, P.J., ed. *The British Discovery of Hinduism in the Eighteenth Century*. Cambridge: Cambridge University Press, 1970.

Mayer, Henry. *All on Fire: William Lloyd Garrison and the Abolition of Slavery*. New York: St. Martin's Press, 1998.

McAfee, David G. "The 'Alt-Right' and ISIS Agree On More Than You Think." No Sacred Cows, July 1, 2017. www.patheos.com/blogs/nosacredcows/2017/07/alt-right-isis-agree-think/. Accessed April 3, 2018.

_____. "White Nationalist Richard Spencer Says He's an Atheist." The Friendly Atheist, January 22, 2017. www.patheos.com/blogs/friendlyatheist/2017/01/22/white-nationalist-richard-spencer-says-hes-an-atheist/. Accessed February 10, 2018.

McClellan, Robert. *The Heathen Chinee: A Study of American Attitudes toward China, 1890–1905*. Columbus: Ohio State University Press, 1971.

Mehta, Uday Singh. *Liberalism and Empire: A Study in Nineteenth-Century British Liberal Thought*. Chicago: University of Chicago Press, 1999.

Miller, J. Joseph. "Chairing the Jamaica Committee: J.S. Mill and the Limits of Colonial Authority." In *Utilitarianism and Empire*, edited by Bart Schultz and Georgios Varouxakis, 155–78. Lanham, MD: Lexington Books, 2005.

Moore, James. "Freethought, Secularism, Agnosticism: The Case of Charles Darwin." In *Religion in Victorian Britain*. Vol. 1, *Traditions*, edited by Gerald Parsons, 274–319. Manchester and New York: Manchester University Press in Association with the Open University, 1988.

Nash, David. *Blasphemy in the Christian World: A History*. Oxford: Oxford University Press, 2007.

_____. "Charles Bradlaugh, India, and the Many Chameleon Destinations of Republicanism." In *Republicanism in Victorian Society*, edited by David Nash and Anthony Taylor, 106–24. Stroud, Gloucestershire: Sutton, 2000.

_____. "Taming the God of Battles: Secular and Moral Critiques of the South African War." In *Writing a Wider War: Rethinking the South African War, 1899–1902*, edited by Greg Cuthbertson, Albert Grundlingh, and Mary-Lynn Suttie, 266–86. Athens: Ohio University Press, 2002.

Nelson, Craig. *Thomas Paine: Enlightenment, Revolution, and the Birth of Modern Nations*. New York: Viking, 2006.

Bibliography

Nethercot, Arthur H. *The First Five Lives of Annie Besant*. London: Rupert Hart-Davis, 1961.

_____. *The Last Four Lives of Annie Besant*. London: Rupert Hart-Davis, 1963.

Niblett, Bryan. *Dare to Stand Alone: The Story of Charles Bradlaugh*. Oxford: Kramedart Press, 2010.

Nisbett, Richard E., Joshua Aronson, Clancy Blair, William Dickens, James Flynn, Diane F. Halpern, and Eric Turkheimer. "Intelligence: New Findings and Theoretical Developments." *American Psychologist* 67, no. 2 (2012): 130–59.

Nongbri, Brent. *Before Religion: A History of a Modern Concept*. New Haven and London: Yale University Press, 2013.

Norrell, Robert J. *Up from History: The Life of Booker T. Washington*. Cambridge, MA, and London: Belknap Press of Harvard University Press, 2009.

Osofsky, Gilbert. *Harlem: The Making of a Ghetto: Negro New York, 1890–1930*. New York: Harper & Row, 1963.

Pagden, Anthony. "The Savage Critic: Some European Images of the Primitive." *Yearbook of English Studies* 13, "Colonial and Imperial Themes" special number (1983): 32–45.

Painter, Nell Irvin. *The History of White People*. New York: W.W. Norton, 2010.

Perry, Jeffrey B. *Hubert Harrison: The Voice of Harlem Radicalism, 1883–1918*. New York: Columbia University Press, 2009.

Phipps, William E. *Mark Twain's Religion*. Macon, GA: Mercer University Press, 2003.

Pinn, Anthony. "What If God Were One of Us: Humanism and African Americans for Humanism." In *Varieties of African American Religious Experience: Toward a Comparative Black Theology*, 20th Anniversary Edition, 175–212. Minneapolis: Augsburg Fortress Publishers, 2017 [1998].

Pitts, Jennifer. *A Turn to Empire: The Rise of Imperial Liberalism in Britain and France*. Princeton: Princeton University Press, 2005.

Podmore, Frank. *Robert Owen: A Biography*. 2 vols. London: Hutchinson & Co., 1906.

Popkin, Richard H. *Isaac La Peyrère (1596–1676): His Life, Work, and Influence*. Leiden and New York: Brill, 1987.

_____. "The Philosophical Basis of Eighteenth-Century Racism." *Studies in Eighteenth-Century Culture* 3 (1973): 245–62.

Porter, Andrew. *Religion Versus Empire? British Protestant Missionaries and Overseas Expansion, 1700–1914*. Manchester and New York: Manchester University Press, 2004.

Porter, Bernard. *Critics of Empire: British Radicals and the Imperial Challenge*. 2nd ed. London and New York: I.B. Tauris, 2008 [1968].

Post, Albert. *Popular Freethought in America, 1825–1850*. New York: Columbia University Press, 1943.

Pybus, Cassandra. "Thomas Jefferson and Slavery." In *A Companion to Thomas Jefferson*, edited by Francis D. Cogliano, 271–83. Hoboken, NJ: Wiley-Blackwell, 2011.

Radest, Howard B. *Toward Common Ground: The Story of the Ethical Societies in the United States.* New York: Ungar Publishing, 1969.

Rectenwald, Michael. *Nineteenth-Century British Secularism: Science, Religion and Literature.* Houndmills, Basingstoke, and New York: Palgrave Macmillan, 2016.

Rich, Jeremy. "Heresy Is the Only True Religion: Richard Lynch Garner (1848–1920), A Southern Freethinker in Africa and America." *Journal of the Gilded Age and Progressive Era* 12, no. 1 (January 2013): 65–94.

Richards, Evelleen. "The 'Moral Anatomy' of Robert Knox: The Interplay between Biological and Social Thought in Victorian Scientific Naturalism." *Journal of the History of Biology* 22, no. 3 (Autumn 1989): 373–436.

Richards, Robert J. "Myth 19 – That Darwin and Haeckel Were Complicit in Nazi Biology." In *Galileo Goes to Jail: And Other Myths about Science and Religion,* edited by Ronald L. Numbers, 170–77. Cambridge, MA: Harvard University Press, 2009.

Robertson, J.M. *A History of Freethought Ancient and Modern to the Period of the French Revolution.* 2 vols. London: Dawsons of Pall Mall, 1969 [1929].

_____. *A History of Freethought in the Nineteenth Century.* 2 vols. London: Dawsons of Pall Mall, 1969 [1929].

Royle, Edward. *Radicals, Secularists and Republicans: Popular Freethought in Britain, 1866–1915.* Manchester: Manchester University Press, 1980.

_____. *Victorian Infidels: The Origins of the British Secularist Movement 1791–1866.* Manchester: Manchester University Press, 1974.

Ryan, Alan. *Bertrand Russell: A Political Life.* New York: Hill and Wang, 1988.

Said, Edward. *Orientalism.* London: Penguin, 2003 [1978].

"The Sam Harris Debate." Vox, April 9, 2018. https://www.vox.com/2018/4/9/17210248/sam-harris-ezra-klein-charles-murray-transcript-podcast. Accessed May 23, 2018.

Sanford, Charles B. *The Religious Life of Thomas Jefferson.* Charlottesville: University Press of Virginia, 1984.

Schmidt, Leigh Eric. *Village Atheists: How America's Unbelievers Made Their Way in a Godly Nation.* Princeton and Oxford: Princeton University Press, 2016.

Schwartz, Laura. *Infidel Feminism: Secularism, Religion and Women's Emancipation, England 1830–1914.* Manchester: Manchester University Press, 2011.

Schwartz, Thomas D. "Mark Twain and Robert Ingersoll: The Freethought Connection." *American Literature* 48, no. 2 (May 1976): 183–93.

Seaman, Ann Rowe. *America's Most Hated Woman: The Life and Gruesome Death of Madalyn Murray O'Hair.* New York and London: Continuum, 2006.

Secord, James A. *Victorian Sensation: The Extraordinary Publication, Reception, and Secret Authorship of Vestiges of the Natural History of Creation.* Chicago and London: University of Chicago Press, 2000.

Seligman, Scott D. *The First Chinese American: The Remarkable Life of Wong Chin Foo.* Hong Kong: Hong Kong University Press, 2013.

Spencer, Nick. *Atheists: The Origin of the Species.* London: Bloomsbury, 2014.

Bibliography

Stanton, William. *The Leopard's Spots: Scientific Attitudes Toward Race in America, 1815–59*. Chicago and London: University of Chicago Press, 1960.

Stedman, Chris. "Too Many Atheists Are Veering Dangerously Toward the Alt-Right." Vice, April 2, 2018. https://www.vice.com/en_us/article/3k7jx8/too-many-atheists-are-veering-dangerously-toward-the-alt-right. Accessed April 3, 2018.

Stenhouse, John. "Imperialism, Atheism, and Race: Charles Southwell, Old Corruption, and the Maori." *Journal of British Studies* 44, no. 4 (October 2005): 754–74.

Stepan, Nancy. *The Idea of Race in Science: Great Britain, 1800–1960*. London: Macmillan, 1982.

Stephens, Mitchell. *Imagine There's No Heaven: How Atheism Helped Create the Modern World*. New York: Palgrave Macmillan, 2014.

Stocking, George W., Jr. *Race, Culture, and Evolution: Essays in the History of Anthropology*. New Edition. Chicago and London: University of Chicago Press, 1982 [1968].

———. *Victorian Anthropology*. New York: Free Press, 1987.

Taylor, Miles. "Imperium et Libertas? Rethinking the Radical Critique of Imperialism during the Nineteenth Century." *Journal of Imperial and Commonwealth History* 19 (1991): 1–23.

Thrower, James. *Western Atheism: A Short History*. Amherst, NY: Prometheus, 2000 [1971].

Touba, Mariam. "Paine's Antislavery Legacy: Some Additional Considerations." First International Conference of Thomas Paine Studies, Iona College, 2012. http://thomaspaine.org/front/2016/04/16/paines-antislavery-legacy-by-mariam-touba/. Accessed March 9, 2018.

Trautmann, Thomas R. *Aryans and British India*. Berkeley and Los Angeles: University of California Press, 1997.

Tribe, David. *President Charles Bradlaugh M.P.* London: Elek, 1971.

Tunick, Mark. "Tolerant Imperialism: John Stuart Mill's Defense of British Rule in India." *Review of Politics* 68, no. 4 (Fall 2006): 586–611.

Turner, Frank Miller. *Between Science and Religion: The Reaction to Scientific Naturalism in Late Victorian England*. New Haven and London: Yale University Press, 1974.

Utley, Freda. *Odyssey of a Liberal*. Washington: Washington National Press, 1970.

Varouxakis, Georgios. "John Stuart Mill on Race." *Utilitas* 10, no. 1 (1998): 17–32.

Vetter, George, and Marin Green. "Personality and Group Factors in the Making of Atheists." *Journal of Abnormal and Social Psychology* 27, no. 2 (1932): 179–94.

Warren, Sidney. *American Freethought, 1860–1914*. New York: Gordian Press, 1966.

Weikart, Richard. *From Darwin to Hitler: Evolutionary Ethics, Eugenics, and Racism in Germany*. New York: Palgrave Macmillan, 2004.

Wheeler-Barclay, Marjorie. *The Science of Religion in Britain, 1860–1915*. Charlottesville: University of Virginia Press, 2010.

Bibliography

Williams, Vernon J., Jr. *Rethinking Race: Franz Boas and His Contemporaries.* Lexington, KY: University Press of Kentucky, 1996.

Williamson, Scott C. The *Narrative Life: The Moral and Religious Thought of Frederick Douglass.* Macon, GA: Mercer University Press, 2002.

Wood, Forrest G. *The Arrogance of Faith: Christianity and Race in America from the Colonial Era to the Twentieth Century.* Boston: Northeastern University Press, 1991.

Woodhead, Linda. "The Rise of 'No Religion' in Britain: The Emergence of a New Cultural Majority." *Journal of the British Academy* 4 (December 2016): 245–61.

Wright, T.R. *The Religion of Humanity: The Impact of Comtean Positivism on Victorian Britain.* Cambridge: Cambridge University Press, 1986.

Zuckerman, Phil. "Atheism: Contemporary Numbers and Patterns." In *The Cambridge Companion to Atheism,* edited by Michael Martin, 47–65. Cambridge: Cambridge University Press, 2007.

Index

Index

Index

Index

God
belief in 14, 17–18, 86–89, 93
powers of 57
Goetz, Rebecca Anne 5
Gordon, George William 168–69
Gossett, Thomas 199
Gould, F.J. 112–13, 195
Grant, Madison 194
Graves, Kersey 37, 152
Gray, Asa 53, 142
Gray, Robert 90
"great chain of being" 56–57, 60, 67
Greenspan, Ezra 154

Haddon, Alfred 197
Haeckel, Ernst 68
Haiti 7–8
Haldane, J.B.S. 209
Ham and the curse of Ham 9, 118, 193–94
Hansberry, Lorraine 208
Harlem Renaissance 159, 195, 207–8
Harris, Sam 214–16
Harris, W.S.T. 160
Harrison, Frederic 19, 109
Harrison, Hubert 159–60, 194, 206, 208
Harte, Bret 131
Hawley, George 213
Hemings, Sally 7
"hereditary heathenism" 5
Heston, Watson 49–50, 79–80, 98–101, 131, 148, 151, 185, 205–6
Hilmi, Abbas II 199
Hinduism 118–26
Hittell, John Shertzer 58, 77–78, 81–82, 118, 120, 128
Hoffman, Frederick 182–83
Hogben, Lancelot 209
Hollick, Frederick 75
Holyoake, George 15–21, 36, 91–92, 122, 142, 147–48, 157–58, 206
Home Rule League (for India) 125
Hose, Sam 165–66
Houston, John 139
Hughes, Langston 208
human nature, formation of 177
humanitarianism 97, 112
Hume, David 7

Hunt, James 9, 30, 37–45, 51, 168, 180, 205
Hurston, Zora Neale 207–8
Hussain, Murtaza 214–15
Hutchins, Zachary McLeod 156
Huxley, Julian 209
Huxley, Thomas Henry 17–18, 22, 36, 41, 59–63, 66–67, 73–74, 82, 93, 121, 129, 131, 159, 167–69, 184, 194, 205, 209

Ilbert Bill 125
images of black people 144–45
immigration restrictions 11, 136
imperialism 25, 84–86, 97, 111–18, 125–28, 134, 180–81, 187, 195
imprisonment for blasphemy 21, 56, 96, 105
Inden, Ronald 116
India 26, 29, 57, 116–28, 140, 206
Indian Mutiny (1857–58) 122
Infidel Association of the United States 151–52
Ingersoll, Eva 158, 162
Ingersoll, Robert 18, 20, 49, 78–79, 101, 120, 132–37, 144, 157–66, 173, 196, 206
intermarriage and interbreeding 64–65, 69–70, 75
Irish nation and nationalism 57, 182, 205–6
Irvine, Clarke 139
Islam 41, 87, 116, 214–15

Jacoby, Susan 153, 170
Jamaica 177
Jamaica Committee 168–69, 180
Japan 64, 116, 129–32, 135, 140
Jefferson, Thomas 6–8
Jesus Christ 6, 9–10, 29, 46, 51, 104, 131, 134, 152, 160
Jews and Judaism 4, 20, 38–39, 79–82, 134, 211
see also anti-Semitism
jihadism 215
"Jim Crow" laws 160–61
Johnson, Brian L. 200
Johnson, James Hervey 210–11

Index

Index

Index